**THE WHITE DEATH:**

*The Epic of the Soviet-Finnish Winter War*

Marshal Mannerheim at his Headquarters during the Winter War
Courtesy of the Finnish War Museum

# THE

# WHITE DEATH:

## The Epic of the Soviet-Finnish Winter War

by

ALLEN F. CHEW

MICHIGAN STATE UNIVERSITY PRESS

DEDICATED

TO

THE MEMORY OF

*The More Than 23,000 Finns Who Gave Their
Lives in the Winter War Defending Their
Nation's Freedom*

Hail, ye halls with heroes peopled. *The Kalevala*, RUNE XXV

# Foreword

Those who recall the journalistic coverage of the "Winter War" of 1939–1940 are familiar with the myth that the Finns were superhuman, fearless, deadly efficient defenders of Western civilization against a brutal, godless, blundering communist horde which outnumbered them fifty to one. The contemporary slogan "one Finnish soldier is worth ten Russians" was but one manifestation of that emotional attitude. Like most myths, this one contains elements of both fact and fantasy.

This study is based on interviews with veterans who held significant posts, research in the official Finnish archives, and examination of the scant Soviet literature on the subject. As a professionally skeptical historian, I have deliberately pried into Finland's dirty linen: questionable personalities, social discords, and frank records not intended for publication. In searching for the whole truth, I discovered a few exceptional cases of treason, cowardice, incompetence, and other human failings among the Finns. I even found some cases of heroism among the invading troops of the Red Army. Yet no matter how deeply I probe into the realities, I remain amazed at the degree of validity of that journalistic myth. While the true pictures of most wars are studies in shades of gray, this one is basically a contrast in stark black and white.

The epigraphs in this book are taken from John M. Crawford's translation of the Finnish national epic, *The Kalevala*. That title, which may be translated "The Land of Heroes," is singularly appropriate for the Finland of that immortal winter.

ALLEN F. CHEW
*Colorado Springs*
1971

# TABLE OF CONTENTS

## LIST OF MAPS

# THE WHITE DEATH:

*The Epic of the Soviet-Finnish Winter War*

*Those that war without a reason*
*Will be slaughtered for their folly . . .*
**RUNE XXXVI**

# Undeclared War

AT TWENTY MINUTES PAST NINE ON THE MORNING OF 30 NOVEM-
ber 1939, a Soviet bomber showered propaganda leaflets over
Helsinki, the beautiful "White City of the North." A few minutes later, other aircraft delivered more lethal messages to
Viipuri in the first of many devastating raids on Finland's second largest city.[1] Earlier that fateful morning, the Red Army
had struck with artillery, tanks, infantry, and aircraft at numerous points along the 900-mile Soviet-Finnish border—from
Petsamo on the Arctic Ocean to the Terijoki region on the Gulf
of Finland. Surprised by overwhelming forces, the guards at
tiny frontier posts—most of whom had never seen a tank before
—were quickly killed, captured, or dispersed.

The same morning a calm, resolute old man hastened from
his home in the fashionable legation district of Helsinki to the
office of the General Staff, and then on to the Presidential Palace. Withdrawing his recently tendered resignation from the
frustrating post of Defense Council Chairman in an economy-
minded government, Marshal C. G. E. Mannerheim was immediately appointed Commander-in-Chief of Finland's
military forces and entrusted with the uncertain fate of his
troubled nation.[2] This was not the first time he had been called
upon to defend Finland against Soviet armies—nor would it be
the last.

In his heavily guarded office in Moscow's ancient Kremlin,
Stalin confidently awaited the victory reports that would be
relayed from his field commanders via the Headquarters of the
Leningrad Military District. A few Soviet bombs, a few tanks,

a few propaganda leaflets—and the unpopular bourgeois government of the Finnish White Guards would topple. The Finnish proletariat would rise again to resume the civil war where they had paused in 1918—only this time the people would greet the mighty Red Army of the world's first socialist state as a liberating ally. Within a few days Soviet forces would enter Helsinki to sign a peace treaty with a Finnish Soviet Government.

Stalin had reason to believe this fantasy. The TASS correspondent in Helsinki had been reporting that Finland's oppressed workers were predisposed for another revolution, needing but a slight spark to transform their latent class antagonism into open conflict.[3] The dispatches from Derevyanski, Soviet Minister in the Finnish capital, echoed the TASS appraisal. The Minister had even confirmed this evaluation during the abortive negotiations at the Kremlin just a month earlier. But, in common with most Soviet bureaucrats, he reported only what Stalin wished to hear, and Finnish intelligence sources were aware of his completely misleading messages. Derevyanski was flustered when Colonel Paasonen, the military adviser to the Finnish delegation, had bluntly asked him—in Stalin's presence—if he had been reporting the truth.[4]

The Soviet dictator had personally tried to persuade the Finnish delegates to yield to his demands at seven different meetings in October and early November, but they broke off negotiations without giving in. As Foreign Commissar Molotov laconically remarked to the recalcitrant Finns, "Now it is the turn of the military to have their say."[5]

Stalin had obviously expected a victory parade, not a serious fight. Shaposhnikov, Chief of the General Staff of the Red Army, was less optimistic; anticipating stubborn Finnish resistance, he presented a plan to the Main Military Council which called for extensive preparations and the employment of units drawn from all over the nation. Stalin ridiculed this plan, and the task of putting the "Finnish reactionaries" to flight was assigned to the Leningrad Military District alone.[6] The Red Army had already completed the conquest of Poland, a nation with eight times the population of Finland, in a matter of days. Of course, the Poles were weakened by Hitler's previous invasion on 1 September 1939—which triggered the Second World War—but the speed and results of the Soviet offensive launched on 17 September appeared impressive. At a cost of only 737 fatalities, the Red Army added 196,000 square kilometers and thirteen million new subjects to the U.S.S.R.[7]

It had all started on 23 August, when Molotov and Hitler's Foreign Minister, von Ribbentrop, signed the treaty which divided eastern Europe between Germany and the Soviet Union. The Soviet share of the spoils included eastern Poland and all of Latvia, Estonia, and Finland. The treaty's secret protocol was amended on 28 September to add most of Lithuania to the Soviet sphere of influence, in exchange for modifications in the division of Poland. The little Baltic states bowed to the inevitable, and by 10 October each had signed a treaty granting the U.S.S.R. the right to station troops and aircraft on its territory. In the case of Estonia and Latvia, the Soviet Baltic Fleet also acquired bases along their shores. Only the Finnish Government was obstinate. It did not respond in the expected manner to Molotov's invitation of 5 October to visit Moscow for discussion of "concrete political questions." Whereas the Baltic states had signed the prescribed treaties within a week, the Finnish delegations haggled from 12 October to 9 November and even then did not sign.[8]

Allegedly fearing an Anglo-French attack thru the Gulf of Finland and via Finnish territory, and also mentioning the possibility of an attack by its new German "friend," the Soviet Government demanded the relocation of the boundary on the Karelian Isthmus to a point some 20 miles from Viipuri and the demolishing of the fortifications on the Isthmus. In addition, the Finns were asked to cede the islands of Suursaari, Lavansaari, Tytärsaari, and Koivisto in the Gulf of Finland, along with the western parts of the Rybachi Peninsula on the Arctic coast. In exchange for these strategic areas, Stalin promised to cede about twice as much territory, of little military importance, in the wilds of the central frontier region. Finally, the Soviet Government demanded a 30-year lease on the Hanko Peninsula, with the right to station 5,000 troops there.[9]

The Finnish Government was willing to compromise on the Isthmus boundary and on the cession of some of the islands and part of the Rybachi area demanded by the Soviets. Stalin finally

FINLAND IN 1939                                              MAP 1

Arctic Ocean
Rybachi Peninsula
PETSAMO
MURMANSK

N O R W A Y

F I N L A N D

U S S R

WHITE SEA

ARCTIC CIRCLE
ROVANIEMI

S W E D E N

TORNIO
KEMI

OULU

GULF OF BOTHNIA

UMEÅ

Murmansk R.R.

VAASA

KUOPIO

JOENSUU

PORI
TAMPERE

MIKKELI

LAHTI

Lake
Ladoga

TURKU

Kotka        Virolahti        VIIPURI

Porkkala                      Koivisto        Terijoki
                              Suursaari              Mainila
HELSINKI                      Lavansaari
HANKO        GULF OF FINLAND

PALDISKI                                              LENINGRAD
        TALLIN
        E S T O N I A

Main Finish Defenses  ·····
MILES  0        50        100

indicated that he might be willing to accept certain islands just off the Hanko Peninsula in lieu of that mainland base. But Soviet units stationed southwest of Helsinki would still pose a serious threat to Finland's over-extended defense forces. And the destruction of the Isthmus fortifications would eliminate the only important Finnish defense line, exposing the major population and industrial centers of the country to easy attack. If these concessions were granted at the expense of their defense posture, worried Finns asked themselves, how could they possibly resist more extreme Soviet demands in the future? The stalemated negotiations terminated indefinitely and inconclusively on 9 November, and on the 13th the Finnish delegation departed Moscow for Helsinki.[10]

After a diplomatic lull of two weeks, the calm was shattered on 26 November by the Soviets' own shelling of Mainila, a village just inside their border. Using this transparent pretext —and ignoring the Finnish offer of a joint investigation of the incident—the Soviet Government denounced the Soviet-Finnish Non-Aggression Treaty on 28 November, and the next day Moscow severed diplomatic relations with Helsinki.[11] Although Finnish border guards in the far north at Petsamo were attacked on the 29th,[12] the Finns mistook this as merely another frontier incident. But the extensive attacks of 30 November could not be misinterpreted.

Thus abruptly began one of the most dramatic wars in modern times—a war that was to hold rude surprises for both Stalin and Marshal Mannerheim. What faith or folly inspired a nation less than four million strong even to attempt military resistance when invaded by a state commanding more than 183 million subjects?[13] What sort of man was this Marshal Mannerheim, to be entrusted with such an impossible burden at the age of 72? And what, in the ledger of history, were the debits and credits of that brief but deadly war which began the final day of November 1939?

*In these mournful days of evil,*
*Evil times our race befallen.*
**RUNE III**

CHAPTER I

# Fools Rush In

ALTHOUGH THE INVASION WAS NOT A COMPLETE SURPRISE, THE SCOPE and intensity of the initial offensives came as a shock to the Finnish General Staff. Four Soviet armies hurled sixteen of the nineteen divisions immediately available, supported by 1,700 tanks and strong artillery, against nine smaller divisions with obsolescent artillery and negligible armor—all the Finns were able to field. Even more disturbing than these odds was the fact that over half the Soviet infantry, with a fourth of their tanks, was advancing virtually unopposed along wilderness roads from Lake Ladoga to the Arctic Ocean. The Finnish Army had grossly underestimated the strength which the enemy could deploy in a region thought to be entirely dependent upon the Murmansk-Leningrad railway (mainly single-tracked) and the primitive roads leading some 50 to 150 miles from the rails to the border. As a consequence, along the northernmost 600 miles of the boundary there were only nine weak covering troop units of battalion size or smaller to oppose Soviet forces which streamed across nearly every frontier road in division strength. This unexpected situation, in Marshal Mannerheim's words, "exceeded our worst apprehensions."[1]

Understandably, those columns progressed rapidly, pursuing the hopelessly outnumbered defenders. As antitank weapons were generally lacking, the first sight of Russian tanks created panic in many areas. Initially, home-front confidence was not substantially greater: recalling the Nazi-Soviet blitzkrieg in Poland three months earlier, many doubted the possibility of successful resistance. There was even loose talk of Russian tanks breaching the main defenses and reaching Viipuri in two days. Furthermore, the fear of an immediate aerial blitz against Helsinki created terror. The initial leaflet raid on 30 November was followed later in the morning by the bombing of the harbor defenses, and that afternoon fifteen low-flying SB's (medium bombers) blasted the very heart of the city. Amidst the confusion of racing ambulances and fire trucks, burning buildings, and harassed civil defense officials, a mass exodus of the helpless civilians began, clogging all roads from the capital for days. The terror was intensified that evening by the widely circulated rumor of a Soviet ultimatum demanding complete surrender by 3 A.M. or the obliteration of Helsinki. To those who knew something of the numerical strength of the Red bomber force, as well as those who could only guess at it, such a threat was all too credible. That rumor, of unknown origin, was believed and even spread by an official of the Finnish Press Bureau.[2]

The objectives of the Red Army immediately became apparent: seal off Finland from foreign aid by seizing the Arctic port of Petsamo and by severing the only rail connection with Sweden at Kemi or Oulu (incidentally cutting Finland in two at its narrow "waist" at the head of the Gulf of Bothnia); drive around the northern shore of Lake Ladoga on a broad front to reach the main rail network and to outflank the critical Karelian Isthmus defenses, while simultaneously assaulting those defenses frontally with powerful armored forces; and finally, break through to the population centers of southern Finland, including Helsinki, and thus overrun the entire country.[3] In the first grim days of December, it seemed to both sides that these goals might soon be attained.

From the Finnish viewpoint, and ultimately also the Soviet, the strategic significance of the Red Army's thrusts generally increased progressively from north to south. Thus the loss of Petsamo in the first days of the war, while regrettable, was predictable and not unduly alarming. Because of its remoteness from sources of support, Petsamo was highly vulnerable to attack from the Soviet Navy's powerful Northern Fleet base at Murmansk. When Soviet forces attacked by land, sea, and air, the Finns could only muster the 10th Independent Covering

Troop Company and one battery of four antique field guns, model 1887. The Soviet 14th Army rapidly achieved its first objectives—securing the port itself and fortifying it to prevent any third parties from intervening there.[4]

The next vital point south of Petsamo was the capital of Finnish Lapland, Rovaniemi, which could only be reached from that direction via the 300-mile long Arctic Highway. As winter was already well advanced in that dark inhospitable land beyond the Arctic Circle, supplying any sizeable force over that single-lane road—which winds through virtually uninhabited fjeld, bog, and forest—would have been difficult even if there were no enemy to consider. Of course, the Soviet drive had to be checked short of Rovaniemi, which was connected by rail with Kemi on the Gulf of Bothnia, but the loss of a few more miles of white wilderness made little difference. After capturing Petsamo, the 14th Army dispatched two regiments of its 104th Division south along the highway towards Rovaniemi, while the retreating Finns tried to gather sufficient forces to make a stand.[5]

Simultaneously, Rovaniemi faced a more imminent threat from the east, where forces based at Kandalaksha were pushing westward along a much shorter route which led through the church village of Salla and the railhead at Kemijärvi. As they did in other areas, the enemy had improved the road from Kandalaksha to the frontier during the autumn. When the 9th Army's 122nd Division swept across the border on 30 November, the only Finnish forces within a hundred miles were the covering troops of the 18th Independent Battalion. By 10 December they had been forced to abandon Salla, the road to Kemijärvi was open, and the invaders were less than 100 miles from Rovaniemi.[6]

Separated from the Salla front by more than 100 miles of woods and lakes, other columns of the invading 9th Army were also marching toward the Gulf of Bothnia. To Commander Zelentsov, leading the 163rd Division, the prospects must have · looked bright indeed. Using a newly constructed road from his base at Ukhta to the border near Juntusranta, he had achieved complete tactical surprise. The Finns initially had only fifty covering troops to defend the road from there to the strategic

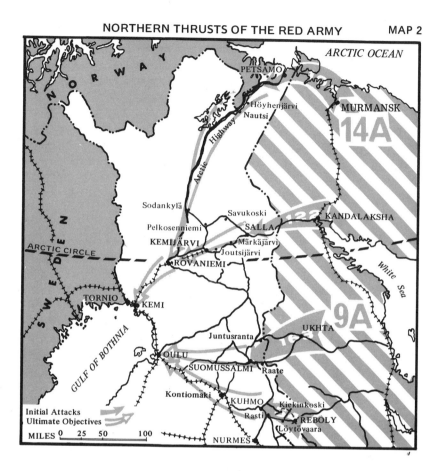

NORTHERN THRUSTS OF THE RED ARMY            MAP 2

road junction at the church village of Suomussalmi. Thus the main force of the 163rd Division (the 81st and 662nd Infantry Regiments, plus a battalion of tanks and cavalry) easily rolled back the despised opposition and in a few days reached the north-south road beyond Suomussalmi, fanning out with motorized columns in both directions. The Finns had expected that any offensive in this region would be launched along the better road which crossed the frontier at Raate, some thirty miles south of Juntusranta. Instead, only the 759th Infantry Regiment and the Division's reconnaissance battalion used the southern route, where the Finns had stationed two platoons at roadblocks about six miles apart. Those defenders, aided by other local reservists of the 15th Independent Battalion and the 4th Field Replacement Battalion which was rushed there from Kajaani on 4 December, harassed the enemy in bitter fighting for the whole twenty-five miles from Raate to Suomussalmi, but the outcome was never in doubt. By nightfall of the first day the Red Army controlled six miles of the Raate road, and on 7 December the two Soviet columns joined to capture the church village. Then the entire 163rd Division was poised to continue its thrust to the vital rail link with Sweden at Oulu, only 150 miles to the west by road.[7]

Here, as everywhere else in the path of the advancing Red Army, the few roads were clogged with civilians fleeing from the "liberation" offered by a steady barrage of Soviet propaganda broadcasts and leaflets. Infants bundled on sleighs or carts in the subzero cold hugged their stoic elders, as the family cattle trudged alongside or were driven off the roads and shot to make way for troop movements along the narrow passages between the high snowbanks. Scorched earth was a painful but prudent policy in a country where nature itself was hostile to the invaders. The reactions of the Finnish troops to these spectacles varied from a feeling of hopeless depression to grim determination to be avenged.[8]

About sixty miles southeast of Suomussalmi a third element of the 9th Army was moving northwest along two roads from its base at Reboly, where the Finnish rail net was in places less than fifty miles from the frontier. The immediate objective was the crossroads at the church village of Kuhmo. Possibly because the 9th Army command was confident of the success of their offensive farther north at Suomussalmi, which was considerably closer to the ultimate objective at Oulu, they initially dispatched only part of the 54th Division towards Kuhmo. Although encountering the stubborn resistance of the 14th Independent Battalion, the main column of the Division was within fifteen miles of that village crossroads by the end of the first week's fighting.[9]

More ominous than any of those isolated thrusts through the northern wilds were the powerful and more concentrated attacks of the 8th Army directly north of Lake Ladoga, in the region known as Ladoga-Karelia, dangerously close to the communications and population centers of southern Finland and the rear of the Karelian Isthmus fortifications. Although the Finnish General Staff anticipated an outflanking attempt around the northern shore of the Lake—indeed, they had rehearsed the appropriate counter moves during years of peacetime maneuvers in that very terrain—they were especially surprised at the size of the enemy forces employed here. Marshal Mannerheim shared their view that the maximum flow which the local road network could support was three divisions. Therefore, when the war began the Finns had only the IV Army Corps, comprising two divisions and three battalions of covering troops, on a sixty-mile front north of Lake Ladoga. During the autumn the Soviets had improved the roads and speeded up the construction of a spur line of the Murmansk Railroad from the 8th Army's main base at Petrozavodsk towards the frontier near Suojärvi. The Red Army was thus able to throw five infantry divisions and one armored brigade across the border on 30 November, and to deploy an additional eight divisions in Ladoga-Karelia as the fighting progressed.[10]

Only bad news issued from the IV Army Corps during the first week of the unequal fight. On 30 November there was heavy fighting in the Suojärvi region, and during the darkness of that winter evening both Leppäniemi, five miles to the southeast, and Salmijärvi, some thirty miles to the northwest, were abandoned. The northern spear of the 8th Army, the 155th Division, was advancing against negligible opposition in the direction of the Ilomantsi road junction. On that Division's southern flank, the 139th Division was moving just north of the Suojärvi Lake region towards the Korpiselkä-Värtsilä road. Both offensives posed extremely dangerous threats to the Joensuu-Sortavala-Isthmus railroad. Marshal Mannerheim was also alarmed by the thrust of the 56th Division straight down the tracks from Suojärvi towards Loimola. If this force captured Kollaa, the planned counterattack against the divisions moving along the shore of Lake Ladoga would have to be scrapped. Along that shore the 168th Division was making rapid progress, as was the 18th Division on its right flank.[11]

To oppose the 139th Division there were only some 4,000 troops of Task Force R. This shaky force was improvised from three unrelated units, reinforced in the first days of the war by another independent battalion and Bicycle Battalion PPP* 7 (Bicycle units used skis in winter). The Task Force was under the overly cautious command of Lt. Colonel V. Räsänen, whose headquarters was too far behind the front to be effective. On 1 December the headquarters moved back from Vuontele to Äglajärvi, although most of the Task Force continued fighting at the Aittojoki River—some six miles to the east—for another two and one-half days.[12]

On 2 December Suojärvi fell, Task Force R continued its retreat, and the enemy moving down the rail line from Suvilahti (the Suojärvi station) was reported halfway to Kollaa. The Marshal was so furious when he heard of the fall of the Suojärvi region that evening that he relieved Major General Juho Heiskanen of command of the IV Army Corps, replacing him with Major General Johan Hägglund. The Commander-in-Chief had expected the covering troops to take better advantage of the natural defenses of the region to hold, or even to counterattack, the enemy. Believing that the defense lacked the requisite vigor, he ordered a general counteroffensive for the next day. At 2 A.M. on 3 December orders went out from IV Army Corps for full-scale attacks that morning. However, Bicycle Battalion PPP 7 was an hour and forty minutes late in moving out, and Task Force R's fighting at the Aittojoki River that day was inconclusive. Early the following morning the river line broke and the Task Force continued retreating, its headquarters moving all the way back to Tolvajärvi about noon.[13]

The IV Corps' counterattack on 3 December to regain the Suvilahti rail station and the lost areas on both sides of the tracks did not fare much better. One regiment, supported by four batteries, advanced along the railway and the parallel road, but at Liete (northwest of Suvilahti) it encountered a strong tank force and was forced to beat a hasty retreat. By 7 December renewed tank attacks had thrown the regiment back to Kollaa, where it managed to hold on precariously.[14]

The demoralization of Task Force R accelerated. In a futile attempt to hold the village of Äglajärvi, the 7th Bicycle Battalion was routed and lost all its machine guns to the enemy on

*PP = Bicycle, P = Battalion (infantry); Finnish unit designations are used where appropriate.

## THE THREAT TO LADOGA-KARELIA                    MAP 3

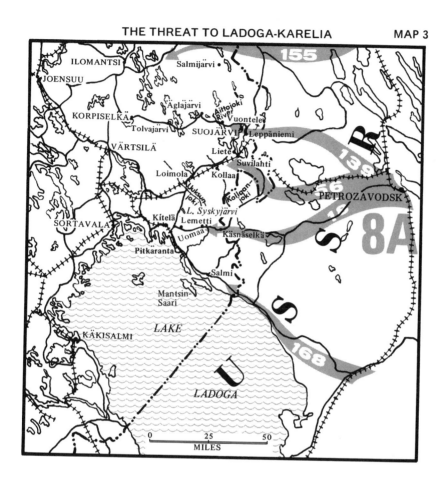

5 December. The continuous retreat—over forty miles in a week—was threatening to become a debacle: jittery troops fired on their own men by mistake, some were irrationally afraid of night attacks, and many panicked at the sight of Soviet tanks.[15] If the next week brought another forty-mile retreat, the vital rail link at Värtsilä would be lost, and a desperate situation might become a disasterous one.

The Finns also had worries behind the front lines, where there was an unspoken, nagging fear of treason within the ranks. Enemy agents were also a threat. The most elusive were those from the region of the Inkeri, descendants of a small tribe living west of Leningrad whose speech was indistinguishable from that of the native Finns. Although the "descanti," as the parachute intruders were nicknamed, were neither as numerous nor as effective as rumor credited them, they were an additional source of concern, and it was mainly because of them that Marshal Mannerheim consented to the presence of a small personal bodyguard at his headquarters.[16]

*If any Soviet agent had been watching the entrance to the Marshal's temporary headquarters in the Hotel Helsinki on the evening of 2 December, he would have seen an unfamiliar officer arrive in a state of agitation.[17] Could the agent have but known what that visit portended, he might have merited the Order of Lenin merely by shooting that deceptively cherubic-looking Finnish colonel.*

During these first hectic days of alarming surprises, Marshal Mannerheim was also disturbed by events in the main theater of war, the Karelian Isthmus. Onto this narrow bridge linking Leningrad directly with the heart of southern Finland, the enemy threw his major forces—eight infantry divisions and five armored brigades of the 7th Army.[18] Communications across the Isthmus, which is only 25 to 70 miles wide, were better than all those along the hundreds of miles of border to the north. Two rail lines linked Leningrad with the Finnish rail net (one of these split to follow two separate routes across most of the Isthmus), a third Finnish line in the central sector terminated at Valkjärvi within ten miles of the frontier, and there were also several good motor roads. The hub of these routes and the logistic center for the Finnish forces on the Isthmus was the ancient stronghold of Viipuri, only 70 miles northwest of the main Soviet support base at Leningrad.

Viipuri (also known as Viborg), which had developed around a Swedish castle dating from 1293 A.D., had witnessed countless Russian invasions during the intervening centuries. Finally captured in 1710 by the army of Peter the Great, the town passed to Russia under the terms of the Treaty of Nystad in 1721. Although Tsar Alexander I annexed Finland in 1809 as an autonomous Grand Duchy, he returned Viipuri Province to Finnish domestic administration in 1812. To the Finns, Viipuri was both a fortress city and a symbol—a bastion athwart the centuries-old invasion route of the traditional Russian foe.[19]

Anticipating that the major blow would fall on the Isthmus, it was there that the Finnish Army concentrated its main force, five front-line divisions, in its strongest positions—the so-called Mannerheim Line. This defense system stretched some 80 miles in a generally southwest to northeast arc from Kyrön-niemi (southeast of Koivisto) on the Gulf of Finland to Taipale on Lake Ladoga. While the Line inspired justifiable confidence, developments in the frontier zone—the sector twelve to thirty miles deep between the main fortifications and the border—caused considerable concern to the Finnish General Staff. Here about 21,500 Finns, organized into Groups U, M, L, and R, were tasked with delaying and harassing enemy legions which included approximately 1,000 tanks. Although there was fierce fighting at certain points from the very first hours, Marshal Mannerheim thought that many other good defensive positions were abandoned without offering sufficient resistance.[20]

After an intensive half-hour barrage by some 600 field guns shattered the early morning calm on 30 November, the intended blitzkrieg assault was launched along the entire Isthmus frontier. Near the Gulf of Finland the 70th Division surprised and captured some of the border guards, and by nightfall it pushed the covering troops of the U Group back as far as the eastern end of the town of Terijoki—soon to achieve notoriety. The defenders blew up the railroad bridge (which alone delayed the tank advance by ten hours), set the buildings afire, and launched four counterattacks during the night, but they had to abandon the town the next morning.[21]

The adjacent M Group withdrew even faster, falling back as far as the vicinity of Pamppala by the late afternoon of 2 December.[22] One of its battalions nevertheless scored the only notable Finnish victory up to this time: after being surprised by a strong enemy force which penetrated the forest near Korpikylä, it retreated through Vuottaa to Ahijärvi, where it successfully counterattacked on 2 December. Amidst the pessimistic events on all other fronts, that minor Finnish triumph was deliberately stressed to bolster morale.[23]

Farther north, in the center of the Isthmus, the Red Army encountered stubborn house-to-house fighting at Lipola village on 30 November. The battles were so heated in this sector that

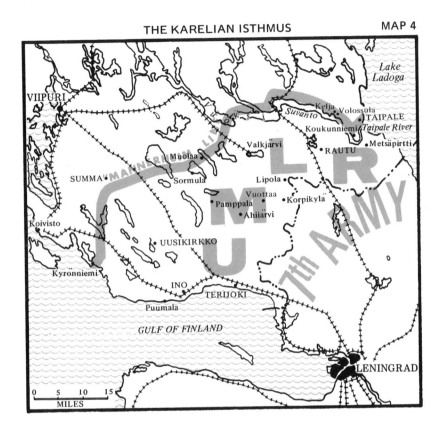

THE KARELIAN ISTHMUS                              MAP 4

some of the Soviet infantry ran out of ammunition on that first day. Finnish snipers, nicknamed "cuckoos" by the surprised invaders, were already taking their toll behind the enemy lines in this area.[24]

Near Lake Ladoga, the invaders captured the village of Metsapirtti during the first night. The successful Soviet regiment was supported by *heavy* tanks—seldom used at this stage of the war. The counterattack of R Group on 2 December failed to dislodge them, and by the next day the regiment reached the shores of Lake Suvanto and the Taipale River.[25]

Towards evening on 2 December the Headquarters of the Kannas Army (the Isthmus Army, commanded by Lt. General Österman) received two alarming reports from Headquarters II Army Corps (defending the southwestern half of the Isthmus, under the command of Lt. General Öhquist). One announced an enemy landing at Puumala on the Gulf coast, behind the right flank of the covering troops. On the basis of this report, General Öhquist ordered the U Group to withdraw to the Uusikirkko region. The other report stated that a tank column had penetrated into Sormula village, close in front of the main positions in the center of the Isthmus, and thus had cut the frontier zone in two. Consequently, General Österman directed the III Army Corps (the units in the northeastern half of the Isthmus, commanded by Major General Heinrichs) to pull back its left wing, the R Group, mostly to the vicinity of Lake Suvanto. Both flanks were withdrawn so hurriedly that—when the reports were subsequently proved false—it was impossible to carry out Marshal Mannerheim's orders to retake the lost areas. Terrain that afforded good defensive possibilities had thus been handed to the invader gratis, and the Marshal had another reason to blister the phone lines to his subordinates on that dismal night of 2 December. The origin of those false reports was never determined—it may have been treason, Soviet deception, or merely Finnish confusion.[26]

On the evening of 3 December Supreme Headquarters was transferred—in accordance with existing peacetime emergency plans—from the capital to the little town of Mikkeli in the lake country.[27] With excellent communications to the principal theaters of war, St. Michel (as it was known to the Swedes) was well situated for its role. Since it had been the Marshal's final headquarters during the civil war in 1918, there was a certain nostalgia connected with the move, perhaps even an unconscious symbolism—Saint Michael, the guardian angel, the conqueror of Satan.

As the rapid withdrawal continued, on 4 December the Commander-in-Chief stopped enroute to Mikkeli to visit General Österman's headquarters at Imatra, where General Öhquist was also summoned. Angered by Österman's failure to carry out his orders to commit the Army reserves to the forward zone, Marshal Mannerheim expressed his dissatisfaction in no uncertain terms. According to Österman's memoirs, both he and the Marshal offered to resign at this point. Among other repercussions of this stormy visit was a directive of 8 December to

Groups U, M, and L for detailed written postmortems of their entire operations from 30 November to 6 December.[28]

The divergence of views on the roles of the covering troops had emerged even before hostilities began. Österman's directive of 25 October to his corps commanders stated that those forces were "perhaps even too strong," and he ordered that they should *not* engage in decisive battles. He obviously viewed their mission in its original restrictive terms—to delay the invader until the reserves could man the main defense positions. Since the Mannerheim Line had already been garrisoned during the prewar mobilization, he believed that a stubborn defense of the forward zone at the risk of heavy casualties was unwarranted. Marshal Mannerheim, on the other hand, wanted the covering troops to maintain "the most effective possible defense much closer to the border region," utilizing forces large enough to inflict heavy losses on the enemy, while taking maximum advantage of the excellent defensive terrain and the field works already constructed there. (His views were contained in a directive of 3 November to Österman's headquarters, strongly reiterated in a clarifying letter of 10 November.) In spite of some redeployments ordered by Österman on 22 November, when the war began the grouping of the troops still did not conform to the Marshal's desires. The inherent problems of the frontier zone defense had been further complicated by the reorganization of the command structure shortly before the war. As a consequence of the changes, there was some ambiguity concerning the respective missions (and considerable friction) between the Kannas Army (Österman) and its subordinate corps, especially Öhquist's II Corps.[29]

As an immediate result of the Imatra meeting on 4 December, stronger resistance was offered on 5 and 6 December, including destructive night raids focused on the enemy's camp fires. Parts of the forces in the Mannerheim Line also participated in the violent fighting of those two days. However, by this time most of the frontier zone had been lost, and there was little more the covering troops could hope to accomplish. On the 6th the Soviet right wing managed to cross the Taipale River and seize the hamlet of Koukunniemi. By their own admission, the attackers suffered heavy casualties in this engagement, and they had to fight off ten Finnish counterattacks that night. The Koukunniemi positions were situated on the lowland meadows within the horseshoe bend of the river, exposed to highly effective fire from the main Finnish positions on the commanding heights to the northeast.[30]

The Soviet claim to have broken through the "main defense line" along the Vuoksi water system on 6 December was misleading, but their tanks did briefly penetrate deeply in another sector, reaching the outskirts of Summa village on the 7th. At this stage most of the weary covering troops were withdrawn through the main positions. As the Marshal had feared, the retreat from the border was too hasty, causing some panic, but it was localized and the Line held.[31]

The defeats and demoralization in this period were almost always caused by the appearance of enemy tanks, which rumbled through the frontier zone by the score. The relentless approach of these mechanical monsters, spewing deadly fire from the mouths of their cannon and machine guns, created in the hapless infantryman armed with only a rifle a sense of desperation and terror. He might as well have been a naked savage, armed with only a spear, facing a charging rhinoceros. During this opening round the Finns' only weapons against armor were mines, field artillery, and some 100 Bofors 37mm antitank guns. Those Swedish-made antitank guns, mostly assigned to the Kannas Army, were quite effective against the light T-26 tanks generally encountered in the December fighting. However, the Bofors were too few, too heavy, and too cumbersome for the changing situations of mobile warfare in the frontier zone. Although 80 tanks were knocked out by the Bofors and the regular artillery by 5 December—and many others were destroyed by mines—their replacements appeared inexhaustible to the harried covering troops. Simple weapons which enabled the individual soldier to cope with the tanks, such as the famed "Molotov cocktail"—which the Finns ironically named after the hated Soviet Foreign Commissar—were not generally available until after most of the frontier zone was lost.[32]

As the first week of war drew to a close, there was an air of apprehension in Mikkeli; the enemy was still advancing in force along the entire eastern border, and Finnish troops were on the verge of collapse at several widely separated points. Their officers, mostly unseasoned reservists recalled a few short weeks ago from their peaceful offices, schools, farms, and shops, were often somewhat paralyzed in their reactions to the overwhelming Soviet offensives. They thought more about the safety of their men, the security of their communications, hoped-for reinforcements, and guidance from higher echelons than about bold counterattacks and dashing flanking maneuvers. That these were natural reactions under the circumstances is undeniable. But to Marshal Mannerheim it was equally unquestionable that this passive attitude must be dispelled immediately, lest an epidemic of panic sweep through both army and nation—forfeiting the fight before it had even begun in earnest.[33]

Aware of their vast superiority in manpower and weapons, Soviet leaders exuded optimism at the outset of the campaign. Potemkin, Deputy Commissar of Foreign Affairs, confided to the French Ambassador on 30 November that it would all be over "in four or five days," with the Red Army occupying Helsinki.[34] Deputy Commissar of Defense Kulik ordered the chief of Red Army Artillery to prepare for a maximum of twelve days of warfare.[35] An order found on a Russian officer killed early in December even cautioned Soviet troops not to violate the Swedish border.[36]

This supreme confidence in a speedy victory explains Stalin's uncharacteristically rash action in creating the "People's Government of Finland" in the frontier town of Terijoki on 1 December. At six o'clock that evening Radio Moscow, which had first informed the Soviet public of the war only seventeen hours earlier, announced the formation of the new government and declared that it would be transferred to Helsinki as soon as that city was liberated. The puppet President (and Foreign Minister) of that "People's Republic" was Otto V. Kuusinen, the exiled leader of the Finnish Communist Party who had spent the years since the unsuccessful Red revolt of 1918 in the service of the Communist International. Mauri Rosenberg, the Vice-President (and Finance Minister), erstwhile member of the Finnish Parliament, had also been working in Moscow for years. Stalin even committed his personal prestige to this gambit. On the front pages of the 3 December issues of *Pravda* and

*Izvestiya* he was pictured witnessing the signing by Molotov and Kuusinen of an "historic" treaty of mutual assistance and friendship between their governments. Naturally, that treaty granted to the U.S.S.R. all of the territorial concessions* it had previously demanded from the legitimate Finnish Government.[37]

Soviet overconfidence had its roots not only in their apparent military superiority, but also in the turbulent social history of the young Finnish Republic. When the Finns finally achieved their independence in December 1917, after some six hundred years of Swedish domination and a century of Russian rule, they immediately plunged into the bloody civil war[38] of January–May 1918. The causes of that tragedy are not directly pertinent here, but some of the effects are. As usual in civil warfare, atrocities were committed by both sides, and—as is also common—the losers nurtured their hatreds longer than did the victors. Otto Kuusinen was one of the tens of thousands of losers.

Probably no one will ever know precisely how many Finnish Red Guards were summarily shot when captured, or starved in prison camps after that war. A reasonable estimate is approximately 8,380 executions and about as many cases of starvation. This, of course, was no worse than the numerous political murders perpetrated earlier by radical Finnish Marxists and their Bolshevik cohorts from the Russian garrisons in Finland. But it was never forgotten by the one Finn in five who still considered himself a communist, even after all communist-front activities had been outlawed in 1930. The democratic experiment in Finland was also plagued during the 1930s by a noisy minority of right-wing extremists, of whom the leaders of the Lapua movement were the most notorious. With such troubled waters to fish in, the Soviet political hierarchy anticipated a very easy catch.[39]

This optimistic political appraisal had certain obvious military repercussions. Since the Finnish proletariat was expected to welcome the Red Army as its liberator, elaborate preparations for the invasion were not considered essential. Stalin did not deem it necessary to assign first-rate units to the campaign;

*See Map No. 16, page 233

consequently, many ill-trained reservists were used, some of whom—by their own admission—knew little more than how to fire a rifle. It was almost the unanimous opinion of the Finnish professional officers that the Red Army troops initially encountered were inferior, even by Soviet standards. And, as the Red Army itself subsequently acknowledged, men were sent into the frozen wilds of Finland in December lacking even adequate winter clothing. While the units from northern regions were better able to endure the severe frost, other troops from southern climes succumbed to it, freezing to death in the safety of their own lines. Mikhail Soloviev, a former Red Army correspondent, reported the freezing of about 100 Uzbeks, Tadzhiks, and Turkmen in one division which had been transferred directly from Turkestan to Finland.[40]

Yet so pervasive was the Marxist interpretation of the Finnish domestic situation that most of the Red Army believed its own propaganda: a war-mongering bourgeois government had deliberately provoked the fight by shelling Mainila village and by invading Soviet territory (the latter fabrication was voiced in the Radio Moscow broadcast which announced the opening of hostilities). The oppressed Finnish workers would join the Red legions in driving the hated White Finns out of the country. A young *Politruk** named Oreshin recorded in the privacy of his intimate diary on 27 November 1939 that he believed "the swine [the Finnish Government]" would refuse to move back their border on the Isthmus as Molotov had demanded after the Mainila incident. The next day he confidently welcomed the "majestic symphony of war," and when his unit fired its first barrage on the 30th, he noted "noisy shouting interrupted by cheers!" That naïve enthusiasm to "liberate" the Finns was shared by countless others before they experienced the sobering realities of the war.[41] The 2 December issue of *Krasnaya Zvezda* (Red Star) reported the disappointment of a soldier stationed in Siberia that the fighting would end too fast for him to participate in this "historic liberation mission."

There was heavy emphasis on propaganda in the initial period. The Finns were feted by Russian bands and loudspeakers playing both the Internationale and the Marseillaise.[42] Appar-

*Politicheskiy Rukovoditel', a political instructor assigned to a military unit.

ently the Soviet leaders remembered the walls of Jericho, even if they had forgotten about David and Goliath.

To a detached observer aware of only the military resources of the opponents, Soviet expectations of a speedy victory seemed credible. Not only was the Finnish infantry outnumbered on the battlefield more than two to one, but—because of peacetime budgetary limitations—it was also critically short of much essential equipment. Below the regimental level there generally were not even field radios; when the vulnerable phone wires were cut by enemy artillery, commanders lost contact with their battalions. Basic items like skis were also scarce in the beginning; the 13th Division fighting near Lake Ladoga was short 10,766 pairs on 6 December! Many shivering reservists lacked even proper uniforms and boots during the first trying weeks.[43]

Although the clothes of the Red Army men were often poorer still, they had a tremendous superiority in arms and ammunition. When the shooting started, the Finns had small-arms munitions adequate for just two months of fighting and artillery shells for only about three weeks. The Soviet artillery could afford the luxury of concentrated barrages lasting for hours on end, whereas the Finns had to ration their shells from the start, and they had so few field pieces that even antiques like the 1887 model 107mm guns, which were manufactured before the counter-recoil mechanism was invented, were pressed into use on the Isthmus as well as at Petsamo.[44]

The only qualitative advantage in weapons that the Finns enjoyed was the "Suomi" machine pistol, a short-range but light and rapid-firing submachine gun which was ideal for forest fighting; its cylindrical magazine held 70 rounds. Not until February 1940 did Soviet units in Finland receive submachine guns, although their Army had tested the Suomi and shortsightedly rejected it in the early 1930s. Even the supply of these Finnish-made arms was limited; only 250 were authorized for each Finnish division.[45]

The Red Army had thousands of modern tanks and armored cars; the Finns had 28 obsolete Renault tanks and a few Vickers, only 13 of which were armed. The air power situation was similar; some 150 Finnish aircraft, including obsolete models with open cockpits, faced a Soviet air fleet which could muster 800 planes for the start of the Finnish campaign and still keep a large reserve for other regions.[46]

If these initial odds were startling, the prospects for replacing battle losses were even more discouraging. The U.S.S.R., frantically accelerating the Third Five Year Plan, was already an industrialized giant geared for military production. With a better than 40 to 1 advantage in manpower, its labor force and armed services could crush their tiny neighbor by sheer mass if necessary.

However, the position of the Finns was not without hope; they possessed certain intangible assets that partially compensated for their materiel weaknesses. Foremost among these were an unprecedented degree of social unity and a courageous determination to preserve their hard-won independence. On 1 December, the very day that Moscow announced the formation of the illusory Kuusinen government, a national coalition cabinet was organized in Helsinki. The acceptance of the Foreign Minister's portfolio by Väinö Tanner, the able Social Democratic leader who had been interrogated in 1919 by a rightist government, was symbolic of the closing of the ranks by all classes.[47]

Far from dividing public opinion, Kuusinen's farcical "People's Government" served to unify it as nothing else could have. Finns of all political persuasions now realized that the issue was not merely this or that territorial concession, but the actual survival of Finland as an independent nation. An overwhelming majority of even the communists rallied to the defense of their country. Veterans of the Red Guards of 1918 volunteered in large numbers for the front or for civil defense tasks. A typical reaction was that of General Öhquist's tailor, who had concealed his communist predilection from the General until the Soviet attack, when he remarked that "this is too much for me!" Even Arvo Tuominen, the General Secretary of the Finnish Communist Party, then in Stockholm, broke with Stalin and declined to head the puppet government planned for Finland.[48]

There were, of course, a few die-hard Stalinists among the communists, but their subversive efforts were not significantly effective. In 1939 forty were sentenced for high treason and fifteen for betrayal of their country.[49] A few others defected to the Red Army during the course of the war.

The general feeling was probably more anti-Russian than anti-communist. Many families still had personal recollections of the senseless repressive measures imposed upon the law-abiding citizens of the autonomous Grand Duchy by the last Tsar of Russia, Nicholas II. Those versed in history could cite numerous earlier instances of Russian aggression. Marshal Mannerheim struck a responsive chord in his first Order of the Day to the Finnish soldiers, noting that "our centuries-old enemy has again invaded our country . . . We are fighting for home, faith and country." Although this could hardly have reflected his personal feelings (he was thoroughly anti-communist, but was sympathetic towards the Russian state which he had served for thirty years prior to the 1917 revolutions), it expressed the prevailing sentiment of the nation. Others echoed the Marshal's words more sincerely; for example, a battle order dictated by a battalion commander just before the decisive engagement at Tolvajärvi on 12 December began with the words "Our traditional enemy having attacked our country . . ."[50]

The Finns also profited from the fact that their opponent had telegraphed his punch. The implications of the 5 October summons from Moscow had been made unmistakably clear even before the talks began on the 12th; in the interim, the last of the tiny Baltic states, Lithuania, had yielded to Soviet extortion and signed a treaty similar to those just concluded by Estonia and Latvia which granted the Red Army bases on their territory, foreshadowing their complete subjugation ten months later. Thus alerted to their own danger, the Finns immediately began preparations which eliminated the possibility of strategic surprise; the Red Army could hope for no more from a sneak attack than local tactical surprise.

The transfer of regular army units to the vital Isthmus region to serve as covering troops began on 6 October. The next day part of the reserves were mobilized under the diplomatic guise of "supplementary reserve training (YH)."* Additional re-

---

*The Finnish term has no precise English equivalent; hereinafter it will be rendered YH, as it is commonly abbreviated in Finnish reports. In addition to the diplomatic implications, the substitution of the euphemistic term "YH" for the word "mobilization" was an economy measure—the reservists did not receive full pay. Nevertheless, the lengthy YH period preceding the war strained Finland's economy, as it cost approximately $200,000 a day. (U. S. State Dept. files 760 D.61/476 and 1046)

serves were called up on 10 October. By the time of the attack on 30 November, mobilization and the concentration of defense forces had been almost completely carried out. This meant, as Marshal Mannerheim noted:

> To a large extent our defensive struggle commenced un-der more favorable conditions than we had dared to ex-pect. The nightmare of the General Staff during the last twenty years had been the problem of how our weak cover-ing troops would be able to hold the gate to the Karelian Isthmus until the main forces of the field army had oc-cupied their positions.
> Now the situation was different—one almost dared to say that we had won the first round. The covering troops, as well as the field army, had in good time and in the best order been directed to their sectors. During the period of four to six weeks we had been enabled to complete the training and equipment of the troops, to make them famil-iar with the country, to continue to build field fortifica-tions, to prepare work of destruction, and to lay mines and minefields. The homogeneity of the units thus became very different from what is usually the case with hastily mobilized troops immediately thrown into battle. These circumstances were calculated to produce calm and confi-dence before the trials in front of us.[51]

Civilians were also marshalled for the grim days ahead. On 10 October the Government broadcast an appeal for the volun-tary evacuation of the large towns and provided special trains and buses for that purpose. In Helsinki the University, the pub-lic schools, and the stock exchange were closed by mid-October. Air raid shelters were constructed throughout the cities to pro-tect those workers who could not leave for the relative safety of the countryside. Prohibition was decreed—a drastic measure for the Finns! However, by late November some of these precautions were abandoned as people became accustomed to living in a protracted state of crisis.[52]

In addition to the regular army and reserve units, the Finns mobilized their unique Civic Guards* organization and its

*The Finnish "Suojeluskunta" is variously translated as Civic Guards, Civil Guards, Territorial Corps, Protective Corps, or Defense Corps. It resembled the National Guard of the individual states of the U.S.A. in many respects.

female auxiliary during the YH period. Formed by local initiative during the fall of 1917, the Civic Guards were the nucleus of the White Army in the 1918 war. Charged with the defense of the fatherland and "its lawful social order," this voluntary organization fostered such peacetime activities as rifle and skiing competitions, mass athletics, concerts, and fund raising for arms purchases. An average of 80,000 to 100,000 members annually participated in its training programs. Their Commander-in-Chief, General Malmberg, was directly responsible to the President of the Republic, and Marshal Mannerheim was their honorary commander. A large percentage of the Guards officers were also army reserve officers. Upon mobilization, the Civic Guards served to augment the field army, as well as to train recruits and to perform civil defense duties.[53]

The women's auxiliary of the Civic Guards was designated Lotta Svärd, after the heroine of an epic by Johan Ludvig Runeberg, Finland's national poet. That legendary patriot accompanied her husband to the war of 1808–09 as a canteen worker, remaining to serve his comrades after he fell in battle against the Russians. Considering Finland's limited manpower, the services of the 100,000 modern Lottas were indispensable. They served as air raid spotters, assistant nurses, switchboard operators, military clerks, cooks, laundresses, and in many other capacities which relieved men for combat duties. "Little Lottas," aged 8 to 17—closely resembling the Girl Scouts of other nations—also helped by writing letters to lonely servicemen, collecting and mailing gift parcels (often simply addressed to "soldiers at the front") and performing other services. Letters from the troops reflected the men's appreciation of these invaluable contributions. One principle of the Lottas was the admonition "Be not ostentatious either in habits or in dress. Humility is a priceless virtue."[54] Their uniform, apparently designed to insure chastity, reflected those Puritan virtues: heavy black stockings; very long, shapeless, somber-gray dresses; and floppy garrison hats. By contrast, the modest uniform of the Women's Army Corps of the U. S. Army was daringly provocative.

Another major asset was the Finnish soldier's thorough adaptation to his peculiar environment. In a land of long snowy winters and few paved roads, virtually all Finns became skilled cross-country skiers in childhood. Robust lumberjacks and woodsmen felt assured in their beloved forest, which covered some 70 percent of the country. A popular prewar sport was "orienteering," in which competitors raced through unfamiliar woods in any season—often at night—aided only by map and compass. The combination of forest lore and skiing ability produced deadly efficient offensive patrols which, moving silently and almost invisibly in their white snow capes, spread consternation deep behind the enemy's lines.

In marked contrast, many Red Army men were terrified by the dense woods, where lurked, in their own words, *Belaya Smert'*, the White Death.[55] Politruk Oreshin wrote that Finland's "countless ridges and hills covered with forest, its lakes and marshes make it grim and gloomy."[56] There is an undertone of awe in this description by Captain Shevenok, who fought on the Karelian Isthmus:

> No, the Finnish woods are altogether unlike our Ukraine. Tall pines stand all together in the snow like paintings. Above are branches and down below it is bare, as if you are standing not in groves but in some sort of grotto with pillars. The stars wink—frigid, still. The snow falls silently, straight in the eye. The firing of the guns sounds like a long drawn-out echo from afar, as if from a tube.[57]

Moreover, many of Finland's 60,000 lakes—in conjunction with marshes and rivers—channeled invading columns along narrow passageways where they were vulnerable to flanking attacks. Finnish peacetime training had stressed precisely such active defense tactics.

Even the season favored the defenders during most of the Winter War. The long hours of midwinter darkness limited the activity of the enemy's vastly superior air force. Snow hampered his roadbound mechanized columns, while facilitating the maneuvering of Finnish ski patrols. And the killing frost of that severe winter—lower temperatures had been recorded only twice since 1828[58]—caused the ill-prepared Red Army much greater casualties than it did the acclimated and survival-equipped Finns. While Red Army men froze to death by the hundreds in icy foxholes at 30° below zero, the Finns, camouflaged in the surrounding woods, were often enjoying the warmth of their inexpensive but practical twenty-man tents, heated by portable woodburning stoves.[59]

Finnish morale was also sustained during those trying days of early December by the hope and expectation of substantial assistance from the West, however illusory this subsequently proved to be.

Finally, in those hours of peril the nation reassuringly looked to Marshal Mannerheim, a man who was already a living legend. Although divided on his political leanings, virtually all Finns shared a sound confidence in his military leadership.

While maintaining his habitual external composure, the Marshal spent many troubled hours during that first hectic week deciding how best to employ his scant reserves to counter the far-flung thrusts of the rapidly advancing enemy. Originally intending to retain all available reserves for the main front on the Karelian Isthmus, he was compelled instead to disperse many of them piecemeal towards Kuhmo, Suomussalmi, and Tolvajärvi, where the unexpectedly strong penetrations of the 8th and 9th Armies were causing alarm. Apart from a few battalions of poorly trained and equipped reservists, and the nine supply battalions which had been reluctantly earmarked during the YH period for their unaccustomed role as combat troops, the Commander-in-Chief's reserves consisted of only two incomplete divisions—the 6th at Luumäki in southern Finland and the 9th at Oulu.[60]

One of the 9th Division's three regiments, JR 26* had been sent to the Isthmus during the YH period. On 4 December JR 25 was made the nucleus of a brigade which was dispatched towards Kuhmo. The remaining regiment, JR 27, then in Kemi, was ordered on 7 December to depart for Suomussalmi; it, too, was to serve as the kernel of a new brigade.[61]

The 6th Division was also fragmented: on 5 December JR 16 was ordered to proceed towards Tolvajärvi as the major unit in a special combat force under the direct command of the Marshal, an indication of the gravity of the situation developing north of Lake Ladoga. The remaining two regiments, JR 17 and

*JR = Infantry Regiment

18, were sent to reinforce the main theater of war southeast of Viipuri.[62]

With these hasty troop dispositions, the stage was being set for some of the most dramatic battles in modern history. Although the odds were staggering, Marshal Mannerheim discerned in the situation opportunities for daring countermoves. Each of the enemy's thrusts through the northern wilds was a serious threat in itself, yet none of the Soviet motorized columns could cooperate with those on its flanks because they were separated by tens of miles of roadless woods. Under the circumstances, the best Finnish defense was a vigorous offense. But it would not be enough merely to check and contain the enemy columns. In order that the Finnish reserves flung against them might later be redeployed to the decisive Isthmus front, it was essential that the northern units of the Red Army be thoroughly defeated. Given the invader's marked superiority over the Finnish forces which could be spared for the counterattacks, the Marshal's strategy was extremely bold. Its successful execution depended largely on finding field commanders who could match it in aggressiveness and imagination.[63]

*Ere the pigmy full unfolding,*
*Quick becomes a mighty giant.*
**RUNE II**

CHAPTER II

# Tourist Season Ends

WHEN HE LEARNED THAT SUOJÄRVI HAD FALLEN ON 2 DECEM-
ber, Colonel Paavo Talvela rushed straight to the Hotel Helsinki to see Marshal Mannerheim. The Colonel had led the 1919
campaign in Ladoga-Karelia, and he later studied the region in
detail at the Finnish War College, where he graduated first in
his class. The strategic implications of a successful enemy advance in that area were all too clear to him. If the Red Army
seized the railroad running through Värtsilä and Sortavala to
the Karelian Isthmus, both the communications of the IV Army
Corps operating north of Lake Ladoga and the rear of the entire
Mannerheim Line would be imperiled.

Although the Commander-in-Chief shared his concern and
welcomed his expert opinions, he did not immediately grant
his requests. Colonel Talvela asked for a front command, but he
was then performing valuable service on the War Materiel
Council. Because there were so few reserves, his suggestion to
reinforce the threatened area with Infantry Regiment JR 16,
led by an esteemed fellow veteran of the 1919 campaign, Lt.
Colonel Aaro Pajari, also required further consideration.[1]

In the following days the Finnish defense rapidly deteriorated: on 3 December Task Force Räsänen's counterattack
against the 139th Division failed; on the next day the improvised holding positions along the Aittojoki River were abandoned; on the 5th Ägläjärvi fell and the 139th Division pushed
on towards Tolvajärvi, halfway from the border to the railroad
at Värtsilä. Meanwhile, by 5 December the Red Army's 155th

Division, advancing in two columns just north of the 139th towards Ilomantsi, had reached Korkeakangas.* If it captured the Ilomantsi road junction it would threaten Korpiselkä, some 25 miles to the south, which, in turn, was only 15 miles to the rear of the Finnish units at Tolvajärvi.[2]

To cope with the impending catastrophe, Marshal Mannerheim summoned Colonel Talvela to his headquarters in the evening of 5 December. On the same day he ordered Lt. Colonel Pajari to proceed to Värtsilä with Regiment JR 16. One artillery battery was also dispatched to the area.[3]

The Marshal had already replaced the IV Army Corps commander; now he decided that organizational changes were also required. To simplify the command problems of the harassed Corps, its northern sector would be detached and reconstituted as a Group subordinated directly to Supreme Headquarters. The mission of this Group was simple and straightforward: defeat the enemy advancing on Ilomantsi and Tolvajärvi, then recapture Suojärvi—accomplish this with forces which, when all the reinforcements arrived, would total less than half the enemy's known strength![4]

When Colonel Talvela arrived at Mikkeli at 4 A.M. on Independence Day, 6 December, he found the Marshal—whom he had expected to see in pajamas at that hour—in his customary immaculate uniform. The Colonel was given the command of the new Group, Marshal Mannerheim considering him "a fearless and strong-willed commander, who possessed that degree of ruthlessness required in an offensive against a greatly superior adversary."[5]

Everything in Paavo Talvela's past confirmed a strong will. As a youthful Finnish patriot, he had volunteered for service in the 27th Jäger Battalion which received its baptism of fire in the Imperial German Army fighting tsarist Russia. After the Jägers returned to Finland in 1918, he rose to the rank of major in just three months during the Finnish civil war. Thereafter he was instrumental in displacing the clique of senior officers who tried to prevent Jäger influence from dominating the Finnish Army. Although promoted to full colonel in 1928 at the age of 31, he resigned two years later because he considered his

*See Map No. 6, p. 38

superiors in the General Staff "visionaries."[6]

During the 1930s, while holding various executive positions in business, he was a frequent guest in the Marshal's home in Helsinki. Naturally, he was recalled to active duty in 1939. A keen judge of men, Marshal Mannerheim recognized in the Colonel precisely those qualities required for this difficult assignment.[7]

Shortly after arriving at Värtsilä on 6 December, Lt. Colonel Pajari received a call from Colonel Talvela at Mikkeli, ordering him to drive to the front at Tolvajärvi, thoroughly acquaint himself with the situation, then return to Värtsilä to brief the Colonel, who would arrive later that night. Pajari reached Tolvajärvi at 10 P.M. and returned in time to meet Colonel Talvela when he arrived at 3 A.M.[8]

The briefing was anything but encouraging: after a week of continuous retreat under heavy enemy fire—interrupted only by costly but futile delaying actions—the officers and men alike were physically exhausted and mentally in a state bordering on panic. As was the case elsewhere, enemy tanks were a major cause of this demoralization. In contrast with other Russian units, moreover, the leadership of the Red Army's 139th Division was able and energetic. The attackers repeatedly employed daring flanking maneuvers through wooded terrain under cover of darkness. In Ladoga-Karelia there had not yet been sufficient snow to hamper such tactics, nor to permit the Finns to capitalize on their skill with skis. Given the enemy's initial four-or five-to-one numerical advantage, plus a much greater superiority in artillery and a monopoly of armor, the situation seemed almost beyond redemption.[9]

Lt. Colonel Pajari returned to the front on the 7th, determined to hold at least the western shore of Lake Tolvajärvi, which was ideal terrain for defense. When he took over command from Lt. Colonel Räsänen at 5 P.M., Task Force R was redesignated Task Force P. The situation was steadily worsening: Bicycle Battalion PPP 7 had retreated five miles that day, from Ristisalmi to Lake Hirvasjärvi.[10]

However, the odds against the defense were narrowing somewhat: a second artillery battery (5/KTR*12) had arrived in the

*KTR=Field Artillery Regiment

GROUP TALVELA'S INITIAL AREA OF OPERATIONS    MAP 5

Tolvajärvi area on 6 December and two additional batteries (7 and 8/KTR 6) were enroute; a battalion (ErP*9) detached from the IV Army Corps was ordered to start early on 8 December for Honkavaara at the northern end of Lake Ala Tolvajärvi; and— most significantly—the main elements of Pajari's own Regiment, JR 16, arrived in the Korpiselkä-Tolvajärvi area on 7 and 8 December.[11]

On the 8th the defense at the Lake was hard pressed. The First Battalion of JR 16 arrived from Värtsilä in the morning

*Er=Independent (or detached), P=Battalion

and took up positions north and west of the Kivisalmi bridge at the narrows between Lakes Tolvajärvi and Taivaljärvi.* The Third Battalion arrived the same day and was stationed along the western shores of Lakes Tolvajärvi and Hirvasjärvi. In the afternoon, the front of the First Battalion broke and Colonel Talvela arrived that evening in time to witness its panicky retreat—some elements fleeing as far as Korpiselkä. He ordered his officers to stop them and form a reserve in the Varolammi area, but the retreat was not entirely checked and the ground lost would prove costly to regain. The enemy now held Kotisaari Island and the strategic peninsula which jutted almost to the western shore at the northern end of Lake Tolvajärvi. They commandeered for the headquarters of the 609th Regiment an attractive new two-story tourist hotel, situated on the peninsula atop a hill overlooking the picturesque lakes. Finland's uninvited guests were going first class.[12]

The Third Battalion of JR 16 could only be kept in its positions by the personal exhortations of Lt. Colonel Pajari, who calmly strolled among its front line troops. He was especially worried about this unit, which consisted mainly of workers from industrial Tampere, a center of leftist sentiment. Unlike the First and Second Battalions, the cadre of the Third contained very few Civic Guards—troops whom he considered superior to other reservists in military training, discipline, and morale. An incident which had occurred in Tampere on Ascension Day in 1933 also bothered him. As the ranking officer attending a celebration marking the 15th anniversary of the fall of that Red stronghold to the Whites during the civil war, Lt. Colonel Pajari led about 200 unarmed Civic Guards officers down the city's main street to haul down ten red flags which the Social Democrats had hoisted beneath the national colors. This created considerable resentment against Pajari personally, as well as aggravating class tensions in the district. Who could predict how these men would now follow him in battle?[13]

Colonel Talvela's comments about the state of affairs at this juncture reveal the aggressive quality of his leadership: "A total catastrophe seemed imminent, as the superior enemy . . . could continue the attack anytime and pierce the front

*See Map No. 7, p. 45

... In situations like this, as in all confused and hopeless situations, an energetic attack against the nearest enemy was and is the only way to improve the spirits of the men and to get control of the situation."[14]

Lt. Colonel Pajari, in agreement with that concept, volunteered to lead a raiding party composed in part of fresh troops from his Second Battalion which had been held in reserve at Tjokki. Shortly before midnight his raiders (the Fourth Company, commanded by Lt. Urho Isotalo, and Lt. Eero Kivelä's Ninth Company) set out across the ice of Lake Tolvajärvi south of Kotisaari Island for the enemy-held shore.[15]

About 1 A.M. on the same night, the Seventh Bicycle Battalion began a coordinated attack on Kotisaari, but it retreated back across the ice in disorder when its commander, Captain R. A. Ericsson, was killed. The unit's original combat commander, Major J. E. Saarva, had been shot through the chest only five days earlier. This grim and rapid turnover in leaders increased the demoralization of the battalion.[16]

The success of the entire operation now rested with the troops led by Pajari in person. Their adventure, in the words of another distinguished Finnish officer, General Heinrichs, was "almost unbelievable." The Ninth Company encountered water on the ice, turned southward, lost contact with Pajari, and fought its own engagement. It rejoined the Fourth Company during the return trip the next morning. Meanwhile, Lt. Isotalo's men reached their target area. Both Pajari and Isotalo were partially deaf, and—in spite of the need for stealth—they had to shout their orders into each other's ears. Nevertheless, they completely surprised the enemy sleeping around campfires at Kivisalmenkangas, south of the Kivisalmi bridge. The sentinels were unaware of the ghostly figures in white snow capes stealing thru the dark woods around them. When the raiders were within small arms range, they simultaneously opened a withering fire on the unsuspecting foe. The drowsy Russians, awakened by the shattering noise, saw only the flashes from rifles and automatic weapons in the shadows of the trees. In their confusion, they shot wildly in all directions. Different elements of the Soviet unit began firing on each other, while the Finns withdrew from the battle without losses. Pajari's

weary but exhilarated troops reached the relative safety of Tolvajärvi village about 5 A.M.[17]

Probably because both sides were tired, the 9th was a fairly
uneventful day in this sector. Lt. Colonel Räsänen temporarily
resumed command of the Task Force, while Pajari, who suffered from chronic heart trouble, recuperated from the night's
exertions. Some of his raiding party companions had only four
hours' rest before an artillery barrage drove them out of their
farmhouse refuge.[18]

The next day was also "relatively quiet," to use that headquarters' phrase which was meaningless to those individuals
who found themselves in the thick of the isolated skirmishes
which never ceased. Numerous patrol actions, artillery fire,
and snipers continued to take their unspectacular but tragic
toll. As one example, the Third Machine Gun Company lost two
of its three messenger runners that day.[19]

On 10 December Colonel Talvela visited his other Task Force
at Ilomantsi, where the advance of the 155th Division threatened to wreck his contemplated counterattack at Tolvajärvi
before it began. Here the forces at his disposal were considerably weaker than even those opposing the 139th Division. [20]

By 7 December the enemy had taken the high ground overlooking Möhkö, barely twelve miles from the Ilomantsi-Kor-
piselkä road. Major Nikoskelainen, commander of ErP 11, the
exhausted battalion which had fought alone all the way from
the frontier, received permission from Colonel Ekholm to withdraw to Oinaansalmi, but Colonel Talvela emphatically intervened by phone to insist on holding Möhkö. The defenders
repelled several attacks there, but they were finally forced back
to Oinaansalmi on the 9th.[21]

Colonel Per Ole Ekholm, a fellow veteran of the Jägers who
had once been Colonel Talvela's senior in the Civic Guards, had
been in command of Task Force A in this region for the first few
days. When Group Talvela was formed, Task Force A was
subordinated to the Group and redesignated Task Force E. Initially this created some confusion, because Colonel Ekholm did
not receive the orders subordinating him to Colonel Talvela for
about two days.[22]

Task Force Ekholm soon reached its full strength of only four

THE ILOMANTSI SECTOR                          MAP 6

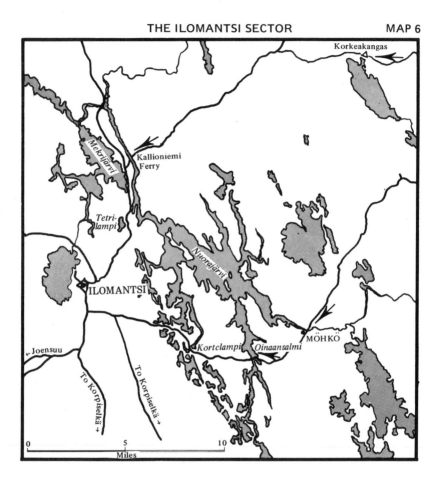

battalions. Since two of these had been part of Colonel Ekholm's Supply Brigade in peacetime, their men were inade-
quately equipped and poorly trained for combat missions. A
mortar detachment which arrived on 8 December provided the
first heavy weapons. A short while later one incomplete battery
of artillery (Ptri* II/KTR 6) was assigned, but of the two obsolescent French 75mm guns, only one was serviceable. In comparison, the opposing 155th Division had over a hundred
artillery pieces, counting the antitank guns which it employed
against infantry targets because there were no tanks in Group
Talvela.[23]

*Ptri=Battery

With these modest resources, Colonel Ekholm achieved the first "total" victory of the war. On the evening of 9 December an enemy battalion of 300-350 men slipped unnoticed through the lines north of Tetrilampi, near Kallioniemi Ferry. Discovered later by a Finnish patrol, it was quietly encircled in the darkness by forces heavily equipped with machine guns. Just before dawn the Finns opened fire simultaneously, killing every single Russian. This, the first of numerous battles of annihilation, boosted the morale of the entire Group. (Even the enemy's boots were prized, as many of Ekholm's troops were still improperly clothed for the increasingly severe weather.) That engagement, like the Pajari raid of the previous night, was undoubtedly a severe shock to the Soviet commanders who had so far experienced only the victorious pursuit of a demoralized adversary.[24]

In the evening of 10 December, Colonel Talvela issued preliminary orders to both Pajari and Ekholm for major counteroffensives on the 11th.[25]

The tempo of the fighting in the Tolvajärvi region picked up during the night of 10–11 December. In the quaintly apt language of the Finnish participants, the largest of that night's engagements became known as the "Sausage War." An audacious enemy combat group of two or three companies had outflanked the defenses north of Lake Tolvajärvi on the 10th, reaching Detachment Pajari's only supply road about two miles northwest of the village of Tolvajärvi. In this area were the Headquarters Company of Regiment JR 16, all of the supply elements of the Third Battalion, and some artillery positions. About 11 P.M. the raiders struck in the vicinity of the Third Machine Gun Company's field kitchen, where sausage soup was being prepared. Fortunately, the Russians paused to eat their prize, giving the Finns a little time to organize their defense.[26]

By chance, Lt. Colonel Pajari was passing the spot when the firing began. He hastily formed a human chain with about 100 men who were in the immediate vicinity—clerks, cooks, supply NCOs, and other housekeeping troops. Not even the artillerymen present were adequately trained for such infantry combat. Pajari conducted the counterattack in the manner of a platoon leader, shouting simple commands which were repeated down the line. In the pitch darkness of the forest, the fighting developed into fierce hand-to-hand conflict in which even bayonets were employed. At Pajari's side, Sgt. Vilho Reinikka had just shot one member of an enemy machine gun crew when his automatic jammed on an empty cartridge. While trying to fix it, the artillery NCO was hit in the left arm, which went lame. He then cleared his gun while holding it between his teeth— meanwhile receiving two more machine gun bullets in his arm and one in his left side. In spite of the pain, he managed to kill the remaining Russian machine gunners before quitting the battle to have his arm amputated at the shoulder. Nearby, a two-man team was taking a heavy toll of the enemy; while his partner flashed a strong light ahead, Sgt. Miinalainen fired his Suomi machine pistol at the hapless Russians caught in its glare.[27]

Later, two Finnish companies from the front line reserves attacked from the east, and the intruders finally scattered in retreat about 4 A.M. Both sides suffered heavy casualties, but few of the Russians lived to reach their own lines. Daylight revealed the grisly scene of corpses near the field kitchen still clutching their costly last meal. Many others who survived the battle were subsequently found frozen in the woods.[28]

Lt. Isotalo laconically entered into his report on this affair a seemingly trivial item which concealed tremendous potential: during the height of the fighting, he heard from a distance the traditional battle cry dating from the Thirty Years War, "Hakkaa Päälle!—Cut them down!"[29] The fighting spirit of the Finns was reawakening.

While the Sausage War was raging, the preliminary maneuvering for another bitter engagement was taking place about three miles away, within earshot of the first battle. Around 1 A.M., the Ninth Company of Regiment JR 16 received information that a battalion from Kotisaari Island had crossed the ice and was attempting to outflank the Finns from the south. The Company commander, Lt. Eero Kivelä, leaving his machine guns and two platoons in position south of Tolvajärvi village, led three rifle platoons in a sweeping night march to outflank the outflankers. When dawn broke about 7 A.M., the Finns surprised and routed their quarry, killing scores as they fled back across the ice to their island base. Almost two Soviet companies were destroyed, and the booty included 16 very useful machine guns.[30]

Although these victories strengthened morale, the all-night battles exhausted both the participants and their neighboring units which had been alerted for possible action. A Soviet frontal attack and additional flanking attacks were repelled during daylight hours. By noon on 11 December some units had been fighting for four days without rest; these included the entire Third Battalion and two other companies of Regiment JR 16, the Eighth Company of JR 37, and certain elements of the 112th Independent Battalion. Consequently, Lt. Colonel Pajari requested postponement of the counteroffensive which had been scheduled for that day. Colonel Talvela, in daily contact with Mikkeli, was on this occasion encouraged by the optimism of Colonel Aksel Airo of the Supreme HQ Staff, who agreed that the counterblow need not be rushed.[31]

Pajari felt that his troops would not even be sufficiently refreshed by the 12th. Talvela's Chief of Staff, Lt. Colonel Stewen, therefore proposed that the initial attack be staged by the rested units then in the Group reserve, Battalion ErP 9 and two companies of the First Battalion of JR 16.[32]

Accordingly, on 11 December Colonel Talvela issued a revised battle order for the 12th, based on the expectation that the success of the reserve units would inspire the others to advance. The reinforced battalion, commanded by Major J. A. Malkamäki, was to deploy to the northern end of Lake Hirvasjärvi. Its ultimate mission was to attack the enemy-held peninsula northeast of Kotisaari Island from the rear. At H hour (the time of the attack) Malkamäki would be subordinated to Lt. Colonel Pajari. The latter's Task Force would hold its present positions along the western shore of Lake Tolvajärvi until Malkamäki's strike progressed, at which time Pajari's troops would take the offensive in their sector. For this operation Task Force P was reinforced with the Tenth Independent Battalion and the Eighth Company of Regiment JR 37.[33]

In the Ilomantsi sector, enemy attacks were repelled on the 11th at both Oinaansalmi and Kallioniemi Ferry, the enemy losing 134 men at the Ferry. Although Task Force Ekholm had

no antitank guns, two tanks were destroyed at Oinaansalmi
that day. By this time the Finns were employing two simple
weapons for in-fighting with tanks: a cluster of small charges
bound around a wooden grip or a long-handled grenade, and
the "Molotov cocktail"—a bottle containing kerosene, ignited
before throwing by an attached wick or saturated rags (later,
refined versions were ignited by chemicals and an attached
capsule of sulfuric acid). Either was quite effective against
light tanks, but it took great courage to lie in wait in a foxhole
until advancing tanks were within throwing range.[34]

Colonel Ekholm was also ordered to prepare to attack on 12
December. During the discussions at Ilomantsi on the 10th, he
had proposed an offensive against the weaker units at Kallioniemi Ferry, but Colonel Talvela decided that the nearer and
more threatening forces had to be checked first. Therefore, the
battle orders specified that one of the Task Force's four battaltions should hold the positions at the Ferry, while the other
three attacked Möhkö from the front and both flanks.[35]

For the past several days, the jittery defenses of Group Talvela had barely withstood strong enemy probes. Now the die
was cast for a major counteroffensive against that same superior enemy. One way or the other, 12 December would be a
day of decision.

On paper, the plan of attack looked good. Major Malkamäki's
troops would get an advance start, cross the northern end of
Lake Hirvasjärvi at dawn in a surprise attack against the Hirvasvaara ridge sector, then proceed south towards the rear of
the enemy forces defending the peninsula at the northern end
of Lake Tolvajärvi. A second pincer would capture Kotisaari
Island to bring the enemy's center communications under fire.
Only after the invader had weakened his center to counter the
threat posed by Malkamäki would Pajari throw his main force
across Hevossalmi Strait to capture the strategic peninsula and
drive down the main road.[36]

From the very early hours of 12 December, actual operations
and the neat theoretical plan went their divergent ways.
Around midnight, the Second and Third Companies of the First
Battalion of JR 16 began moving from their rest area to Malkamäki's assembly point, which was about one-half mile west of

the northwestern shore of Lake Hirvasjärvi. The first ac-
cumulative snows had fallen in the Tolvajärvi region the week
before, and by now the depth was about a foot. Because of rough
terrain and the failure of the trail-breaking detachment to
make sufficient tracks, it took until dawn to cover the few miles
to the rendezvous. Malkamäki's attack was therefore delayed
until daylight, and all chance for surprise was lost. [37]

In fact, it was the Finns themselves who were astonished.
About two battaltions of the Soviet 718th Regiment had moved
undetected into position for their own flanking attack around
the northern end of Lake Hirvasjärvi. The intended surprise
attacks therefore developed into a confused meeting engagement in which each side cancelled out the other. The Third
Company, which was on the flank most exposed to the unexpected enemy force, encountered withering fire from ten machine guns before it even reached the western shore of the
Lake, and it retreated rapidly all the way back to the Tolvajär-
vi-Kokkari road. The Second Company succeeded in crossing
the Lake without losses and turned south towards its objective
at Hirvasvaara. However, its advance stalled around 11 A.M.
when it received heavy fire from the rear and simultaneously
lost contact on its right with Battalion ErP 9.[38]

That Battalion had also encountered disruptive enemy fire
early in the attack. By 10:20 A.M., its First Company had retreated down the western shores of Lakes Hirvasjärvi and Myllyjärvi to Tolvajärvi village. By 11:30, enemy flank attacks had
also stopped the Second and Third Companies which—along
with the Second Company of JR 16—had reached the Hirvasvaara ridge. Around noon, Major Malkamäki ordered the retreat. The remaining units of ErP 9 then withdrew in a wide arc
around Lake Hirvasjärvi, to a point west of Tolvajärvi, continuing that night to their bivouac in Tjokki.[39]

When Malkamäki retreated, the commander of the Second
Company of JR 16 also ordered a withdrawal along the same
general route, parts of his unit reaching Kokkari during the
night. Nevertheless, parts of the Second Company remained in
the Hirvasvaara area until evening, making the most significant contribution of the Malkamäki venture by tying down
forces which might otherwise have endangered Pajari's entire
operations.[40]

While Malkamäki's reinforced battalion was being routed in the north, reverses were also experienced by the southern pincer which attacked an enemy battalion, supported by machine guns and two batteries of artillery, on Kotisaari Island. The First and Second Companies of ErP 112 assaulted the southern tip of the Island about 8 A.M., but the Ninth Company of JR 16 did not launch its scheduled coordinated offensive on their left flank because it had not received word from its Battalion Headquarters explicitly defining H-hour. Although elements of Battalion ErP 112 reached Kotisaari and even the shoreline east of the Island, by early afternoon they were forced to retreat to the small islands south and southwest of Kotisaari.[41]

Meanwhile, Pajari's forces in the center, at Hevossalmi, had also fallen behind schedule. Originally planned for 7 A.M., their attack was postponed until 9:15 because the snowy terrain had delayed the movement of the supporting artillery. Consequently, the Second Battalion of JR 16, the spearhead of the center thrust, had to storm across the ice towards the strong enemy positions on the Tolvajärvi peninsula in broad daylight. This was doubly unfortunate because the long-awaited artillery support was very weak when it finally arrived.[42]

Lt. Isotalo's Fourth Company managed to cross the Hevossalmi Strait on the southern side of the roadway with few casualties, thanks to the highly effective supporting fire of the Second Machine Gun Company. The Sixth Company, which started its attack at the same time on the northern side of the road, was unable to proceed. Heavy machine gun fire from two directions pinned the commander, Lt. Martti Siukosaari, and seven others down flat on the ice in the middle of the Strait, while artillery shells burst around them. Miraculously, only two of those exposed human targets were hit before friendly machine gun covering fire enabled the others to reach the southern side of the road embankment. As was usual at this stage of the war, Soviet artillery units tried to compensate in volume for their lack of accuracy. Barrages of shells tore into the western shore of Hevossalmi, ripping up the barbed wire and blackening the snow, but otherwise inflicting little damage. The majority of the Sixth Company joined the Fourth Company south of the roadway when they realized the futility of trying to advance on the northern side. Lt. Aarne Heinivaho's

THE BATTLE OF TOLVAJÄRVI, 12 DECEMBER 1939     MAP 7

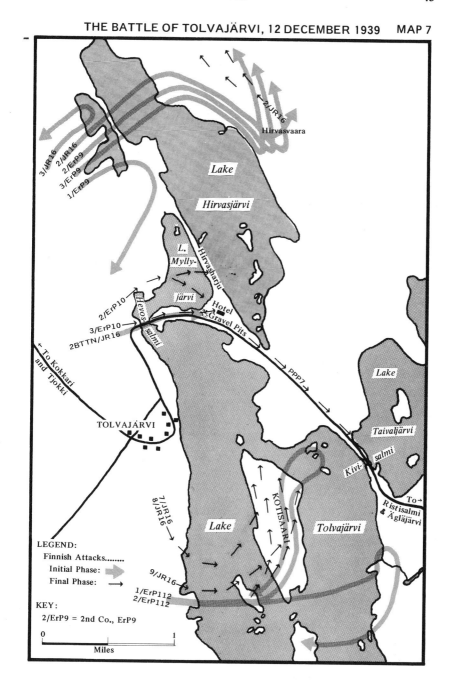

Hirvasvaara

2/JR16

Lake

Hirvasjärvi

3/JR16
2/JR16
2/ErP9
3/ErP9
1/ErP9

L.
Mylly-

L. Hirvasjarju

järvi

2/ErP10

Hevossalmi

Hotel
Gravel Pits

3/ErP10
2BTTN/JR16

To Kokkari
and Tjokki

PPP7

Lake

Taivaljärvi

Kivi-
salmi

TOLVAJÄRVI

To→
Ristisalmi
& Ägläjärvi

7/JR16
8/JR16

KOTISAARI

Lake

Tolvajärvi

9/JR16

1/ErP112
2/ErP112

LEGEND:
Finnish Attacks........
   Initial Phase: 
   Final Phase: →

KEY:
   2/ErP9 = 2nd Co., ErP9

0                    1
Miles

Fifth Company now joined the battle, and by the time they secured a firm foothold across the Straits, the troops of all three companies were intermingled, making leadership very difficult.[43]

The Second Machine Gun Company and a platoon from the First Machine Gun Company continued to provide excellent support, silencing one artillery battery before it could even zero in on the Strait, compensating as well as possible for the weak Finnish artillery and the shortage of mortar shells. Several of the machine gun squads crossed the Strait as soon as the rifle squads were in position. They first assisted in clearing out enemy foxholes in the western end of the peninsula, then directed their barrage against the enfilading fire from Hirvasharju. There was fierce fighting along the entire length of the peninsula leading to the tourist hotel, during which several platoon leaders fell. Lt. Isotalo was hit in the hand, but he continued leading his company after having the wound bandaged.[44]

The enemy made a determined stand some 200 yards west of the hotel hill, where gravel pits afforded protective cover. Here they emplaced more than ten machine guns, plus other automatic weapons. In a bitter and costly engagement, the Finnish infantry drove them from the pits towards the hotel. At this moment a few light tanks appeared, but Group Talvela's only antitank platoon was on hand with its 37mm guns. Since the narrow wooded roadway prevented a concerted tank attack, they could be dealt with one at a time. Three tanks were disabled and abandoned between the Strait and the hotel.[45]

When the Second Battalion reached the slope of the hotel hill, it was stopped in a hail of artillery and automatic weapons fire. At noon, Lt. Heinivaho ordered the entire Battalion to pull back to the shelter of the gravel pits to rest and regroup. During the ensuing lull in the fighting, the men were reassembled in their own platoons for more effective leadership. By now, a Finnish mortar platoon had reached the ridge behind the pits, from where it was able to cover the approaches to the hotel. An hour later, the enemy attempted a counterattack, but Finnish machine guns and mortars quickly halted their advance.[46]

About 12 o'clock, by which time Malkamäki's force should have been threatening the rear of the hotel position for at least two hours, Lt. Colonel Pajari received the first substantial and alarming report from that sector, delivered orally by an exhausted lieutenant. Almost simultaneously, a report from the Second Battalion informed him that it was stalled at the gravel pits and could not take the strong hotel position without reinforcements. From his Command Post near the road west of Hevossalmi, Pajari witnessed the steady stream of casualties being evacuated to military hospitals. A disquieting proportion were key NCOs and junior officers from his own regiment. [47]

He now faced a crucial question: Should he use part of his slim reserves to bolster the northern flank against an obvious threat from that direction, or should he commit them in the center to try for a rapid decision on the only front where even partial success had been achieved? When nothing had gone as planned that day, dare he gamble further? While he was pondering the alternatives, a new report came in from the north— at least some troops were still holding out there, tying down the enemy on his flank. That decided the issue: Pajari threw his support to the center. The Third Company of ErP 10 was dispatched on skis along the peninsula to the gravel pits, while that Battalion's Second Company was flung over the ice of Lake Myllyjärvi against the enemy positions on Hirvasharju.[48]

About 1:30 P.M., the Second Battalion of JR 16, now supported by the Third Company of ErP 10, resumed the attack on the hotel hill. The building, atop a 60-foot knoll, was a miniature fortress. The ground floor walls were stone, and a second floor with many windows overhung the first. Machine guns were posted on opposite corners outside, as well as inside at the windows. Since the command post and headquarters of the 609th Regiment had not had time to evacuate the hotel, the enemy used all available men in its defense. The hill was furiously contested in repeated attacks for an hour, with heavy casualties on both sides. While trying to hurl a grenade thru a window, Lt. Heinivaho was hit in the left arm and side, but he was able to crawl back to the aid station to begin the long trek by sleigh and bus to the hospital. Another officer of the Fifth Company, Lt. Lehtinen, was killed near the crest of the hill, his body rolling down the slope.[49]

Gradually the attackers gained the upper hand. The Second Company of ErP 10, advancing under the protection of Finnish machine gun fire, reached the peninsula on the northern flank of the hotel, bringing it under attack from a second angle. Finally, some of the assaulting troops secured a favorable position on the opposite flank, where the Russians could not return their fire. Realizing their hopeless position, many of the enemy rank and file fled at this time, and the chase of the demoralized foe began. Pajari threw his last reserve battalion, PPP 7, into the pursuit. Others dashed up to the hotel's stone wall, from where they threw grenades thru the windows, silencing the defenders on the ground floor.[50]

While the decisive battle was underway around the hotel, another important operation was developing to the south. About two o'clock in the afternoon, the First and Second Companies of ErP 112 resumed the offensive against Kotisaari Island, supported this time by the Third Battalion of JR 16. Their coordinated attack gradually succeeded in rolling up the defense from south to north. By evening they had cleared the entire Island, capturing two artillery batteries and some twenty machine guns. This victory possed a threat to the enemy's only good supply road at Kivisalmi, thereby contributing to the day's final outcome.[51]

Pajari's bold decision now paid off. Brigade Commander Belyaev, shaken by reports that the center of his line was broken and one of his regimental command posts overrun at the hotel, his artillery fire control disrupted, and his retreat route threatened, ordered the entire 139th Division to withdraw. For the first time since the beginning of the invasion thirteen days earlier, a major unit of the Red Army was retreating! This electrifying news flashed thru the entire Finnish Army, skyrocketing its sagging morale. That night, the official press release announced it to the world in more circumspect terms.[52]

There remained the job of mopping up. The enemy still held the second floor of the hotel, firing intermittently from the windows at the troops passing by. Towards dusk the Second Battalion assigned the task of clearing the hotel to the Sixth Company. Lt. Siukosaari suggested burning it to avoid further losses, but Major Paloheimo, the commander of ErP 10 who happened to be present, would not permit this. Having ordered the Fourth Platoon to capture the building, Lt. Siukosaari crawled on hands and knees along the front wall, pistol in hand. Turning the corner, he was startled by an equally shocked Russian officer, pistol drawn, in the kitchen doorway less than a yard away. The Finn fired first. After the fighting near the hotel ceased, the body of the commander of the 609th Regiment was found there. When the platoon burst thru the main entrance, only dead bodies greeted them on the first floor, and by tossing hand grenades to the second floor they were able to take the hotel without a single casualty. Venturing upstairs, they captured 28 survivors, many of them wounded, huddled together in a back room. In addition to useful documents, the booty included eighteen machine guns and an enormous supply of rifle ammunition.[53]

The other platoons of the Sixth Company joined the remainder of their Battalion in mopping up as far as the destroyed Kivisalmi bridge that evening, after which they returned to the vicinity of Tolvajärvi village for much-needed rest. Colonel Talvela now intervened to order Pajari to continue the pursuit, with at least two companies, four miles farther to the Ristisalmi bridge, blown up by Task Force Räsänen during its retreat five days earlier. However, the exhaustion of the men was so great that this order was not executed.[54]

Task Force Ekholm's 12 December offensive failed in its objective of capturing Möhkö. The two flanking battalions reached the western edge of the village from the north and the south, but instead of turning towards the enemy's rear as ordered, they returned in their own tracks. Colonel Talvela, attributing the failure to the difficulties of maintaining tactical contact in such a dispersed maneuver, ordered the attack renewed the next day on a more restricted scale.[55]

In the Kallioniemi Ferry sector, four more Soviet tanks were destroyed on the 12th, and additional Russian attacks were repulsed on the 13th. However, the Finnish attack on Möhkö that day again failed, and the contending forces were stalemated. This in itself was quite an achievement for Colonel Ekholm's ragged troops. Had they not been able to hold the enemy, the victory at Tolvajärvi would have been impossible. [56]

This front soon froze, both literally and figuratively, at Oinaansalmi. The Finns held good positions here, behind a watercourse and higher than the enemy. Their best defenses, however, were the cold and the snow. It was never above freezing, and on 26 December the temperature dipped into the twenties below zero (Fahrenheit), reaching the minus thirties in January. The Soviet 155th Division, which had no skis until late in the war, was virtually immobilized when the snow reached a depth of two feet in January.[57]

Colonel Talvela insisted on his policy of active defense: continued offensive patrol activity, probing attacks, and limited offensives. Until the snow prevented it, the enemy followed similar tactics. On 14 December a Russian force of about a battalion slipped thru the lines and struck the Task Force's communications near Kortelampi. Colonel Ekholm personally led a company or so of cooks, supply men and other rear-echelon troops in a successful counteraction which resembled the "Sausage War."[58]

The smaller forces opposing each other at the Kallioniemi Ferry were also stalemated. An unsuccessful attack which Colonel Talvela ordered on 22 December got underway that evening and continued until about six o'clock in the morning. The badly battered Finnish battalion had to abandon nine machine guns and seven light machine guns during its retreat. In spite of this, enemy activity remained confined to artillery and aircraft harassment and small patrol actions.[59]

Meanwhile, the pursuit of the foe in the Tolvajärvi sector continued. While most of Lt. Colonel Pajari's weary troops rested on the day following their initial victory, Battalion PPP 7 advanced as far as the defile at Ristisalmi, where it stopped before strong enemy positions. The 139th Division was severely battered but not yet completely defeated; it stubbornly contested every favorable terrain feature along its line of march. The Finns bitterly acknowledged the Russian soldier's superiority at digging in for defense. Under those circumstances, both Colonel Talvela and Pajari believed that the policy best calculated to reduce casualties was to drive their troops mercilessly in unrelenting attacks to keep the enemy off balance. It is likely that even the letup on 13 December, although possibly unavoidable, caused additional losses later on. While some of Pajari's subordinates at the time considered him too harsh, in retrospect most of them understood the reason for his orders.[60]

When the Task Force resumed its full-scale counteroffensive on the 14th, the Finns did not know that they were now fighting a new opponent. The Eighth Army's reserve, the 75th Division, was thrown into the battle to replace the 139th Division. It was not until 16 December that Colonel Talvela learned that he had, in effect, a whole new campaign on his hands, when the new division and its three regiments were identified. Fortunately, by this time the remnants of the 139th Division were rapidly withdrawing: air reconnaissance on 17 December reported traffic moving both east and west in the Äglä järvi area, and heavy traffic to the east was sighted on the following two days. The main forces of the 75th Division were marching past the demoralized survivors of the 139th Division while enroute to face the confident victors—hardly the best preconditioning for their baptism of fire.[61]

The fighting near the Ristisalmi Strait, where enemy machine guns commanded the open field of ice, raged on 14 December from 8 A.M. until late in the day. At one point the spearhead battalion, ErP 9, spent a hectic hour pinned to the steep slopes of a narrow ridge, while two Soviet tanks drove back and forth along the road above them, firing in all directions. There was not so much as a Molotov cocktail on hand to oppose them. Finally, word of this situation reached Corporal Mutka of the antitank platoon a mile to the rear. He immediately hitched a gun to the nearest horse, galloped to the front, and swiftly knocked out both tanks. With the support of the Third Battalion of JR 16, the Strait was finally secured, and the enemy withdrew to Metsänvaara,* a mile to the east.[62]

During the entire campaign, Colonel Talvela alternated his few battalions between front duty and reserve status like a skillful football coach relieving his tired players. On 15 December, 355 fresh troops arrived at Kokkari and all but seven were immediately assigned to Pajari to fill in vacancies in his units. At this early stage of the war, it was somewhat disheartening to greet these relatively old, poorly trained and badly equipped replacements.[63]

On the 16th, a costly engagement was centered near In-

*See Map No. 8, p. 53

goinaho and Point 194 on the road to Äglajärvi. Here the Second
Battalion of JR 16 encountered fanatic resistance sparked by
about 200 crack troops from a Red Army officers' school, the
toughest opponents Talvela's Group ever had to face. These
tall, young, well-equipped Russians took a heavy toll of the
attackers; the First Platoon of the Sixth Company alone had five
of some twenty men killed here, including its leader, Lt. V.
Rantanen. After the battle, the Company commander, Lt. Siukosaari, found his brother's body among the dead outside the
first aid station. On the other hand, only two members of the
force from the officers' school escaped. The booty included
many machine guns, which were highly prized since the Finnish light machine gun, because of too close a tolerance, froze up
in cold weather.[64]

While the main forces were locked in combat along the Tolvajärvi-Äglajärvi road, Battalion ErP 10 was engaged in wide
flanking actions. Its First Company skirted about five miles
south of the road to Vieksinki, from where it staged guerilla
raids against the enemy's communications. Captain Lahtinen
led the Battalion's other two companies in a wide sweep to the
north, reaching the road at Yläjärvi to attempt a surprise attack
against Äglajärvi from the northwest.[65]

On the 17th Colonel Talvela subordinated all the forces in
reserve at Tolvajärvi to Pajari, urging his field commander to
push the attack vigorously. As his order stated, "The last ener-
gies of the troops must be used to achieve the great victory
looming ahead." He also authorized the immediate use of all
captured tanks, but Pajari soon received a report that these
were "mere junk." That same day, Lt. Colonel Pajari was promoted to full Colonel.[66]

On 18 December the preliminary skirmishing for Äglajärvi
village began. The enemy was again in strong positions supported by artillery. At this time his air activity—which had not
been significant in this region—also increased; bombing and
strafing attacks were launched against the Finnish batteries
and communications immediately behind the front. Captain
Lahtinen's outflanking companies were checked in heavy battles at Välimäki, two miles northwest of Äglajärvi. Five miles
to the southeast, a second ambitious flanking maneuver was
attempted in the evening. After a difficult march through dense

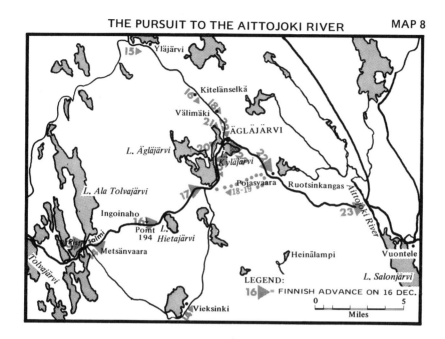

THE PURSUIT TO THE AITTOJOKI RIVER          MAP 8

LEGEND:

16 ▶ = FINNISH ADVANCE ON 16 DEC.

0           5
Miles

woods, Battalion ErP 112 emerged on the main road near Pojas-vaara. The tired troops, without artillery support, encountered strong enemy positions and had to retreat swiftly the next day. [67]

On the morning of 19 December, Marshal Mannerheim telephoned Colonel Talvela to inform him that he had promoted him to Major General. The Commander-in-Chief had been in close contact with Talvela, following the course of the campaign from the dismal succession of retreats to the present amazing reversal of fortunes. Although the full extent of the 139th Division's losses had been partially obscured because its defeat occurred over a period of several days and many of the fallen lay hidden in the snowy forest, the magnitude of the achievement was fully appreciated by the Marshal. At the same time, he was acutely aware of the heavy price of the victory. The mounting losses caused him to consider breaking off the attack, and he attributed it largely to General Talvela's insistence that he decided to continue trying for complete victory on this front. In contrast to his concern with many of his other field commanders, his main problem with General Talvela was in restraining him.[68]

Heavy fighting on 19 December and early on the 20th failed to achieve significant results. An attack against Äglajärvi village was scheduled for 8 A.M. on 20 December, but before it could get under way an enemy battalion surprised the outpost unit, the Second Company of ErP 9, near Kyläjärvi. Nine tanks penetrated to the center of the Company's position while it was still too dark for the antitank platoon to fire its guns. After the leading vehicle rammed and disabled the forward gun, Corporal Mutka destroyed the tank with a cluster of charges. This halted the tank column until dawn, when Corporal Mutka was able to sight his remaining antitank gun. He first set fire to the rear tank, then hit two others in the column. The last five were captured undamaged. After this, the planned Finnish attack began, but the results were again inconclusive. By the end of the day the village was still in enemy hands, although it was now surrounded on all but the eastern side.[69]

Meanwhile, General Talvela had requested Supreme Headquarters to assign to his command Lt. Colonel Kaarlo Viljanen, another experienced veteran of the Jägers and the civil war. Concerned about Colonel Pajari's physical limitations, Talvela had Viljanen accompany his Task Force commander at the front for orientation. Worn out himself, Pajari advised Talvela that his troops were too exhausted to continue the offensive. The General disagreed, but he ordered Colonel Pajari personally to take a few days' rest. Lt. Colonel Viljanen then assumed acting command of the Task Force, from 21 to 23 December, leading the weary troops into renewed assaults on the strongly entrenched enemy positions.[70]

Their losses and fatigue were so great, however, that efforts during daylight hours on the 21st were limited to battle reconnaissance and the regrouping of forces. Soviet air activity continued at a relatively high level, concentrated along the Tolvajärvi-Äglajärvi-Yläjärvi road. During the course of bombing and strafing runs that day, three Soviet planes were shot down behind the Finnish lines.[71]

Late in the evening, full-scale fighting resumed. The plan called for the Second Battalion of JR 16 and the First and Third

Companies of ErP 9 to advance across the eastern end of Lake Kyläjärvi to Äglajärvi, while two companies of ErP 10 and Battalion ErP 112 simultaneously attacked the village from the north. The operations began at 10:10 P.M., when the Fourth and Fifth Companies of the Second Battalion, camouflaged in snow suits, reached the middle of the Lake before being detected. Although they were then the targets of heavy machine gun fire from the shoreline, in the darkness it was inaccurate, and the first wave reached the outskirts of the village without losses. The Sixth Company, the Second Machine Gun Company, and the Battalion command-post unit followed next. Finally, the two companies of ErP 9, which had been delayed by marching difficulties, crossed the ice without losses.[72]

The misleading ease of the Lake crossing was mainly due to surprise; thereafter, the enemy retreated to barns, cellars, houses, pits, and any other cover the village provided. These he stubbornly defended with automatic weapons which took a terrible toll of the attackers. As the commander of ErP 9 described it, "The houses were shot full of holes like sieves, hand grenades were thrown in, but when we tried to enter there was always some Russian alive who fired.... From several units fell all the officers and a notable part of the NCOs who were the bravest in storming the nests." In the first hours of the engagement, the Second Battalion lost all three of its company commanders. The recently-appointed commander of the Fifth Company, Lt. Lipola, was killed just after midnight, about the same time that the Fourth Company's Lt. Isotalo was wounded. In the unlucky Sixth Company, the last remaining platoon leader died shortly before midnight, and Lt. Siukosaari, the commander and only surviving officer, was wounded in the early hours of 22 December. As he was being carried off, Siukosaari told Sergeant Rauhalahti to take command of the Company, which he did until Lt. Korppoo arrived from the Second Machine Gun Company to relieve him. The Third Company of ErP 9 retreated to the southern shore of the Lake after losing all of its officers and many of its NCOs, but officers hastily detached from the headquarters were able to return the company to the fight. The nerves of the middle-aged commander of the Second Battalion cracked under the stress of this battle. He directed machine gunners to fire towards their own troops, threatened to shoot an officer who refused to execute this order, and later broke down and cried at the sight of the wounded. Under these circumstances, only the remarkable fortitude of men and officers alike enabled them to persist in the attack.[73]

While the Fourth and part of the Sixth Companies advanced towards the village, the Fifth Company and a machine gun platoon turned to the southeast to prevent any reinforcements from reaching Äglajärvi along the main road. The larger part of the Sixth Company covered the rear of the Second Battalion, and the Second Company of ErP 9 remained in position on the southern shore of Lake Kyläjärvi, on the right flank of Battalion PPP 7. The Sixth Company reserve soon had to be flung into action alongside the Fifth Company, when an enemy relief force, including several tanks, arrived from the direction of Pojasvaara. Aided by field works constructed here during the YH period, the Finns at the roadblock stopped the reinforcements in their tracks. Nevertheless, the tanks were able to fire both at the troops defending the roadblock and over their heads at the units assaulting Äglajärvi.[74]

When the northern jaw of the pincers—Battalions ErP 10 and ErP 112—fought its way into the outskirts of the village, it was no longer possible for the Finns to employ artillery or mortars against the strongpoints for fear of hitting their own men. Thus the final phase of the battle for Äglajärvi was simply bloody house-to-house fighting. The decisive break came when the Second Company of PPP 7, which had retreated after its initial attack early in the morning had miscarried, finally stormed the very center of the village around noon. By 2 P.M., the entire 75th Division was in retreat towards Vuontele; a prisoner reported that its commander was lying wounded at Pojasvaara.[75]

Lt. Colonel Viljanen wasted no time in celebrating the fall of Äglajärvi; he immediately directed the First Battalion of JR 16 and the rested elements of PPP 7 to continue the battle towards Vuontele. About 3 P.M., the Soviet rear guard engaged PPP 7 in tough and costly skirmishes near Pojasvaara. The front held there until noon the next day, when the pursuit to the east resumed. By 8 P.M. on 23 December the Finnish vanguard reached the Aittojoki River, and the main forces of the Task Force were at Ruotsinkangas.[76]

When the Aittojoki line was attained, Marshal Mannerheim called a halt to the entire offensive. Although the objectives outlined to General Talvela on 6 December had included the recapture of Suojärvi, Finnish losses were already alarming. During the week of the pursuit, the Commander-in-Chief had cautioned his field commander more than once that his casualties were becoming excessive. The frontal attacks at the Tolvajärvi tourist hotel and at Äglajärvi had been especially costly. The 630 men killed and 1,320 wounded included 30 percent of the Task Force's officers and NCOs and 25 percent of the rank and file. Proportionally, these were the heaviest losses of the entire war. To stem this unacceptable rate of loss, the Marshal ordered General Talvela to take up defensive positions along the Aittojoki River.[77]

Tragic as the Finnish casualties were, those of the enemy were far greater. Along the main Tolvajärvi-Aittojoki road alone, the Red Army lost 4,000 dead and 580 prisoners. The number of wounded probably exceeded the number killed. And these figures do not include those fallen in the snowy woods on the flanks. The vast amount of materiel abandoned along the same road included 59 tanks and 220 machine guns.[78]

It would be difficult to exaggerate the significance of the Finnish victory at Tolvajärvi and the pursuit to the Aittojoki. In conjunction with the successful defense of Ilomantsi, they decisively eliminated the most acute threat to Ladoga-Karelia, with all that this implied for national survival. The dispatch of the Eighth Army's reserve, the 75th Division, to the wilderness beyond Äglajärvi was also an important contribution to the operations of the Finns engaging other Eighth Army divisions near Lake Ladoga. These considerations alone justified the costs of the victory.

However important those strategic factors were, the psychological impact was even more significant. From a defeatist attitude verging on total despair, both nation and army responded to the first great offensive victory of the war with optimism and self-confidence. Other spectacular feats of Finnish arms followed on the heels of Tolvajärvi, augmenting this spirit of hope and determination, but Group Talvela's exploits provided the first tangible proof to the Finns themselves that they could stop the Red Army colossus.

It is intriguing to speculate on why the Finns won the Tolvajärvi-Aittojoki campaign against odds which were never less than two to one in manpower and much greater in munitions, artillery, and armor. It was *not,* as was the case in certain later Finnish victories in the northern wilds, because the enemy was completely roadbound while the Finns were able to maneuver on skis; each side at Tolvajärvi launched flanking attacks—which were not decisive. Although Finnish soldiers generally enjoyed superiority in educational level and individual initiative, it was *not* a question of experienced troops defeating vastly inferior reservists; both forces included many poorly trained units.

This leaves two factors: esprit de corps and leadership. The morale of the bewildered Soviet infantryman was understandably low. He had been told that he was liberating the Finnish working class from its hatcd oppressors. He had been led to expect an easy victory, because the Finnish soldier would welcome him in that spirit. What was he to make of the fierce resistance he encountered from those same "oppressed" Finns? Prisoners captured by Battalion ErP 10 on 16 December reported that "hordes" of their comrades would surrender if they knew they would be well treated (their commissars instilled the belief that the Finns shot their captives). The 580 prisoners taken by Task Force Pajari represented over 10 percent of all prisoners captured during the entire war.[79]

Yet, if morale was a key factor, it must be recalled that in the initial stage of the fighting the Finns themselves were in a state bordering on panic. It was only after the arrival of Colonels Talvela and Pajari that success was attained, first in defense and then in counterattack. Thus, leadership emerges as the decisive factor. As General Heinrichs expressed it, "Before long the initiative and will power of the new leaders overturned the depressed mood and fatigue . . . Tolvajärvi was and remains a fascinating example of what, in a war, can be accomplished by strong will power and strong mind." Pajari appraised his superior's contributions in these terms, "The commander of

Group T . . . was the driving force in creating the belief in victory and the active battle spirit of Tolvajärvi and retaining them through the greatest mental and physical fatigue." Events had fully justified Marshal Mannerheim's confidence in Paavo Talvela.[80]

*Let our contests be in winter,*
*Let our wars be on the snowfields.*
**RUNE XXXII**

Chapter III

# White Christmas

While Group Talvela was locked in deadly combat in the wilds north of Lake Ladoga, the first assaults were being launched against the main Finnish defenses west of that Lake. By the time of the climactic Tolvajärvi battle on 12 December, the advance units of Commander Meretskov's 7th Army had reached the Mannerheim Line in all sectors across the Karelian Isthmus.[1]

Because the Red Army was stalled before it for an embarrassingly long period, that Line assumed mythological proportions in the Soviet press and literature, where it was consistently equated with the Maginot and Siegfried Lines. In reality, there were only 109 reinforced concrete bunkers in the entire Line (over 80 miles long), and about half of them were obsolescent ones constructed in the 1920s. By way of perspective, in the strongest 87 miles of the Maginot Line there were reinforced concrete pillboxes backed up by larger casements, which, in turn, were supported at 3–5 mile intervals by veritable underground fortresses. The latter were garrisoned by as many as 1,200 men and serviced by their own electric railways; not a single fortification in Finland approached that strength.[2]

The Finns relied heavily on natural defenses; more than half of the Mannerheim Line ran along rivers and lakes.* Unfortunately, the shortest route from Leningrad to Viipuri was also the most vulnerable. The ten-mile gap between the Summajoki River and Lake Muolaanjärvi—the "Viipuri Gateway," tra-

*See Map No. 14, p. 161

versed by good road and rail communications—was a region of open farmland and sparse, nearly level woods.* In this exposed sector, where enemy tanks and artillery had room to deploy en masse, the Finns had constructed 35 reinforced concrete bunkers, including 15 modern ones, to support 14 miles of winding front line. The only other segments strongly fortified with concrete installations were the extreme flanks of the Line. Those terminals on the Gulf of Finland and Lake Ladoga were also protected by five batteries of heavy coast artillery (120 to 254 mm guns). In the main, however, the defenses were merely strong field works: earth-and-timber bunkers, trenches, dugouts, korsus (small underground sleeping quarters), granite antitank obstacles, barbed wire, and mine fields. This Line was formidable by the standards of 1914–1918, but it was unimposing in comparison with the Maginot and Siegfried Lines and the technology of the Second World War. Moreover, except on the flanks, it lacked an element essential to the strength of any static defense system—powerful supporting artillery with ample ammunition.[3]

While the fighting lasted, neither side was motivated to dispel the myth of the invincible strength of the Isthmus defenses. However, an unintentional effect of this Soviet propaganda was to instill fear in the attackers. Soloviev noted that rumors of its impregnability, underground towns, etc. circulated among Soviet troops.[4] A captured battle order, issued by a Red Army Corps Commander on 9 December, included this revealing passage:

> If a machine gun is suddenly observed it should not be regarded as belonging to a permanent strongpoint; in general, there has been too much talk about such points. ... It must be explained to the infantry that it is completely wrong in believing that every emplacement is a strongpoint.[5]

The 7th Army's offensive began in earnest on 15 December, when a new attack was launched against the eastern sector of the Line near Taipale. After an intensive artillery barrage, Russian infantry advanced en masse. Lighter but more effec-

*See Map No. 9, p. 66

tive Finnish artillery fire raked the attacking formations just as they began moving out, causing heavy casualties. The same bloody scenario was repeated with fresh Soviet troops the next two days. Having an excellent field of fire, the Finnish gunners inflicted prohibitive losses on the enemy who had to advance across open fields and ice. By the time these futile assaults were halted on 17 December, the Red Army had lost 18 tanks and countless men from three infantry divisions.[6]

As was generally the case, these attacks in the Taipale region were a diversion intended to draw Finnish reserves away from the main objective, the Viipuri Gateway. As was also the rule, the Finns were aware of this strategem in time. In this instance, Soviet troop transfers from the eastern to the western sectors of the Isthmus were the warning signs detected by Finnish Intelligence. As early as 9 December General Österman's headquarters alerted Colonel Isakson, the commander of the 5th Division holding the critical Muolaanjärvi-Summajoki gap, to expect a major offensive against his positions. The next day, the First Brigade (of the First Division) was deployed along the railway, and one Regiment (JR 14) of the Fifth Division was subordinated to the First Division, which then assumed responsibility for the sector from the railroad to Lake Muolaanjärvi. Beginning 12 December enemy probing attacks in the strength of an infantry battalion, supported by a few tanks, were carried out sector by sector along the front of the Viipuri Gateway. The intensity of the artillery preparations for these attacks increased daily as more and more field guns were brought into line.[7]

The anticipated offensive began on 17 December with an ear-splitting barrage in the early morning darkness, accompanied after dawn by the crash of exploding bombs. The large-scale infantry and tank assaults were first concentrated against the Lähde sector, defended by Lt. Colonel K. Vaala's Task Force with about the strength of a regiment. Vaala's front-line unit was the First Battalion of Regiment JR 15, commanded by Captain A. Kuiri. About 35 of 50 tanks storming the battalion's positions penetrated the Line during the morning. Fortunately for the defenders, Red Army tactics were very poor at this stage of the war; the lack of coordination between different arms was striking. The tank breakthrus were not effectively exploited because Soviet infantry did not follow them closely or willingly, and this rendered the tanks vulnerable to close-range attack with Molotov cocktails, draw mines, and explosive clusters, in addition to antitank artillery. At least 15 tanks were destroyed in Vaala's sector alone that day. Although a few penetrated as far as the support line, the majority circulated between the front and the First Battalion's command post, trying to get the infantry to follow them.[8]

When darkness fell, most of the tanks returned to their own lines. However, a few remained at one of the support positions on the Lähde road, where they were joined by heavily armed Soviet infantry. The concrete bunker in the middle of that position remained in Finnish hands, although completely surrounded by the enemy for the next several days. All other Soviet gains in Vaala's sector were cancelled by successful Finnish counterattacks that same day.[9]

The attack on 17 December was also serious in the vicinity of Summa village, which—like the Lähde sector—was situated in relatively open country. Here, too, a few tanks broke thru, but four were destroyed and all infantry assaults were repulsed by Lt. Colonel I. Karhu's Task Force, which approximated a regiment in strength.[10]

The next day brought a repetition of the same tactics on a larger scale. Air attacks were intensified, and 68 tanks in close formation were flung against the Lähde sector. Finnish artillery fire caught them while they were still a mile from the front, destroying or immobilizing more than 10. Although Soviet fire was so intense that all of Colonel Vaala's phone lines were cut, the defenses held.[11]

By late afternoon the center of action had shifted to the Summa sector, where the attackers suffered heavy losses. An infantry force of about a battalion advanced in tight formation —almost in parade-ground manner—making hapless targets for Finnish machine guns.[12] These childish tactics, employed again and again during the December battles, resulted in senseless slaughter. The apparent rationale for such suicidal mass attacks was embodied in a cynical remark attributed to L. Z. Mekhlis, Chief Political Commissar of the Red Army, "They can't kill all!"[13]

When the offensive reached its peak on 19 December its center of gravity was still in the Summa area, but heavy attacks also extended eastward as far as Lake Muolaanjärvi. The weary troops of the 5th Division, along with part of the 1st Division, fought off four Red Army divisions and several hundred tanks, including numerous 30-ton models. The granite tank obstacles proved to be too small to withstand concentrated fire, and some 40–50 tanks penetrated as far as the northern edge of Summa village, about a mile behind the front. Other tank waves rolled over the barriers in the Lähde sector early in the morning, harassing the infantry all day. One of the strongest Finnish bunkers (nicknamed Poppius after its commander) was rendered partially inoperative that day by close-range tank fire which virtually welded shut its metal embrasures. Its garrison nevertheless continued the fight until a Finnish counterattack drove the besiegers off two nights later.[14]

Although the Finns lost many antitank guns and sustained considerable casualties during the fierce engagements of the 19th, they regained nearly all of their lost positions by determined counterattacks. At nightfall most of the Soviet tanks again withdrew to their own lines. When the fighting subsided and the results of the day's actions were reported to Supreme Headquarters, Marshal Mannerheim relayed his personal thanks to the troops for their steadfast defense.[15]

The attacks were resumed on the 20th, but their reduced scale indicated that the major offensive had spent its force. Some 20 tanks again entered Summa village, but eight of them —including three 30-ton heavies—were destroyed. In addition to their huge manpower losses, the attackers were now experiencing acute supply shortages. An entire battalion of tanks stalled near Summa that day when it ran out of gasoline.[16]

Since the start of the main offensive the Red Army had lost 58 tanks, including 22 heavy models. The commander of one tank battalion defected to the Finns because he feared to face his superiors after losing too many of his machines. Interrogation, confirmed by captured maps, revealed that the optimistic objective of the tank force had been Viipuri.[17]

Desultory fighting continued in the 5th Division's sector and elsewhere along the Isthmus front after 20 December, but large-scale attacks were not resumed in the Viipuri Gateway for many weeks. The Isthmus Army had weathered a severe storm; the Mannerheim Line had passed its first serious battle test.

Their successful defense led the Finns to underestimate the opponent's resiliency. Exaggerated reports of supply problems and demoralization in the enemy camp led some to consider the moment opportune for a major counterattack. General Öh-quist was especially eager to strike before the Red Army could deploy additional units opposite his Second Corps. On 20 December he revised an earlier attack plan, which General Österman forwarded to Supreme Headquarters with some mis-givings. Because Marshal Mannerheim had rejected a similar plan on 11 December, the Army commander was greatly sur-prised when this proposal was accepted. The Marshal appar-ently authorized the counterattack, with hesitation, because it was virtually a fait accompli by the time the detailed plan reached his Headquarters around noon on 22 December, only 18 hours from H-hour. By that time preliminary preparations were well underway in the units involved.[18]

The plan outlined a major attack on a front of approximately 25 miles, from Lake Kuolemajärvi to Lake Muolaanjärvi, with supporting strikes southeast of the latter extending this area considerably. Parts of five divisions participated, making this the largest offensive operation ever undertaken by the Finnish Army to that time. The 6th Division, which had not yet engaged in battle, and the 1st Division formed the spearheads of a large pincers. On the right, the 6th Division was to attack from the Karhula region, moving southeast between the Summajoki and Työppölänjoki Rivers to sever the main Soviet supply route east of Lake Kaukjärvi. On the left, the 1st Division was to advance from positions west of Lake Muolaanjärvi, striking south and southeast to the crossroads at Perkjärvi Station; from there it was to continue west towards Kaukjärvi to link up with the 6th Division. Limited missions, to tie down enemy forces and to secure the flanks of the spearheads, were assigned to the other Second Corps' divisions: the 11th to attack east of Lake Muo-laanjärvi, the 4th on the southwestern flank, and the 5th in the center between the 1st and 6th Divisions.[19]

An obvious weakness in the plan was the wide dispersal of Finnish forces and the lack of a definite point of concentration

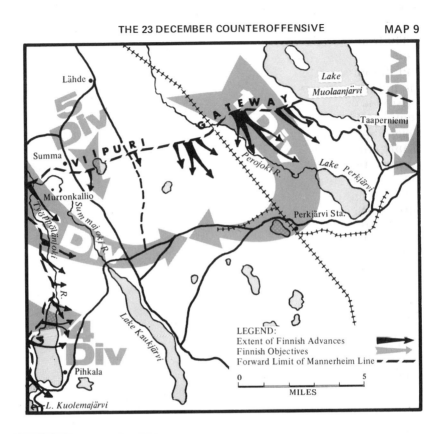

THE 23 DECEMBER COUNTEROFFENSIVE                    MAP 9

for the attack. Furthermore, the location of enemy units was largely unknown, since contact had been lost and reconnaissance was inadequate. Another serious shortcoming was the undue haste with which the plan was implemented, allowing very little time for troop preparation. For example, regimental commanders in the 5th Division only received their preliminary orders late in the evening of 21 December, when they were instructed to present plans the next day for the attack scheduled for the morning of the 23rd. When they were first informed that they would be required to detach reserves for an offensive to commence within 36 hours, their troops were still involved in clearing the front line of the last Soviet units which had penetrated their sectors. Consequently, the hasty scheduling of troop movements, logistic support, artillery coordination, and

all of the other details essential to the success of a large operation resulted in confusion, costly delays, and other serious errors in the execution of the plan.[20]

The general offensive was scheduled for 6:30 A.M., but many
units were late in reaching their starting points due to the
difficulties of crossing unfamiliar terrain in the darkness of
that midwinter night. Poor planning aggravated the march
problems; the 3rd Brigade took along its entire supply column,
clogging the single road to the front so much that elements of
the 2nd Brigade, which had to share the same poor road, were
two hours late in launching their attack. Some of the supporting artillery units did not even reach their firing positions until
the afternoon. Artillery coordination was negligible at best,
partly due to inadequate knowledge of enemy dispositions, but
especially because communications with the advancing infantry were generally severed. The failure to provide the army
with reliable field radios was once again paid for in blood; few
units were able to maintain phone contact under combat conditions. General Öhquist even lost contact with two of his division
commanders. These same factors accentuated the dispersal of
the attack formations, which generally fragmented into isolated battalions waging their own separate infantry battles. In
the best cases they gained only about two miles before stiff
enemy resistance halted their advance.[21]

The fortunes of the battalions varied in relation to the
strength of the enemy units they stumbled upon. For example,
in the 2nd Brigade of the 1st Division, the Third Battalion encountered little opposition (except for artillery fire) until it
reached a fortified bivouac area in a clearing in the woods near
the Perojoki River south of the Suursuo Swamp. There it killed
some 40 Russians and several horses and set fire to a few tents
before Soviet tanks halted its progress. Because of the rough
terrain and woods, the battalion could not bring antitank guns
with it; nevertheless, its own losses that day were only seven
killed and nine wounded. The adjacent First Battalion, on the
other hand, encountered much stiffer resistance, suffered
heavier casualties, and had to be rescued from a dangerous
situation by the Brigade's reserve battalion.[22]

The other spearhead unit, the 6th Division, had the worst
luck of all the Second Corps' forces that day. It's combat bap-

tism occurred in relatively open country where it was vulnerable to enemy machine gun and artillery fire; the latter was exceptionally accurate because it was directed in this sector from two captive balloons. It also appeared that strong Russian forces had been grouped for an attack here when the 6th Division advanced. The Third Battalion of JR 17, whose assigned role was merely that of a regimental reserve, found itself under withering machine gun fire about 8:30 A.M. near Murronkallio, about a mile beyond the front lines. The 9th Company retreated in haste when its commander was killed here, and the attack of the remainder of the Third Battalion was checked by 10 A.M.[23]

The other two battalions of Regiment JR 17 advanced southeast of Murronkallio, where they were stopped by Soviet infantry reinforced with tanks. The regiment received no artillery support until after noon. When it tried to compensate for this shortcoming with mortars, it was discovered at that untimely moment that the mortar shells did not fit the firing tubes![24] When these battalions began to withdraw shortly after 2:00 P.M., the Third Battalion was already retreating in disorder.

On the left of JR 17, the main force of Regiment JR 18 struck at thin air; only its First Battalion engaged the enemy in force. Nevertheless, the entire Regiment came under Soviet artillery fire. Although JR 18 was ordered about 1:00 P.M. to join forces with JR 17, the two units were not able to establish contact.

The third regiment of the 6th Division, JR 22, was involved in stiff fighting on the right flank of JR 17. By 8:00 A.M. its Second Battalion had been halted by heavy fire; after suffering considerable losses, it finally withdrew under cover of darkness around 4:30 P.M. Meanwhile, the Third Battalion and part of the First continued their attacks until a strong Soviet counterattack, supported by tanks, threw them back. Here, too, coordination between neighboring units was very poor. Those responsible for joining the fronts of the 6th Division and the 4th Division on its left later engaged in mutual recriminations because the enemy was able to dominate that sector.[25]

In General Heinrich's words, the 6th Division showed "signs of disintegration" by the end of the day. Some of its elements, notably the Third Battalion of JR 17, were so shaken by their first exposure to heavy concentrations of artillery fire that even their redeployment for the defense of the Mannerheim Line was difficult. Moreover, the demoralization was not entirely confined to the ill-fated 6th Division; Detachment Vuori, a regimental-sized unit attached to the 1st Division, sustained 140 casualties and its survivors were temporarily in a state of panic.[26]

When granting permission for the offensive, Marshal Mannerheim had stipulated that no risks were to be taken—if the advance encountered major difficulties it was to be recalled. General Österman apparently supported this view completely. As one unfavorable report piled upon another at the Second Corps Headquarters, General Öhquist ordered the attack halted about 2:40 P.M., eight hours after it had begun. Fortunately, the enemy did not pursue the Finns when they withdrew in the darkness; most units had retired in good order to the safety of the Mannerheim Line by late evening.[27]

Thus the only large-scale counteroffensive of the war ended ignominiously, except for the searching postmortems which began that same evening. Total casualties in the Second Corps exceeded 1,300—counting those killed, wounded, and missing in action. In addition, there were some 200 cases of frostbite. Morale in general also suffered; General Österman admitted that the failure tended to reduce the troops' confidence in their leaders, and he, himself, was deeply depressed.[28]

Sporadic Soviet admissions indicate that Russian casualties also must have been considerable. In one isolated battle near Sormula a combat engineer company was surprised by a superior Finnish force which engaged it for two hours. When those Finnish troops were withdrawing, they surrounded a Russian battalion; the division commander, Chernyak, had to send strong reinforcements to rescue that unit. Elsewhere, the Finns surrounded the First Battery of the 28th Corps Artillery Regiment and inflicted serious losses on that unit.[29]

The abortive attack may have had one redeeming result—the suspension of major Soviet assaults on the Viipuri Gateway for a long time thereafter. Marshal Mannerheim speculated that this was attributable to the Finnish counteroffensive.[30]

However, the trials of December were not yet over for the entire Isthmus Army. On Christmas Day a new Soviet offensive struck the front of the Third Corps, and, as usual, the 10th Division in the Taipale sector bore the brunt of the fighting. While Taipale was under attack, other Soviet forces tried to cross frozen Lake Suvanto in the Volossula-Kelja area,* some 4–6 miles to the northwest. For three days, these costly advances across the half-mile stretch of ice continued. Elements up to company size temporarily gained the northern shore—one unit even reached the Finnish artillery positions near Kelja—but the main attacking forces were stopped or destroyed on the Lake, which was littered with hundreds of bodies.[31]

The endurance of the 10th Division at Taipale was remarkable. No other sector was subjected to such prolonged punishment—by artillery, aircraft, and ground attacks which frequently developed into major offensives. Because it was strategically much less vital than the Viipuri Gateway, very few reserves could be spared to relieve the troops on this front. Under nearly constant pressure, the weary defenders remained in their positions to the end. The price of their resistance was high: in December the Third Corps suffered 2,250 casualties, mostly men of the 10th Division.[32]

Their opponent's losses will probably never be known precisely, but at least three divisions were terribly mauled in the futile December attacks. One of these divisions left 2,000 bodies on the ice and on the northern shore of the Suvanto in just three days of the last offensive.[33]

With the failure of these attacks, the fighting on the Isthmus reached a stalemate. Already on 27 December Soviet troops had been observed building field fortifications in the Summa sector, indicating a defensive posture.[34] Reviewing the course of operations of the 7th Army to date, the Main Military Council of the U.S.S.R. reached the decision to temporarily suspend further offensives on the Karelian Isthmus.[35] By its tenacious resistance, the Kannas Army had won a much needed breathing spell.

The gifted Soviet journalist, Aleksandr Tvardovski, has preserved a vivid picture of the efforts of one unit (the 90th Division) to crack the Mannerheim Line. On a late December day, the Russian infantry was pinned down on the snow by well

*See Map No. 4, p. 16

aimed fire, unable either to advance or withdraw. The attackers lay there helpless while the entrenched defenders picked
them off one by one. Towards evening the narrator witnessed
the evacuation of the wounded by every conceivable means,
even on tanks. This sensitive, intelligent observer acknowledged a sense of perplexity and incomprehension: what was
wrong that the Red Army could experience such costly failures?[36] Others in higher positions were asking the same question.

Meanwhile, in the midwinter darkness far beyond the Arctic
Circle the front had also been stabilized by late December. By
the middle of the month the strong elements of the 104th Division which were pursuing the weak Finnish force down the
Arctic Highway from Petsamo had captured the nickel mines
at Salmijärvi, and a few days later they reached the vicinity of
Nautsi.* There the Finnish forces, which had been brought up
to battalion strength, made a successful stand in the hilly country, driving the numerically superior enemy back a few miles
to Höyhenjärvi on 21 December. At that bleak point, fifty miles
southwest of Petsamo, the front remained relatively quiet for
several weeks. Cold, snow, darkness and the inherent logistic
difficulties of this remote region were the Finns' best allies.[37]
Some 150 miles to the south, there was heavy seesaw fighting
west of Salla in December. The 122nd Division, joined early in
the month by the 88th Division, was advancing towards Kemijärvi via two routes from the Salla road junction. The Finns
hastily reinforced the Salla Battalion (ErP 17) with the Eighth
Field Replacement Battalion, Battalions A and B, and the
poorly equipped Regiment JR 40. Thus, by 17 December they
had mustered seven battalions to oppose two divisions. This
substantial drain on Finnish manpower resources—even
though it still conceded the enemy a 3 to 1 numerical advantage
—was an indication of the anxiety created here in mid-December. Marshal Mannerheim's concern was also reflected in an
organizational change: on 17 December he separated this sector from General Tuompo's overextended Northern Finland
Group, creating a Lapland Group to direct the fighting from

*See Map No. 2, p. 9

Salla to Petsamo. The able but politically controversial Major General Kurt Wallenius was entrusted with this new command.[38]

The northern Soviet thrust from Salla was aimed at Pelkosenniemi,* from where it could attack either Sodankylä or Kemijärvi—to cut the only supply route of the Finnish battalion in the Petsamo sector, or to outflank the Finns fighting due east of Kemijärvi. By the evening of 16 December this column, comprising a regiment reinforced with a reconnaissance battalion and medium tanks, reached the eastern edge of Pelkosenniemi village. Four Finnish companies held them off for one day, until Regiment JR 40 arrived by truck the following night. The crucial battle of the entire Salla front was fought here on 18 December. The Soviet attack developed into deadly close combat at the village, where the Finnish defense was several times on the verge of collapse. However, the Finns were simultaneously undertaking their usual flanking attacks, to the north and to the rear of the enemy column. The decision came about 8 P.M., when the First Battalion of JR 40—striking the enemy flank under cover of darkness—created panic among the Soviet troops. Abandoning much of their equipment, they fled 25 miles to Savukoski, where they paused only for a brief encounter before continuing the retreat another 30 miles to Raatikka, about 10 miles northwest of Salla.

Meanwhile the invaders' southern column, moving directly on Kemijärvi, had fought its way to Märkäjärvi by 11 December, and by the time General Wallenius took command on the 17th the fighting was close to Joutsijärvi, about 20 miles from Kemijärvi. Because there was less than a foot of snow, the attackers were also able to execute flanking maneuvers here. On 20 December an entire battalion slipped undetected to Mäntyvaara, five miles west of Joutsijärvi, where Battalion ErP 17 had just arrived to rest after 20 days of continuous combat. Despite their fatigue, the Finns dispersed the flanking battalion, which left 600 dead behind. This was the high tide of the Soviet threat to Kemijärvi. After the defeat of the northern column at Pelkosenniemi and its hasty retreat, the Finns were able to redeploy two battalions of Regiment JR 40 to reinforce

*See Map No. 2, p. 9

the Joutsijärvi sector. By the end of the year, General Wallenius was preparing to mount counterattacks in this area also.

Here, as elsewhere, primitive tactics contributed to the Soviet defeats. A company commander in the 122nd Division described his battalion's futile mass frontal attacks against a Finnish village. Twice their ranks were decimated by deadly small arms fire from close range as they charged in the open across a frozen lake. By the time the second advance had been routed, all but 38 of the more than 100 men in his company had fallen. Yet the battalion commissar, who took charge when the commander was wounded, ordered a third frontal assault a few minutes later. When that attack met its predictable fate, several hundred men, more than two-thirds of the battalion, lay dead or wounded on the ice. Only then did the regimental commander authorize a retreat.[39]

The 163rd Division, which had captured Suomussalmi on 7 December and threatened to cut Finland in two at its narrow waist, was decisively defeated late in the month. The sensational Finnish victories in this region merit their own chapter, which follows this one.

The 54th Division, directed towards Kuhmo, was halted short of that village in the middle of December. Despite stubborn delaying actions, the Finnish battalion originally stationed here had been forced to yield ground. However, this front became static soon after the 25th Infantry Regiment from Oulu arrived.[40]

In the Lieksa sector, just south of the Kuhmo front, two minor Soviet columns were decisively defeated in December. The Northern Karelian Group, led by an experienced forest fighter, Colonel Raappana, drove one enemy unit back across the border at Kivivaara (some 40 miles southeast of Kuhmo) and another—a reinforced regiment—at Inari (about 30 miles farther to the southeast). These victories were so complete that most of this Finnish force could soon be transferred to the Kuhmo area. The single battalion which remained in the Lieksa sector conducted daring guerilla raids deep into Soviet territory.[41]

North of Lake Ladoga, not only Group Talvela, but also other Finnish forces were successful in checking the 8th Army's progress by mid-December. The 18th Division, supported by the

34th Tank Brigade, and the 168th Division—advancing by different routes—had joined forces in front of the Finnish field positions near Kitelä.*[42] In spite of their superiority, these forces could not break the Finnish resistance between Kitelä and Lake Syskyjärvi, about eight miles to the northeast. The Finns launched counterattacks here 12–13 December and again 17–19 December; although both failed in their major objectives, the latter attack did wrest the initiative from the enemy, who hastily prepared defensive positions. From 26 to 29 December the Finns renewed their push southwards from Syskyjärvi—again with very limited success. However, their simultaneous flanking blow against the Soviet supply route at Uomaa fared better. On the 27th the attackers reached the vicinity of the road, and on 3 January they completely cut that vital communications link at Lavajärvi, about six miles west of Uomaa. At the same time, 27 December, another Finnish unit reached the outskirts of Uomaa village, initiating bitter fighting which lasted for many weeks.[43]

The Soviet 56th Division, which had reached Kollaa by 7 December, was unable to proceed any farther down the railway towards Sortavala. Four Finnish battalions, making good use of field fortifications on both sides of the railroad, fought off repeated attempts to break through this key position. Even the appearance of a second Soviet division, the 164th, did not significantly change the situation. Both sides suffered heavily in the constant fighting in this region.[44] Politruk Oreshin's revealing diary includes these entries (he was with a unit of the 56th Division):

> 9/12 . . . The men have lain in the snow for three days and didn't dare to lift their heads. . . . Our casualties are heavy . . . more from frostbite than from enemy fire. . . . We can't even put our noses out of the trenches. Our men have launched several attacks but have always been beaten back. The barbed wire is man-high. Tank obstacles are everywhere. The marshes and splendidly camouflaged posts around us make the Finns invulnerable.
> 19/12 . . . We are still unable to advance and are suffering heavy casualties. Yesterday the butchers became so

*See Map No. 3, p. 13

cheeky that they began to attack our positions. They were warmly received and many of them given peace for eternity.[45]

Heavy snowfall late in December reduced Soviet activity in Ladoga-Karelia and gave the Finnish skiers one advantage over their immobilized foe. The two reinforced divisions which made up the Finnish Fourth Corps, plus the heterogeneous forces of Group Talvela, were more than holding their own against the entire 8th Army, which by then included at least seven divisions, one tank brigade, and various special artillery units.[46]

The cumulative effect of the Red Army's widely publicized reverses in the first month of its war with little Finland was disasterous to its prestige. War correspondents from the world over, bored with that winter's "phony war" or "sitskrieg" along the Rhine, flocked to Finland for more exciting news. Their reports filled the wires with the amazing feats of Finnish arms, often presented in the most flamboyant prose. As early as 1 December there were accounts of how well the "Finnish David" was meeting the challenge of "Goliath." By the 19th, even the moderate *New York Times* was editorializing on the "Rift in Russia's Armor," asserting that "all the well-fed political commissars in the world cannot make up for the officer-victims of the Red firing squads." Three days later, that paper's headline read:

## RUSSIANS RETREAT IN ARCTIC FROM FINNS, COLD, AND SNOW.

On 28 December the headline proclaimed:

## FINNS AGAIN CROSS BORDER, IMPERIL RUSSIAN RAILROAD: SOVIET CALLS MORE TROOPS.

In mid-January, 1940, Assistant Secretary of War Louis Johnson voiced a widely held opinion when he publicly stated that "Finland has taught the world again the age-old axiom that a free man is worth a dozen serfs."[47] A week later, Winston Churchill echoed this sentiment more eloquently—

Only Finland—superb, nay sublime—in the jaws of peril,
Finland shows what free men can do. The service rendered by Finland to mankind is magnificent. They have
exposed, for all the world to see, the military incapacity of
the Red Army and of the Red Air Force . . .[48]

French, Swiss, and other Western observers drew the same conclusion about the "myth" of the Red Army's power.[49]

On 23 December the major Soviet papers featured a front-
page summary of the first three weeks of hostilities in which
these depreciatory reports were explicitly refuted:

The foreign press, especially the French and British,
regards the rate of advance by Soviet troops as too slow,
attempting to explain this by the "low fighting capacity"
of the Red Army. . . . such vilification of the Red Army can
be explained either by overt and crude slander . . . or by the
ignorance of its authors in military affairs.[50]

Stalin was highly sensitive to those disparaging news stories
and editorials, for practical as well as prestigious reasons. He
angrily questioned Meretskov on the 7th Army's failure to
break the Finnish defenses. As that harried commander reported, Stalin emphasized that

ineffective military action could reflect on our policy. The
entire world is watching us. The authority of the Red
Army is the guarantee of the security of the U.S.S.R. If we
get bogged down for a long time before such a weak
enemy, then by that very action we will stimulate anti-
Soviet activities of imperialist groups.[51]

Concrete anti-Soviet measures had already been taken; on 14
December the moribund League of Nations expelled the Soviet
Union and appealed to its members to render all possible aid
to Finland.[52] Humanitarian contributions flowed from the sympathetic West. By February little Sweden had raised the astonishing amount of 28 million dollars. Despite their own war
needs, the British public contributed $1,200,000. In America,
Herbert Hoover headed a Finnish Relief Fund which collected
$2,000,000. In addition, all three countries made sizeable contri-

butions in other forms—food, medicines, voluntary services of medical personnel, etc.[53]

On 2 December President Roosevelt declared a "moral embargo" on the sale of aircraft and related strategic items to the U.S.S.R. More important were the arms shipments the Finns received from Sweden, France, England, Italy, Belgium, and Hungary. And from the very beginning of hostilities, many Swedes and a few Britons, Americans, and others volunteered to fight for Finland. Stalin had reason to ponder where all of this anti-Russian activity might lead.[54]

It is apparent that the Soviet dictator undertook an "agonizing reappraisal" of the situation before the end of December. The different, more sober tone of the Soviet press has already been suggested. The exuberant optimism of the first days gave way by the third week of the war to a restrained apologia. The summary published on 23 December correctly noted that "Finland presents most serious difficulties for troop movements. Lack of roads, rugged terrain, impassable forest, innumerable lakes divided by innumerable isthmuses . . .," but it concluded on a misleading note, claiming that "the Red Army knew of these difficulties . . . and therefore never expected to annihilate the Finnish troops by one lightning blow."[55]

That may have been true in the case of Chief of Staff Shaposhnikov, but we have seen how cavalierly Stalin had brushed aside his cautious recommendations for the Finnish campaign. Now that the poorly prepared and badly executed blitz had ground to an awkward halt, Shaposhnikov's plan was retrieved from the wastebasket. He and other responsible General Staff officers were drawn into the direction of military operations. A highly professional soldier, one of the few former tsarist officers remaining in Stalin's good graces (and long an intimate neighbor of his all-powerful leader),[56] Shaposhnikov brought to the task far more sophistication and efficiency than the staff of the Leningrad Military District had displayed. His hand can be discerned in the decision to suspend offensive operations on the Isthmus pending thorough preparations for a well organized attack.

The revised Soviet strategy called for a greater concentration of forces and effort on the decisive front, the Karelian Isthmus, and a more cautious approach to adventures in the

northern wilds. A directive issued by the High Command on 28
December pointedly recalled the experiences of the Russian
Army in 1808–09, when, it stated, Finnish troops under Swedish
commanders intentionally lured the Russians into the depths
of their country in order to encircle and capture their pursu-
ers.[57]

The plan entailed reinforcing the units on the Karelian Isthmus to bring them up to the overwhelming strength of 21 infantry divisions (plus one rifle-machine gun brigade), 20 artillery
regiments (plus four heavy artillery battalions), six tank brigades (plus four independent tank battalions), 15 supporting
air regiments, and one cavalry regiment. In addition, two infantry divisions were to be held in reserve. In connection with
this projected dense concentration of troops, a reorganization
was ordered on 26 December. The group, originally three divisions, which had been fighting in the eastern sectors of the
Isthmus was transformed into the 13th Army; Corps Commander V. D. Grendal', who had led the unsuccessful assaults
against Taipale, assumed command of the new army. Commander Second Rank Meretskov retained control of the 7th
Army, which was now responsible for the remainder of the
Isthmus front.[58]

The state of troop morale—Finnish or Russian—was seldom
affected by either opponent's propaganda, which was about
equally inept. In quantity the Soviets, inveterate practitioners
of the art, had the advantage, but the quality was very low.
Their farcical "People's Government of Finland" was a major
psychological blunder, not only uniting the Finns more solidly
in face of this obvious threat to their national survival, but also
straining Russian credibility when the loudly heralded
proletarian uprising in support of "President" Kuusinen failed
to materialize. As the war dragged on, less and less was heard
of the "Terijoki Government." To be sure, Kuusinen's greetings
to Stalin on his sixtieth birthday on 21 December were published in *Pravda* on the 23rd, and two days later the same paper
carried Stalin's reply to "Tovarishch Otto Kuusinen,
Terijoki."[59]

That illusory "Government" even had a phantom army; on 2
December *Krasnaya Zvezda (Red Star)* and other papers

hailed the formation at Terijoki of the "First Finnish Corps" of volunteers, the alleged nucleus of a future "People's Army of Finland." However, at the end of the month *Red Star* could only claim that it numbered 5,775 men. The great majority of this force was probably recruited from communists who fled Finland in 1918 and from Finnish-speaking inhabitants of Eastern Karelia and Ingermanland ;[60] however, there was a small but indeterminable number of traitors who joined its ranks. A Finnish border guard captured in the first moments of the war revealed that in mid-December Kuusinen and four of his "ministers" visited the building where he and some 70 other POWs were held. Kuusinen persuaded 19 of the prisoners—including some who had been Red Guards in 1918—to join the "People's Army."[61] Of 600 Finns held in the largest Soviet POW center used during that war, 16 are known to have enlisted in Kuusinen's motley force.[62] For a gambit calculated to entice thousands of Finnish volunteers, the whole venture was a dismal failure.

Nor were other Soviet psychological warfare measures more successful. A vast shower of leaflets, radio broadcasts in good Finnish, and loudspeaker appeals to front-line troops failed to convince the Finns that life was better in the Soviet Union or that Finland's defeat was imminent—two major themes of this incessant barrage. Even the paper on which the leaflets were printed—of very poor quality—tended to belie the first claim. Moreover, Soviet propagandists were so misinformed that they promised the Finnish workers an eight hour day—something which had been in force in Finland for two decades! The reaction to such crude appeals was one of mirth; Finnish officers permitted their troops to listen to Russian broadcasts for entertainment.[63]

Finnish efforts to influence their enemy were not significantly more effective. Defections from the Red Army were generally due to other, subjective reasons. For example, a deserter who shot the other members of his tank crew and then surrendered to the Finns wanted revenge for the persecution of his peasant family during Stalin's collectivization drive in the early 1930s.[64]

Politruk Oreshin entered these telling comments in his diary on 24 December:

I read a Finnish leaflet today. What a lot of tripe! I must admit that I thought better of them. The writer of this leaflet should have gone to a political elementary school— tripe without a single redeeming feature.

He calls the Kronstadt mutineers* "pioneers of liberty." He doesn't appear to know that our people have cursed these men. The leaflet is also full of grammatical mistakes. In general, the stupid composers of the leaflet appear to think that the Red Army soldier is a useless and uneducated lout.

This is stupidity. Some of our men are good enough to be their statesmen.[65]

The "grammatical errors" were sometimes lapses into the obsolete orthography in use when the older Finns were students; in 1918 certain archaic letters had been eliminated from the Russian alphabet.

One preposterous leaflet addressed to Soviet airmen offered $10,000 (literally dollars, not expressed in Finnmarks) and free passage to the country of their choice for a bomber in undamaged condition. To illustrate the rosy life awaiting defectors in the West, it pictured a Florida mansion. It also reproduced, without identification, a still from the 1938 movie *Test Pilot* showing Clark Gable and Spencer Tracy walking away from an airplane, arm-in-arm with a smiling Myrna Loy. It may have been fortunate for Miss Loy that there were no takers for this offer! Attempts to purchase tanks in similar fashion also drew a blank.[66]

One theme frequently featured in Finnish propaganda was more effective—the death awaiting the Russians in the frigid wilds of Finland. A typical example was a leaflet which simply pictured a corpse with snow in its eyes, under the bold caption WHITE DEATH. The brief accompanying text stated a truth all too apparent to the shivering Russians:

You cannot fight against this enemy—frost. You do not see him, but he is around you.[67]

Other tracts showed actual photographs of heaps of corpses frozen in grotesque postures at the scene of Red Army disasters

*There was an anti-Bolshevik revolt at the Kronstadt naval base in 1921.

in the northern woods. In postwar conversations, Soviet officials termed the Finns very cruel for using such pictures—thus
attesting to their effectiveness.[68]

Sometimes stories of Russian casualties were accompanied
by pictures of starving children—grim reminders that the soldier's family would be destitute if he were killed. This also hit
home; many of the reservists called away from the farms worried about the survival of their dependents. Soloviev related the
tragic fate of a combat engineer who daringly attacked a Finnish strongpoint with explosives in the vain hope that he would
be wounded and sent home to help his starving family.[69]

Another common topic was how well the Finns treated their
prisoners. Pictures of captives smoking cigarettes and chatting
merrily in cozy quarters abounded, even in the press. As Finnish field commanders pointed out, such articles angered the
troops who were enduring great hardships at the front, and it
was possible that they might therefore decide not to take any
more prisoners.[70] The common soldier's hatred of the Russian
invaders was so strong in any case that prisoners were occasionally shot by front-line troops, despite orders to the contrary.[71]

The propaganda of both sides which was designed for domestic consumption was generally as devoid of finesse as that directed at the enemy. Generals Heinrichs and Walden were both
highly critical of the entire Finnish effort. Walden even phoned
Marshal Mannerheim on several occasions to complain about
specific items released by Supreme Headquarters. The Marshal
agreed with the criticisms, but he could not personally super-
vise everything. Much of the material in the wartime press was
flippant, and the enemy was treated with derision. Heinrichs
described it in these words:

> It is apparently rarely that propaganda has shown a more
> primitive psychological instinct and such absolute igno-
> rance of the tide of opinion. . . . Rarely has a . . . field army
> been fed with such low class propaganda.[72]

In the Russian camp, the Party line was even less successful.
Although many in the Red Army initially believed that they
were engaged in a worthy crusade to free the Finnish proletar-

iat from an oppressive ruling class, the determined resistance which the common enemy soldier offered to his "emancipation" rapidly dispelled that hoax.[73] Yet this transparent lie was constantly reiterated in the press; as late as 23 February 1940 *Izvestiya* declared that the Red Army was "rendering brotherly aid to the Finnish people in their struggle against the Mannerheim-Tanner gang."

The official daily communiqués of the Leningrad Military District were also unlikely to inspire confidence in the veracity of Soviet leadership. The retreating survivors of the battle of Tolvajärvi on 12 December must have been amazed to read that "Soviet troops continue to advance on all fronts."[74] For the entire period 27 December thru 4 January the daily bulletins merely stated that "nothing significant occurred at the front" (sometimes accompanied by a brief note on air activity); this was the period when the Red Army was suffering its most humiliating defeat of the war at Suomussalmi.

After the great ballyhoo of early December, the virtual silence of the Soviet press at the turn of the year must have been both puzzling and annoying to the combat soldiers. That terse phrase "nothing significant occurred at the front" was the sole reference to the war in the entire 31 December issues of *Pravda* and *Krasnaya Zvezda.* On New Year's Day *Izvestiya* carried only a similarly brief communiqué, although it devoted seven paragraphs to military action in China and ten to the war in Western Europe and operations at sea. Under those circumstances, the *politruk's* job of motivating the troops was indeed difficult![75]

While morale in the Red Army was generally low by late December, the Finns' spirits had risen in proportion to their battlefield successes. At Christmastide they felt they had much reason to give thanks unto the Lord, even if there were some forebodings about the New Year. To the amazement of both belligerents, the Red Army had still not captured and retained any important objectives, with the sole exception of virtually defenseless Petsamo. Moreover, everywhere north of the stalemated Karelian Isthmus the Finns had wrested the initiative from their avowedly godless foe. In the relative calm of those Christmas holy days, Finns of all walks of life sang the traditional hymns with feeling and prayed with fervor. *A Mighty Fortress Is Our God* took on a very special significance.

As sometimes happens in times of great stress, a religious revival was in full bloom. Not only those from the customarily pious regions of south central Finland, but even the "soulless" drew close to the church in those days; this phenomenon was part of what later became known as the Spirit of the Winter War. (Other ingredients were the unprecedented national unity and the stoic determination to fight on against all odds.) The regimental chaplains were busy, not only with the melancholy duties of writing letters to the next of kin of all the fallen and arranging for the shipment of the bodies to their home towns, but also with conducting as many religious services as possible for the front-line troops. Most of the Finnish Army worshiped in nature's cathedral on that memorable Christmas Day; during the early morning services the moon bathed the snow-laden spruce and pine trees in splendor. It may have been the spiritual awareness of the moment that caused many a rough-hewn warrior—from whom one might not expect poetic insights—to remark on the beauty of his beloved woods on that holy day.[76]

The traditional Christmas ham dinner was served to the entire army; some units received it as customary on the 24th, others as necessity dictated on the 25th. The field army and the many wounded in military hospitals ate better than the civilian population. A small ration of liquor, a few ounces per man, was issued for the occasion. There were plenty of gift parcels of food and warm clothing—from relatives, hometown organizations, and unknown Lottas. Even some of the transport horses were remembered with blankets from those donors.[77]

In quiet sectors of the front, modest celebrations were held. Spruce trees, decorated with a few plain candles, were hung in tents and korsus. Colonel Pajari, visiting his units at the Aittojoki River line, brought a star for the tree in the command tent of one of the battalions. Colonel Ekholm, a true gourmet, shared about a half pound of caviar with his staff officers at Ilomantsi.[78]

Although during the holidays the Red Army took the offensive only in the Taipale sector (failing miserably, as we have seen), Soviet aircraft were active everywhere. Poor flying weather, which had settled in on 2 December, lifted after the 18th; enemy bombers then took advantage of the clear skies to roam far and wide over Finnish towns and villages. Attacks on civilian centers became intensive during the last week of December. Members of the U. S. Legation, which had relocated from Helsinki to Bad Grankulla for safety, observed as many as 30 bombers in their vicinity alone on Christmas Day.[79]

The combat zone also received increased attention from the air. On 24 December Pajari's headquarters was badly damaged. Among those killed there on the eve of that sacred holiday was Chaplain Vahervuori. Task Force Pajari was again harassed from early dawn on Christmas, but the attacks in this sector stopped after Finnish fighters arrived later in the day and shot down four bombers. Many front line religious services were interrupted by air raids that morning.[80]

Christmas at Mikkeli was also observed with quiet dignity. There was a little party for the Headquarters staff officers at the Seurahuone Hotel, where Marshal Mannerheim was lodged. This was the only occasion during the war when champagne was served at the Headquarters, although liquor was always served at the Marshal's table.[81]

Marshal Mannerheim preferred to adhere to a rigid schedule at Headquarters whenever possible. Regardless of the time he retired, he was awakened at 7 A.M. Precisely an hour later, immaculately groomed, he had breakfast in the small room at the back of the hotel where he ate all of his meals; the larger and better-furnished dining room was left for the junior staff officers.

After breakfast he went to his office in the elementary school, about a third of a mile from the lodgings. He enjoyed walking to and from work, as this afforded exercise and relaxation from the tensions of the day.

At noon he dined with the senior officers: Lt. General Oesch, Chief of the General Staff; Colonel (Major General from 26 February 1940) Airo, Quartermaster General;* Major General Kekoni, who had been the Commander-in-Chief's aide in 1918 and now served as a trusted liaison officer and an entertaining

*The Finnish title Quartermaster General—like its German counterpart—is roughly equivalent to the U. S. Army's Deputy Chief of Staff for Operations.

raconteur at the Headquarters; and his ever-present aide, Major Grönvall. Other officers were occasionally invited to join them.

A simple but rigid formality was observed at the Marshal's table, varying slightly only when important guests were present. The host was served first, waiting until everyone received the first course before eating. Between the first and second courses, large schnapps glasses were filled to the very brim. When the host raised his glass, arm outstretched in silent toast, the others did the same. Many an embarrassed guest spilled his drink during this ceremony, which was deliberately prolonged to tease the visitor. After the first glass was emptied "bottoms up," another half glass was enjoyed at leisure. One glass of beer accompanied the warm dish, and exactly one cup of coffee followed the meal. Smoking was permitted with the coffee, but only after the Marshal lit his own specially made cigar.

If very important guests were present, formal toasts were exchanged and wine and brandy were served. On these occasions printed menus were prepared; normally the aide merely advised the kitchen staff in advance of the Marshal's desires. A fastidious gourmet, he was so fond of lingonberry porridge that he ordered it almost daily.

When the host was in a good mood the conversation might turn on horses, a subject dear to the ex-cavalry general's heart, or some other diverting topic. Smoking-room jokes were completely foreign to his nature, but he enjoyed innocuous military humor. On other occasions, the meal might pass in silence. Private conversations at his table were unheard of, and he did not discuss the urgent problems of the war at mealtime.

After lunch he returned to the school building to work. When the situation permitted, he sometimes took a nap, while sitting upright in his chair. Major Grönvall saw that he was not disturbed at such times.

The evening meal at the Seurahuone Hotel was ordinarily as punctual as the noon dinner. When it was finished, at 8:30 P.M., the Marshal returned to the office to receive the evening reports. Colonel Airo briefed him on all military operations twice a day. The Commander-in-Chief was invariably concerned about Finnish casualties, as manpower was a scarce and irreplaceable resource; he wanted to be informed of losses man by man, and even—in the case of officers—by name.

The main variable in this daily routine at Mikkeli was in the time he retired. Sometimes he managed to return to the hotel by midnight, but often the 72-year-old Marshal did not get to bed until 3 or 4 A.M. He liked to have a drink or two of Scotch and to read his newspapers before retiring, being especially partial to the *Journal de Genève* for its coverage of international news.

On the rare occasions when a relatively quiet situation permitted it, the old warrior-statesman sometimes reminisced with his closest associates about his two long and eventful careers, the strange and winding trail that led to Mikkeli and to his present momentous responsibilities. Although he never confided his thoughts to anyone completely, he was more candid in discussing his service in the Imperial Russian Army than his subsequent role in Finnish affairs.[82]

Baron Carl Gustaf Emil Mannerheim's first career began by a fortuitous twist of fate, when in his late teens he was expelled from the Finnish Corps of Cadets in 1886 for going AWOL. As the son of a distinguished Swedish-Finnish family (a Finlander, rather than an ethnic Finn) he soon had entrée into the Nikolaevski Cavalry School in St. Petersburg, and from there—after a year's duty in Poland—into the exclusive Chevalier Guards Regiment. Ethnic origins (other than Jewish) were not a serious handicap in Imperial Russia, provided loyalty to the régime was beyond question. Thus the horizons spreading before the young Guardsman were infinitely broader than those of a graduate of the parochial Finnish Corps of Cadets.

The tall, handsome nobleman was sometimes responsible for the resplendent interior guards at the Winter Palace; he was invited to the great receptions and balls; he came into contact with the Imperial family; in short, he enjoyed the privileges of the capital's most glittering society. In 1892 he married Anastasia Arapova, daughter of a general and former Chevalier-Guards officer. She bore him two daughters before they separated seven years later (they were divorced in 1919). At the last Romanov coronation in 1896, he was one of four officers chosen for the honor of standing ceremonial guard at the steps to the thrones of Nicholas and Alexandra. Despite the discomfort of his uniform and the ordeal of standing motionless for four and one-half hours, he found the pomp and circumstance "indescribably magnificent."

In 1901 he accepted a position under the Master of the Horse which enabled him to travel to Germany, Austria-Hungary, Belgium, France, and England to purchase thoroughbreds for the Imperial stables. In addition to satisfying his passion for horses, this assignment involved such broadening experiences as lunch with Kaiser Wilhelm II and the German Empress.

The gay, easy, and profitable life of a courtier-officer remained open to him, but he chose instead the harder service of the serious professional officer. In 1903 he requested transfer to the Officers' Cavalry School, where he served under the famous and talented tactician, General Brusilov. When the Russo-Japanese War broke out in 1904, Lt. Colonel Mannerheim volunteered for duty with the 52nd Nezhinski Hussars, in spite of Brusilov's optimistic counsel that this affair was too insignificant to bother with.

As usual, Russia was poorly prepared for a war which her diplomacy had done much to provoke. The energetic and observant staff officer learned much by contrasting the bungling Russian leadership with the adroit Japanese tactics and their skillful employment of modern weapons. During one reconnaissance his charger was fatally wounded, but he managed to complete his mission before the horse collapsed. For this feat he was promoted to Colonel.

Returning to St. Petersburg after the war in the fall of 1905, Colonel Mannerheim was granted a long leave of absence because of rheumatism contracted in the field. He took advantage of this respite to visit his native land, where, as a member of the archaic Nobles Estate, he attended the final Diet of the Four Estates in 1906. At that meeting the Estates voluntarily yielded their authority to a single-chamber Parliament elected by all men and women over twenty-four. This was the future President of Finland's only direct involvement in Finnish politics prior to the upheavals of 1917–1918.

The sojourn in Helsinki was terminated by a summons from the Chief of the General Staff, offering him a unique and challenging assignment: a two-year journey through Central Asia, from Russian Turkestan to Peking—a distance of some 5,000 miles, most of which could only be covered on horseback. The object was to report on conditions in northern China and to collect topographical and other information of military value. Realizing that there would also be many opportunities to gather scientific data, Colonel Mannerheim volunteered his services to the Fenno-Ugrian Society and the National Museum in Helsinki, meanwhile reading everything he could find— starting with the writings of Marco Polo—to prepare himself for the epic journey. The visible results of that endurance test were two large volumes of meticulous data and travel descriptions definitely *not* designed to entice the fun-seeking tourist, plus a lifetime interest in Orientalia.[83]

It was with great relief that the epicurean aristocrat returned from the primitive environment of Central Asia to the comforts of European society in the summer of 1908. His next assignment was command of the 13th Vladimir Uhlans Regiment, stationed in central Poland. Improving the training of that undistinguished unit won the approval of the Inspector of Cavalry, and two years later he was promoted to Major General and posted to Warsaw as commander of the Emperor's Uhlans of the Guard. This was followed in 1914 by command of the Brigade of Cavalry of the Guard in Warsaw. These were happy years, combining satisfying military duties with the pleasures of Polish society. He had many friends among the local nobility, and he was admitted to the exclusive Cercle de Chasse, the "Jockey Club" of Poland. He also accompanied the Tsar's family when they were shooting at Spala, the Imperial hunting lodge near Warsaw. There, in 1912 he was made a Général à la Suite de Sa Majesté, an honor which entitled him to informal admission to the Tsar's presence.

During the First World War the Eastern Front witnessed large-scale battles of maneuver, unlike the static trench warfare in France. Cavalry became a key factor, and General Mannerheim saw plenty of action, both offensive and defensive. He served under his old commander, General Brusilov, who entrusted him with command of the 12th Cavalry Division early in 1915.

In June 1917, three months after the downfall of the monarchy and the formation of the pusilanimous Provisional Government in Petrograd, he was promoted to Lt. General as commander of the Sixth Cavalry Corps. By then the Russian army had advanced far along the road to complete disintegration. When (in August) he was unable to secure appropriate punishment for mutinous soldiers who had molested a junior officer, and when (in September) Premier Kerensky arrested the Commander-in-Chief, General Kornilov, General Mannerheim resolved to quit the army. As it had begun, his service ended with a lucky twist of fate. A fall from his horse afforded a pretext for withdrawing to Odessa to recuperate from a sprained ankle. There he learned of the Bolshevik Revolution of 7 November. Everything the Bolsheviks represented was anathema to his conservative and aristocratic predilections. He was even disgusted at the sight of generals carrying their own luggage. The new Soviet régime posed a threat to his life and also presaged great troubles for Finland. When his suggestions to fellow-officers and members of the royal family for a counterrevolution fell on deaf ears, his determination to return to his native land was reinforced. The termination of his distinguished 30-year career was marked by an adventurous train ride thru revolutionary Russia to Petrograd, then an illegal border crossing into Finland—which had just declared its independence on 6 December.

Although not everyone realized it immediately, the fateful year 1917 was to prove a radical turning point in the lives of all Russians and most Finns. At least one 50-year-old Finnish-Russian general was acutely aware of this fact.[84]

Civil conflict had long been smoldering in Finland. By October of 1917 class relations had deteriorated to the point where both camps had their own private armed forces—the proletarian Red Guards countering the bourgeois "White" (Civic) Guards.[85] This dangerous situation was complicated by the presence in Finland of some 40,000 Russian troops whose status—after the Bolshevik Revolution in November and Finland's declaration of independence in December—was ambiguous. At the end of January 1918 the mutual fears and hatreds burst into open warfare.

It was not until January that General Mannerheim learned that some 1,800 Finnish volunteers had been trained in the 27th

Jäger Battalion which was organized in the German Army in
1915. When he had dined with old fellow-cadets and former
Finnish Army officers in Helsinki eleven months earlier, they
had not confided that secret to him. Among those Jäger veterans—the intended and actual nucleus of the future Finnish
officers corps—there was considerable suspicion of the General
who had spent thirty years in the service of the nation widely
regarded as Finland's oppressor. However, when leading Jäger
officers met him in person early in 1918, they immediately
recognized his outstanding leadership qualities.[86]

General Mannerheim assumed the challenging position of
Commander-in-Chief of an army which existed only as scattered groups of poorly trained Civic Guards volunteers (the
majority of the Jägers did not reach Finland until late in February),[87] whose main initial source of arms would be those they
could capture from the Russian garrisons. It was a tribute to the
General's administrative ability, as well as to his strategic talents, that in only three and one-half months he succeeded in
organizing and leading to final victory this first army of an
independent Finland. Skilled command and discipline tri-
umphed over mere numbers.

By the time the fighting ceased in the middle of May, the man
who had been virtually unknown in his native land in January
was popularly hailed as the "savior" of Finland. Unfortunately,
to a sizeable minority he had become known as "White Butcher
Mannerheim." From that brief civil war to the present, he has
always been a highly controversial figure to his countrymen.[88]

Scarcely had the guns been silenced when, at the end of May,
the Commander-in-Chief resigned and immediately departed
for Stockholm. His stated reason was the Government's plan to
place the Finnish Army under German direction. Earlier, he
had unsuccessfully opposed the Government's request for German intervention in the fighting in Finland.[89]

In the brash, naïve new Finnish state—where few of the inexperienced leaders fully appreciated the relationship between
goals and means in foreign policy, and few had a practical
understanding of Great Power politics—Baron Mannerheim
was virtually the only sophisticated statesman with broad international contacts. This was belatedly recognized by the Gov-

ernment when it called upon him to try to rescue Finland from the consequences of its blindly pro-German policies. As late as October 1918, only a month before Kaiser Wilhelm fled from his defeated Germany to Holland, the Finnish Parliament had voted to offer a crown to his brother-in-law, the Prince of Hesse. Now that the victorious Allies distrusted Finland, the Government requested him to visit England and France to mend the broken fences. He initially traveled as a private citizen, but while in Paris in November the Parliament voted to appoint him Regent, and he received formal confirmation of that position in London on 12 December. That action, along with a reorganization of the Finnish Cabinet, facilitated the accomplishment of his mission: the British Government promised to recognize Finland once the offer to the Prince of Hesse was withdrawn, other pro-German policies were reversed, and a new Parliament was elected. Influential French statesmen indicated that those same measures would result in a resumption of diplomatic relations with France—severed when German armed forces were invited to Finland in the spring.[90]

As Regent, Mannerheim enthusiastically supported the project of sending Finnish volunteers to aid Estonia in its fight for freedom from Soviet Russia early in 1919. It is apparent that only the chauvinism of the White Russian leaders, who refused to acknowledge Finland's independence, prevented deeper Finnish involvement in the Allied intervention in Russia. Even so, the Regent authorized Finnish volunteers to join the East Karelian irregulars in attacking Petrozavodsk in the spring of 1919. Although that effort failed, the Finns did capture Reboly (Repola) and Porosozero (Porajärvi) at that time. (They were returned to Soviet control by the terms of the Peace of Tartu signed by Finland and the R.S.F.S.R. in October 1920.)[91]

Although Baron Mannerheim favored a monarchy for Finland, that cause had been discredited by the Prince of Hesse affair. Instead of a king, the new constitution adopted in 1919 created a Republic with a strong executive. In the first Presidential election in July, Mannerheim—who refused to join any political party—experienced the humiliation of overwhelming defeat. Professor Kaarlo Ståhlberg won by 143 Parliamentary votes to his 50.[92]

The end of the First World War also marked the end of an era. The archaic Romanov, Hapsburg, and Hohenzollern dynasties collapsed in chaos. No longer restrained by the stagnant but outwardly serene domination of the hereditary aristocracy, the Continent was buzzing with the tumultuous contentions of inexperienced parvenue bourgeois (or ostensibly proletarian) politicians. Baron Mannerheim's familiar orderly world— where a self-perpetuating élite governed and the commoners knew their place—had suddenly disappeared; an agitated and boisterous new régime replaced it. He never became fully reconciled to democracy; when the new constitution was being formulated, he had urged empowering as head of state "a strong hand that will not be moved by party strife or forced to fritter away the power of government by compromise,"[93] not appreciating the fact that compromise is the essence of democratic rule. Understandably, he was an isolated and lonely figure in the new Republic of Finland.

For the next twelve years the man who had played so prominent a role in launching the ship of state held no official position. As a private citizen he remained an apostle of anti-communism. In the fall of 1919, when the successes of the Red Army had shaken the White Russian intransigence on the question of Finland's independence, he tried to promote Finnish participation in an anti-Bolshevik crusade. Visiting London, he found a kindred spirit in the War Secretary, Winston Churchill. From Paris, where he conferred with Premier Clemenceau and other interventionists, he sent an open letter to President Ståhlberg on 28 October urging Finnish participation in an attack on Petrograd.[94] It was probably fortunate that his counsel was rejected, as the time when the Soviet régime might have been overthrown with ease had passed.

Although the intervention issue died when the Allies and their last Russian protégés withdrew from European Russia in 1919–1920, the problem of domestic communism continued to concern Baron Mannerheim. The extreme right-wing Lapua Movement of 1929–32, which arose as a reaction against Finnish communist activities, received his sympathy.[95]

Citizen Mannerheim devoted his time to various social and civic projects. As honorary Commander-in-Chief of the Civic Guards, he maintained an active interest in that organization and its Lotta Svärd auxiliary. He was also honorary President of the Mannerheim Child Welfare Association which he founded in 1920; that society flourished and expanded to hundreds of branches engaged in charitable work in the fields of health, education, and youth care. In 1922 he became Chairman of the Finnish Red Cross. Applying his usual zeal to this task, he attended the international conference in Switzerland and visited the Stockholm association, laying the foundation for future Swedish-Finnish cooperation. In 1925 he proposed the absorption of the Mannerheim Association by the Red Cross, to increase efficiency and reduce expenses; it became an autonomous section for child care and health.[96]

Those activities—although contributing to the nation's welfare—were not sufficient to fully occupy the vast energy and talents of the former Commander-in-Chief and Regent. He was probably bored, and there can be no doubt about his loneliness. He lived alone, with a few servants, in a large house in the Kaivopuisto section of Helsinki. In 1919 he had the good fortune to recover his belongings intact in Warsaw, where they had been stored for five years since the outbreak of the World War.[97] He furnished his home to his masculine taste, filling it to the limit with momentos of his travels, hunts, honors, and careers. Even while he lived there, the house was taking on the air of the museum it was to become after his death.

Here he entertained his many influential acquaintances, sometimes inviting an individual for the evening on a moment's notice. Yet he could never unbend enough with those bourgeois generals and civilians to enjoy the warmth of true friendship. As one who worked for him aptly expressed it, "he was a prisoner of his own splendor." He apparently had only one intimate friend in Finland, the wealthy industrialist Rudolf Walden, whom he first met in 1918. From that time on, Mannerheim considered Walden a trusted friend and "counselor," a unique term for him to use in referring to others.[98]

During those years of relative inactivity the Baron found time to indulge his fondness for hunting. In the beginning of the 1920s he rented a lodge in the Tyrol, where he hunted deer and chamois every autumn. In 1928 he hunted in India and visited other parts of Asia unfamiliar to him—Sikkim, Burma, and Baghdad. As usual, the cosmopolitan aristocrat met the leading personages wherever he traveled. In India he was presented to the Viceroy, the future Lord Halifax—who was British Foreign Secretary during the Winter War. On his second trip to Nepal, in 1937 when he was approaching 70, he shot his first tigers.[99]

The early Depression years witnessed a rightist reaction in Finnish politics. In 1930 all communist-front organizations were outlawed, and the next year the conservative "strong man" Svinhufvud was elected President. The new President appointed General Mannerheim Chairman of a reorganized Defense Council, with the private understanding that the Chairman would become Commander-in-Chief of the Armed Forces in event of war. In peacetime he was responsible for the organization of the army, planning the defense budget, and related matters concerning military preparedness. From his appointment in 1931 until the very outbreak of the war on 30 November 1939, the Chairman found himself in an endless hassle with the Parliament over appropriations, a conflict which caused him more than once to consider resigning from his frustrating office.[100]

There were a few rewarding moments, however. In 1933 the Government promoted him to Field Marshal and presented him with a marshal's baton; he remains the only Finn honored in this fashion.[101]

Marshal Mannerheim had occasion to observe developments in military aviation firsthand. In 1934 he was invited to the Royal Air Force display at Hendon, and the next year he visited Germany to inspect its bustling aircraft industry. After both trips he returned home to urge increased preparations to meet the challenge posed by this newest form of warfare.

In 1936 he was again in England, this time representing Finland at the funeral of King George V. He took advantage of that opportunity to confer informally with Foreign Secretary Eden and King Edward VIII on the international situation. He was keenly interested in this subject, foreseeing the likelihood of a general war with its inherent dangers for Finland. When he had to return to the Continent in 1938 for his health, he again visited London and Paris to discuss the gathering clouds of war with key military and diplomatic figures. Convinced that war was imminent, he was able to secure a modest increase in Finnish defense appropriations early in 1939.

No one knew better than the Chairman of the Defense Council the weaknesses of the Finnish Army, nor had a better appreciation of the threat it faced. In spite of his consistently anti-Soviet views, he urged Foreign Minister Erkko to make concessions when the Soviet Government requested a lease on certain strategic islands on the approaches to Leningrad in March 1939. He also tried to persuade President Kallio and Prime Minister Cajander that those defenseless islands were useless to Finland and that the exchange of territory offered by Foreign Commissar Litvinov would preserve Finnish prestige. He even went to the extent of proposing something that Litvinov had not even mentioned—moving the frontier nearest Leningrad 5 or 6 miles to the west. His advice fell on ears deafened by considerations of domestic politics; the special Soviet representative was forced to return to Moscow emptyhanded.

When Stalin reopened the discussions in October, the Finnish bargaining position had worsened drastically. The blunt Molotov had replaced the genial Litvinov, a move related to Stalin's rapprochement with Hitler; the notorious Molotov-Ribbentrop pact had in effect handed Finland over to the U.S.S.R.; England and France were preoccupied with their own war problems; and Soviet demands were significantly and ominously harsher than they were in March. Again Marshal Mannerheim counseled concessions, but only those which could be made without jeopardizing Finnish security.

The danger of war was acute after the negotiations broke down and the Finnish delegation left Moscow on 13 November. When—at that late hour—the Government would not approve the additional defense appropriations he had recently requested, Mannerheim asked to be relieved of his responsibilities as Chairman of the Defense Council.[102]

The Red Army's invasion on 30 November 1939 catapulted the Marshal from the wings of Finnish history to center stage —where he remained the principal actor for the next six years. The Government which had ignored his advice toppled, and the new wartime Cabinet entrusted him with a task he knew was impossible.

And now he was back in Mikkeli, nearly 22 years after he had used that quiet town as his Headquarters in an earlier battle with communism. This new war was in essence one long delaying action, trying to stave off the inevitable defeat in the desperate hope that a compromise peace might be negotiated. But what a magnificent delaying action it was! One battle which the world would long remember was reaching its climax at the turn of the year.

*He will drive thee back dishonored,*
*Sink thee in the fatal snow-drift*
**RUNE III**

CHAPTER IV

# Belaya Smert´

THE STRATEGIC CROSS-ROADS VILLAGE OF PUOLANKA LIES MID-
way between the Soviet border and Oulu; the latter is a key
junction on the only railroad linking Finland with Sweden, the
ultimate objective of the 163rd Division. Puolanka can be
reached from the northeast by the road to Peranka, and from
the southeast by the road to Hyrynsalmi. When the two regiments of the 163rd which advanced from Juntusranta reached
the Peranka-Hyrynsalmi road in the first days of December,
they split up to attack both of those villages. The leading regiment, the 81st, drove south to Suomussalmi where it joined
forces on 7 December with the 759th Regiment advancing from
Raate; their mission was to proceed to Puolanka via Hyrynsalmi. Most of Commander Sharov's 662nd Regiment wheeled
north, intending to attack Puolanka from the Peranka road.[1]

Major General W. E. Tuompo, commanding the Northern
Finland Group, deployed his slim forces to counter the unexpected thrust from Juntusranta. From distant Kuusamo he dispatched Major I. Pallari's Independent Battalion ErP 16 south
via Peranka. The first company arrived in the Lake Piispajärvi
area at 1 A.M. on 6 December, and the remainder of the battalion joined them around noon. The Finns immediately engaged
elements of the 662nd Regiment which Division Commander
Zelentsov had ordered to occupy Peranka that very day. Although outnumbered two to one, Pallari's troops—occupying
good defensive positions at the Piispajärvi straits—checked
Sharov's advance a few miles short of its objective. On the 7th

GENERAL LOCALE OF THE SUOMUSSALMi BATTLES      MAP 10

KUUSAMO

TAIVALKOSKI

Peranka

Ketola    *Piispajärvi*
          *L.*

Haapavaara

Yli-Näljänkä                    Juntusranta

Tervavaara

Palovaara      Linna

Vääkiö    *Myllyjoki R.*

*L. Pirttajärvi*
*L. Kovajärvi*
*L. Alajärvi*
*Vuonanlahti*

                    SUOMUSSALMI

PUOLANKA
                                        Vasovaara

                    *Alan-
                    teenjärvi*        Raate
                    *Pärsämönselkä*
                    *Vuokkijärvi*

HYRYNSALMI

                    Moisiovaara

                    LEGEND:
                    Progress of 163rd Div to 7 December
                    Intermediate Soviet Objectives

Kontiomäki

          0                    25                    50

                         MILES

KAJAANI

U S S R

the invaders still held the initiative, but the next day the Finns counterattacked and threw the Russians on the defensive.[2]

In the battle on 8 December Major Pallari was wounded. He was replaced by Lt. Colonel Paavo Susitaival, who had requested relief from his duties as a Member of Parliament to serve at the front. Colonel Susitaival was soon given command of all units operating against the enemy north and east of the Palovaara road junction (Task Force Susi), and Captain Salske then assumed command of ErP 16.[3]

The Finns encountered less opposition than they expected from the 662nd Regiment. Commander Zelentsov had retained its Third Battalion for division use, leaving Commander Sharov slightly less than 2,000 men. However, the quality of the Russian unit was more of a limitation than its numbers. As Sharov complained on 11 December in a report to the 47th Army Corps, his troops lacked warm clothes and boots, camouflage suits, and even adequate rations. By 13 December he had found it necessary to send back 48 men suffering from frostbite, and he had received no replacements for them or for his 160 combat casualties. He further admitted low morale and combat efficiency, desertions, and the fact that "part of the reserve officers cannot handle their men." A week earlier Political Commissar Boevski, attached to a supporting artillery unit, had been murdered by two of his own men.[4]

By 11 December the 662nd was holding defensive positions around Haapavaara, facing Finnish forces based at Ketola across Lake Piispajärvi. On 14 and 15 December Sharov directed a determined attack during which his First Battalion reached Ketola village, but it then retreated under heavy machine gun and mortar fire. The only results were an additional 150 casualties in the Russian regiment.[5]

Meanwhile, the major Soviet forces concentrating at Suomussalmi for the advance on Hyrynsalmi posed a more serious threat. On 7 December, the very day that Suomussalmi fell, Marshal Mannerheim ordered Regiment JR 27 to depart Kemi for this trouble spot. Colonel Hjalmar Siilasvuo, a Jäger veteran, learned when he reported to General Tuompo in Kajaani that he was to use JR 27 as the nucleus of a new brigade charged with destroying the 163rd Division. That was a formidable task for a reserve force which had no artillery, no antiair-craft or antitank guns, and not even enough tents and winter clothing.[6]

However, there was already about a foot of snow in this area, which facilitated the maneuvering of the Finnish skiers while restricting their enemy's movements. Moreover, most of the men of JR 27 were hardy lumberjacks who were happy to be sent to fight in the northern woods rather than on the Karelian Isthmus, and their rapid deployment to the battle zone came as an unexpected shock to Commander Zelentsov and the staff of the 163rd Division. While the Soviets had surprised the Finnish Army with their new road towards the border in the direction of Juntusranta, they, in turn, were apparently unaware that the Finns had just completed the Kontiomäki-Taivalkoski Rail-road as far north as Hyrynsalmi, about 25 miles from Suomus-salmi. Thus, as early as 8 December Colonel Siilasvuo and the first elements of his brigade arrived at the railhead. When the Russians tried to advance towards Hyrynsalmi the next day, they were repulsed by machine guns which covered the road at the ferry just south of Suomussalmi. By the 10th Siilasvuo's entire brigade (JR 27 plus the two battalions which were al-ready fighting here—some 4,700 men in all) was deployed for a counterattack set for the following day.[7]

For the harried covering troops and border guards who had fought two entire regiments from the very beginning, the ap-pearance of JR 27 on the scene was barely in the nick of time. Lt. Elo, a young school teacher whose exhausted detachment had suffered heavy losses while fighting for a week without rest —unaware of the reinforcements enroute and feeling the situa-tion hopeless—shot himself just before their arrival. Upon reaching the battle area, the first action of Colonel Siilasvuo's chief of staff, Captain Alpo Marttinen, was to spread the exag-gerated report that a Finnish division was on the way. That big white lie had the intended morale-boosting effect![8]

During the long night of 10–11 December, JR 27 moved to an assembly area southeast of Suomussalmi, about 5 miles south of the Raate road. Advancing thru the woods on the 11th, the Finns succeeded in cutting that vital communications link in spite of the reinforcements the Russians sped to the scene by truck. The main forces of JR 27 then pushed westward towards

Suomussalmi, occupying a few miles of the Raate road before stiff resistance halted their progress. Two companies were dispatched eastward to establish a roadblock at the ridge between Lakes Kuivasjärvi and Kuomasjärvi, some six miles southeast of the village, to prevent any reinforcements from reaching the 163rd Division along this route.[9]

Simultaneously, another Finnish battalion struck at the enemy's northern communications line near Hulkonniemi, just northwest of Suomussalmi. The Russian forces in this area were too strong for a single battalion to overcome, but the Finns were able to harass traffic on this last road remaining open to the village.[10]

For the next two weeks Siilasvuo's brigade maintained the initiative, recapturing most of the village and launching constant raids against the northern supply route. These attacks against well-entrenched and numerically superior forces supported by artillery and numerous tanks were costly to the Finns; nevertheless, they achieved their objective of containing the enemy until sufficient reinforcements could be mustered to destroy him.[11]

The first Finnish artillery reached the front on 16 December —four old 76.2mm guns, model 1902. Two days later a second battery arrived, and on the 20th two antitank guns were received. On 22 December Colonel Siilasvuo learned that his unit would be reorganized as a division, assuming its former designation, the 9th Division. For Christmas he received the welcome "gift" of five battalions: the three poorly equipped ones of Regiment JR 64, the newly formed guerilla battalion, Sissi* P1, and Captain Paavola's light battalion; these reinforcements brought the strength of the 9th Division up to 11,500 men.[12]

Meanwhile a lone Finnish bicycle battalion, PPP 6, was concentrated early in December at Yli-Näljänkä, which was being menaced by deep cavalry raids. The battalion commander, Major Järvinen, received the mission of protecting this area by driving the enemy from the minor road which joins the Peranka-Hyrynsalmi road about two miles north of Suomussalmi. Early in the attack phase PPP 6 was attached to Task Force

*Sissi = guerilla unit

Susi, but when its advance brought it closer to the operational area of the 9th Division it was subordinated to Colonel Siilasvuo. On 17 December Järvinen's force began its attack, reaching Vääkio the next day. By the 22nd it had closed off the isthmus between Lakes Alajärvi and Kovajärvi, and it was in position to coordinate further operations with those of the 9th Division.[13]

Simultaneously with the advance of PPP 6, the main forces of ErP 16 deployed to Tervavaara for a flanking attack on the Palovaara road junction, while the remainder of the battalion continued to tie down the major part of the 662nd Regiment in the Lake Piispajärvi region. By 23 December the flanking units had skied close to Palovaara, where they harassed Soviet supply columns for several days.[14]

At this time Task Force Susi was reinforced by Lt. Colonel K. Mandelin's newly formed regiment, JR 65, which travelled more than 100 miles from Oulu by truck in weather reaching 25 degrees below zero (F). Colonel Susitaival positioned this unit north of Lake Piispajärvi, from where it fought its way south to the vicinity of Haapavaara by Christmas.[15]

Thus the main parts of the 662nd Regiment were under heavy pressure from Task Force Susi during the holidays, in no position to assist the remainder of the 163rd Division when the decisive battles were fought near Suomussalmi village. On the contrary, Susitaival's forces captured the important Palovaara road junction on 27 December, the very day that Siilasvuo's climactic offensive began.[16]

With the reinforcements he received at Christmas time, Colonel Siilasvuo quickly hurled a full-scale attack against the 163rd Division. Time now became the critical factor because parts of a new unit, the elite 44th Motorized Infantry Division, had been observed by Finnish aircraft approaching from the east as early as 13 December. It had been this report which prompted Marshal Mannerheim to increase Siilasvuo's strength from a brigade to a division. On 20 December an intercepted Soviet radio message—a prime source of Finnish intelligence—indicated that a strong enemy force would reach the area on the 22nd. The Finns estimated that the main components of this new division were on the Raate road on 24 December.[17]

This was alarming because there were only the two infantry companies, reinforced by additional mortars and guns, at the roadblock to keep the 44th Division from the scene of the battle with the 163rd. Captain Mäkinen, Siilasvuo's staff intelligence officer, had been entrusted with this important task. To prevent these meager defenses from being overrun or outflanked by the new enemy force, ski detachments were flung in hit-and-run raids against its vulnerable flanks which stretched along the road mile after mile.[18]

On 21 December Captain Mäkinen left his roadblock to lead a small reconnaissance patrol which reached Lake Kokkojärvi, five miles to the east,* without encountering strong enemy forces. On the 23rd, he threw his two companies at the vanguard of the enemy division, the 25th Regiment, to tie it down while three other detachments simultaneously hit its flanks. Captain Kontula's detachment (about 200 men) struck from the south in the vicinity of the Haukila farm, slightly more than a mile east of the roadblock. It succeeded in killing about 100 horses of an antitank unit before withdrawing. Captain Lassila's battalion (I/JR 27) hit the Raate road from the south at Kokkojärvi about 11 A.M., fanning out in both directions. Although they destroyed one tank, two trucks, and a field kitchen, Russian tanks prevented them from blowing up the highway bridge south of Kokkojärvi. They suffered only two fatalities, while slaying an estimated 100 of the enemy, before Colonel Siilasvuo ordered their return to bivouac early the next morning. The third and smallest unit, Lt. Larvo's TO 1 of about 50 men—which was to attack the Kokkojärvi area from the north —failed even to reach the road.[19]

In spite of its limited success, this first sizeable strike against the new opponent created so much confusion and fear that the 44th Division never recovered its balance. Small but mobile raiding parties continued to harass the road-bound enemy day and night—disrupting supply, preventing restful sleep, and convincing the overly cautious Commander Vinogradov that much larger forces were threatening his division behind the

*See Map No. 12, p. 115

dense pine curtain which enveloped it. Such forays also provided the 9th Division with excellent intelligence for planning
future operations.[20]

A farsighted measure which facilitated these flitting raids,
and later made an even greater contribution to the final outcome, was undertaken while the decisive engagements with
the 163rd Division were still in progress. This was the plowing
of an ice road along the chain of frozen and snowcovered lakes
(Alanteenjärvi-Pärsämönselkä-Vuokkijärvi) which parallel
the Raate road some four to six miles to the south.* Here ski
troops could move swiftly—without the exhaustion of long
cross-country treks—to their attack sectors, and supplies could
be transported by truck or horse. At the same time work was
begun to clear a supply route linking Moisiovaara, which was
connected by road to the Hyrynsalmi railhead some 20 miles to
the west, with the Vuokkijärvi area.[21]

With the support of these daring raiding parties the weak
roadblock held, but Siilasvuo's main forces had to face the
163rd Division with the uneasy feeling that an entire new division, just six to eight miles away, might break thru to their rear
at any moment.

Commander Zelentsov's main units, virtually surrounded in
the Hulkonniemi-Suomussalmi area, launched a violent attack
on 24 December. After a heavy artillery preparation which cut
all Finnish phone lines to the front, they advanced at noon
along both sides of the road leading south from the church
village. At first the Finns were forced to yield some of their
positions, but at the last moment the lost ground was regained
in a counterattack by the Second Battalion of JR 27.[22]

The Russians renewed the attack the next day in the same
direction, but on a reduced scale. Elements of the 163rd Division also tried to break thru the Finnish lines to the west on
Christmas; they crossed the ice from Hulkonniemi to the Vuonanniemi peninsula, but they were thrown back there as well.
When the enemy's storm had spent its fury without results,
Colonel Siilasvuo issued his own attack orders on 26 December.[23]

*See Map No. 10, p. 98

THE DEFEAT OF THE 163RD DIVISION                        MAP 11

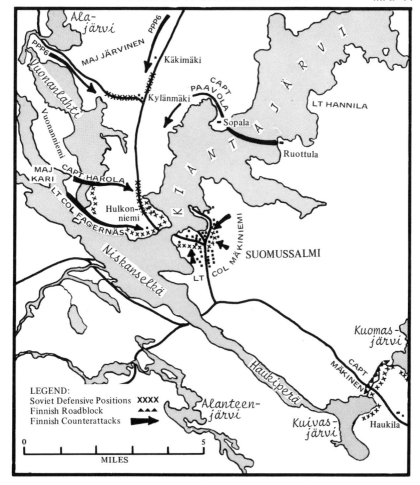

The main Finnish blow was directed toward the Hulkonniemi positions from the northwest. Major Kaarle Kari, a
proven leader who had been fighting on this terrain from the
first week of the war, was given command of four battalions for
this operation. He split his force into two strike columns, pair-
ing his experienced veterans with the green troops of Regiment
JR 64 who had just arrived at the front. Lt. Colonel Frans Fagernäs was to direct the First Battalion of his own JR 64 and the
Fourth Replacement Battalion in an attack from the southern
tip of Vuonanniemi towards the Hulkonniemi farm and the
main road beyond. About a mile to the north, Captain Martti
Harola was to strike directly for the main road with the Second

Battalion of JR 64 and Independent Battalion ErP 15; after blocking the road to the north, Harola's main forces were to move south towards Suomussalmi. The 9th Division's two antitank guns were divided between Kari's two strike forces, which were also augmented with combat engineers. Both of Siilasvuo's artillery batteries were also deployed to support this assault on the Hulkonniemi positions. The offensive was set for 27 December at 8 A.M., when it would still be dark.[24]

About eight miles to the north, Battalion PPP 6 was set to launch a coordinated attack at 7:30 A.M., sending its main forces down the eastern side of Lake Pirttajärvi towards the Kylänmäki road junction.[25]

Lesser detachments were assigned supporting roles: Captain A. Paavola's three companies, also newly arrived, were deployed at Ruottula on the eastern shore of Lake Kiantajärvi three miles northeast of Suomussalmi. Paavola was to start across the ice at 7:30, cutting off any enemy movement on the Lake; upon reaching the western shore near Sopala he was to push south to join Major Kari's main forces. A light company commanded by Lt. T. E. Hannila was instructed to remain east of Kiantajärvi, a mile or so north of Ruottula, to observe traffic on the ice and to provide security in the north.[26]

During the night of 26–27 December one of Captain Harola's infantry companies, supported by engineers, cut the road a half-mile north of the column's main objective. By felling heavy trees across the road and mining these obstructions, this small force held the roadblock against a tank attack.[27]

The furious battles of 27 December were indecisive. Colonel Fagernäs' column encountered strongly fortified positions from the moment it crossed the narrow strait at Vuonanniemi, and it did not reach the Hulkonniemi farm, two miles to the east, until 1 P.M. Although the main road was little more than half a mile farther, the exhausted attackers failed in three separate attempts to reach it.

Captain Harola's column, on the northern flank of Colonel Fagernäs, managed to fight its way to the road, but it was thrown back by a determined Russian counterattack supported by the inevitable tanks. The battle at this road point raged all night.

Captain Paavola's detachment was delayed in crossing Lake

Kiantajärvi by armored trucks on the ice and by small enemy forces which it engaged east of the Lake during the morning. It was after noon by the time Paavola reached the western shore at Sopala, and he was unable to establish contact with Major Kari that night.

PPP 6 achieved limited success on the 27th; one of its detachments cut the road east of Lake Pirttajärvi,* destroying five Russian trucks in the ensuing fray. South of the Myllyjoki River the main forces of the Battalion ran up against strong positions which they finally carried in heavy fighting. However, a company which was progressing towards the Kylänmäki road fork around noon encountered stiffening resistance which culminated in a strong Russian counterattack. The fierce engagement continued late into the evening; the Finns repelled the counterattack but could not take the Klyänmäki junction.

On 28 December PPP 6 finally secured the road fork, holding it against violent new counterattacks. Captain Harola's column also reached the main road in its sector by noon; its main forces then continued south towards the church village, but a detachment was sent north to assist PPP 6 in its unequal struggle with about a regiment of infantry supported by a battalion of artillery.[28]

Colonel Fagernäs renewed his attack at Hulkonniemi early that morning, seizing the road and pushing the defenders south towards the strait. At that point, Captain Marttinen, the daringly aggressive chief of staff of the 9th Division, urged Colonel Siilasvuo to throw in his only remaining reserve (the First Battalion of JR 27) to close the last few hundred yards of the ring tightening around the enemy's main forces. The cautious commander refused this request, possibly concerned about the 44th Division which was marking time just a few miles to the east. Around 9 A.M. Russian resistance suddenly collapsed in front of Fagernäs; the men bolted from their positions, some towards Suomussalmi village, others onto the ice of Lake Kiantajärvi— a few throwing away their weapons in their haste. This retreat sealed the fate of the 163rd Division, although the battle continued against its remnants for two more days.[29]

*See Map No. 10, p. 98

When the Finns captured Suomussalmi and Hulkonniemi, the Russians still had considerable forces to the northwest in the Kylänmäki-Käkimäki region. Shortly after noon, when Colonel Siilasvuo finally agreed to commit his reserve, Captain Lassila's battalion was dispatched to Sopala to intercept those enemy groups trying to reach Lake Kiantajärvi thru the woods. Colonel Fagernäs was also thrusting his column up the east side of the road to prevent the Russians' escape. Around midnight, Captain Harola's main forces began to push north to the same general area, still encountering intense resistance in some places.[30]

At 10 A.M. on the 29th, Major Järvinen requested additional assistance for PPP 6 because the enemy was desperately fighting to break its encirclement. Colonel Siilasvuo sent almost all of the remaining units which the collapse of the Hulkonniemi-Suomussalmi sector had freed for action elsewhere; only the Second Battalion of JR 27 was dispatched in the opposite direction—to bolster Captain Mäkinen's force at the Raate roadblock against any possible action by the 44th Division.[31]

Lt. Colonel Mäkiniemi was put in command of an imposing task force assembled to crush the last enemy stronghold in the north. It included the First and Third Battalions of Regiment JR 27, the First Battalion of JR 64, and part of the 4th Replacement Battalion. He began his attack at 3 P.M. when the winter day was fading into dusk. Movement was very slow in the dark forest where the Finns encountered isolated enemy units trying to reach Lake Kiantajärvi. The First Battalion of JR 27 fought one group of about two companies for four hours before the surviving Russians scattered in all directions. Another fleeing unit of some 50 men stumbled upon the battalion's supply train at Sopala on the western shore of the Lake. The logistics officer, Lt. Miettunen, improvised a combat force from the horse drivers and in a short skirmish killed all of the enemy.[32]

Isolated fighting continued throughout the night of 29–30 December, as more and more of the Russians tried to escape to the Lake. The trap was not fully effective until visibility improved in the morning. The final coordinated effort to break out to the north at 10 A.M. terminated in the death of some 300 Russians and the capture of eight field guns, 50 trucks, and 100 horses. By noon the last organized resistance west of Lake Kiantajärvi had ceased.[33]

The 163rd Division no longer existed—there were only a few hundred cold, hungry, frightened men who abandoned their weapons and fled in panic towards the Soviet border beyond Juntusranta, some 20 miles to the northeast. The rout developed into a slaughter, as the Finns called in an air strike and also sent five truckloads of troops equipped with heavy machine guns, automatic rifles, and even one antitank gun in pursuit of the hapless infantry struggling thru the snow on the ice.[34]

This first and only bombing mission against the 163rd Division was flown by two of the 18 bombers Finland then possessed —all twin-engine Bristol Blenheims. Although three of the trucks sent out at 8 A.M. from the Suomussalmi area turned back because of the snow, two of them continued on and caught up with an enemy column twelve miles to the north. Virtually all of the 400 Russians were annihilated on the ice; one Finn was wounded. On the return trip, the truck detachment encountered and destroyed another enemy group.[35]

Mopping up actions continued. Task Force Susi was ordered to destroy a small enemy concentration at Linna on the northeastern shore of Lake Kiantajärvi, and it cleared the Juntusranta road, where a few stragglers had managed to escape.[36]

About 500 prisoners were taken, and ten times as many Russians lay dead in the snow. Some 30 artillery pieces and a larger number of antitank guns were captured intact—along with thousands of rounds of ammunition. With these modern weapons the Finns were able to replace their own obsolete artillery and to equip new units.[37]

The world took notice. On 1 January 1940 the headline of *The New York Times* read:

## FINNS SMASH A RED DIVISION

and the author of the accompanying article termed this "the greatest victory of the month-old conflict." Marshal Mannerheim's Order of the Day for 31 December announced the award of a Freedom Cross to Colonel Siilasvuo for this achievement.[38]

The 9th Division did not pause to celebrate, as the 44th Division was still only a few miles away. Incredibly, Commander

Vinogradov had not even made a determined attempt to rescue the 163rd Division while it was being destroyed virtually within earshot. On 24 December his forward unit tried to cross the Kuomasjoki River, close to Lake Kuomasjärvi. On Christmas Day the attack was renewed on the ice of the Lake, but Captain Mäkinen's small forces repelled these blows by a counterattack. On 27 December Vinogradov belatedly scheduled a new assault on the roadblock for 10:30 the next morning, but raids by only two Finnish companies early on the 28th led him to revoke that order and to instruct his division to dig in for defense on the Raate road.[39]

Although the 44th was reputedly a crack unit, its heavily motorized forces, trained for mobile warfare in open country where their many tanks and trucks could maneuver freely, were at a great disadvantage in the dense forests of northern Finland. Since the troops were untrained in the use of the skis with which they had been supplied at the last moment, they could not pursue the Finnish raiders who appeared suddenly and vanished at will. Air supremacy also made little difference here, as there were only 5 to 6 hours of daylight, the weather was changeable, and the forests effectively concealed the elusive Finns. Consequently, the 44th Division, like the 163rd, had to fight blindly—unable to determine the strength or disposition of the opponent's forces—while nakedly visible itself.[40]

While mopping-up operations were still underway in the woods north of Suomussalmi, Colonel Siilasvuo had already begun the execution of a well conceived plan to segment and then destroy the 44th Division, whose vulnerable flanks stretched nearly 20 miles along the Raate road from the roadblock to the border.

On New Year's Eve Captain Häkkinen's guerilla battalion, reinforced with an independent company, carried out a probing attack to the Haukila farm area. Flanking Lake Kuivasjärvi from the south, they encountered and fended off an enemy battalion east of the Lake. Their report confirmed that this area was heavily defended; in fact, the largest concentration of the 44th Division (the 25th Regiment, reinforced by the Second Battalion of the 146th Regiment and most of the division artillery and tanks) was strongly entrenched in a two-mile sector just east of the roadblock. The attack planned in this area would obviously have to be made in considerable strength.[41]

On 1 January a 50-man reconnaissance unit (TO 2) reported that the enemy had recently occupied the Eskola area, about a mile and a half south of the Raate road along another road which branches off it near Lake Kokkojärvi and runs in a southeasterly direction to the Soviet border.* As this branch road was potentially important as a supply or retreat route for the 44th Division, Siilasvuo considered it essential to secure it immediately. That same day he dispatched Captain Paavola's light battalion to the Sanginlampi area, about three miles south of Eskola. Now the ice road which had previously been cleared south of and parallel to the Raate road proved its worth. Paavola's unit easily travelled 15 miles on New Year's Day, camping for the night in the vicinity of the Mäkelä farm house.[42]

Two larger strike groups, Task Forces Kari and Fagernäs, also sped along the ice road during the first two days of January, deploying from the vicinity of Suomussalmi to positions far to the southeast from where they could later launch coordinated flank attacks. Major Kari's battalions bivouaced in the Mäkelä area, while most of Lt. Colonel Fagernäs' troops camped near Heikkilä. One reinforced company moved as far east as Vänkä, just south of Raate.[43]

The first sustained effort to cut up the 44th Division was undertaken during the night of 1–2 January by Captain Lassila's unit, the First Battalion of Regiment JR 27, numbering approximately 1,000 men. At 2 P.M. on New Year's Day, the Battalion commander sent one rifle company ahead as a trail-breaking party, starting the remainder of his unit from its assembly area southwest of Lake Kuivasjärvi an hour later. At 5 P.M. the battalion reached the end of a horse trail paralleling the Raate road, where the troops had a hot meal before proceeding to battle. From there to the objective three miles farther, the column advanced silently on skis thru dark woods in deep snow and subzero weather. About 11 P.M. the advance guard reached a ridge some 400 yards from the Raate road, from where they could see enemy troops huddled around innumerable camp fires.

After a hasty reconnaissance and a brief conference with his company commanders, Captain Lassila deployed his battalion

*See Map No. 12, p. 115

for the attack. He split his heavy machine gun company, positioning six guns on each side of the attack force on the ridge, with orders not to shoot until the enemy opened fire. Two rifle companies were to advance abreast and very close to one another. Upon reaching the road, one company would push east, the other west, to secure about 500 yards of the roadway. Then the engineer platoon would rush forward to construct roadblocks in both directions, felling trees and mining them. The third rifle company was held in reserve behind the ridge, near the battalion command post. During the hour and a half required for these dispositions, the Russians remained blissfully unaware of the thousand Finns a few hundred yards away.

A half hour after midnight the assault companies advanced, overran the enemy sentries posted about 60 yards from the roadway, and reached the road with little opposition. Expecting to meet Soviet infantry, the Finns were surprised to encounter an artillery battalion. Due to the difficulties of navigating in woods at night with unreliable maps, Lassila's unit had accidentally arrived about 500 yards east of its objective, the Haukila farm. This error proved to be a lucky break, as the intended objective was strongly defended, whereas the artillery positions were easily captured. When the surprise attack struck from the south, all of the field guns were pointing west; the Russians managed to turn two pieces towards the Finns, but their crews were cut down by small arms fire before they could get off a single round. Soviet four-barreled antiaircraft machine guns were also ineffective, because they were mounted high on trucks and thus fired over the heads of the advancing infantry. Lassila's battalion was therefore able to complete its mission in about two hours with only light casualties; the reserve company was not even needed.

All night long the battalion supply troops labored to construct a winter road from the end of the horse trail to the battle area. About 7 A.M. the first priority shipment arrived via this route—the two 37mm antitank guns which were assigned to the battalion for this operation. These guns were barely emplaced when the Russians launched their first counterattack from the east. Within a quarter of an hour the Finns destroyed seven tanks on or near the road, making the roadblock even more effective. The Soviet infantry attack was also repelled.

Later in the morning hot meals were sent up from the support area, and tents were erected near the command post behind the ridge. The troops were then rotated so that they could warm up and enjoy hot tea inside this welcome shelter.

In the afternoon about two companies of Russian infantry waded thru the deep snow to hit the roadblock from the west, but Lassila's reserve company caught them from the flank and forced their withdrawal. On this first day, as on subsequent days, the Russians counterattacked from both east and west, but never from both directions simultaneously. Thus the Finns were able to strengthen their positions and to counter the enemy's moves one at a time.[44]

In contrast to the relative comfort of the Finns, who enjoyed hot meals throughout the contest with the 44th Division, the Russians were both cold and hungry in their encircled positions. Finnish patrols deliberately sought out field kitchens as targets, and the Russians soon learned that it was dangerous to light camp fires during the bitterly cold nights. Every day that the roadblocks held, the Russians grew weaker and more demoralized. The Finnish term for such an encirclement—which became a common feature of the battles in the northern wilds —was "motti," their word for a stack of firewood piled up to be chopped.

On 2 January Captain Airimo's Third Battalion, JR 27, assaulted the Raate road at Haukila on the left flank of Lassila's Battalion. As noted above, this area—Lassila's intended objective—was very heavily defended. Consequently, although the Third Battalion stubbornly maintained a grip close to the south side of the roadway, it could not cut the road. That evening Colonel Siilasvuo ordered Captain Häkkinen to position his guerilla battalion closer to Haukila, where it could support the First and Third Battalions in the event a withdrawal should become necessary. Häkkinen also sent out reconnaissance patrols east of Lassila's roadblock.[45]

Captain Paavola's light battalion advanced cautiously on 2 January, moving from its bivouac at Mäkelä towards the Sanginlampi farm house where it was stopped by small arms fire. Here the secondary road from Kokkojärvi enabled the Russians to deploy considerable forces, and when it became obvious that Paavola's unit could not clear the road alone, Siilasvuo sent Major Kari to his assistance.[46]

Kari threw the Fourth Replacement Battalion into the attack at 4 P.M. on the 3rd. When this fierce engagement ended the next day with the capture of Sanginlampi, 260 of the enemy were dead and 40 had surrendered. As the Finns also suffered in that bloody encounter, Kari rotated Battalion ErP 15 into the forward position. While this battle was raging, a guerilla company from Sissi P1 cut the road north of Eskola on 3 January. As a result of that raid, ErP 15 easily captured Eskola from the south in the morning of the 4th. Kari's third unit, the First Battalion of JR 64, also reached the Eskola area that day. Thus by 4 January Task Force Kari had secured an excellent attack position, within two miles of the Kokkojärvi road fork.[47]

Meanwhile, Task Force Fagernäs (the Second and Third Battalions of the Colonel's own Regiment, JR 64) had been improving its communications from the base camps towards the Raate road, but not close enough to alert the enemy. The company at Vänkä constructed a winter road as far as Linnalampi, while the main units at Heikkilä opened a poor road part way to Honkajärvi. By 4 January both forces had relatively easy access to points within four miles of the Raate road.[48]

On the 4th, Colonel Siilasvuo issued orders for the attack designed to destroy the 44th Division the next day. Colonel Mäkiniemi was to command his own Regiment JR 27, including the Second Battalion which had been supporting Captain Mäkinen at the western roadblock. A less experienced battalion from JR 65, which had just arrived from Colonel Susitaival's northern sector, replaced the Second Battalion as Mäkinen's reinforcement. Captain Häkkinen's guerilla battalion Sissi P 1, already operating alongside JR 27, was attached to Task Force Mäkiniemi for the offensive. Because this task force had to attack the strongest known enemy concentration—in the Haukila area—Siilasvuo allocated it six of his eight field guns. Elements of Colonel Mandelin's Task Force, which consisted of two battalions of JR 65 and three serarate units of company size or smaller, were instructed to hit Haukila from the north in coordination with Mäkiniemi's attacks from the south.[49]

Operating just east of Mäkiniemi's sector, Task Force Kari's mission was to destroy the strong enemy units in the Kokkojär-

DESTRUCTION OF THE 44TH DIVISION          MAP 12

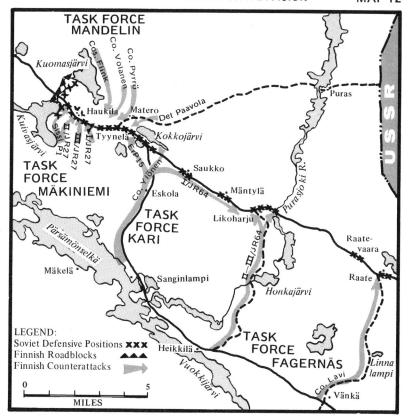

vi-Tyynelä region by flank attacks. With part of his troops he was also to drive east to link up with Task Force Fagernäs. Major Kari had three battalions and the remaining two field guns at his disposal.[50]

Task Force Fagernäs, comprising two battalions of JR 64, was charged with preventing the 44th Division from receiving any new reinforcements from the east. To accomplish this it was ordered to cut the Raate road about a mile from the Soviet border and at the Purasjoki River, destroying the enemy known to be in the latter area.[51]

Russian resistance on 5 January was so fierce that none of the Finnish attacks succeeded completely. In Mäkiniemi's Task Force, Captain Häkkinen's veteran guerilla battalion struck towards the Raate road just east of Lake Kuivasjärvi at 6 A.M., maintaining contact with Major Sihvonen's unit (the Second Battalion of JR 27) which was advancing on its right. Both battalions made good progress against the light patrols encountered deep in the woods. Along the Lake shore Häkkinen passed field positions which the Russians had abandoned, but enemy resistance stiffened drastically when the Finns came within a half mile of the roadway. In the stretch nearest to the Lake the Russians were massed so densely that Häkkinen's force was stopped dead in its tracks. Sihvonen's unit moved ahead slowly in heavy fighting, but by evening it too had been halted.[52]

Captain Airimo's Third Battalion, JR 27, on Sihvonen's right flank, attacked from the positions near the road at Haukila which it had held for the last three days. By noon it reached the road, but it was stopped in a murderous hail of fire from the Haukila hills. The battle in this sector did not subside until after midnight, and even then Soviet artillery was active and their tanks continued to patrol the road.[53]

Just east of the Third Battalion, Captain Lassila's men endured their hardest day since making the initial break in the 44th Division during the night of 1-2 January. Attacking at 8:30 in the morning, the First Company by early afternoon had pushed north of the road to widen its positions. In that relatively open terrain the Finns were exposed to devastating artillery fire; after its commander, Lt. Miettunen, was killed and both other officers wounded, the Company withdrew to the south of the road. At that point a medical sergeant volunteered to lead the Company. A few hours later Captain Lassila met the sergeant as he was being evacuated with a bullet through his lung. In reply to his commander's sympathetic inquiry about the pain, the sergeant joked that he could breathe easier with two holes in his chest. The Finns call this *sisu*—in any language it equates to sheer guts![54]

The Russians counterattacked fiercely in this sector, desperately trying to force a passage to the east thru the First Battalion's roadblock. Lassila lost 96 of his men, killed and wounded, that day—roughly ten percent of his strength. When he requested permission to pull the entire battalion back just south of the roadway to reduce casualties—still keeping the road closed by firepower—Colonel Mäkiniemi threatened to have him shot. The battalion held its positions in spite of its losses.[55]

Major Kari ordered Captain Mankonen's battalion (I/JR 64) to secure the Kokkojärvi road fork. The attack began at 6 A.M., but in heavy fighting which lasted all day the battalion only reached a point a quarter of a mile east of that junction. Part of Mankonen's troops also moved east to try to establish contact with Task Force Fagernäs. Due to the First Battalion's heavy losses and the lack of tents on that bitter night (the mercury dipped to 31° below zero F), Kari relieved it with Lt. Karhunen's Fourth Replacement Battalion which had been in reserve south of Eskola all day. Mankonen's men then pulled back into the woods where they could safely rest around small camp fires.

Kari's other attack force, Captain Harola's Independent Battalion ErP 15, skied cross-country to hit Tyynelä from the south. As they approached their objective, Harola observed that the road was heavily defended in this sector and three tanks were patrolling it. Without their antitank gun, which was delayed due to transport difficulties, they could not cope with the tanks in the open terrain. After two hours of futile fighting, Harola ordered his men to pull back into the woods to await the gun.

In the afternoon, Major Kari ordered Harola to make a full-scale attack on the road; this effort began at 7 P.M. Although all three companies reached the road, they could not cross it in the face of the tank and infantry fire. At midnight the Finns again fell back into the cover of the forest. Colonel Siilasvuo informed Major Kari that he *must* secure the road the next day.

Task Force Fagernäs achieved the day's most significant results, although it accomplished only half its mission. Lavi's reinforced company—tasked with cutting the road at Raate, a mile from the border—found movement difficult north of Linnalampi due to swamps and heavy snow. While the supply train advanced slowly, the main force skied ahead, reaching Raate around noon. About a company of Russians were camped there in the houses, which were protected by bunkers. Lavi's troops brought the road under fire and destroyed a few trucks,

but because of the open terrain they could not establish a roadblock. Since they also lacked tents, the main forces of the company withdrew about three miles to the first houses that night.

The larger part of Task Force Fagernäs, advancing via Honkajärvi towards Likoharju, experienced similar difficulties in
the snowy terrain. Nevertheless, the forward elements contacted the enemy early in the morning near the road northeast
of Likoharju. About two and a half miles farther east, an engineer detachment had already blown up a bridge over a stream.
However, it had failed in an attempt to destroy the important
Purasjoki River bridge.[56]

Colonel Fagernäs decided to attack the Likoharju positions
without waiting for his antitank guns. He concentrated the
strike force in the woods some 300 yards south of the Likoharju
farm house and began the advance at 10 A.M. Drawing heavy
automatic fire from bunkers near the road and from tanks
which rushed to the scene of battle, the Finnish attack faltered.
Soon more Russians were observed approaching from the west
by truck. Fagernäs dispatched a platoon toward Mäntylä,
which ambushed several truckloads of troops and successfully
delayed other reinforcements. These new arrivals belonged to
the Third NKVD Regiment which had just been sent to assist
the 44th Division at the beginning of January.[57]

During that cold moonlit night, Fagernäs renewed the attack
and captured a stretch of the road just north of Likoharju. The
enemy immediately launched a counterattack from the east,
supported by tanks and artillery; this forced the Finns to pull
back their right flank. Fagernäs then threw into battle his reserve company, which broke up the Russian attack. Colonel
Siilasvuo released a company of the 9th Division's reserve for
the use of Fagernäs, who had encountered much stronger resistance in this sector than had been anticipated. After several
more failures, the Task Force finally succeeded in blowing up
the Purasjoki bridge about 10 P.M. Now the Finns no longer had
to worry about additional truck traffic beyond that point.[58]

While those attacks were underway against the southern
flank of the 44th Division, small elements of Task Force
Mandelin were simultaneously active north of the Raate road.
Lt. Volanen's light company and the small reconnaissance de-

tachment, TO 1, both experienced guerilla units, had been on
patrols the previous night along the Raate road and the minor
road to Puras village, where they had destroyed several enemy
patrols. On the morning of the 5th, Volanen's company moved
to Kotvala and TO 1 took up positions near the Puras road. In
order to forestall any Russian attempt to escape via the latter
route, Volanen was reinforced with Lt. Pyrrö's company from
the Third Battalion of Regiment JR 65. The remaining companies of the Battalion, led by Captain Flink, the commander of
III/JR 65, took up positions nearby, just southeast of Lake Kuomasjärvi. The region between Kotvala and Matero was covered
by Finnish patrols.[59]

When Captain Harola's battalion was stalled on the southern
approaches to Tyynelä, Colonel Siilasvuo ordered Colonel
Mandelin to put more pressure on that sector from the north.
Pyrrö's company advanced from Matero towards Tyynelä, but
Russian machine gunners stopped it short of its goal. At night
the main forces were pulled back to the shelter of the few
houses in Matero and Kotvala.[60]

Although Siilasvuo's offensive had not brought the desired
victory on the first day, the Russians had lost their last chance
to seize the initiative. A radio message from 9th Army Headquarters to the 44th Division, transmitted at 10 A.M. on 5 January, ordered Commander Vinogradov to launch an attack to the
south at 1 P.M. with at least two battalions, to be joined by the
Third NKVD Regiment. The Finnish attacks preempted this
belated Russian plan.[61]

The 6th of January was another bloody day, with both sides
launching attacks and counterattacks.

Task Force Mäkiniemi encountered stubborn resistance
when it renewed its offensive early in the morning. The Third
Battalion of JR 27 finally succeeded in establishing a roadblock
west of the one held by the First Battalion. The Second Battalion reached the road in the evening, after tearing open a gap
in the bunker defenses and then rolling up other bunkers from
the flank. Battalion Sissi P1 also smashed its way to the road by
nightfall, but the Russians still held a few bunkers on its left
flank along the shore of Lake Kuivasjärvi. The battered First
Battalion at the main roadblock was repeatedly attacked by

tanks, but it held its positions. The Russians even drove horses against the road obstacles to detonate the mines, but the only result was a slaughter of the helpless animals.

Around 2 A.M. on the 7th the Finns renewed the assault. After about an hour's fight, the enemy facing the Second and Third Battalions abandoned their heavy equipment on the road and fled towards Haukila hill, firing in all directions, while their attackers remained in positions near the road to await the morning.

During the night of 5–6 January, Major Kari resumed the attack in the vicinity of the Kokkojärvi road fork with the Fourth Replacement Battalion. As the Russians held artillery positions and bunkers very close to the road junction, a direct attack along the southern route was very difficult. Lt. Karhunen therefore dispatched Lt. Ylönen's Third Company, reinforced with a heavy machine gun platoon and one antitank gun, cross-country to cut the Raate road about a mile east of Kokkojärvi. The Finns reached their objective about 3 A.M. and established a roadblock. Early in the morning the enemy counterattacked from the west in such strength that Major Kari reinforced Ylö-nen's unit with the heavy machine gun company from Man-konen's battalion and two additional infantry platoons. Around 2 P.M. the Russians renewed their drive, but the roadblock held.

Captain Harola's battalion, ErP 15, also resumed its advance in the morning of the 6th. At 11 A.M., after three hours of heavy fighting, the attackers attained the road just east of Tyynelä. Some of the troops remained there to guard against possible attack from the east, while the main forces of the battalion turned west towards Tyynelä. Close to the farm houses they succeeded in establishing still another roadblock, which they defended against more counterattacks from the west. The 44th Division, desperately fighting to break out to the east, was being systematically cut into smaller and smaller fragments.

In the afternoon it was noticed that the Russians here were abandoning their Raate road positions and fleeing along the Puras road, where there were only the companies of Volanen and Pyrrö to check their retreat. Colonel Siilasvuo then committed Captain Paavola's unit to the battle, and by evening the detachment had reached the Matero area to help close this escape route.

Companies Volanen and Pyrrö, as well as Captain Flink's companies, had been pursuing enemy troops retreating thru the woods to the northeast most of the day. The first two companies advanced towards Haukila in the morning, but as the stream of Russians abandoning that area swelled by platoons and companies in the afternoon, the Finns pulled back towards Matero to cut them off. Some of the enemy even reached Määtälä, about four miles north of Matero, but the smoke from their camp fires gave them away and Colonel Mandelin threw his reserves in pursuit. The demoralized Russians trudging thru the snow on foot, easy prey for Finnish skiers, were killed or captured in droves.

In the Likoharju sector, where the freshest Russian troops were encountered, the enemy launched several assaults—supported by artillery and five tanks—against Task Force Fagernäs. When one company commander in Regiment JR 64 was killed and another wounded during the morning, the Finns fell back slightly into the forest where the tanks could not attack them. The antitank guns malfunctioned after a few rounds, and one was abandoned during the withdrawal. After the arrival of their reserves—the Ninth Company—the Finns returned to the attack at the Purasjoki bridge area, where they drove the enemy back and establishd defense positions west of the river. Nevertheless, the Russians were able to continue their attacks against the Finnish positions near Likoharju late into the evening.

Because the pressure against Fagernäs was so great, Colonel Siilasvuo ordered Major Kari to send the First Battalion of JR 64 to destroy the enemy units which were operating between their two task forces. Captain Mankonen's battalion, less the company which had already been detached to bolster Lt. Ylönen's roadblock near Kokkojärvi, started after noon along a forest path from Eskola to Saukko. Overcoming stiff resistance at that tiny settlement, Mankonen pushed on in the evening to Mäntylä, which was also captured after several hours of fighting. By then the numerous Russian stragglers who had bypassed Ylönen's roadblock thru the woods were becoming a threat to the battalion's rear. Accordingly, late in the evening Mankonen turned his front from east to west and destroyed those harassing groups.[62]

At Raate, Lavi's company also resumed the fight on the 6th, preventing enemy movement on the road near the border. Late that evening, Commander Vinogradov belatedly authorized the retreat which had already been underway in many sectors for hours; he tersely advised his subordinate commanders that the situation was "desperate" and that those who could should escape.[63]

Although only mopping up action was required in most sectors on 7 January, the Russians still offered serious opposition near Likoharju, where they again tried to fight thru to the east. About 4 A.M. they succeeded, with the help of tanks, in throwing the Ninth Company of JR 64 back from the Purasjoki River. However, Colonel Fagernäs' troops counterattacked at 10:30 that morning, dispersing the Russians in disorder. The Finns then continued westward to capture Likoharju, where they took many prisoners and five tanks.[64]

The other detachment of Task Force Fagernäs, Lavi's unit at Raate, was the object of the final Soviet effort to assist the 44th Division. During the early morning darkness the Russians advanced here, supported by artillery in positions behind their border. After repelling those attacks, the Finns sent a reconnaissance patrol as far as Vasonvaara, about two miles inside the U.S.S.R., where it found only support elements.[65]

In the Lake Kokkojärvi sector, an armored truck broke thru Lt. Ylönen's roadblock during the night of 6–7 January, but he personally destroyed it. At Tyynelä the fight continued in the morning, but the Russian spirit was broken. Many fled northward to death or captivity at the hands of Captain Paavola's troops.[66]

When morning came, Colonel Mäkiniemi's forces near Haukila crossed the road and pushed north until they met friendly units. The booty on the Raate road in this sector was enormous. Along the shore of Lake Kuivasjärvi, Task Force Mäkiniemi still faced determined resistance; enemy bunkers prevented the use of the road from Haukila to the supply base at Suomussalmi village. Captain Laine's company, assisted by parts of Captain Häkkinen's guerilla battalion, soon cleared this area. Then the roadblocks were dismantled and a new bridge was constructed over the Kuomasjoki River that same day to open the main logistical route. The victors even took time out to round up and feed some 600 horses which were wandering loose here.[67]

The last organized resistance was offered by bunkers near Lake Kuomasjärvi. A platoon dispatched at 10 P.M. to destroy them returned at 4 A.M. on the 8th with 70 prisoners.[68]

Mopping-up actions continued for several days, as half-frozen stragglers were hunted down in the woods along the entire length of the Raate road. The booty was staggering by the standards of this war: it included 43 tanks, 70 field guns, 278 trucks, cars, and tractors, some 300 machine guns, 6,000 rifles, 32 field kitchens, 1,170 live horses, and modern communications equipment which was especially prized. The dead could not even be counted because of the snow drifts which covered the fallen and the wounded who froze to death.[69]

About 1,300 prisoners were taken.[70] Conspicuously absent was Commander Vinogradov, who fled in a tank to a worse fate awaiting him in the Soviet Union. A Red Army lieutenant told his captors that he had seen the Commander on the first day of the battle, but he disappeared on the second day.[71] From a 9th Army staff officer later captured at Kuhmo, the Finns learned that the 9th Army had ordered Vinogradov and three other officers shot. Documents found at Kuhmo confirmed this report. The official reason for this sentence was "the loss of all 55 field kitchens to the enemy!"[72]

Finnish losses in the entire Suomussalmi-Raate campaign totalled some 1,900 men—including approximately 600 killed, 133 missing, and nearly 1,200 permanently disabled; Russian losses were estimated at 22,500.[73] So complete was the destruction of the invading forces that on 18 January General Tuompo ordered Siilasvuo to proceed with most of his troops to another critical front near Kuhmo; only three battalions and one artillery battery were left to watch the Suomussalmi sector.[74]

The reverberations of the "Suomussalmi battle," as the defeats of both the 163rd and 44th Divisions came to be known,

were heard much longer and farther than the shooting. Finnish General Headquarters released a communiqué on 1 January announcing that the 163rd was "virtually annihilated," and
exactly a week later it publicized the defeat of the 44th, enume-
rating the impressive booty taken. On 9 January the headlines
of *The New York Times* read

## "FINNS SMASH A NEW DIVISION."

But the interest of the world press was not confined to these
preliminary reports. The concentrated carnage along the Raate
road—especially in the western sector where thousands of Russians had been isolated for five days before their agony ended
—was the most dramatic evidence of a Soviet military fiasco
that the war produced. Foreign correspondents—denied permission to visit many other battle sectors—were given a tour of
this front even before the mopping up was completed. On 10
January a United Press dispatch vividly described a trip by
journalists from Suomussalmi to Raate, and the next day James
Aldridge sent a report to *The New York Times* in which he told
how he had to step over Russian corpses, "a kaleidoscope of
bodies . . . four miles long." Gruesome details and pictures of
dead soldiers and horses frozen in the snow filled the press for
weeks after the event. *The Times* of London and *The New York
Times* both carried lengthy articles on the Suomussalmi
fighting as late as 5 February 1940. No other battle did as much
to belittle the Red Army in the eyes of the world.[75]

Initially, Soviet authorities tried to ignore this humiliating
defeat. The communiqués of the Leningrad Military District
were silent on this sector during the critical battle phase which
began on 27 December. Then, on 10 January, the first cautious
acknowledgement of any Red Army defeat was published; the
communiqué merely noted that "in the course of 9 January
. . . our units withdrew several kilometers to the east of Suomussalmi." Soviet sensitivity to the notoriety of their defeat was
reflected in the second three-week summary issued on 13 January; foreign press articles, especially those of the French
HAVAS news agency, were explicitly refuted. Concerning the
reports that the 44th Division lost 14,000 men, the Soviet summary claimed that it had no more than 10,000 on the front, and

that only 900 of those were lost—"due more to the sudden cold ... than to actions of the Finnish troops." However, the ghosts of Suomussalmi could not be exorcised that easily.[76]

In some respects the very magnitude of their victory was a liability to the Finns. After such a severe blow to the Red Army's prestige, its commanders were not anxious to see the war end before they could achieve compensating victories. That, at any rate, was the opinion voiced to Foreign Minister Tanner by both the German and the American Ministers.[77]

The Finns reacted to Suomussalmi with justifiable pride. President Kallio's memorandum to Marshal Mannerheim, published in the 14 January Order of the Day, read:

> I congratulate you, Mr. Field Marshal, and thru you our whole army for the great successes that you have attained everywhere, but especially in Suomussalmi where a historical miracle was performed. This will remain a bright star in our military history.[78]

However valid that praise may have been, Suomussalmi tended to make the Finns overconfident. As General Heinrichs later observed, it can be argued that this victory was celebrated excessively, considering that the decisive and heaviest battle of the war would be fought on the Karelian Isthmus under vastly different circumstances.[79]

*Bring me frost upon the snow-sledge,*
*Snow and ice in great abundance.*
RUNE XLVIII

CHAPTER V

# The Lull Before

As 1939 FADED INTO HISTORY, THE FINNS COULD LOOK BACK ON the first month's fighting with considerable satisfaction. Their astonishing victories at Tolvajärvi and Suomussalmi had won them world acclaim, the Mannerheim Line had successfully withstood massive attacks, and the Red Army had been held in check on all other fronts. Yet beneath the surface there were disquieting omens: attrition was already affecting the contestants in reverse ratio to their resources—human and material, and the enemy, learning from his costly blunders, was improving his tactics and reorganizing his command for renewed assaults.

While ground action in general was virtually stalemated, air operations were becoming increasingly serious as extremely low temperatures were accompanied by clearer skies. Marshal Mannerheim witnessed a vivid demonstration of Soviet air superiority on the bright day of 5 January, when wave after wave of bombers showered Mikkeli with incendiaries from morning till dusk. That evening he took his last meal at the doomed Seurahuone Hotel, with the light of the blazing town glowing thru the shattered window by his table. The same night he moved to the little village of Otava, eight miles to the southwest, where the Operations and Supply Sections of GHQ were transferred.[1]

This shifting of key elements of the Headquarters to a less conspicuous village was consistent with a policy which the Government had been advocating for the general public since the YH period. Approximately 400,000 children, women, and elderly men fled from the more exposed urban centers to the relative safety of the countryside. This dispersal of the populace, coupled with bomb shelters and an efficient warning network of aircraft spotters (mainly Lottas), kept the number of civilian casualties at a minimum. Although there were a total of 2,075 bombing raids against 516 localities (exclusive of the battlefronts), only 640 Finns were killed and about 1,500 wounded.[2]

In that more civilized era, before the Nazi's wanton destruction of Rotterdam ushered in this brutalized age of indiscriminate mass killings, even those relatively few civilian casualties aroused world indignation. Most of the Finns bore their personal tragedies stoically; one obituary euphemistically attributed the death of an eleven year old victim to an "accident."[3] Such incidents merely strengthened the nation's resolve to fight on to the bitter end.

The material losses were far greater—nearly 1,800 buildings were destroyed and 5,000 damaged. These figures do not include Finland's second largest city, Viipuri, which—being in the combat zone—was virtually destroyed by artillery fire and more than 11,600 bombs. Of the more remote cities, Turku and Tampere suffered the greatest damage. By mid-January, 48 of the 63 dock sheds in the important port of Turku were reported destroyed. Tampere, a major industrial center and site of the State Aircraft Factory, was the target of some 1,700 bombs.[4]

These raids on southern and southwestern Finland were greatly facilitated by the newly acquired Soviet air bases in Estonia. Together with airfields spread along the route of the Murmansk Railroad, they brought the entire country within range of Russian bombers. Initially, the Finnish home front received more of their unwelcome attention than the battle zones. Rail junctions became a favorite target, especially in the later phases of the war. Bombings caused over 700 rail interruptions, but only two engines and 134 passenger and freight cars were destroyed. In proportion to the effort expended, the results of Soviet air raids were not impressive.[5]

The Finns made good use of their few antiaircraft weapons, destroying at least 327 of the attackers. Their heavier guns, 76.2mm, were mainly deployed in defense of important cities and logistical centers. Front line units relied upon twin-mounted 7.62mm machine guns, 20mm cannon, and a few 40mm guns. The effectiveness of their fire apparently came as a surprise to the Soviet bomber pilots; in the first days they sometimes flew as low as 2,000 feet, sustaining substantial losses from ground fire. When they later increased their altitudes, up to 20,000 feet in cases, the accuracy of their bombing —not notable at best—decreased even more.[6]

To challenge the hundreds of bombers which roamed their skies almost at will (a Soviet source acknowledges nearly 44,000 bomber sorties), the Finns had only 31 Fokker D. XXI fighters in serviceable condition when hostilities began; ten others were then undergoing repairs. The D. XXI's top speed of only 286 mph afforded but a slight edge over the principal bombers it had to intercept, the Tupolev SB-2 (263 mph) and the Ilyushin DB-3 (254 mph). Those few Fokkers remained the mainstay of Finland's fighter force throughout the entire war, accounting for the vast majority of the 235 confirmed kills scored by her pilots. Although they saw action every day that weather permitted, only twelve Fokker D. XXIs were lost.[7]

More than 100 additional fighters were purchased abroad during the war, but the majority arrived too late to participate in the fighting. The most opportune reinforcements were the 30 Morane-Saulnier M.S. 406s which arrived from France in December. These fast fighters (302 mph) were ready for combat when the full fury of the Soviet offensive was unleashed in February.[8]

In addition to those Finnish planes, there were 12 Gloster Gladiator IIs and four Hawker Harts flown by Swedish volunteers during the last two months of the war. Despite the poor combat qualities of their British aircraft, Swedish pilots destroyed six Soviet bombers and six fighters over northern Finland—losing five of their own in combat and one by accident.[9]

The effectiveness of Finnish fighters was not limited to the number of bombers actually shot down or to the hundreds of additional damaged ones which managed to limp back across the lines where their ultimate fate could not be determined. The mere presence of Finnish aircraft affected Soviet air operations. It became Finnish intercept policy to attack every bomber formation within range, even if only one fighter could be sent against each flight, because the enemy frequently

aborted his mission—and invariably expedited his bomb release—at the sight of fighters.[10]

The Finnish air force had to endure appalling field conditions. Aircraft frequently operated from frozen lakes, employing skis instead of landing wheels. Often this meant that all
maintenance had to be performed in the open at temperatures
reaching 30° to 40° below Zero F! Pilots stood alert duty in full
gear near their planes for long hours in such weather, feeling
themselves fortunate if they had even a tent for shelter. With
the number of enemy raids constantly increasing, the same few
pilots had to scramble to meet them week after week, often
several times in one day. As Soviet flying proficiency gradually
improved and better Russian fighters appeared in ever-growing numbers, the strain began to tell. On 28 February 15 Finnish pursuit planes were jumped by 36 enemy fighters just as
they were taking off on a bomber-interception mission. Caught
in that disadvantageous posture, six of the Finns were shot
down. Thereafter, Finnish policy prohibited takeoff when
enemy fighters were actually in sight of the airfield.[11]

Soviet air activity reached its peak in February and March,
when the number of their sorties averaged 400 to 1,000 a day.
A Soviet source puts the daily average for the entire war at 800.
Like their R.A.F. counterparts in the later Battle of Britain,
Finnish fighter pilots performed miracles of skill and endur-
ance in rising against overwhelming odds to the very end.
Amazingly, only 26 Finnish fighters were shot down in air-to-
air combat.[12]

Until January the operational strength of the Finnish
bomber force amounted to only 16 Bristol Blenheim Is. Two
others were being utilized as models at the factory in Tampere.
Twelve more Blenheims (model IV) were dispatched from England that month, but one was lost and another badly damaged
enroute. A final shipment of 12 model Is arrived in February.
Relatively modern bombers, capable of carrying a half-ton pay-
load 1,250 miles at 220 mph, the Blenheims were nevertheless
very vulnerable to fighter attack. The replacements from England hardly kept pace with combat losses; only eleven bombers
were serviceable at the war's end. The Finns used this tiny
force primarily against Soviet march columns and artillery
batteries. After the Mannerheim Line was breached in February, bombers and fighters alike concentrated on targets on the

Karelian Isthmus and Viipuri Bay. Due to the intensity of Soviet fighter activity at this stage, bombing raids were limited to the early morning or dusk.[13]

The Finns also had a motley assortment of obsolete aircraft fit only for reconnaissance duty, planes so old and slow that most could survive only by restricting their flying to the twilight hours from the very beginning of the war. The variety of makes and models also presented tremendous supply and maintenance problems, as was also the case with fighter aircraft, artillery, small arms, etc.

While the contest in the skies was steadily intensifying, by mid-January naval warfare had literally frozen to a halt. This was fortunate for the Finns; their Lilliputian navy could hardly have fought off the Soviet Baltic Fleet, with its battleships and cruisers, indefinitely. The Finns had only two monitors, five submarines, and a few minesweepers, minelayers, patrol boats, gunboats, and torpedo boats in the Baltic.[14]

Because of proscriptions in the 1920 Soviet-Finnish Treaty of Dorpat, the Finns had no naval craft whatsoever in the Arctic Ocean to protect Petsamo, nor did they fortify the outer islands in the Gulf of Finland. Nevertheless, the Soviets bombarded the largest of those islands, abandoned and defenseless Suursaari (Hogland), before they occupied it.[15]

Finnish offensive naval action was limited to laying mines by submarines off Soviet harbors. Two enemy subs were sunk in Finnish minefields. The Soviet navy succeeded in sinking— mainly by submarines—only three Finnish vessels and three neutral merchant ships (one Swedish and two German).[16]

The shallow Gulf of Finland froze fast by late December, and by mid-January the Gulf of Bothnia was also a solid sheet of ice. During that near-record winter the ice became so thick that it supported even heavy tanks. From 21 February to the end of the war, a truck supply route was in operation across the Gulf of Bothnia from Vaasa, Finland to Umeå, Sweden. When these conditions made the conventional use of naval forces impossible, both Finnish and Soviet sailors found themselves converted to infantrymen—no doubt to their mutual chagrin.[17]

Before nature imposed her veto on naval action in the Baltic Sea, a few classic Nineteenth Century-style ship vs shore artillery duels were fought at Finnish islands. On the second morning of the war the Soviet cruiser *Kirov,* accompanied by two destroyers, approached the fortifications at tiny Russarö Island, about two miles south of the Hako Peninsula. At 9:52, when the range was 15 miles, the Finnish commander ordered his heavy batteries to commence firing. The *Kirov* turned its starboard side towards the fort and began firing 35 180mm shells, but they had no effect. At 9:55 a Finnish shell hit one of the destroyers, which thereupon turned away to the south. Ten minutes later the *Kirov* and the remaining destroyer broke off the engagement and departed at full speed; it was believed that the cruiser had been hit, but poor visibility prevented confirmation. The entire exchange of fire had lasted only 13 minutes.[18]

The vital coastal defense batteries at Koivisto, which also secured the right flank of the Mannerheim Line, were involved in a minor naval duel during a heavy snowstorm on 6 December. The first serious attack here occurred on the tenth, when a Soviet battleship under cover of fog bombarded the powerful Saarenpää batteries at the southeastern end of Koivisto Island for an hour. Considering that the ship fired 200 half-ton shells from its 305mm guns, Finnish casualties were slight—two killed and three wounded.[19]

On 14 December two destroyers approached the Finnish battery at Utö, an islet southeast of the Åland Islands. At 11:40 A.M., when they were within seven miles, they turned sharply to port to fire. The Finnish battery scored a direct hit on the leading ship, staring internal fires. After returning some ten rounds with no effect, the attackers turned southeast at 11:50 and fled in a zigzag under cover of a smoke screen. Ten minutes later three huge pillars of smoke appeared above the damaged destroyer and several explosions were heard; when the smoke cleared the ship had disappeared beneath the waves.[20]

After minor contacts at Koivisto again on 13 and 14 December, on the eighteenth a determined attempt was made to silence the Saarenpää batteries, which by then were seriously hampering the Red Army's efforts to smash thru the Mannerheim Line. Waves of aircraft struck throughout the day, the first ones numbering 60 bombers and fighters. At eighteen minutes past noon the old battleship *Oktyabr'skaya Revolyutsiya* and five destroyers appeared, supported by a fire-directing aircraft. A call to a fighter base brought two Fokker D. XXIs to deal

with the spotter plane, but the strain on the Koivisto antiaircraft gunners that day was so great that they shot down one of
their own fighters. The pilot, Eino Luukkanen, survived the
resulting crash landing unscathed to become Finland's third-
ranking ace.[21]

At 12:28 the battleship opened up on the Saarenpää batteries
at a range of 12 miles. The Finns returned the fire with their
254mm (10 inch) guns until about 1 P.M. Their old, nearly worn-
out artillery did not hold up under the stress of its own firing,
and one by one the six 254s fell silent. The *Oktyabr'skaya Revolyutsiya* then drew closer at 1:50 and its fire became more
accurate at shorter range. However, one of the 254s was re-
paired by 2:20 and it soon forced the enemy to withdraw. The
400-odd Soviet shells had obliterated the forest around the battery and disrupted its communications, but the vital guns received no direct hits. The effect of the 49 heavy rounds fired by
the Finns could not be determined.[22]

The attack was renewed the following day, with dawn to dusk
air raids as well as naval action. This time it was the battleship
*Marat* which arrived off Koivisto at 11:20, accompanied by
three destroyers and other escorts. At 12:25 the *Marat* commenced firing with its 305mm guns at 13 miles. Four minutes
later the Saarenpää battery returned the fire with only
one 254mm piece—in order to conserve ammunition and save
wear and tear on the old artillery. When this emboldened the
*Marat*'s commander to close the range to 11 miles, a second gun
was brought to bear on the ship. One of the 35 rounds fired by
the fort hit the *Marat,* whereupon the enemy ships withdrew.
Some 150–170 heavy shells had bracketed the Saarenpää batteries, but the priceless guns again escaped direct hits. Only
one artilleryman was killed and three wounded, although a
number of buildings were destroyed. Air raids continued, of
course, but this was the last serious naval bombardment of the
war—the Finnish coastal artillery had proved its worth against
the Soviet Baltic Fleet.[23]

In northern Finland, the weather in January was generally
more of a problem than the Red Army for the Finns. At Utsjoki,
the northernmost weather station in Finland (70° 5′ N.), the
mercury had dipped to 34° below zero (F) by the end of Decem-

ber. At Rovaniemi, just below the Arctic Circle, it was 31.5° below on 15 January. And at Sodankylä, on the Arctic Highway, the official temperature was minus 36.5° on 23 January (reaching a numbing −42.7° F on 25 February!).[24]

Although temperatures were extreme, snowfall in Lapland was below average that winter, delaying the use of skis—while confronting Soviet motor traffic with less difficulties than in a normal year. At Utsjoki the accumulation was only one and one-half inches on 15 December, 16 inches on 31 December, and less than 2 feet by the end of January. Rovaniemi had less than 10 inches at the end of December, and about 15 inches at the end of January. Sodankylä recorded 13 inches on 31 December and 20 inches on 31 January. The anticipated heavy snows generally did not fall until late March or April, after the fighting had ceased.[25]

In the Petsamo region, the lone Finnish battalion continued to hold the main part of the 104th Division at Höyhenjärvi throughout January, in spite of renewed Soviet attempts to push southward beginning in the middle of the month. Finnish patrols created so much havoc behind the lines that the enemy had to construct a string of heavy wooden blockhouses at 5–6 mile intervals along the Petsamo-Höyhenjärvi road and patrol between them with tanks. This tied down considerable Soviet forces in a purely defensive role.[26]

In the Salla sector,* where seven Finnish battalions had checked two Red Army divisions by late December, the counterattack against the main Soviet forces on the direct Salla-Kemijärvi road began on 2 January. This time the enemy anticipated the Finns' moves, which were intended to sever their communications with Joutsijärvi from the north. By their own successful flanking attack, the invaders forced the Finns back almost to their starting point on 5 January. The front then remained static at Joutsijärvi for about a week. On the 12th, Battalion ErP 17 deployed by truck on a wide flanking move to Kallunki, some 16 miles south of Märkäjärvi. From there it fought its way to within two miles of that crossroads village by 19 January. Meanwhile, the Soviet forces at Joutsijärvi also

*See Map No. 2, p. 9

began to withdraw towards Märkäjärvi; by 20 January they had dug in on a hillside two miles west of that village. There—scores of miles from their objectives—they remained stalemated by the outnumbered Finnish battalions until the ceasefire in March.[27]

Except for the Kuusamo area, where action was limited to patrolling and guerilla raids throughout the war (and the Suomussalmi area where the Soviet threat had been decisively eliminated), the next battle sector—moving south from Salla—was east of Kuhmo. There the main units of the 54th Division had been held in check near the Rasti road junction* since early December. Smaller Soviet forces, which had attacked from Kiekinkoski towards Kuhmo, were driven back across the border early in January.[28]

Most of Colonel Siilasvuo's self-confident 9th Division, fresh from its exhilarating victories at Suomussalmi and Raate, arrived in the Kuhmo area between 20 and 23 January. Two infantry battalions and one artillery battery were also transferred here from the Lieksa region in January, following the decisive victories of Colonel Raappana's forces on that minor but active front. All the units which had already been fighting here, including Regiment JR 25, were subordinated to Siilasvuo by 28 January, and the next day he launched a major counterattack against the 54th Division.[29]

Siilasvuo's men soon learned that the 54th Division was a more worthy foe than the 44th Division had been. Commander Gusevski's units had trained in the wilds of northwestern Russia for several years; the troops were acclimated to cold and familiar with the problems posed by roadless forests. Furthermore, they had more than a month's time to dig in before the Finnish attack began. Nevertheless, by the end of the first day the Finns had severed their enemy's supply road at several points, creating numerous mottis. On 30 January they seized Löytövaara, near the border, further splintering the Russian forces. The 54th Division, now trapped along a 28-mile stretch of road between Rasti and the border, remained cut off from its supply base at Reboly for the duration of the war.[30]

*See Map No. 2, p. 9

Group Talvela's sector remained relatively quiet for a few weeks after the lines became stabilized at the Aittojoki River* and at Oinaansalmi** late in December. The defenders even enjoyed the unaccustomed reassurance of a little air cover here; eight Fokker D. XXIs were assigned to Värtsilä from 25 December to 4 February to patrol the skies of Ladoga-Karelia. During that period Figher Detachment L shot down 11 Soviet bombers and damaged several others. The unit also destroyed three enemy fighters in the air and shot up an additional six on the ice of Lake Tulomajärvi, just across the border, losing only one Fokker in these engagements.[31]

Although the tempo of the Soviet air offensive was increasing, the sporadic attacks in this sector did comparatively little damage because the Finns were dug in and well camouflaged. The horses which were the occasional victims of these raids made good soup. Hare and other game also added variety to the monotonous army diet. Colonel Ekholm even kept hunting dogs behind the lines, and his "fishing commandos" found the ice fishing rewarding in the lakes near Ilomantsi.[32]

Task Force Pajari also experienced a welcome lull in the fighting during the first half of January. Construction of saunas began, and by late January some of the luckier men enjoyed their first baths since early December; others had to wait until February for that rejuvenating ablution. As young soldiers ever have, when temporarily released from the acute tensions of combat, the Finnish "GI" turned his thoughts to women. Homesick and lonely youths skied long distances to the canteen at Äglajärvi—where two Lottas worked—just to steal a glimpse of "real live girls." When a lone Lotta stepped from a truck into the snow near their Aittojoki positions, men of the Second Battalion of JR 16 jovially carried her footprint around in a shovel for all to see.[33]

It was to this calm front that the first Finnish-American reinforcements were assigned late in December. Just before Christmas fifty volunteers, some without any military experience, arrived in Oulu to begin a training program which was to last several weeks. Impatient with that prospect, Captain Albert Penttila recruited (while still aborad the liner *Gripsholm* and

*See Map No. 8, p. 53
**See Map No. 6, p. 38

during the train trip thru Sweden) action-ready squads composed of younger service veterans. The day after their arrival in Finland, Captain Penttila, a former brother-in-arms of General Talvela, departed with these men for Tolvajärvi. This token force of Finnish-Americans served with distinction on patrols at the ill-defined Aittojoki River front, frequently operating behind enemy lines.[34]

The pace of the skirmishing in this region picked up by late January. On the 20th, a Soviet flanking attack between the Aittojoki River and Kivijärvi, some nine miles to the southwest, was repelled with great difficulty. Fresh Russian troops, now equipped with skis, made prolonged and concerted efforts to cut Finnish supply lines. They advanced systematically along wilderness trails between their two main local objectives—the Tolvajärvi-Ägläjärvi road to the north and the Loimola-Kollaa* road to the south. The threat to Group Talvela's communications became ominous when Vieksinki** fell. Finding his southern flank under attack by five battalions, General Talvela hastily recalled two battalions from temporary duty in the Ilomantsi sector to cope with this new threat. Vieksinki was recaptured, and the Finns began extensive guerilla operations behind the attacking enemy forces. This resulted in a series of complex wilderness battles and maneuvers in which each side tried to outflank the other. Both the intensity and the range of these engagements increased considerably late in the war, but the Russians never succeeded in reaching the Tolvajärvi-Ägläjärvi-Aittojoki road.[35]

Serious as the flanking attacks against Group Talvela were, they nevertheless appear to have been intended primarily as diversions to keep Finnish reserves from the Kollaanjoki River area,* where the command of the Soviet 8th Army placed higher priority on an attempted breakthru.[36] The region between Lake Ladoga and the Kollaa road, where the two divisions of General Hägglund's IV Army Corps faced the ever-growing might of the 8th Army, was the only major front to witness continuous heavy fighting throughout the month of

*See Map No. 3, p. 13
**See Map No. 8, p. 53

January. Here Marshal Mannerheim again stole the initiative from the Russians.

Because General Hägglund had recalled one risky counter-attack before its objectives were achieved and had only partially succeeded in two other attacks in December,[37] the Commander-in-Chief sent Lt. Colonel Nihtilä from his Operations Section to the IV Army Corps as his personal representative. Feeling like an unpopular *politruk* in this awkward role, the Lt. Colonel had to prevail upon the cautious General to launch a major counteroffensive against superior forces and to see it through with determination.[38] On 6 January the long-planned attack began with the Finnish 12th and 13th Divisions pushing south from the Lake Syskyjärvi area to the enemy's rear—leaving only slightly more than four battalions at Kollaa to defend the main positions against the Soviet 56th and 164th Divisions. Within two days the main Finnish attack units, bypassing sizeable enemy forces via wilderness trails, cut both the north-south and the east-west communications of the 18th Division and the 34th Tank Brigade. By 11 January a smaller strike group reached the shore of Lake Ladoga at Koirinoja (some four miles northwest of Pitkäranta), thereby also severing the only remaining supply route of the 168th Division. By the 15th the Finns controlled the Lake shore from Koirinoja to Pitkäranta, where they held off ever-increasing Soviet forces until the end of the war. On 16 January a company of NKVD border guards—attempting to rescue the surrounded 18th Division staff—suffered severe losses when they too became encircled. [39]

However successful their offensive appeared, the Finns now held a tiger by the tail. In their dash to the Lake, they had left behind large Soviet groupings which were far from defeated. The 18th Division and the 34th Tank Brigade were cut into ten isolated enclaves, while the 168th Division was surrounded virtually intact. Finnish attempts to destroy these encircled units resulted in the most extensive and bitterly fought motti warfare of the entire war.[40]

The hopeless position of the 18th Division and its supporting tank brigade encouraged the Finns to expect a rapid and conclusive victory, but the Russians continued to offer incredibly stubborn resistance. For example, in one of three companies trapped at Uomaa, the survivors refused to surrender even after 83 of their 85 men were either dead or wounded. The nucleus of the defense of the ten smaller mottis was provided by more than 200 tanks. The two mottis at the twin villages Lemetti East and Lemetti West alone were defended by over 100 tanks. Even when immobilized by lack of fuel, they made formidable artillery and machine gun strongpoints. Combined with field artillery and the automatic weapons of the infantry, they gave the mottis tremendous firepower. It would have been prohibitively costly for the Finns—lacking heavy artillery—to storm the stronger mottis before cold and hunger had time to exact their toll. And starvation was postponed by eating the transport horses, and to some extent because the Soviet aerial supply effort was reasonably effective in this sector.[41]

Colonel Bondyrev's 168th Division was contained in the so-called "great motti," stretching from northwest of Kitelä to Koirinoja on Lake Ladoga; at its widest points it was approximately 4½ by 5 miles across. Anticipating Soviet attempts to supply this unit over the ice of the Lake, the Finns occupied the northwestern islands of the Pitkäranta Archipelago on 20 January. However, the Russians had already seized the islands closest to Pitkäranta, including Pusunsaari. Fierce nocturnal battles were fought among the islands as the Red Army sent horse-drawn and tank-drawn sleds to the relief of its trapped division. Until late in the war, the Finns were able to destroy most of these supply columns enroute to Koirinoja, where hundreds of Soviet horses, sleds, and men cluttered the ice.[42]

On 20 January another Finnish strike force cut the Uomaa-Käsnäselkä road and established a defense line near the Uuksunjoki River, about a mile east of Uomaa, where it held off the greater part of the 60th Division which had been sent to aid the beleaguered 18th Division. By this time the two divisions of the IV Army Corps were confronted by superior forces on three fronts—at the Kollaanjoki and Uuksunjoki Rivers and at Pitkäranta—while simultaneously several battalions were required to maintain the seige of two Russian divisions and a tank brigade far to the rear of those positions. By the end of January a few of the weaker mottis had been destroyed and the entire front was fairly stable, but there were ominous intelligence reports of additional Soviet divisions enroute to Ladoga-Karelia.[43]

Instead of releasing part of the IV Corps for action on the critical Karelian Isthmus front, Marshal Mannerheim was compelled to reinforce this sector from his meager reserves. A cavalry brigade (converted to skis) and three independent battalions were sent to the Corps in January. At the end of the month the newly formed 23rd Division was also assigned to General Hägglund; however, only one of the Division's regiments actually reached the front here—the other two had to be diverted to the Isthmus in February.[44]

To speak of a "lull" on the Karelian Isthmus in January is appropriate only in comparison with the hectic period 17–20 December and the even worse weeks which were to follow January. In accord with the Soviet decision of late December to suspend offensive operations temporarily, infantry attacks were limited to local actions and reconnaissance patrols. However, air units which were augmented by 50 percent and artillery which increased by more than 150 percent during the month of January constantly harassed the Mannerheim Line and its communications. More than 4,000 bomber sorties and nearly 3,500 strafing attacks by fighters were conducted against the Isthmus defenses in this period. Aided by spotter aircraft and observation balloons, artillery fire—much now of heavy caliber—became so effective that Finnish road and rail traffic could move only under cover of darkness. Even field kitchens had to be brought up to the Line at night and removed before daybreak; one meal was distributed when they arrived in the evening, and a second was cooked during the night to be served in the morning darkness. In spite of the extreme cold, korsus and other shelters could not be heated during the day because even a trace of smoke invited artillery fire.[45]

These bombardments, which smashed field fortifications, disrupted communications, and inflicted considerable casualties, were most severe in the Taipale region and in the Viipuri Gateway. The unremitting pressure against these key sectors caused the defenders great physical and mental fatigue. The exhausted 5th Division, which had borne the brunt of the

December offensive in the Summa area, was relieved of its front-line duties during the nights of 2–3 to 4–5 January, moving a few miles south of Viipuri to work on the intermediate line of fortifications. Its positions in the Mannerheim Line were officially taken over on 5 January by the 6th (Reserve) Division, which had been redesignated the 3rd Division on 1 January to confuse the foe.[46]

The 10th Division at Taipale also needed a well-earned rest, but there were not enough reserves to rotate into its sector. All that could be done was to renumber it the 7th Division, in the hope that the enemy would think it was confronted with a new unit here. At the end of January the newly formed and poorly equipped 21st Division was posted to the Pyhäjärvi area, north of the Suvanto and behind the 7th (10th) Division, as the Commander-in-Chief's reserve. By then the Finns were aware of the unmistakable signs of an imminent offensive of unprecedented proportions.[47]

Early in January Stalin summoned Commanders Meretskov and Grendal' to Moscow. Also present at the meeting were Andrei Zhdanov, the top Party organizer in Leningrad and a Politburo member; Commissar of Foreign Affairs Molotov; N. N. Voronov, the Chief of Red Army Artillery; Commissar of Defense Voroshilov; and S. K. Timoshenko, the Commander of the Kiev Military District whose efficient occupation of eastern Poland a few months earlier had won him Stalin's approval. After dinner Stalin announced the creation of a centralized directorate of operations whose basic mission was to seize the Mannerheim Line before the spring floods arrived. (The annual thaw would immobilize traffic for several weeks, keeping large Red Army forces bogged down at a time of potential danger on other Soviet borders.) The bitter lessons of the first five weeks of the war had subdued the optimism of the Soviet dictator; he now acknowledged that it would require large-scale reinforcements and thorough planning to accomplish this task.[48]

On 7 January the Leningrad Military District was transformed into the Northwestern Front, which was entrusted to Army Commander First Rank Timoshenko, with Zhdanov serving on its Military Council. The projected offensive would be conducted as a front operation; the adjacent flanks of the 7th Army (Meretskov) and the 13th Army (Grendal') would strike the main blow on a 25-mile sector in the direction Summa-Viipuri. As the planning was further refined, the ten-mile Viipuri Gateway within that area was selected as the breakthru zone where three-fourths of Meretskov's infantry was concentrated.[49]

The directive of 28 December from the Red Army High Command provided the initial guidelines for the planning of the Front. Timonshenko was instructed not to be carried away with the tactics of speedy, suicidal advances, but rather to move only after proper preparation and with due regard for the security of his communications. Mass bunching of attack formations was forbidden, and the infantry was not to be committed to battle until the artillery had destroyed the concrete bunkers in the forward zone.[50]

The Front commander followed both the letter and the spirit of that directive, devoting the remaining weeks of January to very thorough and effective preparations for the offensive. He even took a page from the book of Generalissimo Suvorov, Russia's most brilliant military figure, who had erected replicas of the walls of the Turkish fortifications at Izmail to train his troops for the successful storming of that fortress in 1790. The key fortifications in the Summa sector were reproduced in detail two miles behind the front, where the 123rd Infantry Division—destined to lead the breakthru—practiced its assault tactics. The storming was rehearsed three times, with emphasis on the coordination of artillery, tanks, and infantry. Other units also underwent intensive training for the entire month of January.[51]

Improved Soviet tactics were already evident in the limited attacks carried out that month. Tanks and infantry closely supported one another, and bomber and fighter aircraft swept the front during these engagements. Tanks rigged to detonate mines in front of them were among the new equipment tested in battle.[52]

Continuous reconnaissance by aerial photography, captive balloons, and ground patrols discovered the location of Finnish bunkers, artillery batteries, and other defensive positions. In the assault divisions, second echelon troops were used for reconnaissance patrols, in order that the first echelon might remain intact for the general offensive. Approximately three-fourths of the bunkers in the forward zone and up to 40 percent of those farther back were pinpointed. Many of the earth-and-timber fortifications were knocked out by heavy artillery or air attacks in January.[53]

Large artillery pieces were furtively moved up to the front lines at night, the telltale noise of the gun tractors obliterated by accompanying barrages. They were hidden in camouflaged positions from which they could fire by direct aiming at the gun embrasures of the strongest Finnish bunkers. For example, on 18 January a 152mm* piece was sited within 500 yards of the "Poppius" fortification near the Lähde road. In one place a long-range cannon was positioned only 300 yards from its target. Guns as large as 280mm** were employed in this manner.[54]

The logistical support for the Northwestern Front was prodigious. The capacity of the railroads—even at Leningrad—was increased. New roads and bridges were constructed, and new cross-country routes established. Food, fuel, munitions, and other supplies for more than half a million combat troops were moved in the congested Isthmus with little apparent delay. Two factors facilitated this enormous buildup—abnormal frost which was so severe that swamps and lakes could be made to support heavy traffic (by plowing the snow and pumping water over the surface), and overwhelming numbers of Soviet aircraft which prevented Finnish attacks on the vulnerable supply columns, munitions dumps, etc.[55]

Except for its front line firing positions, the Red Army did not even bother to camouflage its 2,800 artillery pieces.[56] On 1 February a Finnish pilot defied 40 Soviet fighters to reconnoiter six square miles of the Soviet sector opposite Summa, where he photographed 104 artillery batteries; most of those 416 guns were completely in the open. In comparison, there were approximately 64 Finnish pieces opposite that sector. The Finns were generally cognizant of Soviet preparations, but they were helpless to disrupt them; even their supply of artillery ammunition was inadequate. This was to prove critical, because artillery—basic to the Soviet offensive—also became more and

*about 6 inches in caliber
**about 11 inches in caliber

more the key to Finnish defense on the Isthmus.[57]

The leadership of the Northwestern Front also devoted considerable attention to morale in January. Timoshenko, Meretskov, Grendal' and the members of their military councils inspected forward units and addressed the troops. Zhdanov, responsible for Party-political work, assigned 44 Party assistants to the 7th and 13th Armies, in addition to the usual commissars and *politruks*. That month nearly 1,000 men from those two armies entered the Party, and almost 3,000 were accepted as candidate members.[58]

The old strains of the *Internationale* were heard again at midnight on New Year's Eve. However, along with the trite Party exhortations in the name of the proletariat, a newer theme was also stressed: nationalistic patriotism. During the subsequent years of the Nazi-Soviet struggle, this theme was to become paramount—almost to the total exclusion of earlier class-conscious slogans—but at the beginning of 1940 this still somewhat novel concept shared the spotlight with more orthodox communist propaganda. During the Winter War the un-Marxist slogan *Za Rodinu!* [For the Fatherland!]* was coupled with *Za Stalina!* [For Stalin!]. According to Soviet sources, the Red Army launched the February offensive amid enthusiastic shouts, "To the attack for the glory of the Fatherland!"[59]

There is no question that nationalistic appeals struck a more responsive chord with the Russian soldier than did the alleged glories of socialism. There was a subtle and gradual change in the mood of some of the survivors of the December battles. Soloviev, a veteran of the Isthmus fighting whose defection from the Red Army refutes any charge of blind Soviet patriotism, described this mood as a widespread feeling of humiliation. Although not hating the Finns, some of those Russians felt that the "insult"—the shadow cast on Russia's reputation—had to be avenged; the Finns had to be beaten. Thus a sense of shame and degradation was being transformed into a fighting spirit.[60]

As a fillip to morale, on 16 January the Presidium of the Supreme Soviet awarded medals and citations to 2,606 soldiers, commanders, and political workers of the Northwestern Front,

*Literally, "For the Native Land!"

and on 25 January an additional 891 were decorated. This was the beginning of an avalanche of such awards; by 22 May a total of 48,166 individuals were cited for their military exploits. Merely listing the first 2,606 names filled almost three full pages of both the 16 and 17 January issues of *Pravda, Izvestiya,* and *Krasnaya Zvezda.*[61] From this, one might conclude that the awards were designed as much to raise home front spirits as for troop morale.

The 7th Army's concentrations opposite the Viipuri Gateway were overpowering: nine infantry divisions (more than the defenders had in the entire Isthmus Army), five tank brigades, one rifle-machine gun brigade, and ten artillery regiments. On the average, there were 80 field guns per mile of front. The 123rd Division alone was supported by 108 pieces, ranging from 76 to 280mm.* Finnish tank strength was completely negligible, while the 7th Army had hundreds at its disposal. Among them were a few of the new 43 ton KV (Klim Voroshilov) models, which were virtually impervious to Finnish artillery. (One experimental tank employed in this region early in February was so monstrous that it rolled over obstacles and mines undamaged, but it developed engine trouble and had to be towed away by other tanks.) By the end of January this sector of the front resembled a gigantic time bomb ticking off its final seconds.[62]

*about 3–11 inches

*Full of horrors are the highways,*
*On the road are many wonders.*
**RUNE XXVI**

CHAPTER VI

# The Storm

THE BOMB EXPLODED ON THE FIRST DAY OF THE MONTH. COMMAND-
er Timoshenko had ordered Meretskov and Grendal' to conduct
frequent attacks during the first ten days of February to mis-
lead the enemy about the direction of the main blow, improve
the Russian positions, probe the Finnish defenses even more
thoroughly, and wear out the troops in the Mannerheim Line.[1]
The two Soviet Armies failed in their first objective, succeeded
fairly well in the second and third, and achieved the fourth to
perfection. Steady harassing artillery fire sometimes continued
throughout the entire night. Colonel Turbin, commander of a
Soviet howitzer regiment, stated that his unit deliberately
burned the enemy out of their shelters on his sector every day
during this period.[2] Whereas the same weary Finns continued
the struggle day and night—their ranks progressively thinning
due to casualties, the Red Army rotated fresh units to the front
for every significant assault. The cumulative effect was to induce such physical and psychological fatigue in the defenders
that men were at times completely apathetic. After a week of
this incessant pounding, some of the Third Division's troops
were so exhausted that even tanks did not keep them awake.[3]

Following the heaviest artillery preparation to date, the Russians launched an offensive along the whole front of the Finnish Second Corps on 1 February. The attacks were strongest in
the Summa sector, where infantry and tanks surrounded concrete bunker number 2, while numbers 5 and 6 were partially
destroyed by artillery fire. Tank activity also increased in the

Taipale sector of the Third Corps, where powerful assaults were launched on subsequent days.[4]

There was a general pattern to these operations, although their timing, intensity, and location varied considerably. First came a strong artillery preparation, accompanied—weather permitting—by aerial bombardment; then followed the infantry onslaught, supported by large numbers of tanks. Such attacks were often repeated three or more times a day on a narrow front, with fresh troops committed to each wave. On the sector of the Finnish Third Division (the Suokanta-Summa-Lähde-Merkki front), three divisions and a tank brigade were employed offensively, while a fourth division served as a local reserve. On 6 February parts of these units, supported by some 200 aircraft, struck Summa and Suokanta four times. The main attack, mounted after dusk in division strength, was repelled when Finnish artillery decimated the closely jammed infantry formations. The defenders hoped that those extremely heavy losses—possibly reaching several thousand men—would bring these engagements to a halt, but the very next day fresh forces wcrc thrown against both Summa and Suokanta.[5]

Because Summa village lay astride a major highway, the most direct road to Viipuri, it was the object of particularly intensive probes. However, Regiment JR 7—taking full advantage of the scattered woods and the 16 concrete bunkers in this sector—defended the area so successfully that the Seventh Army finally shifted the main weight of its attack eastward to the much poorer road to Lähde.[6]

A few weapons innovations were battle-tested during this period. Armorplated troop-carrying sleighs, some equipped with machine guns, were either pushed by tanks or towed behind them. Individual shields mounted on skis were used to protect riflemen as they crawled forward, firing thru portholes in the armor. Flame-throwing tanks were another novelty.[7]

More ominous was the fact that infantry and tank advances were generally well coordinated; at times the riflemen even rode into battle on the tanks. The tanks also supported each other closely. Both of these changes made it increasingly difficult and dangerous for Finnish "tank commandos" to employ Molotov cocktails or other close-defense weapons. The few available antitank guns were not able to cope with all of the attack formations, which at times included as many as 100–150 machines.[8]

Under these conditions the regular field artillery became increasingly critical to the defense. Unfortunately, the reserves of ammunition were so short that as early as 2 February General Österman's Headquarters had to urge the Second Corps to use its shells sparingly. Although General Öhquist resented this advice, by 8 February he was forced to limit artillery fire to cases absolutely essential to holding the Line—ignoring other lucrative targets. By comparison, Soviet gunners could afford the luxury of expending 10,000 shells against the Kuolemajärvi Church area on 5 February merely for interdiction and deception in support of a probing attack in another sector, and on 9 February they fired approximately 35,000 rounds against the relatively minor front of the Second Division. Furthermore, Soviet aircraft, roaming the Isthmus by the hundreds, pounced upon Finnish batteries when they fired— thus further restricting their use.[9]

The resourcefulness of the Finnish command was severely tested in parrying the shifting heavier blows—now at Summa, now at Taipale, now in the Kuolemajärvi sector, now along the Vuoksi, now somewhere else, now at several points simultaneously. Frequently an infantry battalion or an antitank unit had to shuttle hurriedly from one trouble spot to another, under constant danger from the air while enroute to the next battle. The attackers succeeded in penetrating the front lines at numerous points. Tanks broke into Summa village almost daily; at one time on 5 February there were nearly 100 in that vicinity. Most of these advances were immediately rolled back by counterattacks, but every such action took its toll in lives. In the hectic fighting near Summa on the fifth, one company in Regiment JR 7 lost its commander three times. Similarly, in the devastating attacks at Taipale on 8 and 9 February, more than one company lost all of their officers. By the time the Second Battalion of JR 9 took over the exposed frontal sector at the Lähde road on 8–9 February, its strength was only 375 men. As early as 1 February Colonel Paalu, commander of the Third Division, had to relieve the commander of Regiment JR 8 and a battalion commander in JR 7 because of their nerves. On the sixth, Colonel Paalu requested that his entire division, which had held the critical Viipuri Gateway since early January, be replaced by reserves.[10]

Damage to the Mannerheim Line was serious. Bunker number 2 in the Summa sector changed hands several times in fierce skirmishes before the Finns finally set its wooden parts afire and abandoned it on 3 February. Russian sappers dragged tons of explosives to other bunkers at night, and heavy artillery pounded them by day. Among those damaged were two of the largest and most modern, "Poppius" and "Million," which were the keys to the best tank terrain in the Line.[11] Many of the weaker earth-and-timber fortifications, as well as trenches, antitank ditches, korsus, and other field installations, were pulverized by the incessant barrages. A single direct hit on one large shelter on 7 February killed 18 men and wounded 11.[12]

Soviet casualties were much greater than the Finnish, but their commanders could afford to ignore them. It was not unusual for an attacking unit to lose 500 or more men in a minor sector on one day, only to renew the assault with fresh troops the next morning. The Third Division alone killed an estimated 1,000 of the attackers by 3 February, and by the sixth its score of destroyed tanks reached 42. That was the day it inflicted casualties on the Russians which would have been truly crippling had the scales been reversed. The cumulative Soviet losses during those first ten days, just on the front opposite the Finnish Second Corps, totalled a minimum of 86 tanks and thousands of men.[13]

At times some of the Finnish commanders appear to have been unduly complacent. Because the artillery fire was not as strong on his sector from 2–5 February as it had been on the first day, Colonel Paalu concluded that the enemy was experiencing supply problems. On 7 February General Öhquist felt sufficiently confident that he left his headquarters for an hour and a quarter to go into town on personal business. More troops and ammunition were obviously needed, but the situation seemed far from desperate. The large losses sustained by the Russians should force them to suspend the attack, as they had in December. The Second Corps commander stated that the offensive was expected to "ebb out" momentarily. Prime Minister Ryti and Foreign Minister Tanner visited Marshal Mannerheim at Otava on 10 February, the same day that the Defense Council held a meeting there. Describing the discussions, Tanner observed that "the generals were perhaps a little overoptimistic."[14] For the sake of their own morale, it was probably best that the Finnish leaders did not know that the Red Army command considered those ten days of fierce battles a mere dress rehearsal!

It was not until the third day of these attacks, 3 February, that Timoshenko approved the final version of the operational plan for the main offensive. This called for the major thrust towards Viipuri from the Lake Muolaanjärvi-Karhula sector, with a strong secondary drive towards Antrea Station from the Muolaanjärvi-Vuoksi front,* and a third advance aimed at Käkisalmi* from the Taipale region. On 9 February the commander of the Northwestern Front issued orders setting the attack for the eleventh, and the Military Council exhorted the troops ". . . to forever guarantee the security of . . . the city of Leningrad."[15]

On the night of 10–11 February the assult units occupied their front line positions. Additional artillery intended for point-blank firing was moved forward by hand in order not to alert the Finns. No one in the 123rd Division slept that night. Captain Soroka, commanding the vanguard battalion destined to storm the key "Poppius" bunker, told his subordinates that "on the eleventh of February Comrade Stalin will be following our battle operations from Moscow, the whole country will be thinking of us."[16]

Sunday morning, 11 February, dawned hazy and cold—the mercury a chill 7 below zero (F) at General Öhquist's headquarters. Across the lines, Commanders Meretskov and Grendal' reported on their state of readiness to Timoshenko at five A.M. (four o'clock Finnish time). The Russians were issued vodka at breakfast—to ward off the cold, perhaps to erase memories of comrades who had fallen in previous futile attempts to crack that "impregnable" Mannerheim Line. By eight o'clock the 123rd Division and the supporting 35th Light Tank Brigade were in their jumping off positions, the tanks about three miles from their objectives. An hour and forty minutes later the

*See Map No. 14, p. 161

morning stillness was shattered by the roar of the hundreds of guns massed on their sector. With slight variations in timing, the entire Mannerheim Line was pounded by an unprecedented barrage that morning. Along most of the front of the 13th Army, from Lake Muolaanjärvi to Taipale, the shriek and crash of shells were heard for three full hours. Along the Seventh Army's zone, from Muolaanjärvi to the Gulf of Finland, the nerve-wracking hurricane of steel lasted two hours and 20 minutes. The fire in the Lähde road sector followed a predetermined pattern: 15 minutes of deliberate fire, five minutes concentrated, transference to rear targets for a quarter hour, 10 minutes of concentrated fire, 20 minutes deliberate, etc. For the final ten minutes, which seemed interminable to the groggy Finns crouching in their dugouts, the salvos rose to a deafening crescendo. By the time this terrifying storm subsided, several additional concrete bunkers were destroyed and weaker fieldworks were crushed like matchsticks.[17]

Behind the 1½-mile front between Lake Summajärvi and the Munasuo Swamp were five concrete bunkers, including the modern "Poppius" just west of the Lähde road and "Million" about half a mile farther west. All five had been extensively damaged even before the massive barrage of 11 February. The three older ones, dating from the early 1920s, were nearly useless. Each of the two larger ones was garrisoned by a platoon of about 36 men, but some of their firing embrasures were no longer serviceable. In addition to these permanent fortifications, there were a number of earth-and-timber machine gun nests here, plus the usual fireworks, most of which were obliterated by the preparatory fire. The support line in this sector ran from one-half to seven-eighths of a mile behind the forward positions. To defend the entire 1½ miles of front line there was only Major Lindman's woefully understrength unit, the Second Battalion of JR 9, down to approximately one-third of its normal strength of 1,000. Its three rifle companies were all on the line: Lt. Ericsson's to the west, Lt. Hannus' behind the Munasuo Swamp, and Lt. Malm's in the center near the Lähde road.[18]

While 18 other Soviet divisions and five other tank brigades were simultaneously engaged across the entire Isthmus, the attack in the Lähde road sector began at noon, Leningrad time.

MANNERHEIM LINE BREAKTHRU, 11 - 15 FEB. 1940    MAP 13

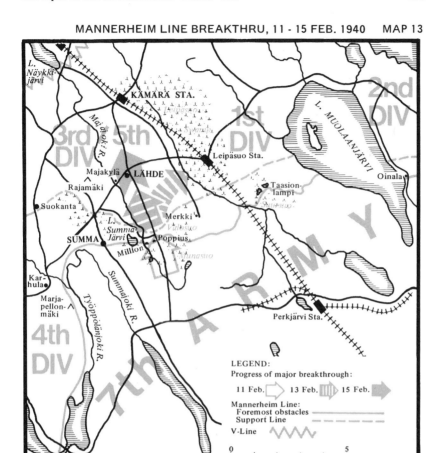

Holding one regiment in reserve, Brigade Commander Alyabu-
shev ordered two regiments of his 123rd Division to commence
their well rehearsed assult on the fortifications. One regiment
—several thousand men—was hurled against Lt. Ericsson's
company near the "Million" bunker, while the other regiment
advanced against the eastern sector. The Lähde road and the
"Poppius" bunker were the objectives of Captain Soroka's battalion which was supported by two companies of tanks. Lt.
Kharaborkin's heavy tank company led the advance against
the defense works on Hill 65.5, which included "Poppius."
However, the few bleary but staunch survivors of Lt. Malm's
company delivered such effective fire from the damaged bunk-

ers and the remaining fieldworks that they held up the advance of Captain Soroka's infantry and the light tanks. The assault wavered momentarily and the Third Division optimistically reported to General Öhquist twenty minutes after it began that the attack had been repelled.[19]

Correspondent Tvardovski, following the offensive from a regimental command post of the 123rd Division, recorded some of the excitement of those moments. When one of the subordinate unit commanders was a few minutes late in advancing because he failed to see the signal rocket, the regimental commander hastened his departure by phone, using the strong Russian expletive, *". . . tvoyu mat'"* [. . . your mother!]. A few moments after the tank and infantry attack began—following the barrage which seemingly nothing could survive—Finnish shells burst near the command post. The Soviet officers were amazed that the "sons of bitches" could still return their fire.[20]

The second echelon of the attack regiment was committed to the battle, while scores of tanks pounded the defenses at point-blank range. In the furious fighting at least four heavy tanks were damaged before the last antitank gun was smashed. When the Finns abandoned one of the smaller bunkers, a bloody skirmish was fought with hand grenades. As both sides were wearing white camouflage garments, the battle resembled a deadly game of blindman's bluff. According to their own report, at least one Soviet infantry company lost most of its men in the assault. When tanks halted right in front of the embrasures of "Poppius" to screen them off, the garrison finally abandoned that strongpoint to continue the battle in the open. At 12:28, their time, the Russians hoisted a red banner atop the captured bunker, the key to this sector and—as events developed—to the entire Line west of Lake Muolaanjärvi.[21]

Lacking adequate artillery support, Major Lindman's battered battalion was doomed from the start. Nearly half of those present on that morning were lost during the savage fighting of the eleventh. About an hour after "Poppius" fell, Lt. Malm—with no antitank guns left and scores of the steel monsters overrunning his sector—ordered the remnants of his company to withdraw to the support line. To the east of that sector, the small company of Lt. Hannus cut down the vulnerable infantry attacking across the Munasuo Swamp, thereafter known to the

Russians as the "valley of death"; but they also were compelled to retreat later in the afternoon when T-28 tanks flanked them along the Lähde road. The battle for the "Million" bunker see-sawed into the night; the Russians repeatedly surrounded it, only to be thrown back by the determined counterattacks of Lt. Ericsson's company.[22]

By the time darkness fell, tanks and infantry had arrived in front of the support line along the Lähde road, where they dug in for the night. Some of the victors broke out the vodka to celebrate the day's success. Subsequently, 22 men of the 123rd Division were designated Hero of the Soviet Union for their part in the breakthru, and nearly 1,000 lesser awards were bestowed within that unit. The Division was one of six units to receive the Order of Lenin during the Winter War.[23] However, a Red Army doctor who was at a Finnish bunker that day strongly implied that there were a number of cowards in that lauded Division. He told the regimental commander:

> You have a lot of "communications men." There you can stumble on one who is lying down: "Why are you lying down?"-"We are communications men." All around are "communications men."[24]

Although Commander Timoshenko's great 11 February offensive extended across the entire Karelian Isthmus, in no other sector was its success as great or as ominous as at Lähde. At Summa, west of the Lähde road penetration, strong attacks which began in the morning continued late into the night, but Regiment JR 7 doggedly held its positions. The regiment was even able to transfer one infantry company to the adjacent Suokanta front, where tank-supported infantry was severely straining the defenses. By evening the Russians had seized a small section of the front line at Suokanta, but the Finns were able to regain the lost ground and repel additional attacks there before midnight. Elsewhere along the front of the exhausted Third Division, the attackers took some forward positions at Merkki during the day, but the defenders also recaptured these and beat back renewed assaults that night.[25]

In the Fourth Division's sector, the Russians penetrated the forward zone a mile south of Marjapellonmäki around noon.

Within an hour and a half that gain was cancelled out by counterattacks, but the invaders retained control of a nearby grove
which they had captured on 10 February.[26]

In the first significant action of its kind—an omen of worse to
come—the enemy also tried to flank Colonel Kaila's Fourth
Division over the ice of the Gulf of Finland. Some two or three
battalions of marines cautiously approached the coast behind
the Mannerheim Line near Muurila.* Nine Finnish fighters
were ordered to strafe the columns on the ice, but due to poor
visibility they could not find the white-caped troops. However,
coastal defense batteries, especially the six 152mm guns at
Humaljoki, created havoc on the ice and thwarted this attack
for the time being. Because of the potential danger from this
direction, Colonel Kaila felt obliged to reinforce the regiment
closest to the Gulf, JR 12, with a company from the reserve
battalion of JR 11.[27]

On the opposite flank of the Third Division, the First Division
met strong advances in the Taasionlampi-Suursuo Swamp
area, where several tanks became stuck in the partially frozen
marsh. When the attackers penetrated into two peninsulas in
the swamp, they were rapidly thrown back from one, but inconclusive fighting continued late into the night.[28]

East of Lake Muolaanjärvi the Soviet 13th Army launched
strong assaults in the Punnusjoki River sector, forcing the river
early in the afternoon. Here, as elsewhere, Finnish artillery
was hampered by enemy aircraft. The commander of the harried Second Division, Colonel Koskimies, requested fighter protection for his guns, but the few Finnish planes were already
engaged on other sectors. Late in the afternoon eleven tanks
broke thru at the mouth of the river, where approximately two
regiments of infantry were attacking. The Russians also
achieved a minor penetration at Oinala, on the eastern shore of
Lake Muolaanjärvi, where they employed an equally large
force. Colonel Koskimies estimated the total enemy infantry on
his front at seven regiments; nevertheless, he was initially optimistic about the prospects for a successful counterattack. However, by late evening the Russians had widened their breach at
the Punnusjoki to about half a mile and he felt that the costs

*See Map No. 14, p. 161

of the counterblow—considering the shortage of artillery shells —would exceed the benefits. Because the main Finnish positions were still intact at the edge of the forest about a mile north of the river, driving the enemy back from the shoreline did not seem essential, and the proposed counterattack was cancelled.[29]

As usual, the Taipale sector was also subjected to heavy attacks on the eleventh. At this end of the Mannerheim Line, flanking attacks over the ice of Lake Ladoga—similar to those over the Gulf near Muurila—were repelled, and the Line from the Vuoksi to Lake Ladoga remained in the hands of General Heinrichs' Third Corps, except for previous minor penetrations of the most forward positions.[30]

That had been a terrible day for the Kannas Army, certainly the worst to date for the Second Corps defending the western Isthmus. Nevertheless, the calm reaction of the Finnish commanders to the widespread penetrations and the serious breach at the Lähde road was their normal, courageous, virtually ingrained order—counterattack! During the evening, elements of Regiment JR 8 succeeded in clearing the enemy out of the western part of the Lähde sector, and two battalions continued the battle along the Lähde road in an attempt to regain the eastern portion. Somewhat hesitatingly, Marshal Mannerheim released his main reserve force, the Fifth Division, to the use of the Second Corps—Regiment JR 15 on 10 and 11 February, JR 13 in the evening of the eleventh, and JR 14 the next morning. The intention was to throw the entire division into counterattacks, but enemy pressure along the Third Division's front necessitated its piecemeal deployment to several trouble spots, and only the last regiment to arrive was actually available for such action. JR 15 was initially divided between the Fourth Division and the Suokanta sector of the Third Division, while JR 13 manned the support line at Lähde.[31]

Meanwhile, the 123rd Division continued attacking to widen the base of its wedge. While Major Rosly's regiment was capturing its main objectives along the Lähde road almost on schedule, the regiment to its west was temporarily stymied by Lt. Ericsson's company and the "Million" bunker, manned by Lt. Skade's platoon. Fierce seesaw battles raged around the damaged fort all afternoon and into the night, when Russian infantry finally surrounded it for the last time. Under cover of darkness, Junior Lt. Lekanov's sapper group hauled up hundreds of pounds of explosives, which they positioned atop the bunker. At 5 A.M. on the twelfth an ear-splitting explosion blasted a 30-foot crater in the fortification, killing Lt. Skade and his entire platoon. Even after that crippling loss, Lt. Ericsson's staunch men held their isolated front line positions until noon, when they withdrew north of Lake Summajärvi to the support line.[32]

Although there was some costly fighting at the Lähde support line on 12 February, the 123rd Division seemed more intent upon consolidating its gains than in deepening its wedge in the Finnish defenses. General Österman considered the enemy "surprisingly passive" on this front, a factor which facilitated Finnish dispositions for their projected major counterattack.[33]

Elsewhere on this date, the battles were also inconclusive. In the western portion of the Summa sector, five separate company-to regimental-sized attacks were repulsed. However, the cautious employment of tanks on this sector (only four were destroyed this day compared to nearly 100 knocked out during the previous attacks) indicated that these were merely harassing actions, not serious attempts to penetrate this formidable section of the Line. During the night of 12–13 February the front line battalions of Regiment JR 7—which had endured twelve days of continuous pounding without yielding—were relieved by JR 15.[34]

Early in the afternoon the Russians achieved a minor breakthru between Summa and Suokanta, but by evening the local defenders, reinforced by a battalion from JR 15, threw them out of their lines.[35]

The First Division also succeeded in counterattacking during the afternoon, retaking the main position at Taasionlampi.[36]

The Red Army penetrated the Second Division's front again at Oinala, Parkkila, and Pällilä* on 12 February, but the Finns recaptured all of these areas during the night. The Russians were able to retain only minor gains at the Punnusjoki River.[37]

On the flanks of the Mannerheim Line, the Seventh Division

*See Map No. 14, p. 161

again had to fight off heavy attacks at Taipale on the twelfth, while the Fourth Division's sector was comparatively quiet. The enemy forces which had approached Muurila over the Gulf on the previous day disappeared, abandoning on the ice some of their weapons and about 100 pairs of skis.[38]

Although the Isthmus Army held its front positions tenaciously, its own casualties on that day reached an alarming total of some 1,200 men.[39]

The major counterattack planned for the morning of 13 February was to be a three-pronged strike to recapture the front line in the critical Lähde sector. Two battalions of JR 14 were to move southeast from north of Lake Summajärvi to their initial objective, the Majajoki River valley. Simultaneously, one battalion of the Third Brigade was to advance to the southwest from the area northeast of the Munasuo Swamp. When JR 14 reached the river, JR 13 was to dispatch one battalion from the support line towards the lost front line positions.[40]

At 7 A.M. the Second and Third Battalions of JR 14 began their attack as planned. By noon they had not only reached the Majajoki River, but had thrown the Russians off a hill northeast of Lake Summajärvi after a lengthy skirmish. However, the advance ground to its inevitable halt when the enemy's overwhelmingly superior artillery was directed against the Finns. In the afternoon Soviet tanks smashed thru the regiment's eastern flank, forcing Colonel Polttila to order a retreat to the support line. Losses were especially heavy among the officers; one battalion changed commanders four times, and Colonel Polttila was mortally wounded that evening.[41]

Neither the Third Brigade nor JR 13 had a chance to carry out its part of the counterattack. Most of the Brigade was engaged throughout the morning in checking a new danger near Merkki, east of the Lähde road penetration, where Russian ski troops were threatening the rear of the positions manned by the exhausted Regiment JR 9. After eliminating most of that enemy force in mid-afternoon, the Brigade became tied down on JR 9's front, where five Soviet battalions were attacking.[42]

Colonel Vaala's Regiment, JR 13, on and behind the support line at the Lähde road, was under extreme pressure from early morning on the thirteenth. Good flying weather facilitated the heaviest air attacks to date, and artillery fire was also intensive. In the morning several attacks were repulsed, but early in the afternoon some 50 tanks broke thru just east of the road on a front about a half mile wide. Since there were no antitank guns available, there was little hope of preventing the Russians from exploiting their success. The fighting at the point of the break-thru was so fierce that in one company with a strength of more than 100, only 14 Finns survived. Due to the confusion of those hectic moments, the infantry neglected to warn the artillery of the armor, and ten 150mm howitzers were abandoned when heavy tanks overran their positions east of Majakylä. The last "tank commando" unit in the Second Corps was rushed to the area, but just when these men were preparing for their suicidal attacks in the evening, tens of additional tanks swarmed over them. This time Soviet infantry accompanied the armor, pro-tecting it from the grenades and Molotov cocktails of the com-mandos. The massive tank onslaught was terrifying to witness; Colonel Vaala noted that his muscles involuntarily tightened at the sound of tanks for years afterward. It is understandable that some of the helpless defenders fled in panic, even while other reserves were being rushed to the scene.[43] The Fifth Divi-sion commander, Colonel Isakson, was so demoralized that he reported to General Öhquist at 7:50 P.M. that "it's finished now, they have broken thru."[44]

That gloomy evaluation may well have been justified, but—almost incredibly—the victor deliberately halted after advanc-ing some two miles, stopping little more than a mile short of the very strategic road junction at Lähde. Once it had ruptured the support line, Meretskov's Seventh Army had an open road stretching before it; there were no prepared field positions closer than the intermediate line at Lake Näykkijärvi, some eight miles to the rear. The "Kämärä ridge," stretching from the Soviet side of the Line almost to the Lake—an open, nearly treeless heath which afforded no cover for the Finnish tank commandos—was perfect terrain for the attackers. The Finns had been forced to throw in their last reserves in the vicinity, a Civic Guards battalion from Viipuri. Most of its members were high school boys who hadn't even served their period of military training; only the day before, their use on the front had been forbidden.[45]

General Öhquist acknowledged that within a few hours the

Russians could have overrun both the Lähde road junction and the better road at the Kämärä railroad station. From Lähde they could have fanned out on a road behind the Summa front and also behind the entire First Division, with "catastrophic consequences" for the defenders.[46] Had the back of the Second Corps been broken in that fashion, it would have been mainly a matter of marching time until the spectre of Soviet troops occupying Helsinki became a reality.

Since total victory was apparently within its grasp, why didn't the Red Army take full advantage of this opportunity? Undoubtedly one reason was tardy planning. Special mobile groups consisting of tank brigades with supporting infantry and combat engineers, designed to exploit the breakthrus, were not organized until the middle of the month, *after* the initial break was achieved. Colonel Baranov, commanding the group formed to dash thru the opening blasted out by the 123rd Division, did not even receive orders from Meretskov to attack Lähde and Kämärä Station until 14 February.[47] Every hour of Soviet delay was precious to the Finns, hastily improvising a defense with reserves from every conceivable source.

Yet, even without Baranov's mobile group, the Seventh Army could have continued the offensive with excellent chances for success. Their basic weakness at this crucial moment was probably psychological—Soviet commanders had learned to respect and fear their adversary. The exorbitantly costly failures of December remained a sobering memory, and the cursed Finns were still displaying a remarkable ability to counterattack. Stalin, himself, had shown considerable concern about Finnish counterattacks.[48] Thus, when their tangible defense line was broken, the Finns were saved by an intangible one— their well earned reputation for prowess.

Elsewhere on 13 February the Finns were generally able to counter strong Russian probes. The enemy renewed his attempts to flank the Mannerheim Line across the ice of the Gulf, throwing about one battalion, supported by eight tanks, against the Muurila-Kyrönniemi coastal sector. In good visibility, the attackers made excellent targets on the ice; coastal batteries sank three of the tanks and dispersed the others. However, as dusk fell Russian reinforcements arrived on the scene.[49]

At the opposite end of the Line, massive assaults against the

Taipale region continued. Approximately 100,000 shells pounded this sector between 11 and 13 February, in support of attacks by four or five regiments. Both sides suffered severely, but the Finnish positions held.[50]

The Seventh Army achieved a minor indentation in the Suokanta front around noon; however a mid-afternoon counterattack by a battalion of JR 15 checked any further advance.[51]

The Second Division, east of Lake Muolaanjärvi, was subjected to more serious pressure. The Finns repulsed renewed attacks at Oinala, but a few miles to the east 20 tanks, accompanied by infantry, broke into the support point at Muolaa Church early in the afternoon. Although the defenders regained part of the lost ground after dark, the Soviet forces were too strong to be driven out completely.[52]

At the Punnusjoki River, where the 13th Army had seized a foothold on 11 February, both daytime and night attacks were launched in an effort to exploit this minor success—without significant results. In the Pasuri area one Soviet battalion was repulsed so decisively that a second battalion farther back did not even try to advance.[53]

In the First Division's sector, west of Lake Muolaanjärvi, Soviet pressure was also strong. The weak Finnish forces which had recaptured the Taasionlampi strongpoint the previous day suffered 40 casualties on the 13th. As the Russian attacks continued into the evening, it was necessary to send a battalion to reinforce the harried defenders.[54]

Nowhere—except at the Lähde road—did the great offensive of the Northwestern Front yet achieve results commensurate with its tremendous expenditure of men and resources. Even at Lähde, the Finns were planning another major counterattack for the night of 13–14 February. Sizeable forces, including one and a half battalions of JR 14 and a few companies from the Third Brigade, were grouped during the evening for an attack scheduled for 3:45 A.M. However, the proposed counterblow was cancelled late at night. Because of the critical shortage of artillery ammunition, it was decided that sending infantry against the Kämärä ridge, where scores of tanks were maneuvering at will, would only lead to pointless slaughter.[55]

It was obvious that, sooner or later, the increasingly dangerous Soviet wedge at Lähde must inevitably render the adjacent

MAIN THEATER OF OPERATIONS, FEB.- MAR. 1940        MAP 14

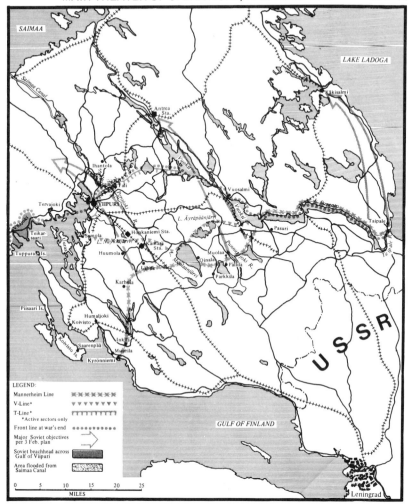

Finnish positions untenable. To consider the long-range alternatives, General Öhquist phoned the Kannas Army Headquarters at 11:20 P.M. to request a meeting with General Österman
the next morning at Second Corps Headquarters. At midnight
Marshal Mannerheim called Öhquist for details on the situation in the Second Corps.[56]

When General Öhquist—who had been up most of the night
—arrived at his headquarters at Saarela Manor at 7:40 on 14
February, he was surprised to find the Marshal and Colonel

Airo awaiting him, along with General Österman and Colonel
Tapola from the Kannas Army Headquarters. The Commander-in-Chief had made the long trip from Otava by car, travel-
ling during the hours of darkness to elude hostile aircraft. As
is true of other matters concerning these three strong-willed
men, there are conflicting accounts of this conference. All parties agreed that the Second Corps positions must be abandoned,
but the extent of the proposed withdrawal is disputed. General
Österman states that he proposed withdrawing the main forces
to the rear line near Viipuri (the so-called "T-Line"), using the
intermediate line ("V-Line")* merely as a delaying position to
cover that retreat. General Öhquist says that there was unanimous agreement to pull back only to the intermediate line for
the time being. Characteristically reticent, Marshal Mannerheim (in his memoirs) merely noted that he subsequently authorized withdrawal to the intermediate line.[57] Österman was
also irked because the Commander-in-Chief discussed specific
operational details directly with Öhquist, while the commander of the Kannas Army listened from the sidelines, in his
own words, "as a totally unneeded party."[58]

In any case, the conferees were able to deliberate in a relatively calm and unhurried atmosphere, because the enemy
spearhead was virtually marking time before Lähde where its
infantry had dug in during the night. Detailed plans for new
troop dispositions were outlined, facilitating an orderly withdrawal. Furthermore, reinforcements were arriving or enroute
from distant points—a heavy artillery section from Pohjanmaa
(Ostrobothnia), two coastal defense battalions from Hamina-
Säkkijärvi, and two regiments (JR 67 and 68) of the 23rd Division which were diverted from assignment to Ladoga-Karelia.
Many of these units were delayed, however, by the extensive
Soviet air raids on road and rail centers.[59]

Bomber formations were so thick over the Viipuri-Saarela
area that day that the Marshal and his entourage had to don
white capes to walk the few hundred yards to the dining hall
at lunch time, and they were forced to duck under the trees in
the park several times to avoid detection. At 4:30 in the after-

*See Map No. 14, p. 161

noon, Mannerheim departed for Otava—without announcing his decision on the vital question of the withdrawal.[60]

Across the shell-torn Karelian Isthmus, combat operations on 14 February followed the pattern of previous days—strong attacks at widely separated points, with only slight tangible results. By this time the Soviet marines on the ice in the Muurila-Kyrönniemi coastal sector had reached the strength of about two regiments, supported by tanks and artillery. The very effective fire of Finnish coastal artillery inflicted heavy casualties and helped to disperse repeated assaults. In futile attempts to silence the Humaljoki battery, four Soviet aircraft were shot down that day.[61]

Severe fighting continued in the Taipale, Taasionlampi, Punnusjoki, and Merkki areas. The attacks at Taipale and Taasionlampi failed, but the 13th Army captured two support points at the Punnusjoki River. A more serious threat developed at Merkki, where 20 tanks broke into the front line in the morning. That attack was later repulsed, but towards evening the Soviet division renewed the advance, forcing the remnants of Regiment JR 9 and part of the First Brigade to fall back to the support line.[62]

In the critical Lähde sector, the Seventh Army was content with widening the base of its breakthru—capturing the remainder of the support line—without trying to deepen its advance. The Finns attempted to contain the enemy wedge from hastily manned positions along its perimeter. Regiment JR 13 deployed along the western side of the Majajoki River between the Majakylä bridge and Lake Summajärvi. Opposite JR 13, the Third Brigade faced west from positions anchored on the Munasuo and Valosuo swamps and a bog south of Kilteenlampi. The dangerous point of the wedge was held by parts of JR 14 along a "line"—existing only on paper—which crossed the Kämärä ridge south of the Lähde crossroads. The Finnish command had no illusions that these weak positions could withstand a determined assult, but they might buy a few more hours in which to muster forces farther back.[63]

As early as 7 A.M., JR 13 received permission—if its front line became untenable—to withdraw from the Majajoki River to improvised positions running south of the road from Leipäsuo to the Rajamäki area. The other units surrounding the Soviet wedge received similar instructions. Although the battalions on his right flank started to pull back an hour later, Captain Laakso—considering the river the best place to make a stand—resolved to keep his Third Battalion there as long as possible. At dusk Laakso's unit annihilated an attacking company almost to the last man. About 8:30 P.M. the battalion on the left also pulled out, leaving the Third Battalion perilously exposed on both flanks. It was nearly midnight when Laakso's determined men withdrew to the Leipäsuo road line.[64]

These developments also made it necessary to evacuate the Summa sector, now in imminent danger of being outflanked from the east. Summa's formidable defenses, which included 16 concrete bunkers, had held out through 70 days of almost incessant pounding. During the night of 14–15 February Regiment JR 15 abandoned the area to the enemy, who had prematurely boasted of its capture over Radio Moscow.[65] The subsequent Finnish denial had wry consequences within the Soviet hierarchy. Commanders Meretskov and Voronov were rebuked by their superiors in Moscow, even though—in Voronov's words—"there was nothing said in the Seventh Army's reports about seizing the damned strongpoint" (he blamed someone on Timoshenko's staff for the erroneous report).[66] On 15 February Voronov witnessed the massive assault by artillery, tanks, and two infantry divisions which resulted in the "capture" of the Summa fortifications—just abandoned by the Finns. The final irony was that no one in Moscow would believe that Summa had finally fallen. Meretskov was trying to convince Defense Commissar Voroshilov by phone that this great news was true when Voronov returned to the Seventh Army's command post. Voronov had to repeat three times that he had seen the sector captured before Voroshilov was satisfied. Undoubtedly, this skepticism stemmed partly from a grudging respect for the Summa defenders, but perhaps it may also be attributed to the probability that, if the Russian and Finnish situations were reversed, Stalin would have required the defenders to perish on the spot—as his ill-considered refusal to permit a timely retreat from Kiev in September 1941 indicates.[67]

A more ominous loss occurred at Lähde, where the Seventh Army finally decided to follow up the 123rd Division's success, after keeping their overwhelming forces immobilized about a mile south of that vulnerable crossroads for two days. Between them and the road junction were only remnants of JR 14, two "tank commando" companies (no antitank guns), and one company of the youthful Civic Guards battalion from Viipuri. In sub-zero weather, these cold and weary troops burrowed into the snow—their only protection on the exposed Kämärä ridge. In the afternoon the fresh tank and infantry forces of Colonel Baranov's mobile group blasted their way thru this thin line to seize Lähde. Finnish losses were severe, especially among the boys from Viipuri, and by evening the survivors were completely apathetic from fatigue.[68]

Once again, the road lay open before Meretskov's army. The only Finnish force between Lähde and Baranov's next objective, the road-rail junction at Kämärä Station, was one battalion of JR 62 which had recently arrived from the Third Corps. Incredibly, the relatively invincible Soviet spearhead halted again when it encountered that negligible opposition about a mile north of Lähde. With notable lack of initiative or daring, the Russians did not even attempt to encircle the Finns on their flanks by fanning out along the east-west road at Lähde.[69]

At 3:50 P.M., about an hour after Baranov's group penetrated the Finnish positions south of Lähde, Marshal Mannerheim authorized General Österman to pull the entire Second Corps back to the intermediate line, in accord with the discussion of the previous day. The Kannas Army commander immediately relayed this anxiously awaited decision to General Öhquist, who then issued detailed orders for the general withdrawal to commence the next day. Instead of the panicky rout that might have ensued if the Red Army had aggressively exploited the breach of the support line on the Lähde Road on 13 February, the Finns were now able to execute a planned, generally orderly retreat.[70]

Timoshenko's two armies scored other gains on 15 February —most notably in the Punnusjoki region[71]—but, because of the Finnish decision to withdraw, they were of only fleeting significance.

The Second Corps' retreat to the V-Line began in the morning of 16 February on all sectors except those of the Second Brigade, just west of Lake Muolaanjärvi, which covered the Corps' withdrawal, and the Second Division (between Lake Muolaanjärvi and the Vuoksi) where enemy pressure was so severe—especially at Punnusjoki—that the defenders could not disengage until evening. Fortunately for the hard-pressed Second Division, the intermediate line was strongest in this region; it had been the intended main line until the YH period, when it was decided to relocate the front positions in this area a few miles ahead. Therefore, the Division was able to withdraw to the shelter of numerous concrete bunkers and well prepared field positions. The remainder of the V-Line, from the northern shore of Lake Muolaanjärvi to Samola Bay on the Gulf of Viipuri, was a sorry contrast. Here the defense works, begun only late in 1939, consisted of half-finished trenches and holes in the ground; some sectors did not even have barbed wire entanglements. General Hanell, in charge of fortification, declared that these positions existed only as a colored line on a map. There were not even any favorable terrain features worth mentioning.[72]

Because the V-Line was only 4–9 miles behind the main positions in the Viipuri Gateway, there was a risk that the momentum of the enemy's drive might carry it thru the second line before the retreating Finns could properly man those positions.[73] On the other hand, the western end of the Mannerheim Line, on the Gulf coast, was so far from the intermediate line (approximately 25 miles) that there was great danger of the defenders in that sector being cut off during the retreat. However, the timid tactics of the Seventh Army negated the first threat, and careful planning by the Finnish command forestalled the second.

One regiment of the Fourth Division was sent to reinforce the coastal artillery on Koivisto Island, while the retreat of the remaining regiments was greatly facilitated by the devastating fire of its heavy batteries. Even after all of the Second Corps reached the V-Line, these guns continued to pound Soviet concentrations and communications. The 70th Division, advancing along the Koivisto Peninsula on the mainland, was one unit which felt the effects of this fire. (Finally, during the night of 22–23 February, the island garrison fired its last rounds, destroyed the gun tubes, and began the long trek across the ice to the western shore of Viipuri Gulf at Ristiniemi. Their perilous march past the enemy's flank on the 23rd was covered by a fortuitous blizzard.)[74]

Beginning on 16 February, the Seventh Army belatedly attempted to employ its mobile forces to encircle the defenders, making deep thrusts with its hundreds of tanks. When Colonel Baranov's group finally seized Kämärä Station early that afternoon, following a fierce three-hour battle, strong tank columns were hurled to both east and west. However, by the next morning virtually all the Finnish troops from the main line reached the intermediate positions. The enemy was hard on their heels —the 123rd Division reached the vicinity of the V-Line near Huumola on the 17th.[75]

Both sides sustained heavy casualties in the confused fighting of these days. In the week ending 17 February, Colonel Isakson's Fifth Division alone lost nearly 800 men. The battalion of JR 62 which Baranov's armor overran enroute to Kämärä Station was so severely shaken by that dreadful baptism of fire that it could only be reformed far beyond the intermediate positions. Other green units received similar shocks in their first encounters with the powerful tank forces. On the other hand, some overconfident Soviet commanders swung from excessive caution to costly recklessness. Believing they had the Finns on the run, they reverted to the careless tactics of December—storming forward in dense formations without artillery preparation, and failing to keep their tanks in contact with their infantry. Tacitly admitting the price of such tactics, Commander Timoshenko ordered a halt to the Seventh Army's main offensive operations on 21 February in order to withdraw and replenish the vanguard divisions, bring up fresh reserves, and regroup the attack forces.[76]

While these momentous battles were raging in the western half of the Isthmus, Commander Grendal' maintained the pressure of the Thirteenth Army's attacks against the eastern end of the Mannerheim Line. February 18 is remembered as the "black day at Taipale" by the survivors of the grueling marathon fighting in that sector. Just before noon, scores of bombers plastered the front southwest of Taipale, between Lake

Suvanto and the Taipale River, while a strong artillery preparation began. Unfortunately, the First Battalion of JR 61, a replacement regiment formed two months previously (which included elderly men and casualties who had recently recovered), arrived at the front just in time to suffer serious losses in the furious barrage. Consequently, when three enemy regiments attacked at 2 P.M., these green troops panicked and abandoned the front line. To their east, elements of the First Battalion of JR 19—for the most part, also recently arrived replacements—likewise abandoned three front line strongpoints. Fortunately for the defense, the attack was not followed up, and the support line held. Nevertheless, this was the greatest reverse the Third Corps had suffered to date.[77]

Although the withdrawal of the Second Corps to the V-Line was a tactical success, its psychological implications were disturbing. Informed circles in Helsinki, until recently hearing of nothing but defensive victories at the Mannerheim Line, were alarmed by the news. To allay their fears, the Commander-in-Chief requested his trusted friend, General Rudolph Walden, to inform President Kallio and Prime Minister Ryti that he personally made the decision to withdraw.[78] The Marshal's optimistic proclamation to the Kannas Army, issued on 17 February, was also carried in the following day's press. It mentioned "new defensive positions against which the enemy's forces will finally exhaust themselves" and concluded with the exhortation, "may we remain firm and immovable in our confidence in the final victory."[79]

That Mannerheim was actually less confident than those defiant words suggest is indicated by the fact that he sent Lt. Colonel Nihtilä on another special mission at this time. That able GHQ officer visited the headquarters of all the front line regiments in the Second Corps, in order to evaluate the conflicting reports which were being received in Otava. Then, because of the illness of Colonel Takkula, the Chief of Staff of the Corps, he remained to substitute in that capacity for about two weeks. General Österman considered this surprise visit a reflection on his own judgment.[80]

The longstanding friction between the commander of the Kannas Army and the Marshal culminated in the former's resignation from his command "for reasons of health" on 19 February. In his overly reserved memoirs, Mannerheim accepted the transparent "reasons of health" at face value. Österman claims that the final crisis in their relationship arose because he could not agree that the V-Line must be considered the new main position. (Orders to hold that line at any price had already been issued.) One can only speculate on the degree to which the conflict of personalities induced the resignation, but it was probably great. General Österman was undoubtedly under additional stress at this time because his wife lay gravely wounded as a result of an air raid.[81]

In selecting a new commander for the Kannas Army, Marshal Mannerheim bypassed Lt. General Öhquist (their relations had also been strained in the past) and promoted Major General Erik Heinrichs to Lt. General to fill that key post. To replace Heinrichs as Third Corps commander, he appointed the victor of Tolvajärvi, Major General Talvela. Colonel Pajari assumed Talvela's former command at the Aittojoki River.[82]

In connection with these personnel shifts, an organizational change which had been discussed at the 14 February conference was put into effect. On 20 February a new command, the First Corps, was established in the central Isthmus, between the Second and Third Corps. Consisting of the First and Second Divisions, its boundary with the Second Corps ran from Lake Lyykylanjärvi, just east of Tali, to the Perojoki River. Major General Laatikainen, commander of the First Division, took over the new Corps, and Colonel Martola took the First Division. This reorganization enabled General Öhquist's Second Corps to concentrate exclusively on the defense of the city and region of Viipuri, where the crucial battles would soon be fought.[83]

When the Finns withdrew to the V-Line and abandoned the Koivisto batteries, the Gulf of Viipuri suddenly assumed great strategic significance. The Red Army might now cross the frozen Gulf to outflank the Viipuri defenses from the southwest. By 22 February Soviet forces had secured a foothold on Piisaari Island, northwest of Koivisto, and they were already threatening Uuras Island, close to Viipuri.[84]

On 18 February the Kannas Army assumed responsibility for

the defense of the Gulf, which was mainly *terra incognita*—no peacetime maneuvers, not even map exercises, had been concerned with the defense of its western shore. More serious was the shortage of men to defend this unexpectedly lengthened front. In order to release a few battalions of experienced troops to reinforce this sector, Marshal Mannerheim turned to the Swedish Volunteer Corps which had been training in northern Finland for several weeks. Their commander, General Ernst Linder, a veteran of Finland's war of 1918, eagerly accepted the Marshal's suggestion on 19 February that the volunteers assume the major responsibility for the defense of the Salla front. Beginning on 22 February some 8,000 Swedes and 725 Norwegians relieved five infantry battalions and two artillery batteries of the Lapland Group, who began the long and perilous journey to the Viipuri Gulf area. (In the lengthening days of late winter, Soviet air raids were increasingly numerous—there were 1,500 sorties on 19 February.) General Kurt Wallenius was summoned from his successful exploits in the northern wilds to direct the defense in the strikingly different surroundings of the Gulf.[85]

There were fierce local engagements at several points along the V-Line even before the Red Army resumed its general offensive. The First Corps repelled strong probes northeast of Lake Muolaanjärvi and north of Lake Äyräpäänjärvi on 22 February. The 13th Army also began attacking between Äyräpäänjärvi and the Vuoksi that day, but these assaults wore themselves out against the permanent fortifications of this sector.[86]

The most critical battles were waged east of Näykkijärvi Lake, where parts of the 123rd Division and Baranov's tank force drove into weak Finnish field positions along a narrow ridge. Repeated counterattacks failed to dislodge the invaders, who by 23 February had seriously bent the intermediate line at the main railroad. It was here, near the small station of Honkaniemi, that the Finns launched their first and only armored attack. In the morning of 26 February six Vickers tanks, accompanied by Finnish infantry, broke thru the lines and approached the command post of a Soviet battalion. However, five of the tanks were destroyed, and this counterattack also failed.[87]

That same day, Commander Timoshenko ordered the Seventh and Thirteenth Armies to be ready to resume the offensive by 28 February. By a happy coincidence which probably saved many Finnish lives, Marshal Mannerheim simultaneously authorized the withdrawal of the First and Second Corps to the rear positions, because the Soviet wedge at the railroad was threatening their communications with Viipuri. At midnight the Kannas Army issued orders to begin the retreat to the T-Line, which ran from the ancient fortress city of Viipuri to Tali and on to the Vuoksi at a point some 15 miles north of the right flank of the Third Corps. In order to cover the opening between the flanks of the First and Third Corps, the latter's front was extended to the northwest along the eastern banks of the Vuoksi, and two regiments of the Second Division were transferred from the First Corps to man that sector. This withdrawal, which began on the 27th, was everywhere executed according to plan. The next day an hour-long barrage ploughed up the intermediate line, heralding the resumption of the general offensive, but the only Finns the attackers encountered were those at scattered delaying positions.[88]

No less than twelve Soviet infantry divisions and five tank brigades were decorated for their part in breaking the V-Line,[89] which had been held by five understrength Finnish divisions and six combat-worthy light tanks! The crude streamroller tactics of the overwhelming invaders were inexorably winning the battle of attrition, at least in the crucial western half of the Karelian Isthmus.

Although the timely retreat was successfully executed, even Marshal Mannerheim later acknowledged his private fears that the exhausted Kannas Army would not be capable of making a new stand at the rear line.[90] The Mannerheim Line had held firm for more than two months, but the intermediate positions survived only twelve days. How long could the weary defenders of the T-Line withstand the pressure of constantly increasing Soviet forces, while their own thin ranks were progressively dwindling? With no fourth line to fall back upon, the Kannas Army finally had its back to the wall at the end of the third month of its unequal fight for survival.

It was small consolation for the Finns who endured the inferno of February on the Isthmus, but during that month thou-

sands of their hated enemies were perishing in their own
frozen hells in the northern wilderness. This was especially
true in Ladoga-Karelia, where large Soviet units had been cut
off from their supply bases since early January, and even larger
forces had failed to rescue them. By February the number of
Russian divisions sent as reinforcements had grown so large—
and their operational control so complex—that the Eighth
Army was split in two. A new 15th Army operated south of
Loimola,* while the Eighth Army continued the struggle
northeast of that important road-rail junction. This increased
pressure from the east did not prevent the Finns from systematically destroying one motti after another behind the main
battle lines. As the situation of the Kannas Army steadily
deteriorated in February, Marshal Mannerheim ordered General Hägglund to press the attacks against the mottis by all
means, in order to free more troops for the decisive battles in
the south.[91]

On 18 February the Fourth Corps captured the so-called
"regimental motti" which stretched for about a mile along a
road between the "great motti" near Lake Ladoga and the
Lemetti mottis. The fall of that strongpoint, which contained
the headquarters of several regiments and separate detachments, marked the end of the 18th Division as an organized
unit. About 250 prisoners were taken, and more than 1,000 dead
were counted.[92]

Three days later the destruction of another motti was completed. Soviet forces attempting to smash their way along the
coastal road to relieve the 168th Division had been surrounded
at Konnunkylä, a mile southeast of the "great motti." Because
of the high cliffs near Lake Ladoga, the reduction of these
defenses was difficult and costly, but it was accomplished by 21
February.[93]

Finally came the day of reckoning for the major part of the
34th Tank Brigade, which was surrounded in the powerful
Lemetti East enclave—the so-called "general motti." (The
smaller forces at Lemetti West had been liquidated by 4 February.) As early as 12 January those hapless Russians had begun
eating their transport horses, and by 16 January they were even

*See Map No. 3, p. 13

out of salt for cooking. Soon they were suffering the pangs of hunger, frostbite, and exhaustion; their combat capabilities declined day by day, week by week. Here the numerically weak Finnish artillery was able to repay in small degree the murderous barrages the Russians were pouring on the Kannas Army. Sporadic harassing fire during the night disturbed the rest of the emaciated Soviet troops, shivering in their frigid dugouts. The long ordeal for most of these Russians ended in death when the Finns attacked during the night of 28–29 February and the few survivors tried to escape in the morning. Indicative of the remarkable tenacity of those tankmen was the fact that the Finns found over 2,000 corpses here, yet only about 100 Russians surrendered. Among the frozen bodies was that of the Brigade commander, S. I. Kondrat'ev, lying face down in a dugout with one arm grotesquely raised as if in supplication. The dead commander of the 18th Division, Kondrashev, was also discovered here, where he had fled with his staff when his own unit had been defeated. The booty included 71 tanks, 12 armored cars, 24 artillery pieces and 133 machine guns.[94]

Up to this time nine mottis had been destroyed, but two strong ones remained unconquered to the very end. One of these was at Uomaa, just behind the Uuksunjoki River front where the Finns were defending their positions against the greater part of the 60th Division. The other was the "great motti," where the 168th Division had been surrounded intact since 11 January.[95]

The prolonged seige of the "great motti" was costly to both sides. By the end of the fighting, attrition had claimed more than half of the 168th Division. Yet, maintaining the blockade also exacted a terrible toll among the Finns. After the 15th Army had massed overwhelming strength near Pitkäranta, on 6 March it launched a powerful attack against the islands from which the Fourth Corps was frustrating attempts to supply the trapped Division over the ice of Lake Ladoga. Artillery and bombers devastated the small islands, which were too rocky for the defenders to dig in. Then came tanks and flamethrowers, followed by masses of infantry. Here the Finns proved that they could also fight to the last man when necessary; a few companies of infantry—several hundred men—perished on that one frightful day. The seige of the 168th Division was partially broken, as the 15th Army was able to utilize the supply route over the ice from Pitkäranta during the final week of the war.[96]

Although the Fourth Corps had destroyed the 18th Division and the 34th Tank Brigade, the Russian Hydra kept confronting it with new heads. After the arrival of the 37th Division late in the war, there were four Soviet divisions attacking in the Pitkäranta sector alone,[97] trying to break or outflank the Finnish line which arced to the northeast from the coastal road. A few days before the ceasefire, the relentless pressure of numbers and the ever-growing enemy artillery strength forced the defenders to begin a withdrawal to shorten their front. Nevertheless, the Finns retained control of Mantsinsaari Island, where their coast artillery and guerilla patrols continued to interdict communications in the Salmi area, far behind the Soviet lines.[98]

The increasing scope of the fighting elsewhere in Ladoga-Karelia in late February and early March was also ominous, because General Hägglund was obliged to transfer troops to the Viipuri Gulf at the very time fresh Russian divisions were hurled against the remnants of his two weary divisions. Significantly, the Chief of the Red Army Artillery, N. N. Voronov, visited the Eighth Army just before the war ended.[99]

On the Kollaa sector, where weak elements of the Finnish 12th Division had been holding back the 56th and 164th Divisions since December, the Eighth Army threw in two additional Divisions—the 24th Motorized Cavalry and the 128th Infantry. The Russians painstakingly constructed roads thru the wilderness around both flanks of the defenders, while maintaining heavy pressure against the existing five-mile front in the center. On 2 March all four divisions launched a concerted offensive, supported by strong artillery and air strikes. The two divisions originally deployed here pounded the center, while the others struck at the flanks. The 128th Division, advancing to the southwest, encountered only minor delaying elements and made some progress. Much heavier fighting developed on the northern flank, where stronger Finnish units engaged the 24th Division and other Soviet forces which were simultaneously advancing from positions southwest of the Aittojoki River front. Faced with this serious threat, Group Talvela (now commanded by Colonel Pajari) coordinated its operations with those of the Fourth Corps, eventually committing its last reserve battalions to the battle. There ensued a complex series of flanking maneuvers and counteractions in the wilderness between the roads Kollaa-Loimola and Tolvajärvi-Äglajärvi, in which the Soviet forces were surprised and at least partially checked in fierce engagements. These contests were still underway at the time of the ceasefire—in some cases even afterwards, due to the problems of contacting long-range patrols. The outcome remained uncertain when the guns were silenced, but the disporportion of forces in Ladoga-Karelia was steadily increasing.[100]

At the remote subarctic battlefront southeast of Kuhmo, there was also heavy action during the final month of the war, and—as in Ladoga-Karelia—both sides suffered terribly in that fighting. Although the 54th Division was better prepared to cope with its environment than most of the Soviet units sent into the northern wilds, it had been cut into numerous mottis along the Löytövaara-Rasti road* at the end of January. However, in addition to constructing strong fieldworks, this crafty division felled the trees for 50 yards or more on both sides of the roadway, making attacks by Finnish troops both difficult and costly. Some of the mottis eventually succumbed—the one at Reukha on 25 February, one at Luelahti East as late as 8 March —but many held out to the end. The powerful "headquarters motti" at Luelahti proper, situated in the middle of the 54th Division, was able to repel yet another strong attack on the last full day of the war. With opportune timing, Brigade Commander Gusevski had regrouped his division, pulling the 118th Regiment back to Luelahti to protect the headquarters on 28 January, only one day before the Finnish offensive immobilized his entire force.[101] For the remaining 45 days of the war, the surrounded troops fought so stubbornly that General Tuompo, commander of the Northern Finland Group, later paid them a unique public tribute, commending their "courage and toughness . . . and the military efforts of . . . Commander Gusevski."[102]

During that final month and a half, the only supplies the mottis received were those dropped from aircraft, and much of

*See Map No. 2, p. 9

these fell into Finnish hands. At times this was due to chance or faulty technique, but often it was the result of poor communications security and alert Finnish monitoring units. Intercepted radio messages specified the signals used to mark the drop zones—usually letters fashioned from tree boughs, or small campfires in the shape of letters if the drops were made at night. An example of the excellent Finnish intelligence is this message from the Ninth Army's Chief of Staff to the 337th Regiment at the Kuhmo front, sent on 17 February and read by Colonel Siilasvuo's staff the same day:

> Finns have misled our aircraft by letter T. We have to start to use a cross made from boughs or cloth.

In this manner the Finns received welcome additions to their field rations, such as large barrels of Estonian butter, while the encircled Russians went hungry.[103]

The Ninth Army made numerous attempts to rescue the 54th Division; although none succeeded in its primary objective, each one taxed the limited resources of the Finns. The most dramatic of these ventures was a flanking raid by three battalions of elite ski troops (about 2,000 men) who advanced more than 20 miles thru the wilderness north of the Löytövaara-Rasti road before they were subdued. Their commander, Colonel Dolin, was killed in a skirmish with a small reconnaissance detachment on 11 February, the second day of their daring expedition. At that time the Finns did not realize that they faced an entire brigade, and they lost the enemy's trail in the falling snow. At noon on 14 February one of the ski companies reached the road at Kesseli, southwest of Keikinkoski, where it surprised the logistic elements of JR 27, part of JR 65, and an engineer company; the raiders captured the latter's supply train and inflicted considerable casualties on the Finnish support troops. During the previous night, another unit, numbering about 100 skiers, attacked the headquarters of Regiment JR 27, keeping Lt. Colonel Mäkiniemi and his staff surrounded until they were rescued on the fifteenth. By this time Colonel Siilasvuo had pulled two battalions from the motti battles to counter this unexpected threat. The brigade was dispersed on 14 February, and its scattered detachments were all caught and destroyed by the 16th. After these battles, 1,500 Russian bodies were counted. Finnish losses were less than might have been expected, because the enemy's automatic weapons—being too heavily oiled for the frigid weather—frequently malfunctioned.[104]

While Dolin's brigade was maneuvering north of the Löytövaara-Rasti road, an independent ski battalion advanced south of that road on 12 February, reaching Jumi, about six miles west of Löytövaara, on the 13th. It too was defeated, losing some 300 men, and the remnants fled back across the border on the following days. Several other detachments tried to break thru to the 54th Division at various times, but their success was minimal. For example, of 200 men who attempted to reinforce the Loso motti on 18 February, approximately half died before reaching their destination.[105]

Simultaneous with Dolin's flanking raid, heavy Soviet attacks were launched near Löytövaara, where Finnish positions behind the Kuusijoki River blocked the road from the border. Towards the end of the war, powerful new forces arrived from the Soviet Union along this road. A vast amount of artillery supported their attacks, which overwhelmed the Finns at the Kuusijoki line on 2 March. The defense was reestablished some 1–2 miles to the west, on a narrower front between two small lakes. Strong Soviet pressure continued here without letup, both sides suffering and inflicting heavy losses. Primarily because of the massive artillery barrages, total Finnish casualties at this roadblock averaged about 100 a day.[106]

At a time when Marshal Mannerheim was desperately seeking manpower for the defense of the Viipuri region, General Tuompo felt compelled to reinforce the Kuhmo front. On 13 February a guerilla battalion arrived, on the 24th a mortar company, and on 7 March two rifle companies and a machine gun platoon. Even with those additions, the Finnish position was so precarious towards the end that Colonel Siilasvuo had prepared contingency plans for withdrawing the Ninth Division closer to Kuhmo.[107]

The ceasefire on 13 March may have saved the survivors of the 54th Division from the fate of other divisions which were destroyed in the northern wilds, but it is also conceivable that it saved the Ninth Division from the necessity of retreating and abandoning the seige. Some 1,400 Finns had already died in the Kuhmo campaign, and their losses were accelerating in March.[108] Furthermore, the Soviet Ninth Army appeared to be willing to pay a high price to claim at least one triumph.

On the other northern battlefronts, the stalemate prevailing after the Finnish victories of December and January continued to the war's end with little noteworthy change. The contest in the Petsamo district was only a minor exception. There the deadlock at Höyhenjärvi* was broken late in February when heavily reinforced Soviet units drove the small Finnish force back to Nautsi. Early in March that tiny settlement also had to be abandoned, but by the 7th the front was again stabilized on the eastern loop of the Nautsijoki River. The Russians seemed to be satisfied with this minor gain, because they concentrated on improving their quarters until the ceasefire. It was obvious that the outcome of the war would not be decided here.[109]

*See Map No. 2, p. 9

*Here to leave our souls and bodies,*
*Here to starve, and freeze, and perish . . .*
**RUNE XXX**

CHAPTER VII

# The Eleventh Hour

ALTHOUGH THE FINNISH COMMAND WAS JUSTIFIABLY WORRIED ABOUT
the endurance of the T-Line, which—like the abandoned V-
Line—consisted mainly of temporary field works, the greatest
menace in the final phase of the war was not there but on the
western shore of the Gulf of Viipuri. The possibility of an attack to flank the T-Line across the ice had been considered at
GHQ; indeed, there was a precedent for this—in March of 1710
Peter the Great's Army marched 80 miles across the frozen Gulf
of Finland and Viipuri Bay to besiege that same fortress city.
However, it did come as a shocking surprise that the ice in
March 1940 was strong enough to support heavy tanks and
artillery.[1]

The new commander of the Kannas Army, General Heinrichs, later paid tribute to the boldness and imagination of the
Russian leadership in this connection. At the end of February
sizeable units of the Red Army's reserve were mustered to form
the 28th Infantry Corps, which was transferred to the Seventh
Army with the mission of outflanking the Second Corps across
the Gulf of Viipuri. Plans were also made for simultaneous
diversionary attacks against Finland's southern coast from
Soviet-held islands; thrusts from Suursaari and Lavansaari Islands entailed exposed marches of up to 30 miles across the
Gulf of Finland. The Soviet command was not deterred by an
initial failure, when several tanks drove onto a stretch of
cracked ice at night and sank beneath the frigid waters of the
Gulf. In the continuing cold weather, the strength of the ice

increased daily; cracks which the Finns made by sawing or by detonations quickly froze solid.[2]

Finnish improvisations to meet this new and perilous challenge were beset with frustrations and delays. On 28 February the uncoordinated units hastily deployed to the Gulf of Viipuri, plus the three Coastal Defense battalions originally stationed there, were merged with the Fourth Division to form the Coastal Group. General Wallenius, just arrived from Lapland, was assigned to the Group as commander. However, for the next two or three days, that able and experienced leader was in no condition to provide the direction so desperately needed in this confused and novel situation.[3] In the words of a German intelligence report on the General, ". . . during very important occasions . . . he was completely drunk."[4] Finally, on 3 March Marshal Mannerheim relieved him of his duties (never again permitting him to serve in the Army) and transferred the Chief of the General Staff, Lt. General Oesch, to the command of the Coastal Group. That appointment was an indication of the seriousness of the threat which was developing here—on 2 March enemy reconnaissance detachments had already reached the western coast at two points southeast of Vilajoki.* Although they had been repulsed, stronger units had secured footholds on several strategic islands: almost two divisions occupied the southeastern portion of Uuras, two regiments attacked Tuppura, and Teikarsaari was captured. These were full-scale assaults in which strong air and artillery bombardments preceded the advance of tank-supported infantry. The Finns were able to counterattack with some success at both Tuppura and Teikarsaari, but within two days both islands were lost for good.[5]

The Commander-in-Chief concentrated all possible sources of manpower for the defense. One battalion had already been summoned from the Fourth Corps north of Lake Ladoga; when the last motti of the 34th Tank Brigade was destroyed on 29 February, General Hägglund was directed to release another battalion. High hopes had been placed on the five experienced and self-confident battalions of the Lapland Group, but many of these troops were temporarily demoralized by the shock of

*See Map No. 14, p. 161

their first exposure to large scale air attacks; enroute to the coastal sector, they were caught in a heavy raid while detraining at Taavetti.[6]

Operations were also hampered by the absence of lateral communications among these motley units; the pieces of the puzzle could only be put together at General Oesch's headquarters. The task of that nerve center was further complicated by the lack of a middle command echelon. It was only in the final days of the war, after several reorganizations, that the Coastal Group became an efficient and cohesive force.[7]

On the night of 3–4 March the 28th Corps crossed the Gulf of Viipuri in force, followed by the 10th Corps of the Seventh Army. The 28th Corps seized footholds on the Vilaniemi and Häränpäänniemi Peninsulas southeast of Vilajoki, but the Coastal Group threw the attackers back onto the ice the following night. During the fierce counterattack at Häränpäänniemi the Russians lost 15 tanks and 40 machine guns. The 10th Corps directed its offensive east of Tervajoki, closer to Viipuri and the remainder of the Seventh Army. Finnish resistance was stronger in this area, where repeated attempts to storm the coast were repelled as late as the final night of the war, 12–13 March.[8]

On 4 March, at the same time as the massive assaults across the Viipuri Gulf, the first daring attempts were made to seize the coast farther west, along the Gulf of Finland. Sizeable forces advanced from Suursaari and Lavansaari Islands towards the shoreline between Virolahti and Kotka—close enough to give Helsinki the jitters.* A column of some 500 men was six miles off the coast near Virolahti shortly after noon when eight Finnish figher planes caught them completely by surprise. Firing 8,000 rounds from an altitude of about 30 feet, the Finns killed nearly half of the marching troops and destroyed all of their vehicles; the survivors retreated in panic. After that successful mission, Finland's small fighter force was directed to strafe the enemy on the ice every day; this became extremely risky when the Russians provided air cover for their exposed march columns.[9]

Soviet forces made several additional attempts to reach the

*See Map No. 1, p. 4

shore in this sector, but all were costly failures. Coastal batteries spread havoc among the attackers, creating gaping holes in the ice in which the hapless Russians drowned. One regiment which advanced from Suursaari in close formation provided an exceptionally good target for Finnish artillery. Nevertheless, these forays posed so serious a threat that the Finns had to divert scarce manpower to the area. Five Civic Guards battalions, hastily formed in the Kymi Valley from youths and men normally considered too old to serve, were attached to the coast artillery.[10]

On 5 March the 28th Corps continued its offensive in earnest. A full division, supported by 100 tanks, broke thru the shore defenses on the Vilaniemi Penninsula, while other large forces maintained the pressure all along the Gulf of Viipuri.[11] Marshal Mannerheim confided to General Walden that: "we have to be ready for unpleasant surprises ... The last minutes are at hand."[12]

On the sixth, the beachhead at Vilaniemi was deepened and also widened to include the Häränpäänniemi Peninsula, and on 7 March the 28th Corps succeeded in cutting the coastal highway east of Vilajoki, thereby dividing General Oesch's Group in two. The loss of the road also meant that the troops fighting near Viipuri were cut off from Helsinki; the only supply or retreat routes open to them were the highway and railroad to Lappeenranta. That afternoon, the Marshal informed Foreign Minister Tanner that large new units with hundreds of tanks were crossing the Viipuri Gulf and could not be thrown back.[13]

Repeated Finnish counterattacks were successful in containing the enemy's beachhead, but at the time of the ceasefire the 28th Corps still held a five-mile stretch of the coastal road just east of Vilajoki. The 10th Corps, after capturing numerous islands in hard fighting, was then exerting strong pressure east of Tervajoki. At the end of the war the Gulf of Viipuri remained, as Mannerheim stated, the most critical of all the far-flung battlefronts.[14]

Meanwhile, in the main theater of operations on the Karelian Isthmus, the Kannas Army was subjected to unrelenting pounding in March. By the second of the month, the Seventh

Army was in contact with the T-Line near Viipuri. At the opposite end of the Isthmus, yet another attack was repelled at Taipale. That was one more of a long series of Soviet failures in this sector—the Third Infantry Corps had not advanced as planned at the time of the great offensive in mid-February, and the 13th Army in general moved so slowly that it retarded the progress of the entire Northwestern Front. This finally cost Grendal' his position; on 2 March he was replaced as commander of the 13th Army by Corps Commander F. A. Parusinov.[15] This change in leadership had little noticeable effect on operations at Taipale. The Finns were obliged to evacuate a few strongpoints about 10 March, but they were still able to throw back attacks on the twelfth. When the guns were silenced the next day, the Soviet Third Corps was still as far from Käkisalmi as it had been when it was given that objective on 3 February. Although they lost thousands of their comrades, the defenders of Taipale held out to the bitter end.[16]

After General Talvela took over the Third Corps from General Heinrichs, he even depleted the forces in the Taipale region by transferring five battalions of those weary troops to other fronts. Colonel Blick, the commander of the "Taipale Sector" from the early days of the war, opposed that action. Seeing the casualty lists growing week after week, and experiencing the cumulative fatigue of his men, he was understandably concerned primarily with holding his front with the least cost to his troops. But General Talvela, arriving at this area after the enemy had already broken thru the Mannerheim Line at Lähde, brought a wider perspective. He realized that Taipale now held a lower priority for the Soviet command, and he knew that other areas were even more urgently in need of reserves. At the beginning of March Talvela sent three battalions to reinforce the Second Division in the exposed Vuosalmi sector, where strong attacks were anticipated.[17]

As feared, the 13th Army finally succeeded in crossing the frozen Vuoksi where it narrows near Vuosalmi, but this breach was closed by strong counterattacks on 5 March. The Russians renewed the offensive all along the narrow stretch of the Lake, and a few days later they achieved a new foothold southeast of Vuosalmi. Trying to exploit this success, an entire division crossed over at that point, but—undoubtedly to the surprise of its commanders—it was thrown back. The only lasting beach-head the Red Army secured across the Vuoksi was the small area at Vuosalmi seized on 11 March. The bloody fighting in this sector in March cost the Finns nearly 2,000 casualties, but the enemy did not succeed in crushing their resistance.[18]

The weakest link in the T-Line was the open country around Tali, a few miles northeast of Viipuri. In a desperate effort to halt the Seventh Army's offensive here, the Finns opened the sluices in the headwaters of the Saimaa Canal, flooding the lowlands for miles around. This delayed the Soviet advance, but it did not stop it. Near the Tali railroad station, T-28 tanks towed the light T-26s thru water which was more than three feet deep in spots. Combat engineers in the lauded 123rd Division built matted roadways from fir trees to facilitate the crossing of low-lying areas, and the troops of Major Rosly's regiment waded up to their waists to press the attack. General Öhquist paid tribute to the tenacity of the stoic Russians who in some cases advanced thru icy water up to their necks—in subzero temperatures. Their mortality rate must have been appalling! On 6 March Tali Station was captured, and two days later the Finns withdrew to the Talinjoki River. On the ninth they abandoned the River line, but it was later recaptured by a counterattack. As the war drew to an end, the Seventh Army was again advancing in this sector with strong tank and infantry forces.[19]

The prime Soviet objective was, of course, Viipuri, the communications hub of the Karelian Isthmus and the key to the entire operations of the Kannas Army. The city, with its ancient moats and stone fortifications, was a powerful strongpoint. However, it had been subjected to devastating air raids from the first day of the war, and artillery had pounded it from the moment heavy railway guns could be brought within range—at least as early as 11 February. The successful enemy drives to outflank the city across the Gulf and to the northeast compelled the defenders to spread their forces very thin. In addition to deploying the Fourth Division to the western shore, by 7 March one regiment of the Second Corps and a brigade of the First Corps were transferred to Ihantola, northwest of the city; the brigade was subsequently dispatched to the Tervajoki sector on the Gulf coast. On the tenth, the forces fighting in the city's outskirts were sent to Rasalahti (some three miles northeast of Tervajoki), while the defense of Viipuri was entrusted to reserves in strong positions at Patterinmäki Hill. As the Soviet assault began on 11 March, the city came under murderous artillery drumfire. On the final night of the war, Soviet tanks and infantry entered the ancient city, and they continued the attack until the very last moments. Reinforcements were arriving continuously—one tank battalion saw its first action on 13 March in Viipuri.[20]

Stalin was extremely anxious to capture the city. At the moment the Seventh Army began storming its defenses, he ordered Commander Meretskov to capture it "within two or three days." Yet, the Finns still held a strong defense line within the city when the ceasefire went into effect. That did not prevent the Soviet leaders from loudly proclaiming its complete seizure.[21] Thus, three and a half months after Deputy Commissar Potemkin's boastful prediction that Helsinki would fall in four or five days, the only prestigious "victory" the Red Army could point to was the misleading claim that it captured Viipuri on the last day of the war.

During those anguishing final days, Marshal Mannerheim was under unprecedented strain. When Otava was heavily bombed early in March, it was feared that the Finnish nerve center had been discovered. Therefore, on 6 March the Operations Section of GHQ moved northeast to a new location about midway between Mikkeli and Juva, which are some 26 miles apart. This made it necessary for the Marshal to leave his comfortable quarters near Otava, a hunting cabin situated on a beautiful forest slope leading to a lake. He spent the last week of the war at Inkilä, a small manor house about half a mile from the new Operations site. There he received those alarming reports from the Viipuri sector and the generally depressing news from Ladoga-Karelia and Kuhmo. As if the gloomy military situation weren't enough of a burden, he and his associates at Inkilä came down with the flu. Refusing to remain in bed at a time of such crisis, the elderly warrior-statesman issued orders from an armchair, where he sat huddled in blankets.[22]

The weather, earlier an ally of the Finns, now favored their enemies. In a normal year the thaw would have arrived by

March, immobilizing even road traffic for several weeks. In contrast, in March of 1940 tanks clattered across the Gulf of Viipuri by the hundreds. The frozen lakes and marshes on the Karelian Isthmus also permitted the massing of forces in numbers never dreamed of in the most extreme plans of the General Staff. By the end of the fighting, on these two related fronts there were some 90 Soviet infantry regiments (the equivalent of 30 divisions, although not organized exactly that way) plus copious artillery and approximately 1,200 tanks and armored cars. The number of Russian aircraft over Finland reached a peak of 2,000 in a single day.[23]

The situation at the front was verging on the catastrophic. There were numerous places in Ladoga-Karelia where the Russians could probably break thru later in the spring. Far more ominous and urgent were the reports from the Kannas Army. On 9 March Marshal Mannerheim requested General Heinrichs to prepare an evaluation, preferably with the appraisals of the corps commanders attached. Henrichs could not contact General Laatikainen at the First Corps, but he quickly obtained the opinions of Generals Oesch, Öhquist, and Talvela. The report was immediately sent to GHQ, and the same evening the Commander-in-Chief forwarded it to the Cabinet in Helsinki. This "pessimistic report," as Defense Minister Niukkanen dubbed it, speaks for itself:[24]

*To the Commander-in-Chief:*
As commander of the Kannas Army I consider it my duty to report that the present state of the army is such that continued military operations can lead to nothing but further debilitation and fresh losses of territory. In support of my view I set forth the loss of personnel which has occurred and which is still going on. The battle strength of battalions is reported now generally to be below 250 men, with the aggregate daily casualties rising into the thousands. As a consequence of physical and spiritual exhaustion, the battle fitness of those who remain is not what it was when the war started. Considerable losses of officers further reduce the utility of these diminished units. Through enemy artillery fire our machine gun and antitank weapons have been demolished to such an extent that a noticable lack is generally apparent on critical

fronts. Since, in addition, events on the right wing have
made indispensable fresh expenditures of troops on un-
prepared terrain and at the expense of the present front,
the endurance of our defense has been critically weakened. Enemy air activity frequently makes the transfer
and maintenance of forces decidedly difficult. The commander of the Coastal Group, Lieutenant General Oesch,
has emphasized to me the scanty numbers and the moral
exhaustion of his forces, and does not seem to believe he
can succeed with them. The commander of the Second
Army Corps, Lieutenant General Öhquist, has expressed
the opinion that if no surprises take place, his present
front may last a week, but no longer, depending upon how
the personnel, especially the officer corps, is used. The
commander of the Third Army Corps, Major General Talvela, expressed his view by saying that everything is hanging by a thread.

*Lt. Gen. Heinrichs*[25]

The crux of the peril was the problem of manpower. With
progressively thinning forces facing constantly increasing
hordes of attackers, the only question was how much longer the
inevitable collapse could be delayed. Even the quality of the
last available replacements was not up to normal standards;
men in their mid-40s and high school boys—hastily trained,
and encountering overwhelming odds in their first battle experience—could not be expected to perform miracles.[26] If the ultimate disaster were to be avoided, either peace had to be
concluded momentarily, or large contingents of foreign troops
had to come to Finland's aid at once.

Marshal Mannerheim had to wrestle with both of those complex diplomatic alternatives at the same time as he was direct-
ing the last-ditch defense efforts from his blanketed chair at
Inkilä. Although nominally the concern of the Government
alone, questions of foreign policy were so intimately related to
the military situation that the Marshal's recommendations carried tremendous weight in the deliberations of the wartime
Government. For example: when the Council of State was considering a Soviet ultimatum concerning peace terms on 28 February, President Kallio declared that no decision should be
taken until Marshal Mannerheim's opinion was known; Prime

Minister Ryti and five others rushed to Otava that evening and returned the next morning with his views.[27]

As noted, considerable amounts of humanitarian aid and substantial quantities of munitions were sent to Finland from many countries. The largest shipments of arms were from France, England, and Sweden, in that order. Less significant amounts were sent by Italy, Hungary, Belgium, and the United States; and even smaller quantities came from Spain, Norway, and Denmark. Matching spare parts and ammunition calibers for so varied an arsenal proved to be a serious problem. Many of the shipments arrived too late to matter; for example, of the 44 modern Brewster B-239 fighter planes which constituted the major part of American aid, only five reached Finland before the ceasefire. Some of the weapons, like the Swedish antitank and antiaircraft guns, were excellent. However, many others were obsolescent, if not obsolete; some of the French artillery predated the First World War. As one Finnish officer summed it up: "European countries sent us the guns from their museums." Even with these limitations, and other related to distribution difficulties in the face of increasing Soviet air operations, the munitions problems were less critical in the final weeks than the shortage of trained manpower.[28]

The 8,000 men of the Swedish Volunteer Corps (and the 725 Norwegians attached to that unit) were the largest and most opportune contingent of foreigners to come to Finland's aid. The 300 members of the Finnish-American Legion completed their training in time to reach the front near Viipuri only on the 12th of March.[29] Others arrived too late to see any action; in this category were 800 Danes, 350 Hungarians, and the 420-man "Foreign Legion" ("Detachment Sisu") which represented 26 different nationalities. Other would-be volunteers never even reached Finland. In England, the incurable romantic, Kermit Roosevelt, son of former President Theodore Roosevelt, resigned his commission in the British Army to lead a British Volunteer Force of some 1,000 men. However, that self-styled crusader and most of his volunteers were still in England on 13 March; even the few who had already sailed for Finland arrived too late for combat.[30] It was obvious that if reinforcements were to arrive in militarily significant numbers, something more predictable than volunteer forces would be required.

Paradoxically, the question of whether to accept organized military units from abroad when they were actually offered was one of the most difficult dilemmas that faced Marshal Mannerheim and the three or four officials who determined wartime Finland's foreign policy.[31] From 5 February until the very last day of the war, they had to weigh the tantalizing possibility that an Anglo-French expeditionary force would dash to Finland's rescue like the U. S. Cavalry in a contemporary Hollywood epic—but without the guaranteed happy ending. For those five exciting weeks, little Finland may well have held the fate of Europe—if not the world—in her hands.

To understand this novel situation, it is necessary to consider a few facts which seem, at first glance, far removed from the Soviet-Finnish conflict. First, and most important, was the vital significance for Germany's economy of Sweden's iron ore deposits, the largest of which lay in the north. The industrialist Fritz Thyssen had advised Hitler that control of that ore meant victory or defeat for Germany.[32] Knowing this, the British and French Governments were naturally eager to seize any opportunity to interfere with the delivery of Swedish ore to their enemy. Due to geographic and strategic factors, the Allies' only feasible overland route to Sweden's northern ore field was via the railroad which terminated at the Norwegian port of Narvik —which was also their most practical route to Finland.

Secondly, the French were anxious to deflect from their own territory the Nazi war machine which had demonstrated the overwhelming power of its blitzkrieg in Poland. For them, the opening of new battlefronts in distant lands was an enticing prospect.[33]

Finally, it is pertinent that Swedish Government officials were acutely aware of all of the above-mentioned factors.

Accounts of the meeting of the Supreme War Council in Paris on 19 December 1939 make the relationship of this to the Finnish struggle apparent. There the French took the initiative in suggesting that the pro-Finnish sympathies of the Norwegian and Swedish peoples might provide an opportunity for the Allies to occupy the ore field under the guise of aiding the Finns. This cynical operation would wear the moral cloak of action in support of the League of Nations' resolution calling upon member states to assist Finland. Preliminary planning assumed more concrete form at another session of the Supreme War

Council on 5 February, when specific units, mostly British, were designated for the proposed expedition. On 8 February the British Chiefs of Staff recommended a force of 100,000 troops; however, since most of them would be needed to secure communications and to check the anticipated German counter-move into Sweden, only two or three brigades (7,000 to 10,500 men) would be available to help the Finns. By 18 February a timetable for the landings was devised; the initial units were to debark at Narvik on 20 March. To meet that landfall schedule, the first supply ships would have to depart British ports on 12 March—a date which was to prove fateful.[34]

Both the Finnish Minister in Paris, Harri Holma, and the Military Attaché, Colonel Paasonen, worked enthusiastically to foster Allied plans for the expeditionary force. Their initiative exceeded both the instructions and the desires of Foreign Minister Tanner, although probably not those of Marshal Manner-heim, whose contacts with Colonel Paasonen were more intimate than were the Foreign Minister's.[35]

At times the Allies were less than candid about their priorities, and they were amazingly inconsistent about the size of the force destined for the Finnish front and the timing of its arrival. On 24 February the British Minister in Helsinki, Gordon Vereker, told Tanner that 20–22,000 heavily armed troops could reach Finland by 15 April. Four days later he revised that estimate to 12–13,000, to arrive between 15–30 April. On 29 February the French Minister, Magny, informed Tanner that 20,000 men would be available to fight in Finland, "in time." On 3 March Vereker promised only 6,000 English troops, arriving during the first or second week of April. The next day the French military representative, Colonel Ganeval, told Prime Minister Ryti that 15,000 French and 18,000 English troops could reach Finland between 10–15 April. Finally, on 7 March Colonel Paasonen returned from Paris via London with the news that 57,500 French, British, and Polish troops would be sent, and the first echelon (15,500 men) could be in Finland by the end of March. No wonder that many Finns were skeptical about the proffered aid![36]

There was another consideration which seemed to be an insurmountable obstacle—neither the Norwegian nor the Swedish Governments was willing to risk Hitler's wrath by granting transit rights to regular army units of Germany's enemies. England and France made repeated but futile efforts to secure their permission, and the Finns also requested Sweden to acquiesce. To shift the onus for pressuring these Scandinavian states to jeopardize their neutrality, the Allies made a formal Finnish appeal a precondition for sending the expeditionary force. Because of their timetable for the landings in Norway, the British advised the Finnish Government on 24 February that the appeal should be sent not later than 5 March, a deadline which was later extended by one week.[37]

Had the Finns followed the Allies' urgings and requested their aid, the likely results are staggering to contemplate. Hitler and Stalin would probably have been driven into an actual military alliance against the Allies, altering the entire course of the Second World War. Finland and her Scandinavian neighbors would almost certainly have been plunged into the larger war immediately. This was one reason that the Finns did not request the Allied reinforcements which they needed so desperately. Opinion within the Government was divided, but Foreign Minister Tanner preferred any acceptable alternative to that prospect, and Marshal Mannerheim felt that the involvement of Norway and Sweden in the larger war would hurt the Finnish defense effort.[38]

While wrestling with the weighty question of Allied aid, the Finnish Government was concurrently involved in complex diplomatic maneuvers designed to open peace talks with the enemy. The stated objective of forming a new Cabinet on the second day of the war was to install a Government with which the Russians might negotiate. At the request of the Finnish Foreign Ministry, the United States Chargé in Moscow relayed this information to Soviet officials on 1 December. However, on 4 December, in response to a Finnish offer tendered by the Swedish Minister, Radio Moscow broadcast Molotov's chilling announcement that—because the Soviet Union recognized only Kuusinen's "People's Government"—there could be no further negotiations with another Finnish Government. On similar grounds, that same day Moscow rejected the League of Nations' invitation to discuss the conflict. Confronted with that intransigent attitude in the Kremlin, Finnish diplomacy concentrated for the remainder of the month on the procurement of munitions from friendly nations. It was not until the New Year that concerted efforts to initiate peace negotiations were renewed.[39]

From the very beginning, Finland found the seas of diplomacy very stormy. Pro-Finnish circles in Sweden lost their most influential voice on 2 December when Richard Sandler—unable to persuade the cautious Cabinet to join Finland in defense of the Åland Islands—tendered his resignation as Foreign Minister. His replacement, Christian Günther, was an uncompromising neutralist.[40] Although Sweden subsequently served as an intermediary, her role was not always that of the "honest broker."

Nor could the Finns look to Germany for support, as had been their inclination since the First World War. Although the German Minister, Wipert von Blücher, sympathized with the Finnish cause, he was completely frustrated by the unbending attitudes of his boss, Ribbentrop, and Hitler. In this era of the Nazi-Soviet Pact, Germany was "neutral on the Russian side." As State Secretary Weizsacker cabled Blücher on 2 January, "an unexposed flank toward the east means a great deal to us at the present time."[41] It meant so much that on 10 December Hitler agreed to permit German ships to provision Soviet submarines in the Gulf of Bothnia. Ironically, Stalin's subs sank at least two German ships trading with Finland and fired on others. Officials in Berlin refused to sell munitions to the Finns, and they even prevented the Italians from shipping arms via Stettin.[42] At the beginning of December, Ribbentrop instructed his diplomats in all Missions except Helsinki and Moscow to "refrain from any expression of sympathy for the Finnish position" and to express "sympathy with the Russian standpoint." By the end of the war, the unhappy Blücher reported that Germany had "incurred hatred in many circles" in Finland.[43]

In spite of Swedish timidity and German frigidity, Tanner's diplomacy eventually made some progress toward a settlement. Although he was not aware of it at the time, there was a hint as early as 7 January that the Kremlin was considering abandoning the illusionary Kuusinen "Government." On that day Count von der Schulenburg, the German Ambassador in Moscow, casually suggested to Molotov that the Finns would probably be ready to negotiate. As he noted in his report to Berlin,

"Molotov did not, interestingly enough, make an entirely negative reply but answered with the words that it was 'late, very
late' for this . . ."[44] It was three weeks before confirmation of this
essential prerequisite to peace talks was received in Helsinki.
On 29 January Molotov secretly informed the Finnish Government, via Stockholm, that the Soviet Union did not object in
principle to concluding an agreement with the Government of
Ryti and Tanner. The Foreign Commissar also asked what
concessions the Finns were willing to make, noting that Soviet
requirements were greater now that blood had been spilled
thru no fault of the U.S.S.R. Prime Minister Ryti and Ministers
Tanner and Paasikivi were the only Finns who knew about
Molotov's overture, and they alone decided what response to
make. Their reply was sent via the same route, since the Soviet
Government desired to link the Swedish Government to the
negotiations. Tanner suggested that they take the position at
which the pre-war talks had terminated as a point of departure,
and he indicated willingness to grant additional concessions
for the security of Leningrad and the neutralization of the Gulf
of Finland. Territorial adjustments should be in the form of
exchanges, and compensation must be paid for private property in the ceded areas.[45]

Meanwhile, a bizarre channel of communications between
the belligerents was being gingerly explored. On New Year's
Day Mrs. Hella Wuolijoki, an eccentric left-wing Finnish play-
wright, wrote to Tanner offering to visit her old friend,
Madame Kollontay, the Soviet Minister in Stockholm, to enlist
her aid in bringing about peace talks. Aleksandra Kollontay,
now 67, had been a "progressive" feminist and fanatic revolu-
tionist since the 1890s. Outside communist circles, she was best
known as an apostle of "free love," whose earlier beauty en-
hanced the legends which surrounded her. With understandable misgivings, Tanner agreed to let those two volatile and
colorful women informally discuss the fate of Finland. He authorized Mrs. Wuolijoki to visit her friend to try to ascertain
Soviet war aims and to solicit Mme. Kollontay's advice for
reaching a settlement. On 10 January the playwright-diplomat
departed for Stockholm to conspire with the feminist-diplomat.
For the next three weeks, these incredible old women met secretly in the Grand Hotel almost daily, and—even more incredi-

bly—they actually succeeded in initiating peace negotiations.[46]

Molotov sent two agents, Yartsev and Grauer, to Stockholm, apparently to appraise the seriousness of Mrs. Wuolijoki's mission. They first contacted her on 21 January, but they had no authority to begin negotiations. Nevertheless, the mere fact that they were sent from Moscow encouraged the Swedish Foreign Ministry on 25 January to make another official offer to mediate. It was in reply to this initiative that Molotov forwarded his ice-breaking statement of 29 January. From this point forward, the official and unofficial channels converged in Stockholm. Mrs. Wuolijoki, undoubtedly enjoying her real-life drama to the utmost, remained a go-between for Tanner and Mme. Kollontay, but the more formal route Molotov-Kollontay-Günther-Tanner was also open.[47]

At the suggestion of Mrs. Wuolijoki and Erkko, the former Foreign Minister now serving as Chargé d'Affaires *ad interim* in Sweden, Tanner very furtively departed for Stockholm on 4 February to meet Mme. Kollontay. Before his scheduled rendezvous with her, Tanner called on Foreign Minister Günther in the morning. He informed his Swedish counterpart that on that very day, 5 February, the Supreme War Council was meeting in Paris to consider sending an expeditionary force to Finland. This was disturbing news to Günther, who immediately agreed with Tanner's view that it was the least desirable of the three alternatives open to the Finns. The best solution would be a negotiated peace; second would be military assistance from Sweden alone, which would not involve Scandinavia in the major war. Tanner noted that Finland would need 30,000 regular troops within four to six weeks. Thus the Finns initiated the policy of employing the Allied offer of aid as a diplomatic weapon—both to pressure Sweden for assistance and to induce Russia to accept a compromise peace. While Prime Minister Chamberlain and Premier Daladier were plotting to use Finland for their own ends, some crafty Finns were secretly turning the tables on them. This ploy, enthusiastically endorsed by Prime Minister Ryti and Marshal Mannerheim as their only trump, was played out masterfully until the very end. In the case of the Swedes, it was somewhat blunted by their inside knowledge that the Kuusinen "Government" was being jettisoned and that Finland would at least retain its independence.[48] In the case of the Russians, it obviously proved effective, as events were to show. Tanner's success in concealing his negotiations with the Russians from the Allies (until he was ready to tell them) is evident from their earnest and sustained preparations for sending the expeditionary force.

After leaving Günther with much to think about, Tanner proceeded—via a back staircase—to Mrs. Wuolijoki's hotel room for his clandestine interview with Mme. Kollontay. The meeting had been arranged because the recently launched negotiations seemed on the verge of collapsing. Since she received word that the Kremlin was insisting on acquiring Hanko Cape, Mme. Kollontay considered the Finnish reply to Molotov's message of 29 January unsatisfactory; accordingly, she forwarded it "for information only." Sympathizing with the Finns, she was anxious that the peace efforts should continue. In searching for a solution to the impasse over Hanko, Tanner finally ventured—as a strictly personal, unofficial suggestion—that Finland might cede an island at the mouth of the Gulf of Finland in exchange for the Repola and Porajärvi areas. The Soviet Minister agreed to forward the proposal to Moscow, and she asked Tanner to remain in Stockholm another day for the answer. When they met the next afternoon, she sadly read a telegram rejecting Tanner's offer as insufficient basis for negotiations. Not wishing to sever this fragile connection, yet not authorized to make additional proposals, Tanner asked Mme. Kollontay to inform her superiors of those views and to request Moscow's proposals. On that inconclusive note, he returned to Helsinki.[49]

On 8 February Molotov inquired, via Sweden, what island Tanner had in mind. After a deliberate delay in order to consider alternative policies, Tanner replied on 12 February that Jussarö might be ceded. That same day he again departed for Stockholm in order to press for Swedish aid. While at Turku enroute, he learned of the Kremlin's reply to his request for its proposals. Stalin's new terms, delivered while the Mannerheim Line was still holding at Summa, were shocking: in addition to Hanko, the entire Karelian Isthmus and the northeastern shore of Lake Ladoga were to be ceded.[50]

On 13 February Tanner tried in vain to persuade Foreign Minister Günther, Prime Minister Hansson, and Defense Minister Sköld to release forces from the Swedish Army for the Finnish front. The primary reason given for refusing such aid was the fear that it would provoke a German attack on Sweden; Günther asserted that Germany had warned Sweden of this. In the light of the records of the German Foreign Ministry captured in 1945, the statement appears to have been false. During conversations with the Swedish explorer Sven Hedin on 16 October 1939 and 4 March 1940, Hitler indicated that Germany would not intervene if Sweden fought Russia; he merely warned that he would take action if England obtained a foothold in Scandinavia. Tanner also reported that Hermann Göring gave similar assurances to the Swedish Count Rosen on 6 December 1939. In any case, that evening Tanner returned empty handed to Helsinki, where he heard the alarming news of the breakthru at Lähde.[51]

The threat of Swedish intervention may still have had a restraining influence on the Soviet leaders, as long as they continued to believe in that possibility. However, on 16 February a Swedish paper headlined Tanner's secret visit and the Government's refusal of his request for aid, whereupon Hansson publicly confirmed the reports. The resulting controversy within the country, as well as in the foreign press, prompted King Gustaf V to issue a statement on 19 February in defense of Hansson's policy. Although the King's message was more tactful than the Prime Minister's, it nevertheless ended all hope of obtaining substantial military aid from Sweden[52]—a fact which was observed with interest in Moscow. It also narrowed Finnish choices to two alternatives—peace or Allied intervention.

On 21 February Tanner again requested Swedish mediation, in order to escape the risky consequences of the latter alternative. Günther, knowing what the Allied expeditionary force might mean for Sweden, eagerly agreed. He relayed Tanner's suggestion that Finnish and Soviet representatives meet in Stockholm to Mme. Kollontay and also to the Swedish Minister in Moscow. Marshal Mannerheim also favored negotiations at this time, because of the dangerous situation on the Isthmus and the uncertainties and perils of Allied aid.[53]

On 23 February Molotov replied, via Sweden, listing "minimal" conditions for initiating peace talks; in addition to all earlier demands, the cession of Viipuri and Sortavala was now specifically mentioned, and a new term was a defensive union of the U.S.S.R., Finland, and Estonia for the protection of the Gulf of Finland. Tanner may well have been correct in asserting that these harsher terms were the result of the recent Swedish actions; he later told Prime Minister Hansson that his press release, along with the King's statement, had cost Finland both Viipuri and Sortavala. It is little wonder that the Council of State, which had been divided over the wisdom of yielding even Hanko, rejected these terms on 25 February. Instead, the Council decided to send Tanner back to Stockholm for further discussions with both the Swedish Cabinet and Mme. Kollontay.[54]

Tanner's third trip to Sweden was not much more fruitful than his earlier ones. On 27 February General Rappe, Chief of the Swedish General Staff, called at his hotel to express his private opinion—which he felt was widely shared—that Sweden should officially join the war against Russia. Unfortunately for the Finns, the Prime Minister's views were quite different. The most that the Government was prepared to venture was to permit 16,000 volunteers from the armed forces to serve in Finland—if that many were willing. In the discussions in the Foreign Relations Committee of the Riksdag, only former Foreign Minister Sandler had advocated greater aid.[55]

In a private conversation with Hansson, Tanner also raised the question of transit rights for an Allied expeditionary force. The answer was again no, and—according to Tanner—the Prime Minister now added that, should England and France try to send such a force thru without permission, Sweden would enter the war on Russia's side. He advised the Finns to make peace, even on Molotov's harsh terms, promising Swedish financial assistance for reconstruction. He also agreed to take under consideration Tanner's suggestion for a postwar defense pact involving Sweden, Finland, and Norway.[56]

Before returning to Helsinki that day, Tanner had a brief and uneventful meeting with Mme. Kollontay in a private residence. She expressed her personal regret at the new peace terms, and Tanner asked her to inform Moscow that it would require time to secure Parliamentary support before the Government could reply to them.[57]

At 11 A.M. on 28 February, Mme. Kollontay delivered to Gün-

ther a message from Moscow demanding a reply to the latest
Soviet offer within 48 hours. Tanner and Ryti were advised of
this by phone at 2 P.M. An hour later the Council of State met
to discuss this ultimatum and the possible alternatives to accepting Soviet terms; the members were divided on what action
to take. It was at this critical juncture that President Kallio
decided that the decision should be deferred until Marshal
Mannerheim's views could be obtained. That same day Prime
Minister Ryti, four other Ministers, and General Walden visited
GHQ, where they conferred with the Marshal and those generals who were on hand. At Marshal Mannerheim's request, the
generals presented their views to the Governmental delegation.
To his admitted surprise, all but one favored continuing the
battle. During a short recess—while the Ministers were absent
—the Commander-in-Chief managed to change the minds of
his overly confident generals. He then informed the delegation
that he and the generals were unanimously agreed that it was
necessary to conclude peace without delay in order to forestall
a military catastrophe.[58]

All of the Ministers who visited GHQ returned on 29 February convinced that the Soviet terms must be accepted, but of the
other Cabinet members, Education Minister Hannula and Defense Minister Niukkanen were still opposed. That evening,
the Foreign Relations Committee of the Parliament supported
the decision taken by the majority of the Cabinet, with only
Representative Urho Kekkonen strongly opposed. The party
groups within the Parliament met in caucus, and finally a joint
meeting convened at 9 P.M., when most of those present approved the Cabinet's decision. Around midnight the Cabinet
agreed on the language of the reply to Molotov, in which the
Soviet terms were accepted "in principle." The text was sent to
Erkko in Stockholm, with orders not to deliver it until he received further instructions.[59]

That decision, reached so hesitatingly and painfully, was immediately challenged so effectively that another week was lost
before it was implemented. Tanner had informed the British
Minister of the Soviet ultimatum on 29 February, and London
and Paris went to work with unusual speed to block the anticipated negotiations. During the night of 29 February-1
March word was received that Premier Daladier had upped the

ante by offering larger forces and promising their arrival by the end of March. The British also reported urgent preparations for dispatching the expeditionary force, while warning that future aid would be cancelled if negotiations with the Soviets continued.[60]

An hour and a half before Molotov's deadline for a reply, the Cabinet met to reconsider its stand in view of these developments. No one was willing on 1 March to flatly accept the Soviet terms, as most had been a few hours earlier. Only fifteen minutes before the deadline, Tanner phoned Erkko the Cabinet's decision: the reply he was holding should not be sent; instead, he was to ask Molotov for further particulars about the frontier he proposed and to raise the question of compensation for areas ceded.[61]

This reply was designed to purchase time in which to seek clarification of Allied intentions. Cables were sent to London and Paris, asking if at least 50,000 men could arrive by the end of March, requesting 100 bombers with crews at once, and inquiring about transit rights. Daladier readily agreed to the Finnish requests, even though he could hardly have kept his promises; the British replied more guardedly. The bombers would be sent the moment Finland formally asked for Allied aid.[62]

On 2 March England and France approached Sweden and Norway again for transit privileges, encountering emphatic refusals. This Allied démarche sparked an angry outburst by Günther, directed at Erkko. Among other indiscretions, he informed the Finnish Chargé that, if Sweden became involved in the major war because of the Allied expedition, the Swedes would resent their country becoming a battlefield for the sake of Viipuri and Sortavala, which Finland could liberate in the future anyway! Due to either frayed nerves or poor judgment, Günther was also very imprudent in dealing with the British Minister, Mr. Mallet. He implied that England and France were more interested in their own war then in helping the Finns— a truth better left unsaid. When Mallet countered with the statement that the Allied war effort was of vital interest to Sweden, Günther replied with amazing frankness that he did not consider it in Sweden's interest that Germany should be utterly defeated![63]

Meanwhile, the fragile line to the Kremlin was short-circuited in Stockholm. Because Mme. Kollontay and Günther believed that the Finnish reply would be regarded in Moscow as a final rejection of Russian terms, they suggested that a sentence be added accepting the Soviet proposals "in principle." As that would have bound the Finns to the entire Soviet program, Tanner did not agree to the addition. Therefore, Günther did not forward the reply to Moscow, a fact which he concealed from Tanner for two days, until the Finnish Foreign Minister —worried that there had been no further word from the Russians—asked him pointblank if the message had been sent. However, on their own initiative, Günther and Mme. Kollontay had queried Molotov about easier terms. Marshal Mannerheim was so displeased with the way Sweden handled the negotiations in her own interest that he suggested to Prime Minister Ryti that a disinterested country (such as the United States) might serve as a better intermediary.[64]

On 3 March Tanner authorized Günther to tell Molotov that, if the cities of Viipuri and Sortavala were deleted, Finland would accept all other Soviet demands. That message was relayed to Moscow the same day.

There was no word from Moscow on 4 March. Tensions were mounting in Helsinki, Viipuri, and Otava, as well as in Stockholm, London, and Paris. The fifth was a day of difficult decisions for the Finnish Government; that was the date the Allies had set as the deadline for requesting their military assistance. In addition to the serious diplomatic complications involved, both Marshal Mannerheim and Tanner believed the Allied aid would be too little and too late.

The Council of State, meeting in the morning, decided that Günther should be asked to tell Molotov that his terms were accepted, and that he should request an immediate armistice. If Moscow rejected this proposal, there would be no choice but to ask for the Allied expedition. When the meeting adjourned, Tanner phoned Günther, who had been trying to contact him. Molotov's reply to the message of 3 March had just been received; the Soviet Government insisted on annexing Viipuri and Sortavala. Furthermore, Molotov warned that the Red Army was demanding permission to continue its advance; if the terms were not accepted within a few days, the demands would increase. He also threatened to conclude a final treaty with Kuusinen.

The Finnish acceptance of Molotov's terms was delivered to Mme. Kollontay just before noon. Late in the afternoon Tanner informed both the British and French Ministers that the Finnish Government was awaiting a decisive answer from Moscow. If it was negative, they would present their formal request for Allied assistance. The next day the British and French Ministers advised Ryti that the deadline for that request might be postponed until 12 March.

Early on 6 March the Soviet reply was received in Stockholm and telephoned to Helsinki. Molotov announced that his Government was ready to open peace negotiations in Moscow, but the requested armistice was rejected. Tanner viewed this as an attempt to induce the Allies to abandon Finland, while leaving the Red Army a free hand to attack. Nevertheless, the vast majority of the Cabinet and the Foreign Relations Committee agreed that a delegation should be sent to Moscow at once. That evening Prime Minister Ryti, Väinö Voionmaa (Chairman of the Foreign Relations Committee), Minister Paasikivi, and General Walden departed in secret for Stockholm, where a special plane flew them on to Moscow on 7 March. Meanwhile, as a kind of disaster insurance, the Government officially requested (and subsequently received) an extension to 12 March of the deadline for requesting Allied aid.[65]

At this timely juncture, on 7 March, Secretary of State Cordell Hull instructed Ambassador Steinhardt to arrange an immediate interview with Molotov to inform him that the American public would be "deeply impressed were the Soviet Government to take a generous attitude towards Finland." Steinhardt was also permitted to intimate that Soviet-American trade might depend upon "the degree of moderation and generosity arrived at in the Finnish settlement." The next day the U.S. Ambassador conferred for an hour and a half with the Foreign Commissar, who, he reported, "was effusively cordial and expressed great appreciation for the friendly interest now and heretofore shown by the President and the United States Government in the restoration of peace between Finland and the Soviet Union."[66]

Despite the desire for secrecy, rumors of the negotiations

were widespread. On 8 March Tanner permitted the Finnish press to hint at peace moves for the first time, in order to prepare the public for the shock in store for it. At 7 o'clock that evening, the first meeting of the negotiators was held in the Kremlin, but due to communications delays, word of this did not reach Helsinki until 3:30 P.M. on the ninth. In the meantime, Marshal Mannerheim was growing more and more restless. On 7 March he confided to Tanner his fears that the Soviet Government wanted to prolong the negotiations, now that the Red Army was advancing. The next day he suggested that the appeal for Allied aid be made simultaneously with the Moscow peace talks—an idea which Tanner rejected on the grounds that the former measure would certainly disrupt the latter.[67]

When the negotiations finally began, the Finnish delegation found itself confronted by the dour Molotov, backed by Zhdanov and Brigade Commander A. M. Vasilevski. There was no smiling Stalin present to make a magnanimous gesture, as Mme. Kollontay and Günther had predicted. Indeed, had the Swedish Foreign Minister been able to guess the outcome of that meeting, he might have been less eager to arrange it. In addition to all previous territorial demands, Molotov now insisted on a large area surrounding Salla—which was significant in relation to Soviet access to Sweden. This was spelled out in a further demand that the Finns build a railway from the Kemijärvi railhead to the border near Salla, to link up with one the Soviets would construct from the Murmansk Railroad near Kandalaksha; this would provide the shortest route between the U.S.S.R. and Sweden. It was no accident that these new requirements were not mentioned earlier, when communications were passing thru Günther's hands. Predictably but belatedly, when Tanner informed Günther of the demand for Salla on 9 March, the Swedish Foreign Minister protested to Molotov thru Mme. Kollontay, and he also urged Tanner to stick to the earlier terms. The only consolation to the Finns was that the previously proposed defense pact with the Soviet Union and Estonia was not mentioned.[68]

When the Cabinet met in the evening of 9 March to consider the latest Soviet demands, Ministers Hannula and Niukkanen favored appealing to the Allies rather than signing so harsh a treaty. At this point, Tanner read aloud the "pessimistic report" which Marshal Mannerheim had just forwarded from GHQ. The Marshal offered his own "categorical advice" to conclude peace before the front collapsed. His view was decisive; President Kallio admitted a change of mind when he heard that report on the military situation. After midnight it was finally decided, with Hannula and Niukkanen still opposed, to authorize the delegates in Moscow to use their own discretion about the terms, provided they were in unanimous agreement.[69]

The final moments were at hand. The Allies, informed by Tanner on 9 March that negotiations were under way in Moscow, continued to press the Finns to request their aid. However, in spite of the new Soviet demands which seemed aimed at Sweden, Günther persisted in refusing transit rights. At this late date, neither Marshal Mannerheim nor Tanner considered the proposed Allied expedition militarily significant, but both valued it for its diplomatic impact on the Kremlin.[70]

With the situation at the Gulf of Viipuri growing more menacing by the day, the prolonged stress began to affect the nerves and dispositions of those who carried the heaviest burdens of responsibility. Tanner mentioned Ryti's ill-humor as early as 5 March, while noting his own loss of sleep. The ailing Marshal was also affected; he called the corps commanders of the Kannas Army daily to impress them with the need to hold on at all costs. General Heinrichs considered his frequent calls to the Prime Minister and the Foreign Minister a sign of restlessness. Between 10 and 12 March the Marshal phoned Tanner at least seven times—mainly to ask for news from Moscow or to offer suggestions concerning the negotiations.[71]

On the morning of 11 March the report of the second Kremlin conference, held the previous afternoon, reached Helsinki. The same Soviet negotiators stuck rigidly to their same demands, and they refused to consider an armistice until their terms were accepted. The Finnish delegates, therefore, asked their Government for a prompt decision. At a time when daily Finnish casualties numbered in the thousands, it took twelve hours for this cable to reach Helsinki via Stockholm.[72]

Early that morning the Cabinet concurred with Tanner's proposal that the Soviet terms be accepted, and shortly afterwards the Foreign Relations Committee of the Parliament voted 13–4 in favor of that course. Within four hours, that news was known

to a Swedish news bureau in Stockholm, and—in spite of Tanner's efforts to prevent it—it appeared in the afternoon papers.
This was Sweden's final serious disservice to Finland during
the war; the Russian negotiators used these reports to their
advantage at that day's bargaining session.[73]

Earlier the same day, Marshal Mannerheim called Tanner to
suggest that certain areas in the far north might be offered in
order to retain Hanko and part of the southeastern territory the
Soviets were demanding. To Tanner's remark that this would
irritate Norway and Sweden, he replied that those countries
had also thought of their own interests. According to Tanner,
the area suggested was the so-called "heel" in the Petsamo
district. According to the version recently published by Aaro
Pakaslahti, then Chief of the Political Bureau of the Foreign
Ministry, the Marshal proposed ceding a land corridor across
Finland to Sweden, in order to assure Swedish concern for the
fate of postwar Finland. Later in the day, he reportedly
changed his mind because such a corridor would complicate
Finnish defense problems. When a second cable was sent to the
delegates in Moscow cancelling the corridor proposal, Tanner
added to it the idea of bartering parts of Lapland for some of
the southern areas. Neither cable reached Moscow in time to
affect the negotiations.[74] If Pakaslahti is correct, this is further
evidence that Marshal Mannerheim was under exceptional
stress—it was certainly not in character for him to offer a serious proposal before weighing all of its ramifications.

At 6 P.M. on 11 March another meeting took place in the
Kremlin. The most important news from this session, known in
Helsinki at 5:25 the following morning, was that the Soviets
would present their final draft of the treaty on 12 March. The
Finnish delegation requested full powers to sign.[75]

The Cabinet met in the morning to face the final bitter decision. At this late hour, the lure of the Allied expedition still
dangled before them. Troop ships were actually loading in British harbors, and, late in the previous evening, both Chamberlain and Daladier publicly announced their readiness to send
assistance—if the Finnish Government requested it. The two
diehards, Hannula and Niukkanen, still insisted that the Allied
offer should be accepted. However, the majority supported Tanner's recommendation that the treaty be signed at once, and

President Kallio reluctantly agreed to sign the credentials to be cabled to Moscow. On signing them, the elderly President paraphrased an Old Testament verse (Zechariah 11:17), saying "May the hand wither which is forced to sign such a paper." Five months later his right arm was paralyzed by a stroke, and within the year he was dead. The transmission of the credentials was followed by another period of suspenseful waiting.[76]

At 4 P.M. Tanner learned that Radio Moscow had announced the signing of the peace treaty, but no official word was received on the twelfth. In the evening the British Minister called on Tanner to advise him, in a confidence not to be disclosed to the Norwegian or Swedish Governments, that the expedition would be sent *without* their consent, if the Finns would publicly request it.[77]

There still being no official word from Moscow, Tanner waited up all night to learn the outcome of his three months' search for peace. At 2:30 A.M. on 13 March, he received from Stockholm the text of a protocol to the treaty which defined the provisions for the ceasefire and troop withdrawals. As the ceasefire was scheduled to take effect in eight and a half hours, this important text was urgently transmitted to GHQ. Finally, at 6 A.M., a cable arrived confirming that the treaty had become effective on the previous evening.[78] The long ordeal of agonizing indecision was over; the race against total disaster had been won.

*In this way weep bearded heroes;*
*This the hero cry of anguish.*
**RUNE VII**

CHAPTER VIII

# Entr'Acte

THE CEASEFIRE TOOK EFFECT ON 13 MARCH AT NOON, LENIN-grad time (11 A.M. Finnish time). The fierce battle for the remains of Viipuri continued to the last moment, but elsewhere on the Karelian Isthmus and the Gulf of Viipuri the guns began to quiet down during the final hour. The dead-tired troops holding that hundred-mile front experienced a sense of relief unknown since the relentless Soviet offensive began six long weeks before. Thoughts turned again to the wives and sweethearts awaiting their homecoming. Suddenly, at 10:45 by Finnish watches, all hell broke loose as a terrific artillery barrage pounded the entire length and depth of the line. The Russians kept up this senseless slaughter for the full remaining quarter hour.[1] In view of the fact that the new border was nowhere dependent upon the location of the front at the time of the ceasefire, this was sheer wanton murder.

This pointless killing was not confined to the Isthmus. In the Salla sector, the Russians directed an especially heavy barrage against the Swedish Volunteer Force, which suffered its worst casualties on that last morning.[2]

At Löytöjärvi, on the Kuhmo front, heavy Soviet artillery fire commenced at 7:30 A.M. and continued until the ceasefire. Here the Finnish artillery responded, breaking up a tank-supported attack with serious losses in the final hours.[3] At least one Soviet author boasted of this barbarism, noting that, in the Kuhmo sector:

The morning of 13 March began unusually. The radio brought news of peace, and in the sky, one after another appeared our bombers, flying the last "presents" to the White Finns.

Such a bombardment will never be forgotten . . . The bomb explosions were accompanied by artillery shelling, the fire of machine guns, rifles, and automatics. Twelve o'clock . . . peace.[4]

Most of the nation's leaders, army and civilian alike, realized that the military situation was so desperate that a collapse was imminent if the peace treaty were not signed. However, the general public and the lower echelons of the army, who were less informed, were not prepared to face the inevitable. When news of the peace filtered down to the far-flung fronts early in the morning, the reaction was one of shock. Hours later, as the harsh terms became known, this changed to bitterness and dejection—especially among those troops in the northern wilds who believed that they were winning the war. At the Aittojoki River, for example, entries in the war diaries of Colonel Pajari's units read:

. . . [the ceasefire] came as a flash from the sky. All, from men to officers, like struck on the head with a club. The whole day passed in a kind of a stupor . . .

. . . Later in the day, as the changing of the border became known . . . the spirits of the battalion sank low, as we had to cede our battlegrounds so full of memories . . .

. . . Everybody in a miserable mood after conditions became known . . .[5]

At Inkilä, where Marshal Mannerheim and his intimate staff were now preoccupied with drafting the final Order of the Day to thank the nation and the battered but unbowed Army for their heroic sacrifices, the atmosphere was heavy with misery. The Marshal still had the flu, and the entire entourage was suffering with severe head colds. Understandably, they were all in a terrible humor.[6]

At noon, Foreign Minister Tanner announced the terms of the treaty on the radio and explained to a stunned nation why it was necessary to purchase peace at so high a price. There was bitterness in his reference to Norway and Sweden, who "categorically refused" passage to French and English troops "because of their attitude of strict neutrality." He continued "... It is not our fault if others could not or did not wish to help us . . ."[7]

Many papers framed the peace terms in black, and flags were everywhere flown at half-mast. Tears flowed freely on the streets of Helsinki and were fought back with clenched teeth in the army. And no wonder! Finland had to cede approximately 16,100 square miles of territory, an area slightly larger than Switzerland; most of the cession was in long-inhabited areas of the southeast, where the new boundary was roughly the same as that defined by the Treaty of Nystad in 1721. In addition to the cities of Viipuri, Sortavala, and Käkisalmi, the Finns lost many prosperous rural communes, valuable forest, important industrial facilities such as the large Rouhiala power plant and the Enso and Waldhof factories, and the outlet of the Saimaa Canal which was important to the economy of the entire lake district of southeastern Finland.[8]

The most tragic consequence of the treaty was that some 420,000 Finns lost their homes. As 99% of these people were unwilling to live under Russian domination, a mass migration took place. Those whose homes were in the combat zones had already been evacuated, but there remained about 200,000 who had to be moved within twelve days. All available trains and buses were mobilized for this task; even troop movements— other than marches out of the ceded areas—had to wait until the civilians, and as much of their personal property as possible, could be removed. Even so, much property had to be left behind and hundreds of cattle slaughtered. As new homes and livelihood had to be found for more than ten percent of the total population, the Government initiated a vast land resettlement program in June.[9]

The Army had to evacuate the ceded areas at the rate of at least seven kilometers (four and one-half miles) per day. Because Marshal Mannerheim regarded this in the light of a funeral procession, he refused permission for foreign correspondents to witness this distressing and humiliating event.[10]

The final article of the peace treaty specified that ratification

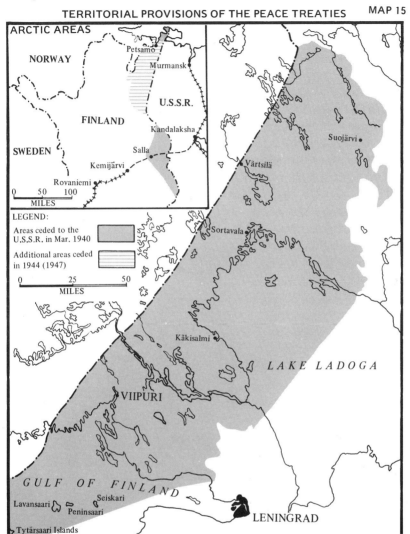

TERRITORIAL PROVISIONS OF THE PEACE TREATIES    MAP 15

ARCTIC AREAS

NORWAY
Petsamo
Murmansk
U.S.S.R.
FINLAND
Kandalaksha
Suojärvi
SWEDEN
Salla
Värtsilä
Kemijärvi
Rovaniemi
0    50    100
MILES

LEGEND:
Areas ceded to the U.S.S.R. in Mar. 1940
Additional areas ceded in 1944 (1947)
0    25    50
MILES

Sortavala

Käkisalmi

LAKE LADOGA

VIIPURI

GULF OF FINLAND
Seiskari
Lavansaari
Peninsaari
Tytärsaari Islands
LENINGRAD

must take place in Moscow within ten days. Echoing the war-time Cabinet debates, the Parliament, meeting on 15 March, was divided on the wisdom of accepting the peace terms. In the balloting, there were 145 votes for ratification, three against it, and nine abstentions. Forty-two members were absent. On 20 March the instruments of ratification were exchanged in Moscow; the war that had never been declared was now formally terminated.[11]

Among other unfinished business was the exchange of war

prisoners, which was not completed until 25 May. By then, some 800 Finnish prisoners were released; approximately 50 others did not return from the Soviet Union. Their treatment had varied from reasonably decent to very harsh, and it generally entailed deficient diet, prolonged and repeated interrogations, and intimidation.[12]

However, the ordeals of the Finnish prisoners were minor, indeed, when compared to the reported fate of the Russian prisoners upon their repatriation. Although absolute proof may never be established, there is considerable evidence that every one of some 5,000 Soviet troops released by the Finns was summarily shot by the NKVD. A former Red Army correspondent, Soloviev, was one person who heard and believed this report. It is all the more credible in view of Svetlana Alliluyeva's confirmation of Stalin's attitude that all POWs were traitors; this even drove his own son to suicide in a German prison camp during the Second World War. She also stated that Beria organized the massacre of returned POWs after that war. Vyacheslav P. Artemiev, a former regimental commander (Lt. Col.) in the Red Army, stated that in 1940 an acquaintance, Major G. B____ of the NKVD, told him about the sub rosa execution of all prisoners returning from Finland. According to him, the interrogations and shootings took place at two special camps in solitary surroundings not far from Petrozavodsk and Kandalaksha.[13] Apparently, the last victims of the Winter War were those Russians murdered by their own Government.

For the Soviet leadership, one final embarrassment was explaining the demise of the Kuusinen "Government." As late as 8 March, *Komsomol'skaya Pravda* reprinted a long article by that shadow ruler in which he boasted that the "bankrupt government of Mannerheim, Ryti, and Tanner is on its way to the bottom. Its days are numbered." On 10 March, just two days before the peace treaty was signed, an editorial in *Krasnaya Zvezda* noted the "exceptionally great significance" of the treaties of mutual assistance between the U.S.S.R. and the Baltic-shore countries and the "Finnish Democratic Republic." What were Soviet readers to make of the treaty now concluded with the "Mannerheim-Tanner gang"?

They had only to wait until 29 March, when Molotov told them what to think in his speech before the Supreme Soviet (which was printed in all major papers the next day). The Foreign Commissar stated tersely:

> ... In the beginning of February the Finns made practical moves for the termination of the war. . . . Before deciding this issue we approached the People's Government of Finland for their opinion on this question. The People's Government expressed the view that in order to put an end to the bloodshed and to ameliorate the condition of the Finnish people, a proposal to terminate the war should be welcomed. . . .
>
> The results of the agreement to terminate hostilities and establish peace are contained in the peace treaty signed on March 12. In this connection the question arose of the People's Government dissolving itself, which it did. . . .[14]

A face-saving device, for Stalin and Kuusinen alike, was the creation on 31 March 1940 of the nominally independent Karelo-Finnish Soviet Socialist Republic, which united most of the ceded areas north of the Karelian Isthmus with the former Karelian Autonomous Soviet Socialist Republic. Otto Kuusinen became its "President," a post he held until this Union Republic was downgraded to autonomous status (A.S.S.R.) again in 1956.[15]

Since the Red Army appeared on the verge of total victory in March, one may ask why Stalin settled for a compromise peace with an independent Finland, thereby scuttling his puppet "Finnish People's Government." His concern that the immense forces deployed in Finland might become bogged down by the spring thaw has been noted. Probably more decisive was the danger that the Anglo-French expeditionary force would involve the Soviet Union in the "capitalistic war" of the Great Powers. The official Soviet history of the war attributes the peace treaty to this very serious threat.[16]

Stalin was well aware of Allied plans and intentions. On 22 February his Ambassador in London, Ivan Maiski, handed the Soviet peace terms to the Under Secretary of the British Foreign Office, R. A. Butler, for transmission to Finland. Two days later, on instruction from Foreign Secretary Halifax, Butler informed Maiski that his Government considered it impossible to forward such terms. As the Soviet Ambassador wrote, this indicated to him that the Chamberlain Government wished to keep its hands free to attack the U.S.S.R. That very day, a Member of Parliament was quoted in *The Times* urging Anglo-French intervention. By 5 March that moderate paper was even considering the possibility of war with Russia in its editorial. The even more militant designs of the French Government were also known in Moscow. In March Stalin specifically mentioned the potential danger of French reinforcements in exhorting Meretskov to capture Viipuri rapidly.[17]

Finally, it is likely that Stalin was confident that the strategic gains extracted by the treaty would facilitate the complete annexation of Finland at a later date—as was the case with the three tiny Baltic countries.

The significant results of those 105 days of bloody fighting were mostly negative for the supposed victor. Precise Soviet casualties may never be known, but they were unquestionably enormous. The truth lies somewhere between Molotov's admission of 48,745 dead (and 158, 863 wounded) and the figure of one million dead ascribed to Khrushchev. The most reliable Finnish source estimates Russian losses at 175,000-200,000 dead and two-three hundred thousand wounded. The official Soviet history merely acknowledges that their casualties were "excessive" and avoidable.[18]

Another "casualty" was the prestige of the Red Army, which suffered even more than the facts merited. The fiascoes of the early phase, such as the Suomussalmi-Raate campaign, received more world-wide attention than the successes of the later stages. A semi-professional British magazine, *The Fighting Forces,* proclaimed in February 1940 that "the vaunted worth of the Russian Army has proved to be a myth," and it continued to deprecate the Red Army in its April issue.[19] Even statesmen who should have had better sources of information than the sensational press ridiculed the "giant with feet of clay." Many German staff officers held that common opinion, which was apparently shared by the Chief of the Army General Staff, General Halder. The following entry is found in his "Journal" for 16 January 1941:

*Russian Armaments:* Obsolete matériel; what is new is copied from foreign nations. Command mechanical! Lack intellectual caliber.[20]

However, it seems that Hitler—contrary to a popular misconception—*did not* miscalculate Soviet strength because of the Winter War. In a letter to Mussolini on 8 March 1940, the German Führer correctly noted:

Russia . . . never intended to take up this fight, for otherwise she would have chosen a different season of the year, and in that event there is no doubt in my mind that Finnish resistance would have been broken very quickly. The criticisms which have been made of the Russian soldiers in consequence of the operations to date are not borne out, Duce, by reality and the facts. . . . Taking into consideration the available supply facilities, no power in the world would have been able, except after the most thoroughgoing preparations, to achieve any other results at 30 to 40 degrees below zero [C] on such terrain than did the Russians at the very first.[21]

Hitler's fatal underestimation of Russian capabilities can probably be attributed to the irrational feeling of invincibility which stemmed from the remarkably easy and swift German conquest of France and the Low Countries later in the spring of 1940.

Whatever the Nazi leader may have thought, Marshal Mannerheim was probably correct in considering the loss of prestige of the Soviet armed forces the most significant international result of the war.[22]

Nor were the Soviet losses offset by comparable gains. The war transformed the alleged danger that Finland might join Russia's enemies in a future conflict from a very questionable assumption into a hard fact. Furthermore, the security of the Gulf of Finland which was supposedly assured by Soviet acquisition of Hanko—the issue which precipitated the war—proved to be an illusion. Less than three months after the German army invaded Russia in June 1941, it overran the southern shore of the Gulf almost to Leningrad. Nazi warships could then enter the Gulf beyond the range of Soviet batteries on

Hanko, which thus became virtually useless. On the night of 2–3 December 1941, the Soviet garrison evacuated that port by sea.[23]

The only substantial advantages which the U.S.S.R. gained from the Winter War were the military lessons which the Red Army learned in what General Zhukov later termed its "acid test." The postmortems began as early as March 1940, when Defense Commissar Voroshilov reported on the war to the Plenum of the Party's Central Committee. That body recommended the convocation of a special session of the Main Military Council, to be augmented by participants in the conflict—the commanders and military council members of the armies, and corps and division commanders—as well as representatives from the Commissariat of Defense, the General Staff, military districts, and service academies. The Council met in the Kremlin from 14 to 17 April. Among other things, speakers criticized the unwieldy organization of infantry divisions, shortcomings in troop supply and motor transport services, the low level of individual instruction for the infantryman, the inadequacy of infantry firepower due to the scarcity of automatic weapons and mortars, and the lack of winter clothing and equipment. These deliberations resulted in demands for radical improvement in the armament, organization, training, and instruction of the troops; the reorganization of supervisory methods; and the revision of service regulations to reflect the experience recently gained. Addressing the Council on the final day of the meeting, Stalin denounced the "cult of tradition" which relied only on the experiences of the Russian Civil War, and he urged all officers to study modern warfare. The Council passed a resolution entitled "Measures to be taken in combat training, organization, and structure of the troops of the Red Army on the basis of the experience of the war in Finland and the combat experience of recent years."[24]

These were not idle words; in the months which followed there were many practical applications of this resolution. Indeed, even before the war ended, the Red Army had issued a *Handbook on the Armed Forces of White Finland* which included translations of Finnish writings on such topics as Reconnaissance and Surveillance, Instructions for Organizing Defense in Woods, etc. Subsequently, numerous articles in

*Krasnaya Zvezda* [Red Star] and *Voennaya Mysl'* [Military Thought] were devoted to the lessons of the war in Finland.[25]

Among the measures to improve their military capabilities which Soviet authorities specifically attributed to the experiences of the Winter War were:

Orders No. 120 (16 May 1940) and No. 30 (21 January 1941) of the Commissar of Defense, which provided detailed policy guidelines to correct deficiencies in the training of troops and their commanders, especially junior officers.

An order issued by the Presidium of the Supreme Soviet of the U.S.S.R. on 12 August 1940 which reinstated unitary command in the armed forces. This reform downgraded the political commissar from a status co-equal with the military commander to that of a *Zampolit* [Deputy Commander for Political Affairs]. Because even purely military orders had required the countersignature of the commissars, this change was essential if field commanders were to display initiative in battle.

Revision of the Field Service Regulations, a task assigned to a special commission in August 1940 and transferred on 31 October to the Main Commission for Service Regulations and Manuals. This project was still incomplete at the time of the Nazi attack in 1941.[26]

As a result of these and other reforms (restoration of the ranks of generals and marshals in May 1940 and the introduction of a strict new Disciplinary Code in October), Red Army organization became more rational and military training more realistic during the fifteen-month interlude between the Winter War and the Nazi-Soviet War. Even if—as Marshal Biriuzov later wrote—there was excessive emphasis on the tactics for storming defenses such as the Mannerheim Line at the expense of training for mobile warfare, the Russian infantryman was more proficient in 1941 than he had been before the war with Finland. The Red Army was also much better prepared for winter warfare during that critical season of 1941–42 than its German opponent. Lt. General Kurt Dittmar, the official military commentator of the German High Command, acknowledged that Russian winter equipment was excellent and their ski troops well organized.[27]

The Finns also noticed improvements in the Soviet units they encountered in 1941; their ability to move, navigate, and use the terrain "had improved remarkably." Timoshenko, who became a Marshal of the Soviet Union and succeeded Voroshilov as Defense Commissar on 7 May 1940, summed it up in these words to the Finnish Military Attaché in Moscow, "The Russians have learned much in this hard war in which the Finns fought with heroism."[28]

In addition to Timoshenko, Meretskov, Shaposhnikov, and Voronov—who subsequently became marshals—a number of less prominent officers gained valuable experience in the Winter War and thereafter rose to the upper ranks of the Red Army. Among them were:

L. Govorov, an artillery officer on the Karelian Isthmus, who later rose to Marshal of Artillery;

M. P. Kirponos, then a Brigade Commander leading the 70th Division, who became a Colonel General by the time he was mortally wounded in the fall of 1941;

A. F. Khrenov, a Colonel who achieved the rank of Colonel General of Engineers;

D. D. Lelyushenko, a Colonel commanding a mobile group in the 13th Army, who was later a General of the Army;

D. G. Pavlov, commander of a tank reserve group which crossed the frozen Gulf, who became a General of the Army by the time he was shot in July 1941; and

I. Rosly, the Major in command of the regiment (123rd Division) which broke thru the key Lähde sector, who was a full Colonel by early 1941; probably the same person listed as Lt. General I. P. Rosly at the victory parade in Moscow on 24 June 1945.[29]

For Finland, the war held even greater significance. The nation's human losses have been established rather accurately—23,157 men paid the ultimate price of battle, and 43,557 others were wounded.[30] In terms of combat statistics, the old bromide that "one Finn is worth ten Russians" was almost exactly true! Of course, in proportion to the national populations, Finnish losses were much more tragic than their enemy's.

For the Finns, the ultimate meaning of the costly conflict lay in the fact that the final peace treaty was not signed with Kuusinen's puppet "Government." They had retained that which they had waited so long to achieve—their freedom and independence. The entire nation had also experienced a heartening sense of unity completely unprecedented in the short history of the Republic. Marshal Mannerheim summarized the meaning of those trying months concisely and eloquently:

> May coming generations not forget the dearly bought lessons of our defensive war. They can with pride look back on the Winter War and find courage and confidence in its glorious history. That an army so inferior in numbers and equipment should have inflicted such serious defeats on an overwhelmingly powerful enemy, and, while retreating, have over and over again repelled his attacks, is something for which it is hard to find a parallel in the history of war. But it is equally admirable that the Finnish people, face to face with an apparently hopeless situation, were able to resist a feeling of despair and, instead, to grow in devotion and greatness. Such a nation has earned the right to live.[31]

*Dost thou other times remember,*
*When we fought and bled together . . .*
RUNE XXX

CHAPTER IX

# Epilogue

FINLAND'S FREEDOM AND INDEPENDENCE, SO GLORIOUSLY DEFEND-
ed in the Winter War, were nearly extinguished in the unfortunate sequel which the Finns call the Continuation War. From
25 June 1941 until 4 September 1944 they again fought their
powerful eastern neighbor. Remarkably, Finland survived as a
democratic nation, but the consequences of her second defeat
were such that her existence as an independent state remains
precarious to this day.

Finland's shining image of the Winter War days was badly
tarnished by the Continuation War, in which she fought side by
side with Nazi Germany against Soviet Russia. It is natural,
therefore, that communist writers dwell on the latter war,
which was far more complex than the Winter War.

There is much controversy, and conflicting and inconclusive
evidence, relating to precisely how and when the Finnish Government became committed to the war which began three days
after the German invasion of Russia. Rather than trying to
fathom that bottomless morass, let us start with the worst possible assumption (by no means proven)—that from the time of
the crushing peace of March 1940 until the renewal of hostilities some 15 months later, responsible Finnish officials were
secretly plotting a war to recoup their nation's losses. Even if
that unlikely supposition were true, who could justly blame
them?

Morally, there was little difference between Hitler and his
head murderer, Himmler, on the one hand, and Stalin and

his chief executioner, Beria, on the other; if there is any justice
in the afterworld, all four are sharing the ninth circle of Dan-
te's Hell. From a practical viewpoint, Nazism may even have
been the lesser evil—considering that it rested upon the charis-
matic powers of a single Führer and therefore may not have
survived Hitler's death in any case, whereas the Soviet brand
of oppression has already endured more than half a century,
and also considering that Nazism held no inherent appeal for
the non-Aryan majority of the world's peoples, whereas communism has attracted the naïve of all races. From the Finnish
viewpoint, the overriding consideration was the simple fact
that the Soviet Union appeared to be a clear and present danger
to Finland, and Germany did not. Finland's main "guilt," for
which she is still paying political ransom, lay in choosing—to
the extent that she had any choice—the losing side.

The practicality of that choice seemed manifestly reasonable
at that time. Most of the world's political and military leaders
expected the till-then-invincible German Wehrmacht to utterly destroy the Red Army within a few weeks. For example,
the U.S. Secretary of War, Stimson, sharing the opinion of the
Chief of Staff of the U. S. Army, General Marshall, advised
President Roosevelt on 23 June 1941 that it would require a
minimum of one month and *a maximum of three months* for
Germany to defeat Russia. The British military estimated that
the Germans would occupy the Ukraine and Moscow within 3
to 6 weeks, although they covered themselves by adding "or
more." Roosevelt was so skeptical of Soviet defensive capabilities that he sent Harry Hopkins as his personal representative
to interview Stalin before deciding on substantial aid to the
U.S.S.R.[1]

Given the widely accepted prospect that the multinational
Soviet state would soon shatter under the blows of the German
invaders, why should not the Finns pick up the pieces which
historically and ethnically belonged to them? Who but Hitler
would gain if they did not?

However, one need not accept the foregoing extreme and
improbable assumption to appreciate Finland's position in
1940–41. Whether or not Stalin planned to annex Finland after
the peace of March 1940 remains a matter of speculation. What

is certain, however, is that he gave the Finns ample reason to believe that he did, and they reacted accordingly. As previously noted, Germany forfeited Finland's goodwill by coldly refusing her any form of assistance during the Winter War. Yet, within a few months thereafter, Soviet pressure on the Finns drove them straight into German arms.

On 20 March, the very day the peace treaty was ratified, relations took a turn for the worse when the Soviet Government authorized a TASS statement denouncing a defensive alliance then being considered by Norway, Sweden, and Finland. Such a coalition might have provided security for Finland without posing the slightest threat to the U.S.S.R., since neutralist Sweden would have been the dominant partner. The Finns suspected ulterior motives behind the Soviet opposition which killed that project.[2]

Subversive propaganda was beamed at Finland from a powerful station in Petrozavodsk, capital of the Karelo-Finnish Soviet Socialist Republic. The creation of that S.S.R. on 31 March, under the direction of Otto Kuusinen, haunted Finland with the spectre of the "Terijoki Government."[3]

International developments in the spring and summer of 1940 increased Finnish apprehensions. After the German conquest of Norway and Denmark, Finland's isolation was nearly complete; her only contact with the Western democracies was via the Petsamo region, which was vulnerable to attack from either Murmansk or German-occupied Kirkenes in northern Norway. After Dunkerque and the fall of France in June, the only counterpoise to the Soviet Union on the entire continent was Nazi Germany. Considering Hitler's attitude during the Winter War, the Finns believed that he may have written them off permanently.

While the Wehrmacht was preoccupied with mopping up in France, Stalin was destroying the foundations of independence in the tiny Baltic states. On 14 June Molotov handed the Lithuanian Foreign Minister, then in Moscow, a 24-hour ultimatum; it demanded free passage for Soviet troops into "the most important centers" of the country, the immediate formation of a government friendly to the Soviet Union, and the trial of two prominent Lithuanian officials. With Red Army units stationed in their country since October 1939, the recipients of these new demands had no choice but compliance; the next day Soviet armored divisions dashed across their border. Molotov presented similar ultimatums to the Latvian and Estonian Ministers on 16 June, and those helpless states also yielded to the inevitable. A week later, on 22 June, Radio Moscow admitted that there were "18 to 20" Red Army divisions in the three Baltic Republics.[4]

During those tense days, the Finns had immediate cause for alarm. On 14 June Soviet fighters shot down an unarmed Finnish civil airliner over the Gulf of Finland. That same day, the communist-front SNS (Finnish-Soviet Friendship Society) issued a circular lauding the Baltic states for yielding to Soviet demands for bases prior to the Winter War. On 23 June Molotov surprised Minister Paasikivi by requesting either a concession to exploit the nickel deposits in the Petsamo region or the creation of a joint Soviet-Finnish company for this purpose. The nickel question, in which both England and Germany also had large stakes, remained a source of recurring friction until the eve of the war the next year. Four days after that démarche, Molotov demanded that the Åland (Ahvenanmaa) Islands be demilitarized and a Soviet consulate be established there to inspect the work; the Finnish Government felt compelled to grant this new demand.[5]

A more ominous request was presented on 8 July, when the Soviet Government asked for unrestricted railroad transit rights to and from its leased base at Hanko; permitting an unlimited number of Russian troops to pass through vital communication centers which outflanked the Finnish capital would obviously pose at least a potential threat of great magnitude. After difficult negotiations, an agreement was signed on 6 September which stipulated that the troops would travel unarmed, and their number was limited to two trains a day in each direction. Coincidentally, on 8 July—the day the Soviet request was received in Helsinki—the Swedish Government granted transit rights for German troops traveling between their homeland and northern Norway.[6]

The political horizon, as viewed from Finland, seemed especially dark in late July and early August. Soviet power was consolidated in the Baltic states in mid-July by rigged elections, and on the 21st all three became Soviet Socialist Republics. In

Finland, the SNS pointedly applauded these acts, calling on the Finns to follow the lead of the Baltic proletariat. Official Soviet endorsement of the subversive SNS appeared portentous. Ivan Zotov, the overbearing Soviet Minister in Helsinki, had ostentatiously received its entire executive committee at his Legation on 19 June; on 26 July he began a tour of the SNS branches in the major urban centers. On 24 July Molotov summoned Paasikivi to the Kremlin, where he criticized the Finnish Government for taking action against the SNS. In his publicized speech before the Supreme Soviet on 1 August, the Foreign Commissar again warned the Finns not to interfere with that organization, although he did not mention it by name. Beginning on 29 July the SNS—numbering over 35,000 members in more than 100 local units—sparked riots in Helsinki, Turku, and other towns. Despite Soviet protests, the Government suppressed these challenges to its authority. By mid-August peace returned to the streets of the capital, but Soviet motives in encouraging such outrages caused continuing concern.[7]

During the interview with Paasikivi on 24 July, Molotov also verbally suggested that Soviet-Finnish relations might improve if Tanner (now Minister of Economics) quit the Government. One of Tanner's sins in Molotov's eyes was his open opposition to the SNS. This blatant interference in Finland's domestic affairs achieved its immediate objective; in mid-August Tanner resigned.[8]

Quite predictably, Lithuania, Latvia, and Estonia were formally incorporated into the U.S.S.R. on 3, 5, and 6 August, respectively. Comparing the Soviet press campaigns against their former governments with the current propaganda directed at the Finnish Government, the U. S. Chargé in Moscow considered the outlook for Finland "ominous." In his cable of 8 August he also reported Soviet troop movements towards the Finnish border during the last few days. German intelligence sources also credited similar reports; Field Marshal Keitel sent an officer to the German Foreign Ministry on 10 August to advise of the danger of a new Soviet attack on Finland. Even Paasikivi, who was inclined to optimism in dealing with the Kremlin, was very pessimistic about Finland's future in August 1940. Unknown to the Finns, decisions had already been made in Berlin which would soon give them some welcome leverage in their dealings with Moscow.[9]

Finnish reactions to Soviet pressures were natural and predictable, given their precarious situation and their limited range of choice. Marshal Mannerheim, who retained the powers of Commander-in-Chief during the tenuous peace, no longer had to argue with a parsimonious Parliament for defense appropriations—the danger was sufficiently obvious even to the politicians. With his trusted friend, Rudolf Walden, serving as Defense Minister in the post-war Cabinet, he enjoyed unchallenged authority in all military matters. Making full and effective use of his powers and the ready funds, he directed the construction of new border defenses, reorganization and reequipment of the army, expansion of the armaments industry, revision of the mobilization plans, and enlargement of the peacetime army to more than double its pre-war strength. Due to these energetic measures, the armed forces—in spite of the serious losses of the Winter War and the peace treaty—were significantly stronger in 1941 than they had been in 1939. Instead of the nine poorly supplied divisions with which Finland had begun the Winter War, by the spring of 1941 she could field 16 well equipped divisions.[10]

Because of Finland's geographic isolation after the fall of Norway, the only country which could supply her with heavy weapons in substantial quantities was Germany. By a twist of fate, this source was suddenly opened in August 1940, when the Finns were at the lowest point of despair. A few weeks earlier, Hitler—flushed with his spectacular victories in the West, yet frustrated by the RAF in his efforts to achieve final victory over Great Britain—seriously began to consider attacking Russia, for the first time since the Nazi-Soviet Pact of August 1939. This automatically caused him to reappraise Germany's relations with Finland.

Late in July Hitler confided his tentative plan to invade the Soviet Union to his military advisers. On the 21st he asked Field Marshal von Brauchitsch, the Commander-in-Chief of the Army, to study the problems involved in a Russian campaign. At a conference in Berchtesgaden on 31 July, he declared that a showdown in the East would take place the next spring. Finland's role in this vast operation "remained to be seen."[11] Three weeks later (22 August) General Halder, Chief of the Army General Staff, recorded in his war diary:

> . . . Reversal of attitude of the Führer with respect to Finland. Support with arms and munitions . . .[12]

The first indication the Finns had of this portentous change in German policy was on 15 August, when a munitions dealer, Joseph Veltjens, visited the Finnish Minister in Berlin, Toivo Kivimäki, to request a letter of introduction to Marshal Mannerheim. Veltjens discussed the nature of his mission with Kivimäki, stressing the need for secrecy. Three days later this retired air force officer, who was serving as Reich Marshal Hermann Göring's personal emissary, paid a surreptitiously arranged visit to Marshal Mannerheim's home. He conveyed Göring's offer to sell arms to Finland, requesting in return transit rights for German military personnel enroute to and from their base at Kirkenes in northern Norway. Marshal Mannerheim disclaimed the authority to make this important decision, but he agreed to obtain an answer for Göring by the following day. According to the Marshal, he consulted Prime Minister Ryti, who was acting President during Kallio's illness, before giving Veltjens an affirmative reply the next morning. Apparently, the only other Finns who were initially privy to this secret were Foreign Minister Witting, Defense Minister Walden, and two Finnish arms importers.[13]

On 12 September a simple technical agreement was signed by representatives of the Finnish General Staff and the German Luftwaffe regulating the transit of German forces thru Finnish territory. To counter the anticipated Soviet reaction, this unvalidated military agreement was followed by an exchange of notes between the Finnish and German Foreign Ministries on 22 September.[14]

Because Sweden had already granted Germany troop transit rights,[15] and because the Soviet demand for railway privileges then under consideration could hardly be rejected outright, the Finns could scarcely have refused the German request even if they had so desired. However, as they feared that a Russian attack was imminent, most Finns at that moment would have welcomed the entire Wehrmacht with open arms. Every German soldier in Finland was tangible insurance against another conflagration sparked by the Kremlin.

This seemingly innocuous agreement proved to be the first step down the slippery path which led to the resumption of hostilities with the U.S.S.R. in less than a year. The immediate effects were reassuring. Germany provided large amounts of heavy artillery, till then a critical weakness of the Finnish Army, as well as modern fighter aircraft and other munitions. Hitler even let the Soviet leaders know that he was aiding Finland (although the exact nature of the armaments was not revealed) in order to inhibit Stalin from further action against the Finns.[16]

These events may have forestalled overt aggression, but they did not terminate Soviet pressure on Finland. At this point, elementary discretion should have dictated a Kremlin policy of reconciliation with Finland designed to insure her neutrality in any future conflict, but Stalin did not have the foresight to abandon the tactics of intimidation until April 1941, when it was too late.[17]

In August certain influential Swedes had initiated a move to reunite Finland and Sweden in a union which would have a common foreign policy and joint armed forces. This idea found support in Finland, and two Parliamentary leaders visited Stockholm in September for exploratory talks. Despite the fact that Swedish domination of such a union would have precluded a Finnish war of revenge, Moscow killed this proposal as effectively as it had buried the earlier plan for a defensive alliance of Norway, Sweden, and Finland. On 27 and 30 September, Molotov denounced the project as being directed against the Soviet Union. As Finnish-Swedish discussions continued, the Foreign Commissar delivered a strong formal protest to Minister Paasikivi on the night of 6–7 December. Due to this Soviet attitude, and because Germany also opposed the union, the idea was abandoned, and Finland in its isolation depended even more on German support.[18]

While Molotov was browbeating Paasikivi that December night, he also read a second note which was another gross affront to Finnish sovereignty. Referring to the upcoming presidential election, he declared that if Tanner, Kivimäki, Mannerheim, or Svinhufvud were elected, the Soviet Government would conclude that Finland did not wish to fulfill the peace treaty with the U.S.S.R. The extent to which this influenced the electors is problematical, but acting President Ryti was chosen overwhelmingly.[19]

In January 1941 Stalin continued the war of nerves by abruptly recalling the Soviet Minister from Helsinki, while simultaneously halting deliveries of flour and other goods purchased under an existing trade treaty. Coming at a time when the Finns were experiencing a serious food shortage, this was a severe blow. Its effect was to increase Finnish economic ties with Germany, then the only alternative source of many essential imports.[20]

Meanwhile, a momentous confrontation of the two giants who dominated Finland's destiny occurred in Berlin on 12 and 13 November 1940. Realizing that its fate might be decided then and there, the Finnish Government requested the German Foreign Ministry (in advance of Molotov's arrival) to strengthen Finland's position in relation to Russia. Finland was, in fact, the main bone of contention between Molotov and Hitler during these pourparlers; no other single issue occupied as much of their time. Molotov raised the question during his first meetings with Foreign Minister von Ribbentrop and Hitler, and Finland was also the subject of a lengthy exchange between the Führer and the Commissar at their second meeting. It was then that Molotov revealed that he "imagined this [Finnish] settlement on the same scale as in Bessarabia" (i.e., Soviet annexation). Hitler expounded several fanciful reasons for opposing a new war in the Baltic, and he stated that, when the current troop transit was completed "within the next few days," no additional German troops would be sent thru Finland. Throughout these discussions, the Führer declaimed in grandiose and general terms about the liquidation of the British Empire and a long-range division of world spheres of influence among Germany, Russia, Italy and Japan. The tactless Molotov stubbornly returned the conversation to prosaic details on specific points of friction, especially regarding Finland.[21]

As a result of the Berlin talks, Stalin correctly understood that he could no longer employ overt force against the Finns without encountering Hitler's opposition. More significantly, his reply of 25 November to Hitler's proposal for a Four Power Pact set future Russo-German relations on a collision course. He would accept the German draft treaty only if numerous preconditions were met, the first of which was that "German troops are immediately withdrawn from Finland, which, under the compact of 1939, belongs to the Soviet Union's sphere of influence."[22]

Hitler was so annoyed at Stalin's proposals that he didn't bother to reply; he would settle their differences on the battlefield. On 5 December Marshal Brauchitsch and General Halder presented to Hitler their preliminary invasion plan, which was already being tested in General Staff exercises. With their Führer's approval, work began the next day on the directive for "Operation Barbarossa," which he signed on 18 December.[23]

Lt. Colonel Veltjens flew to Helsinki on 23 November to brief Finnish military leaders on the Molotov-Hitler talks. He was authorized to allay their fears by revealing that Hitler had informed Molotov that he desired no new complications in the north. His visit brought a sigh of relief in Finland.[24]

In the meantime, military contacts increased and the scope of these conversations broadened. General Talvela had visited Berlin at the end of August to work out the details of the transit agreement. When he returned to Germany in December, he discussed the political and military situation in Finland with both Göring and Halder. As Marshal Mannerheim's personal envoy, he also made numerous other trips to Berlin.[25]

Late in January, 1941, General Heinrichs, then Chief of the Finnish General Staff, lectured on the Winter War to the German General Staff. During a conversation with General Halder, his German counterpart casually remarked that someday their armies might, as in 1918, fight side by side against Russia, in which case it would be natural for the Finns to attack Leningrad. Heinrichs advised Halder that neither Marshal Mannerheim nor the Government would consent to such an operation, which would justify Soviet claims that the Finns threatened that metropolis. However, Heinrichs gave Halder details on Finnish mobilization plans, and Halder's diary notes indicate that a German surprise attack on Russia was probably discussed. [26]

In mid-February, Lt. General Hans von Seidel, General Quartermaster of the Luftwaffe, visited Rovaniemi to check on supply problems in northern Finland. During a stopover in Helsinki, he was very cordially received by Marshal Mannerheim, who decorated him with the Grand Cross of the Finnish White Rose.[27]

Immediately afterward Colonel Buschenhagen, Chief of Staff of the German Forces in Norway, paid a longer visit to Finnish Lapland, where he studied the communications network. He also conferred with the Marshal and other key officers in Helsinki. In his letter to the Intelligence Department of the Army General Staff (which is probaly reliable) the German Military Attaché in Helsinki reported that Buschenhagen "in a very cautious manner" discussed details of *hypothetical* Finnish-German military collaboration against Russia.[28]

The most significant of these contacts were the conferences arranged between General Heinrichs (and four key Finnish staff officers) and the leaders of the Wehrmacht in Salzburg on 25 May 1941, and between that Finnish delegation and General Halder in Berlin the following day. Although still on a tentative basis, these meetings encompassed very detailed planning for joint operations against the Red Army.[29]

There were also other conferences prior to the outbreak of hostilities. Halder's dairy contains this entry for 7 June 1941:

. . . Kinzel's* report on tour to Finland. Conversations with Heinrichs. The Finnish High Command has squared their plans with ours, and seems to be going at it with every ounce of energy . . . [30]

What did all of these military conferences prove? If one is to credit most of the participants, both sides spoke only of hypothetical cases, and the whole truth may never be determined. There is no doubt that Hitler was cautious and devious in dealing with the Finns, as he would not trust any foreigners with the vital secret of the date of his surprise attack on Russia. Apparently, the Finns were genuinely deceived by his pretense that last-minute negotiations with the Kremlin were underway, and that only if he could not reach a new agreement with Stalin would the invasion plans be executed. It is also most

*A Colonel in German intelligence.

probable that the Finns were likewise coy;[31] they would have been naïve to burn their bridges with an unconditional commitment before Hitler revealed his hand. They correctly surmised that Hitler had sold them out in 1939, and history might repeat itself. Nevertheless, when all of this is granted, it is still likely that neither side was so unrealistic as to believe they were discussing purely theoretical operations. Numerous entries in Halder's diaries indicate that he, at least, took for granted Finnish participation in the coming invasion.

In June events moved swiftly towards their inevitable climax. By 8 June the first German transports with heavy reinforcements arrived in Finland; the next day the Finnish covering troops were strengthened by a partial mobilization. Marshal Mannerheim may have learned on 14 June that war was certain, although the date was still a closely guarded German secret. On the 15th, the Finnish corps in the Oulu region began to mobilize, and—as previously arranged—it was subordinated to the German commander in Rovaniemi. Two days later, general mobilization was ordered. Thanks to strenuous defense measures during the interlude since the Winter War, Finland was able to muster more than 475,000 men by the end of the month.[32]

On 22 June Hitler sealed his doom by launching Operation Barbarossa. Although he did not consult the Finnish Government, his bombastic announcement of this historic event included the statement that:

> In *alliance* [im bunde] with their Finnish comrades, the warriors who won the victory at Narvik stand on the shores of the Arctic Ocean . . .[33]

The Finnish censors changed "in alliance" to "side by side;"[34] notwithstanding the close collaboration between the Finnish and German military commands, there was no alliance between their governments.

The Finnish Foreign Ministry issued a somewhat ambiguous statement of neutrality, while warning that the nation would defend itself if attacked. There were sporadic air raids on Finnish targets on 22 June, and heavy raids on ten towns on the 25th;

26 Soviet aircraft were shot down over Finland on the latter day. Up to this time, neither the Finns nor the German forces in Finland had attacked the Soviet Union; the Finnish mobilization was still incomplete, and the Germans were not yet fully deployed for their offensive.[35] Therefore, the Finnish Government was able to present its declaration of war on 25 June as a purely defensive act provoked by the Soviet raids. As Prime Minister Rangell expressed it:

> Finland on Wednesday morning [25 June] was subjected to an attack on the part of the Soviet Union which initiated operations of war against Finland. On the basis of this Finland has begun to defend herself with all the military means available to her.[36]

In reality, the Soviet air raids presented the Finns with an opportune pretext for a war which by then was inevitable. As they well knew, German forces in northern Finland were already deploying for an offensive scheduled to begin on 29 June. On the morning of the 25th, the Government was drafting a statement apparently designed to prepare the Parliament for involvement in the war, when the bombings made that devious declaration unnecessary.[37] Only in a legalistic, technical sense can the U.S.S.R. be accused of starting the war with Finland in 1941.

However, viewed in broader perspective, the Soviet Government initiated that war a year earlier. Stalin's open encouragement and defense of SNS subversion in Finland—at the very time the Baltic states were being subjugated by similar subversion and overt force—coupled with his numerous other attempts to intimidate the Finns, predetermined their decision to join Germany in the war against Russia. The air raids on 25 June were merely the last in a long series of blunders in Soviet policy towards Finland.

In addition to the fact that Finland had no political alliance with Germany, there were other unique aspects of the conflict which the Finns pointedly term the Continuation War. They tried to conduct their operations (and to convince the Western governments that they were so doing) as if they were separate from the clash of the Great Powers. As they informed the British late in June, 1941:

> The Government of Finland desires to maintain unaltered its relations with Great Britain. The Government of Finland is a co-belligerent with Germany solely against Russia.[38]

Nor was their military collaboration with Germany based upon admiration of Hitler or his ideology. During the visit of Colonel Kinzel (early in June 1941), General Heinrichs—probably on the instructions of Marshal Mannerheim—earnestly warned against "any attempt to set up any kind of Quisling government which would immediately paralyze any further cooperation between Finland and Germany".[39] Three years later, on 22 June 1944, Foreign Minister von Ribbentrop queried his Minister in Helsinki about the possibilities of such a coup. Blücher informed his chief that only three percent of the Finns favored authoritarianism, and among that small minority there was not a single person with outstanding leadership abilities.[40]

The Finnish attempt to walk a swaying tightrope across the abyss without falling into the world conflagration was only partially successful. Under Soviet pressure, the British Government reluctantly declared war on Finland, effective 7 December 1941. The coincidence of that date—Pearl Harbor Day—is noteworthy. Had the British waited a few days longer, they may not have felt compelled to yield to the urgings of Stalin, then their only important partner in the struggle with Germany. The entry of the United States into the war radically altered the balance against the Axis Powers. As it was, the British-Finnish "war" was a bloodless affair, except for one British air raid on Petsamo in July 1941—months *before* the declaration of war.[41]

The United States and Finland were never officially enemies, although their relations steadily deteriorated as the global conflict lengthened into the marathon "total war." In 1942 the United States ordered the closing of the Finnish consulates in America. In mid-June 1944 the Minister and three other Legation officials were expelled from the United States. At the end of that month, the United States finally severed diplomatic relations completely.[42]

The Finns were fighting for their own—limited—objectives. The recovery of the areas lost in 1940 was almost universally popular. Even the United States Secretary of State congratulated the Finnish Minister when that was accomplished; however, he coupled this with a warning against further advances. Marshal Mannerheim repeatedly refused German requests to participate in the seige of Leningrad; even some Soviet sources acknowledge that the Finnish advance on the Karelian Isthmus halted at the 1939 frontier. The Marshal permitted only minor adjustments of this borderline for purely tactical reasons.[43]

Unfortunately, many Finns were anxious to advance beyond their 1939 frontier north and east of Lake Ladoga. Marshal Mannerheim, President Ryti,[44] and—if Blücher was a reliable judge of opinion—"the Officers' Corps, rightist circles with the exception of the Finns of Swedish origin, a large part of the Agrarian Party and the Right-wing Socialists"[45] wanted to annex Eastern Karelia as far as the Svir River. Although a temporary advance into that area might be justified on the grounds of military expediency, its annexation was a different question.

At one time, much of the populace of Eastern Karelia had been Finnish-speaking. The Russian border with the Grand Duchy of Finland had been artificial and arbitrary, both geographically and ethnically. However, ruthless Soviet resettlement policies had greatly altered the ethnic composition of the population, which by the 1930s was predominantly Russian. Foreign Minister Witting acknowledged the changed character of the inhabitants of the Repola (Reboly) district and other areas to the U.S. Minister in July 1941. In numerous cases the Finnish troops were viewed quite differently from the welcome liberators some of them fancied themselves.[46]

Perhaps the most that can be said for Finnish annexation of Eastern Karelia (which was never officially advocated) is that it would have been no worse than the annexation *of* Finland *to* Eastern Karelia—which was implied by the treaty signed by Molotov and Kuusinen on 2 December 1939. That "treaty" ostensibly fulfilled "the age-old aspirations of the Finnish people

MAP 16

## TERRITORIAL EXCHANGES BETWEEN THE U.S.S.R. AND THE "PEOPLE'S GOV'T. OF FINLAND" PER TREATY OF 2 DEC. 1939

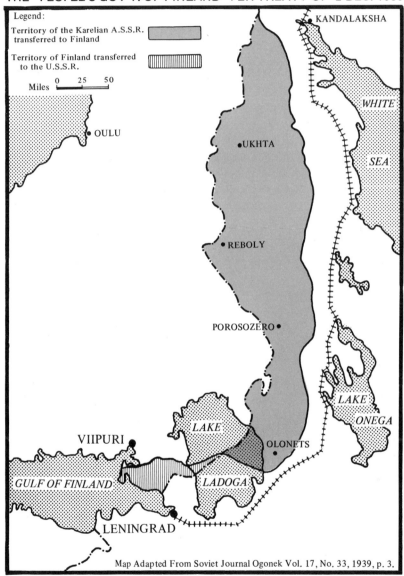

Legend:

Territory of the Karelian A.S.S.R. transferred to Finland

Territory of Finland transferred to the U.S.S.R.

Miles  0   25   50

KANDALAKSHA

OULU

UKHTA

WHITE

SEA

REBOLY

POROSOZERO

LAKE ONEGA

LAKE

VIIPURI

OLONETS

GULF OF FINLAND

LADOGA

LENINGRAD

Map Adapted From Soviet Journal Ogonek Vol. 17, No. 33, 1939, p. 3.

for reunion of the Karelian people with its kindred, the Finnish people, in a single state of Finland" by transferring to "the Democractic Republic of Finland the districts of Soviet Karelia with a predominating Karelian population—amounting altogether to 70,000 square kilometers."[47] The area which the Kremlin leaders were willing to transfer to a puppet Finnish régime was roughly equal to that occupied by the Finnish Army from late 1941 until the summer of 1944; near Petrozavodsk (Äänislinna) the Finns held more territory than Kuusinen's phantom government, but in the Ukhta (Uhtua) region they occupied considerably less.

A detailed study of the Continuation War is beyond the scope of this book. Nevertheless, in view of its significant repercussions, the highlights need to be outlined.

Although there were some Finnish troops in Lapland and some German forces operating with the Finns in central and southern Finland, in general the Germans and Finns fought their own distinct campaigns for their own national interests, with their fronts divided (very approximately) by the Arctic Circle.

The Germans, concentrating in northern Finland, did not achieve either of their objectives—the seizure of the port of Murmansk or the severance of the Murmansk railroad. It is interesting to read admissions in German records that the "master race" was not as effective in that particular environment as the Finnish troops. For example, General Halder noted on 5 July 1941 that "SS Brigade 'NORD', committed at Salla, has been a failure," and in September he acknowledged that "it was the Finns who eventually turned the tide [there] in our favor." Halder also recorded the German Attaché's observation that, as early as 4 August 1941, the Finns could not conceal their "disappointment at the performance of the German troops both on the northern front and in support of the Karelian Army." On the other hand, a German officer returning from Finland on 14 August reported that the "achievements of the Finnish Army as well as those of the entire country are truly remarkable."[48] General Erfurth, the German High Command's liaison officer at the Finnish GHQ, described the reactions of the German troops to the Finnish wilderness in terms strikingly appropriate for the hapless Russians during the Winter War. Beginning in the 1941–42 season, the Finns conducted courses in winter warfare for their German brothers-in-arms.[49]

In marked contrast, the Finns were almost completely successful in achieving their military objectives by the end of 1941. Their first offensive began on 10 July north and northwest of Lake Ladoga, where they reached the Lake shore in eight days, thereby cutting the enemy forces in two. Some of the victors pursued the enemy towards Tolvajärvi, while the main force pushed southeast along the lake-shore road, where they reached the 1939 frontier by 23 July. On the 31st, another offensive was launched west of Lake Ladoga, which freed the Karelian Isthmus north of the Vuoksi within three weeks. On 29 August Finnish troops entered Viipuri, and by the beginning of September they reached their old frontier across the entire Karelian Isthmus. The front remained stabilized here for nearly three years.[50]

Early in September the Finns began a new drive in Ladoga-Karelia. On 1 October they captured Petrozavodsk, the capital of the Karelo-Finnish S.S.R., and they reached the Svir (Syväri) River, which they employed as a defense line between Lakes Ladoga and Onega (Äänisjärvi). Because the best road along their front ran south of the Svir, they advanced beyond the River to secure that important communications link. Their forward positions extended about 12 miles south of the River for approximately 60 miles. Here, too, the front remained relatively stable until the summer of 1944, although there was heavy fighting during an unsuccessful Soviet counteroffensive in April 1942.[51]

The last major Finnish offensive, begun immediately after the conquest of Petrozavodsk, was designed to secure favorable defensive positions between Lakes Onega and Seg (Seesjärvi). With the capture of Medvezh'egorsk (Karhumäki) on 5 December, this operation was successfully concluded, and the Finns went over to the defensive in this area also. A strong Russian counteroffensive shook this sector in January 1942, but by mid-February Finnish reinforcements were able to restore the front —which then remained relatively quiet until 1944.[52]

The only significant failure of the Finnish offensives, as distinct from the German-led operations, was the drive from Suomussalmi towards Ukhta. That crossroads town was never captured.[53]

By December of 1941, the Finns had reached their major strategic objectives, and they began to construct defense works on all the main fronts. Proof of the defensive nature of their war effort from this point on is seen in the sizeable demobilization effected by the spring of 1942. Because the economy was excessively strained with 16 percent of the population serving in the armed forces (counting 80,000 Lottas), the Government had intended to release large numbers of older men as early as November 1941. When the fighting proved more severe than anticipated, this was only possible at a later date and on a smaller scale than had been hoped. Nevertheless, by 1942 approximately 180,000 were released from active service.[54]

During the long period of stalemate, which lasted—with only minor, local exceptions—from early 1942 until June 1944, there were several abortive peace feelers. Various trial balloons were floated by the United States, Finland, and the Soviet Union, but they all burst on the thorns of Soviet conditions and German reactions. The Finns, quick to realize that Germany was losing the war, desired to make peace as soon as that was possible without inviting national disaster from either a German occupation (as happened to Hungary in March 1944 when her support of Germany's war effort wavered) or from unconditional surrender to the Red Army. Their almost total dependence upon Germany for food and military assistance was a serious obstacle to negotiations. Hitler's reaction, when he learned of some of the tentative peace feelers, was to press for a binding political alliance, interrupt food deliveries, and threaten more extreme action.[55]

The Finnish dilemna is illustrated by the negotiations in the spring of 1944. In mid-February Paasikivi went to Stockholm to confer with the elderly but active Mme. Kollontay from whom he received Moscow's terms. These included, among others, restoration of the 1940 boundaries, unspecified reparations, and the internment of the [200,000] German troops on her territory. After lengthy debate, the Finnish Government secretly sent Paasikivi and former Foreign Minister Enckell to Moscow at the end of March, hoping to negotiate a modification of the terms. The only concessions Molotov would grant were to relin-

quish the lease of Hanko and to give the Finns the option of
either interning or expelling the Germans by the end of April.
Clarification of other terms dispelled any illusions of moderation: the Kremlin demanded cession of the entire Petsamo
province and the payment of six hundred million American
dollars' worth of goods within five years. Even the Swedish
Government, which had been urging the Finns to conclude
peace, reportedly considered the Soviet terms regarding the
German troops and the indemnity impossible to fulfill, and
therefore it could not recommend their acceptance. The British
Government suggested that the indemnity be reduced, because
it would require 75–100 percent of the total value of Finnish
exports during the five-year period (which would interfere
with British trade). It is understandable that the Finns, still
unbeaten on the field of battle, found these terms unacceptable.[56]

Hitler reacted angrily to these Soviet-Finnish negotiations.
At the virtual insistence of the Germans, General Heinrichs
flew to Berchtesgaden for a "conference" with Field Marshal
Keitel at the end of April. Keitel rudely and publicly berated his
guest for his Government's dealings with Moscow. Hitler interrupted arms deliveries to Finland in April, and in June he cut
off grain supplies.[57]

After two and a half years of relative calm, the Finnish front
suddenly burst into furious action in June 1944. For once, the
well equipped, battle-seasoned Soviet troops, exhilarated by
their decisive victories over the German Army, had a qualitative advantage over the Finns—demoralized by the years of
enervating inactivity and the sense of impending defeat. The
Red Army also enjoyed the advantages of numerical and technical superiority. The initial strength of the Soviet forces
hurled against the Finns was 450,000 men, 10,000 artillery
pieces and heavy mortars, some 800 tanks and self-propelled
guns, and more than 2,000 aircraft. The official Soviet history
acknowledges that, when this powerful offensive began, the
Finnish forces opposing it consisted of only 268,000 men, 1,930
guns and heavy mortars, 110 tanks, and 348 planes.[58]

When the Russians attacked on the Karelian Isthmus with
more than 15 infantry divisions and strong supporting armor,
there were only three Finnish divisions and one brigade on the

front, plus slightly more than two divisions of infantry and one armored division in reserve. The offensive began on 9 June, when the heaviest artillery and aerial bombardment experienced in either war in Finland was concentrated on a nine-mile sector in the western Isthmus. The devastating barrage resumed at 5 A.M. the following day with even greater intensity.[59]

Marshal Mannerheim described 10 June as the "black day" of Finland's military history. The Tenth Division, which bore the brunt of the withering barrage and the assault which followed, lost its artillery to the enemy, abandoned its positions, and was so severely shaken that it had to be withdrawn from battle the next day. In the afternoon, the entire corps on the right-wing was ordered to retreat to fortified positions some 12 miles behind the front, the so-called VT Line (Vammelsuu-Taipale), while reinforcements were hastily summoned from Eastern Karelia. By the 12th, the Finns were forced back to the VT Line across the entire Isthmus. Two days later, that Line also broke in the Kuuterselkä sector, where a single Finnish battalion was overrun by two reinforced divisions. The Finnish armored division counterattacked during the night, but on the 15th it was necessary to order a general retreat to the VKT Line (Viipuri-Kuparsaari-Taipale). That Line, like the old Mannerheim Line, took advantage of the Vuoksi-Suvanto waterways, but it was weak in the exposed terrain northeast of Viipuri. The Russian pursuit was so vigorous that Viipuri fell on 20 June, and the Line soon wavered again near Tali.[60]

It was at the height of this great Soviet blitzkrieg, on 19 June, that Marshal Mannerheim appealed to Germany for emergency assistance. Although they could not fulfill his requests completely, the Germans promptly sent the 122nd Infantry Division to Finland from the Baltic states, transferred an assault gun brigade from northern to southern Finland, and flew in a group of Stuka dive bombers from the Baltic area. Most helpful, in view of the acute shortage of antitank guns capable of destroying the modern T-34s now encountered, was the speedy delivery by motor torpedo boats of several thousand of the effective bazooka-type weapons called *Panzerfaust*.[61] It is probable that this timely assistance was decisive in preventing a military disaster.

Hitler disclosed the high price of his "generosity" when von Ribbentrop arrived uninvited in Helsinki on 22 June. Two days earlier, General Meretskov opened the Soviet drive to retake Eastern Karelia by throwing the 32nd Army against the Finnish defenses between Lakes Onega and Seg, and on the 21st he launched a stronger offensive by the 7th Army against the Svir front. Since Marshal Mannerheim had depleted the forces in these regions to bolster the tottering defenses on the Karelian Isthmus, these new Soviet drives made rapid progress. The overall military situation was therefore desperate for the Finns, and the German Foreign Minister took full advantage of their plight. On behalf of Hitler, he demanded—as a condition for continued German assistance—a written promise that Finland would not conclude a separate peace.[62]

Simultaneously (22 June), the Finns again inquired, via Stockholm, about Soviet peace terms. The reply, received the following day, amounted to a demand for unconditional surrender. This terrible dilemma, in which Finland's doom appeared certain regardless of which course she chose as the lesser evil, was resolved on 26 June by an opportunistic expedient. Reluctantly, President Ryti signed a *personal* letter to Hitler, pledging not to conclude peace without Germany's consent. Because this document was not ratified by the Parliament, it was not legally binding on the Finnish Government; it could be repudiated at an opportune moment by any successor to President Ryti. Hitler accepted the letter as sufficient[63]—the Finns had cheated the devil at his own game!

One penalty that Finland had to pay was the severance of diplomatic relations by the United States. On Ribbentrop's insistence, the Finnish Government issued a communiqué on 28 June which stated that a "meeting of minds" was achieved on all points between the German and Finnish Governments. As a direct result, President Roosevelt finally agreed to the rupture which Secretary Hull had recommended as early as 28 April; formal notice of the break in relations was presented on 30 June.[64]

Due to the munitions received from Germany, the recall of the demobilized reserves and men on leave, and the lack of coordination of the powerful Soviet offensives, the impending military catastrophe was averted. By 1 July the situation on the Karelian Isthmus was under control, and ten days later the Soviet High Command halted its major offensive in Finland. The 59th Army failed in its attempt to repeat the tactics of March 1940 by crossing Viipuri Bay, mainly because its assault did not begin until the threat in the Tali sector had already been checked.[65]

In Ladoga-Karelia, the Finns conducted an orderly retreat of more than 100 miles to the U Line, which was anchored at Pitkäranta on the northeastern shore of Lake Ladoga. By mid-July, this front had also become stabilized. Just north of this sector, the Finns won a defensive victory early in August, when two Russian divisions were scattered east of Ilomantsi with heavy losses. By 10 August this sector was also relatively static, and at the end of the month the Soviet High Command ordered a stop to offensive operations.[66]

The most fortuitous and decisive factor in Finland's second salvation within approximately four years was the fact that the Red Army had more important objectives in the summer of 1944 than the conquest of Finland. With Allied armies now poised in Normandy for their dash across France, Stalin was, no doubt, eager to beat the Americans and British to Berlin. By mid-July, the Soviet command began to recall the best divisions and much of the armor from the Karelian Isthmus and Ladoga-Karelia for use on the Baltic front. This does not alter the fact that the tenacity of the Finnish troops—once the initial shock was overcome—enabled the defense to endure until the Red Army broke off the attack. Finland's independence was once again saved by the bravery of her soldiers. When the battle for Finland subsided, her Army—now at its peak strength of 530,000 men—stood resolute and unbowed east of the 1940 border on all sectors of the front.[67] When the situation looked darkest in June, Stalin had demanded unconditional surrender; now there was at least reason to hope for a negotiated peace.

As the Red Army drove ever deeper into the Baltic states in the summer of 1944, the prospects for further German assistance progressively decreased, but so did the possibilities of Hitler's retaliation to a Finnish bid for peace. By the end of July, the Germans were so short of troops that they recalled both the

122nd Division and the artillery brigade from southern Finland. Now, at last—with both German and Russian forces withdrawing—there appeared to be an opportunity to lead the nation out of the war without inviting disaster. The first prerequisites to peace were the selection of a new President and a new Cabinet. On 28 July President Ryti visited Mikkeli and arranged a gentlemen's agreement whereby he would vacate his office in favor of Marshal Mannerheim. On 1 August Ryti resigned, and three days later the Parliament unanimously passed a special bill designating the Marshal President. On 8 August a new Cabinet was formed, with Antti Hackzell, a former Foreign Minister and Minister to Moscow, serving as Prime Minister. Carl Enckell took over the Foreign Ministry from Dr. Ramsay. Tanner, definitely *persona non grata* to the Kremlin, was dropped from the Government. A week later (17 August), Field Marshal Keitel flew to Mikkeli, ostensibly to convey Hitler's congratulations to President Mannerheim, but actually to dissuade him from seeking peace. The new President, who also retained his post as Commander-in-Chief, informed Keitel that he did not consider himself bound by the Ryti-Hitler agreement.[68]

On 25 August the Finnish Government inquired, via Stockholm, about the resumption of armistice and/or peace negotiations. The Soviet reply of 29 August set only two preconditions —an immediate and public break in relations with Germany, and the expulsion or internment of all German troops by 15 September. On 2 September Parliament accepted these Soviet conditions by a vote of 108 to 45. That same evening, Foreign Minister Enckell presented a note to Minister Blücher, severing diplomatic relations as politely as possible and requesting that all German troops vacate Finnish territory within two weeks. Simultaneously, President Mannerheim sent a personal letter to Hitler diplomatically explaining the necessity for this action, and expressing the wish of all Finns that the change would not lead to animosity between the recent brothers-in-arms.[69]

The Marshal next proposed to Stalin, again via Stockholm, that a ceasefire be arranged for a day and hour of his choice. The Soviet leader designated 8 A.M. (7 A.M. Finnish time) on 4 September, and orders went out to the Finnish Army to cease firing at that time. However, the Red Army continued its fire for another whole day, until 8 A.M. on the 5th. Without explanation for this unchivalrous behavior, the Soviet Government formally acknowledged it in the first article of the Armistice Agreement. [70]

The Finnish delegation arrived in Moscow on 7 September, but Soviet officials did not receive them until the 14th. There were no negotiations in the normal sense; Molotov simply dictated his terms, and on the evening of 18 September he gave the Finns until the following noon to accept them or face total occupation of their country. A depressed Parliament unanimously accepted the forced decision, and on 19 September the Armistice Agreement was signed in Moscow, taking effect immediately.[71]

The Armistice terms which caused the most critical problems immediately were the requirements to disarm and turn over to the Soviet High Command all German forces remaining in Finland (Article 2), and to return the Finnish Army to a peacetime basis within two and one half months (Article 4). In practice, this necessitated massive demobilization while simultaneously waging a new war against a major portion of the 200,000 German troops still in northern Finland. Far from making a gracious exit, as the Finns had earnestly hoped, the Germans had already begun hostilities against their recent comrades on 14 September with an unsuccessful and pointless attack on Suursaari Island. Heavier fighting, in Lapland, began on 28 September and continued until 27 April 1945 when the Finns drove the last Germans over their northwestern border into Norway. During the withdrawal, the spiteful German commander, General Rendulic, ordered the destruction of nearly everything of value in the whole province.[72]

The deployment of the Red Army was such that it could have assisted the Finnish forces, and perhaps reduced the amount of destruction the Germans could complete, but it generally did not intervene in the conflict. General Meretskov, himself, acknowledged that political considerations overruled military opportunities in the sector west of Kandalaksha and Ukhta. It was only in the extreme north, in the mineral-rich Petsamo district, that the Red Army launched a serious offensive against

The Epic of the Soviet-Finnish Winter War**243**

the Germans. Beginning on 7 October, this drive succeeded so well that Petsamo fell within a week, and the pursuit continued across the Norwegian border, where Kirkenes was captured on 25 October. By early November, with winter setting in, the attack halted near Neiden. In this campaign, some 97,000 Soviet troops engaged approximately 53,000 Germans. Obviously, the Finns were left to cope with the main part of the 200,000 German troops in Finland at the time of the Armistice.[73]

It was in connection with these unfortunate battles between the recent brothers-in-arms, between Germans and Finns who, in many cases, had lived, worked, and fought together for more than three years, that Marshal Mannerheim unquestionably proved to be the *indispensable* leader. Fraternal ties between the professional German officer corps and its Finnish counterpart—dating (in the case of the many influential veterans of the Jäger Battalion) from the First World War—were so close that there was reason to fear a civil war, or at least a mutiny, when the Finns were ordered to turn their guns on the Germans at the insistence of the hated Russians. This was a concern shared by knowledgeable Swedish, American, and Finnish officials. It probably explains why Prime Minister Hackzell invoked the Marshal's prestige in his broadcast to the nation on 2 September, in which he announced the resumption of negotiations with the Soviet Government. His concluding statement was to the effect that the Marshal, "who has more experience and knowledge of prevailing conditions than others, has chosen the road upon which we've now tread." [74] At the time President Mannerheim retired from public office, in March 1946 (at the age of 78), Prime Minister Paasikivi noted that he had led the nation when it disengaged itself from the war, adding that "nobody else could have carried out this task, because nobody else enjoyed as he did the confidence of the great majority of the people."[75] Even the Soviet leaders must have recognized that fact, as indicated by their willingness to negotiate with a Government in which Mannerheim was President. Furthermore, they did not conceal a grudging respect for the warrior-statesman they had publicly damned since 1918; at a luncheon in the Soviet Legation in Stockholm on 30 September 1944, the Soviet Minister, Mme. Kollontay, proposed a toast to the Marshal of Finland.[76] Needless to add, when their Marshal spoke, even the

most Germanophile of the Finnish officers obeyed his orders
without hesitation.

For three years, from September 1944 until the Soviet ratification of the final Peace Treaty in September 1947, the Finns
endured the limbo of life under the so-called "Allied" Control
Commission, which, in effect, meant Soviet interpretation and
supervision of their own ambiguous Armistice terms. Andrei
Zhdanov reigned as Stalin's satrap in Helsinki, with a strong
Russian garrison at his call only a few miles away at Porkkala,
the base which the Soviet Union acquired, under a 50-year
lease, in lieu of Hanko. Other important Armistice terms,
confirmed in the Peace Treaty, included:

> recognition of the 1940 boundaries, plus the cession of
> the entire province of Petsamo;*
> payment, in goods specified by the Soviet Government,
> of reparations valued at 300 million U. S. dollars over a
> period of six years—later extended to eight years (in 1938
> prices, with a 10–15% markup; because of inflation and
> late-delivery fees, the total paid greatly exceeded the
> nominal debt);
> and the trial of persons accused of war crimes. Under
> this clause, the Finns were forced to pass a special law in
> order to prosecute some of their outstanding patriots un-
> der its retroactive provisions; their "crimes" were con-
> tributing to Finland's entry into the war in 1941 and
> preventing the conclusion of peace. As the result of this
> mock trial, which the Finns conducted themselves, ex-
> President Ryti, former Ministers Tanner, Rangell, Linko-
> mies, Ramsay, Kukkonen, and Reinikka, and the former
> Minister to Germany, Kivimäki, were sentenced to terms
> ranging from two and a half to ten years. They were par-
> doned after serving approximately half of their sen-
> tences.[77]

More significant, from a long-range viewpoint, were three
other provisions of the 1944 and 1947 treaties; one of these
limited Finnish military personnel strengths to an army of
34,400 men, a navy of 4,500 and an air force of 3,000 (with a
maximum of 60 aircraft).[78]

*See Map No. 15, p. 209

Under the clause abolishing and prohibiting in the future all "Fascist type" organizations and those "conducting propaganda hostile to the Soviet Union," the Control Commission forced the dissolution of the Civic Guards, the Lotta Svärd, and the Veterans' League.[79] Coupled with other restrictions on military training and equipment, the abolition of the Civic Guards meant that Finland was rendered (and remains) virtually defenseless against the only power ever threatening her. If the Finns were again attacked, their only alternatives might be abject surrender or conducting guerilla warfare in the heart of their country.

Perhaps the most insidious provisions of the treaties, in light of Soviet interpretations, were those which required the Finnish Government to free all persons confined because of their activities in favor of, or sympathies with, the United Nations (read U.S.S.R.) and to repeal all pertinent legislative and other restrictions. Coupled with an innocuous-sounding guarantee of civil rights, these clauses emptied the jails of traitors and subversives and legalized the Communist Party.[80]

Under the transparent guise of a democratic coalition party, the Finnish People's Democratic League (SKDL), the communists have controlled from 36 to 50 of the 200 Parliamentary seats from the time of the first postwar election in 1945 to the present (1970 election). From November 1944 until July 1948, there were communist members in all of the Cabinets; in the Pekkala Government the SKDL held 6 of 18 portfolios.[81] Given all of the leverage at their command (the Control Commission, Soviet funds, the Red Army), it is perhaps more remarkable that they didn't take over the Government completely than that they polled nearly a quarter of the votes.

Significantly, in the 1948 election—the first one held after the departure of the Control Commission—the SKDL vote declined to 20 percent and its Parliamentary representation fell from 49 to 38 seats. From that year until 1966, there were no communists in the Cabinet. The year 1948 was significant in two other respects. There was a purported communist attempt to execute a coup, the exact nature and extent of which are still disputed, and a new Soviet-Finnish treaty (of friendship, cooperation, and mutual assistance) was signed.[82]

Stalin initiated negotiations for the 1948 treaty in February with a publicized letter to President Paasikivi in which he

made ominous reference to "similar" treaties with the satellite
régimes of Hungary and Rumania. The pact, which was signed
on 6 April for a ten-year period and has subsequently been
extended beyond the present time, appears surprisingly innocuous. It was speculated that Stalin had different terms in
mind when he summoned the Finns to Moscow, but that he
moderated them because of the sharp Western reaction to the
communist coup in Czechoslovakia during the intervening
weeks (Jan Masaryk's dramatic death occurred in March). In
any case, Finland won somewhat of a diplomatic victory in
obtaining Soviet concurrence for the statement in the treaty's
preamble acknowledging "Finland's endeavors not to be involved in clashes between the interests of the Great Powers."[83]

The ostensible purpose of the treaty is for mutual defense
against "military aggression on the part of Germany or any
Power allied with Germany," which now includes all NATO
countries. Should Finland, or the U.S.S.R. thru Finnish territory, become the object of such aggression, the Finns are obli-
gated to defend their territory "with the help, if necessary, of
the Soviet Union." In such cases, the U.S.S.R. "shall extend to
Finland any necessary assistance, this to be supplied as mutu-
ally agreed." The second article states that the contracting parties "shall consult together in case there is found to be a threat"
of such aggression.[84] The ambiguities are obvious: what consti-
tutes a threat? who is to decide when a threat exists? and, most
important, must Soviet "assistance" be accepted if it is not
desired?

In the fall of 1961, Soviet Premier Khrushchev publicly demanded military conversations with the Finns to counter an
alleged threat from West Germany and her allies, whereupon
President Kekkonen flew home from Honolulu and subsequently flew to Novosibirsk to meet the Soviet leader. Khrushchev dropped his demand for military talks, but he probably
achieved his goal—the not very subtle influencing of the 1962
presidential elections in Finland, which retained Kekkonen in
office with Soviet blessings.[85]

An article in the 1948 pact reaffirmed Finland's 1940 and 1947
pledges "not to enter into any alliance or take part in any coalition directed against the other . . . party." Under Soviet interpretations of this proscription, Finland has been denied not only

the right to even consider joining NATO (which is at least understandable), but also the right to participate in politically harmless and economically beneficial associations—the European Recovery Program (Marshall Plan)[86] and the European Economic Community (Common Market).

From 1944 until the present, the Soviet Government has continuously labored to expand its influence in Finland by exerting economic, political, and diplomatic pressure. The few conciliatory gestures, such as the return of the Porkkala base to Finland early in 1956 (announced with great fanfare in 1955), were carefully timed to accomplish political ends—in that case, to assist Kekkonen in the 1956 presidential election, which he won by the close vote of 151 to 149, with all 56 SKDL votes backing him.[87]

A very flagrant case of Soviet meddling in Finland's internal affairs occurred in 1958, when SKDL agitators were supported by the Soviet press and radio in their bitter campaign to topple the Government of Prime Minister Fagerholm. The Soviet Ambassador was recalled indefinitely, negotiations for the renewal of a trade agreement were suspended, and Soviet acceptance of a ship built in Finland was postponed. This initimidation succeeded; the Fagerholm Cabinet fell after less than five months in office. From a subsequent statement by Khrushchev, it appears that this vigorous Soviet campaign was not due to any specific policies or statements of the Fagerholm Government, but merely to the fact that it was led by Social Democrats.[88]

These are but a few of countless examples of Soviet interference in Finnish politics. One of the reasons that Finland's independence is so precarious, and that foreigners often consider her virtually a Soviet satellite, is that her Government has generally deferred to Moscow's slightest whim.[89] It is not only the Finnish communists who foster this policy, but certain bourgeois politicians also court the Kremlin to advance their personal interests.

Barring completely unforeseen circumstances, it is improbable that the Soviet Union will ever again attack Finland with its overwhelming army. However, long-term attrition may succeed where brute force has failed. Many thoughtful Finns fear that their nation may eventually become "the 16th Soviet Socialist Republic" as the result of the very gradual but persistent diminution of their latitude for independent action in both political and economic matters. It may be pertinent to note that communists were readmitted to the Cabinet in 1966, for the first time in 18 years, *in spite of their loss of three seats in the Parliamentary elections.*[90] Their influence is obviously greater than their numerical strength.

A peaceful take-over of Finland would be a psychological victory of immense value to the Soviet Government. To succeed, the communists must sell the fanciful advantages of the Soviet system to the gullible; to accomplish that, they must also erode the Finns' faith in their own national values. They must —as they are striving to—distort the facts of Finland's proud heritage, besmirch her true patriots, and belittle those valiant men who fought so tenaciously to preserve her independence.

It is natural that the Finns are war-weary; their small nation lost some 87,000 of its sons in the tragic battles of 1939–1945, which also left 57,000 permanently disabled.[91] It is also natural, given their present situation, that they should strive for true neutrality. But is is not sound to forget those aspects of the Winter War which reveal the true nature of the Soviet régime, merely because their neighbor finds them embarrassing—the phony Mainila incident, the undeclared war, and the Kuusinen "Government." It is not right to forget those glorious pages of Finnish military history—Tolvajärvi, Suomussalmi-Raate, and all the others.

With all the obvious debits that the Winter War entailed, one may ask: was it worth it? Do not ask the cynics among today's youth, in Finland or elsewhere. Do not ask those who shirk freedom's responsibilities, while abusing its hard-won privileges. Ask, instead, the thousands of Hungarians who left all they owned and loved to flee the "liberating" Soviet tanks in 1956. Ask the few lucky survivors of countless escape attempts at the Berlin Wall, civilians shot at for the "crime" of trying to leave their "workers' paradise." Ask the Czechs who remember 1948 and 1968. Ask the Polish workers fired upon by their "People's Government" in 1956 and 1970. For those who have experienced the stark realities of life under Soviet domination, for those who treasure human dignity and individuality, there can be only one answer.

The Finland one likes to remember is the courageous, united nation of the Winter War. Unfortunately, today's Finland is again a class-divided, politically unstable country. The outlook for the next half century is not encouraging. The present challenge is more subtle, in some ways more difficult, than the brutally obvious threats of 1939 and 1940. One can only hope that, from the hidden springs of Finland's strength, there will emerge the leadership, the resolution, and the dedication to preserve her hard-won heritage of freedom and independence.

As this book opened with reference to *The Kalevala,* it is appropriate to close with a few lines from that national epic (Rune XXX) which bear an ever-timely message for those willing to heed it, be they Finns or free men anywhere:

> Let the wizards charm each other,
> And bewitch their magic offspring,
> Bring their tribes to fell destruction.
> Never did my gray-haired father
> Bow submission to a wizard,
> Offer worship to magicians.
> These the words my father uttered,
> These the thoughts his son advances:
> 'Guard us, thou O great Creator,
> Shield us, thou O God of mercy,
> With thine arms of grace protect us,
> Help us with thy strength and wisdom,
> Guide the minds of all thy heroes,
> Keep aright the thoughts of women,
> Keep the old from speaking evil,
> Keep the young from sin and folly,
> Be to us a help forever,
> Be our Guardian and our Father,
> That our children may not wander
> From the ways of their Creator,
> From the path that God has given!'

*This may point the way to others,*
*To the singers better gifted*
*EPILOGUE*

# Postscript and Acknowledgments

THE AUTHOR HAS NO ILLUSION THAT THIS BRIEF ACCOUNT IS A DEfinitive history of the Winter War. One might easily devote a longer study to the complex fighting in Ladoga-Karelia alone. Salla, Kuhmo, Taipale, and many other battles deserve far more attention than they received here. Books in the Finnish language abound on nearly every separate campaign, indeed, even on individual battalions. However, except for those concerned with the Karelian Isthmus in the final stages of the war, their message is everywhere similar: small Finnish units destroying or checking vastly larger Soviet forces by displaying superior skill and daring. Although virtually all Finnish troops merit the highest admiration, the endless repetition of these exploits might become tedious.

A more serious, presently insurmountable, obstacle to writing a definitive history is the inaccessibility of much of the pertinent data. The Soviet Government still finds the whole truth too embarrassing to admit, and consequently it has released only sporadic details about the fighting in northern Finland. Only in relation to the Red Army's belated success on the Isthmus have Soviet authors published substantial accounts, and even these are sometimes of questionable accuracy. The heavy reliance on Finnish sources is thus unavoidable; the author's request for specifics of Soviet military operations, addressed to an agency of the Soviet Government in 1967, remains unanswered four years later. (The same agency had responded promptly and positively to a prior inquiry on a less embarrassing subject.) The Soviet Government finds it easier to admit that its idolized leader for more than two decades was a depraved murderer than to acknowledge, for example, that the Mainila incident was a deliberate provocation.

Furthermore, so delicate are the relations between Finland and her awesome neighbor that the Finnish Government also retains a veil of official secrecy over much material which might embarrass the Soviet Government—captured documents, POW interrogation files, intelligence and counterintelligence records, etc. These are not scheduled for declassification until 1988, and one may predict that not much will be released even at that late date if there has not been a fundamental change in the political situation in either Finland or the Soviet Union by then. It may be significant that the official Finnish history of the Continuation War has been published, while the embarrassing history of the earlier Winter War still awaits the light of day. The diplomatic reasons advanced by the staff of the Institute of Military History for this strange priority are not entirely convincing.

Fortunately, the author had access, in private collections, to a limited amount of material which is still covered by official secrecy. It provided unique insights into the Red Army, but it is frustrating to contemplate the amount of such revealing material which probably exists—or at least *did* exist—in the secret Finnish archives.

Given these serious limitations on source material, the purpose of this book was merely to present a factual (although necessarily incomplete) account of the most significant events of the war, along with representative samples of some of its less important features. The author also tried to recapture some of "the spirit of the Winter War," a remarkable phenomenon which should serve as a shining example for free men in all ages. If he succeeded, even partially, the credit must be shared with a multitude of willing helpers.

I welcome this opportunity to express sincere thanks to the many people who gave so generously of their time and talents in connection with the research on this book. First and foremost, I am indebted to General Staff Colonel Keijo J. Mikola, recently retired Director of the Institute of Military History, Helsinki, for his wholehearted cooperation. Without his invaluable support, this book would not have been possible in its present form. Of the many members of his staff who assisted me, General Staff Major Pertti Kilkki deserves special mention. Among the numerous services Major Kilkki rendered was the verification of the details of Finnish military operations in the first seven chapters. The author, of course, is solely responsible for the opinions and conclusions drawn from these facts.

Also meriting special thanks are two veterans of the Winter War who provided priceless technical assistance, constructively criticizing drafts of the entire book. Colonel Antero Aakkula, U. S. Army, Retired, served in the First Division on the Karelian Isthmus, and Colonel Eino Lassila, U. S. Army, Retired, served in the Ninth Division at Suomussalmi-Raate and Kuhmo.

It is a sad commentary on Finland's present position that several others who assisted asked to remain anonymous for personal or political reasons. These include a Finnish general officer and some civilian officials. More understandably, certain Red Army veterans, now living in voluntary exile from the U.S.S.R., were still too frightened of the long vengeful arm of the Soviet secret police to cooperate at all.

Mr. John E. Taylor of the Modern Military Records Division and Messrs. Wolfe and Bauer of the German Military Documents Section, National Archives, kindly facilitated the author's research in the records of their offices. Dr. Arthur G. Kogan, Chief of the Research Guidance and Review Division, Historical Office, Department of State, provided similar assistance in relation to the pertinent diplomatic correspondence.

It would require an entire chapter to specify the services rendered by all of the others who contributed to this book in one way or another. The mere alphabetical listings of their names are a very inadequate expression of my appreciation for their help.

(1)  Veterans of the Winter War personally interviewed by the author:

General Gustaf Ehrnrooth          General Harold Öhquist
Colonel Per Ole Ekholm           Mr. K. E. Olsoni

General Ragnar Grönvall
Mr. K. V. Kallio
Dr. K. Killinen
Mr. Paavo Korppoo
Colonel Erkki Lahdenpera
Mr. Vilho Manninen
Mr. Lauri Marttala
Colonel Alpo K. Marttinen
Mr. Eino Kaaralainen
Colonel Valo K. Nihtilä

Colonel Andrew A. Paasonen
Mr. Väinö Rauhalahti
Mr. Lauri Rossi
Mr. Arvo Saksala
Major Martti Siukosaari
General Paavo Talvela
Mr. Nestori Uitti
General Kaarlo O. E. Vaala
Mr. Oiva Vuorinen

(2)   Veterans of the Winter War who assisted by corresponding with the author or answering his questionnaire:

Mr. Mikko Asunta
Mr. Paavo Fleming
Mr. Valde Kärkäs
Mr. Arvo Kuusela

Captain Ilmari Miettinen
General Hugo Österman
Colonel Paavo Susitaival
Mr. Eero Sysikumpu

(3)   Others who assisted in various ways:

Colonel Matti Aarnio
Dr. Osmo Apunen
Professor Vyacheslav Artemiev
Dr. William Copeland
Colonel James F. Dunn
Lt. Colonel Theodore Finnegan
Consul Randall Forselius
Commander Jorma Haapkyla
Dr. Eila Hanni
Mr. Viljami Hanni
Colonel Frank B. Hayne
Maisteri Helminen
Colonel T. J. Jackson
Mr. Donald Jacobs
Dr. Ralph Jalkanen
Mr. Jack Kangas
Maisteri K. Kerkkonen
Dr. Fred Kiley
Sergeant Kivelä

Dr. L. Kujala
General M. Kukiel
Mr. Elja Kuorikoski
Mr. Urpo Leskinen
Major Henry F. Lippincott
Mr. Pekka Louhimo
Lt. Colonel Carl Markkanen
Mr. Leon Mitkiewicz
Maisteri Kristina Nyman
Mr. Jon Parssinen
Colonel William L. Roche
Colonel William Ruenheck
Maisteri V. M. Syrjö
Maisteri P. Talvio
Dr. Nicholas Vaslef
Mr. Veikko Virtalaine
Mrs. Maria Voutilainen
Mr. Gerry A. Worsell
Professor John H. Wuorinen

Finally, my wife, Irene, merits an endurance award for the many times she retyped the manuscript of this book.

## COMMENTARY AND DOCUMENTATION

In the first eight chapters the author endeavored to present an objective, factual account of the Winter War in its chronological sequence. In the following pages, controversial aspects and personal reflections are occasionally presented, along with the sources for the factual information. Abbreviated citations are presented in full in the appended bibliography. Parties cited for interviews and questionnaires are fully named in the Acknowledgements section.

## INTRODUCTION: UNDECLARED WAR

1. 30 November Helsinki raids detailed in reports to U. S. Dept. of State from Minister to Finland, Mr. Schoenfeld (U. S. State Dept. files 760 D.61/510 and 512). Also, see U. S. State Dept. *Bulletin,* Vol I, No. 23, 2 December 1939, pp 610–611. These are confirmed by Finnish sources, including J. O. Hannula, pp 25–26. The first (leaflet) aircraft dropped 5 bombs on nearby Malmi airport before departing. An hour later 9 bombers attacked Finnish defenses in Helsinki Bay. First raid on heart of city occurred about 3 P.M., when 15 planes struck near the U. S. Legation, destroying the Technical University and several other non-military structures. As these raids were unexpected, casualties were the highest Helsinki suffered during the entire war—at least 42 killed and many more wounded. An interesting commentary on the accuracy of Soviet bombing is the Finnish Information Central picture of the Soviet Legation with its windows blown out during the 30 November raids. Copy in U. S. State Dept. file 760 D.61/1297. Time of Viipuri raid noted in archives of Sotahistoriallinen Tutkimuslaitos (Military History Institute) Helsinki—hereinafter cited as ST—file 3948:5.

2. Mannerheim, p. 322.

3. An example of misleading TASS reporting from Helsinki found in 18 November 1939 issue of *Pravda,* which claimed that families of mobilized reservists were so impoverished that they lacked clothes and shoes.

4. Author's interview with Colonel Paasonen, 1 April 1967. Derevyanski was confidentially described by a Latvian Foreign Office official in May 1940 as "highly nervous and an accomplished trouble-maker" (U. S. State Dept. file 701.6160 P/22).

5. Tanner, passim. Molotov's remark (made on 3 November), ibid, pp 66–67. (This and subsequent quotes are made with the permission of Stanford University Press, publisher of Väinö Tanner, *The Winter War.*) For other sources on negotiations, see below, footnote 10.

6. Pospelov et al. (ed.), *VOVSS-KI,* pp 46–47. That some Soviet military leaders had (or at least should have had) a realistic appreciation of Finland's defensive capabilities is evident from certain prewar Commissariat of Defense publications, e.g., *Finlyandiya i Eye Armiya* (1937). The author of that 87-page pamphlet knew that all Finnish troops were experienced skiers trained for winter warfare, and that their field exercises emphasized Finland's many natural defense features. It is puzzling to note that —if Marshal Meretskov's memoirs are correct—in July 1939 Stalin had apparently intended to use all the nation's forces if a "counterattack" against Finland developed (Meretskov, pp 178–179). Meretskov was Commander of the Leningrad Military District and subsequently of the 7th Army which carried the main assault against Finland. Sharing Shaposhnikov's apprehensions, on the eve of hostilities he wrote in a report—which the Finns later captured—that "the terrain of coming operations is split by lakes, rivers, and swamps, and is almost entirely covered by forests. . . . The proper use of our forces will be difficult. . . . It is criminal to believe that our task will be easy, or only like a march, as it has been told to me by officers in connection with my inspection" (*Study of Soviet Tactics* . . ., p. 26). In some respects, Soviet *military* intelligence had been very thorough. A handbook issued by the Red Army "for official use" contained detailed data on Finnish air units prior to 30 November 1939—including the dates when 37 officers had been appointed to their latest positions (*Spravochnik* . . ., pp 92–107).

7. The figures on Soviet losses in Poland must be considered minimum, as they are taken from Molotov's address to the Supreme Soviet on 31 October 1939. However, in view of the disintegration of Polish armed forces under the Nazi blitzkrieg prior to the Soviet attack, and because Marshal Smigly-Rydz ordered the Poles not to resist the Red Army, light Russian casualties are credible. Lt. General M. Kukiel, of the Polish Institute and Sikorski Museum, believes that "737 killed . . . seems to conform to the realities of that final period" (Letter to author, 27 March 1969).

8. Informal Soviet overtures to Finland, vaguely foreshadowing the demands made after the Hitler-Stalin pact, had begun as early as April 1938. Those preliminary discussions had terminated inconclusively in March 1939 (Tanner, pp 3–15). Some recent critics (e.g. Oliver Warner, *Marshal Mannerheim and the Finns,* p. 136) have asserted that all the Finns' subsequent hardships were due to the Cajander Government's rejection of those relatively mild proposals. This simplism implies the very questionable assumption that more drastic Soviet demands would not have followed after the Hitler-Stalin pact. Terms of 23 August and 28 September treaties found in U. S. State

Dept., *Nazi-Soviet Relations 1939–1941,* pp 78 and 107. Bessarabia was also allocated to the Soviet sphere, but this is not pertinent to the Finnish problem. Within a year the U.S.S.R. annexed every one of these areas except Finland—which was the only place where Soviet aggression encountered determined and effective resistance. Translations of Soviet treaties with the Baltic countries in U. S. State Dept. *Bulletins,* 11 November 1939, pp. 542–544 and 16 December 1939, pp 705–707.

9. Tanner, pp 28–30, 40–41.

10. A concise summary of negotiations preceding hostilities is found in the introduction to *The Finnish Blue Book.* For more detailed descriptions of these negotiations and subsequent diplomatic activity, see Väinö Tanner, *The Winter War,* and Max Jakobson, *The Diplomacy of the Winter War.* The wisdom of their government's stand is still debated in certain Finnish circles, but there is little reason to believe that Finland's yielding on those vital issues would not have been followed by her complete subjugation, as was the case of the three Baltic States, which were "voluntarily" incorporated into the U.S.S.R. in August 1940. Among the evidence supporting this conclusion is a Memo of 15 November 1940 signed by Hitler's interpreter, Herr Schmidt, recounting the Hitler-Molotov conversations two days earlier. He noted that the Commissar declared that "he imagined this [Finnish] settlement on the same scale as in Bessarabia" (Bessarabia had been annexed by the U.S.S.R. a few months before this conversation), *Nazi-Soviet Relations, 1939–1941,* p 240. On 2 July 1940 Molotov had been equally blunt with the Deputy Prime Minister of Lithuania, Vincas Kreve-Michevicius, remarking that "your Lithuania, along with the other Baltic nations, including Finland, will have to join the glorious family of the Soviet Union" (*House Report No. 2684 . . .* , Part 13, p 12). Molotov's remarks show that even after annexing the entire Karelian Isthmus, which far exceeded any of his objectives expressed in 1939, Stalin was still not satisfied. This is not to say that some further slight compromises by the Finns might not have been judicious—but only compromises which would not have jeopardized the main Finnish defense lines, either directly or from their rear. Even Marshal Mannerheim, albeit an arch villian to the Soviet Government, had advocated making certain territorial concessions to the Soviet Union (Mannerheim, pp 300 and 314–315). This was confirmed in more emphatic terms in a postwar conversation between the Marshal and General Erik Heinrichs (Heinrichs, p 187). Of course, even if it *could* be proven that the Soviet demands in the fall of 1939 reflected their maximum objectives, that would not justify the use of naked aggression to achieve those goals. Finland, as a sovereign state,

had the right to refuse to bargain away any of its territory.

11. Tanner, pp 85–88.

12. Mannerheim, p 321.

13. Figures for the population of the U.S.S.R. illustrate the complexities and reliability of Soviet statistics. The 17 January 1939 census figure was 170.6 million. *Izvestiya,* 16 December 1939 (quoted and reaffirmed in the 1960s by G. Deborin, *The Second World War,* Moscow, n.d., p 68), claimed 183 million, which is consistent with an addition of 13 million from eastern Poland. However, *SSSR v Tsifrakh v. 1967 Godu,* Moscow, 1968, p 7, estimates the 1 January 1940 population at 194.1 million. (There were no territorial changes in the preceding month to account for the 11 million difference.) It is also interesting that various Soviet sources (e.g., *USSR in Figures for 1959,* Moscow, 1960, p 35; *The Soviet Union-Facts and Figures (1960),* Soviet News, London, 1960, p 8) provide two figures for 1939—one prior to the 17 September invasion of Poland and a second (190.7 million) which includes "the Western regions of the Ukraine and Byelorussia [i.e., eastern Poland], Moldavia [i.e., Bessarabia and adjacent areas], Lithuania, Latvia, and Estonia." This appears to be tacit admission that the Soviets already considered the Baltic states part of the U.S.S.R. in 1939, although they were not formally annexed until August 1940.

## CHAPTER I: FOOLS RUSH IN

1. Enumerated Soviet forces are minimum figures, acknowledged in Soviet sources and compiled by Major Seppälä and Major (then Captain) Kilkki of the ST. Mannerheim placed initial Soviet strength at 26 to 28 divisions (p 330) but he did not verify his memoirs with the ST archives, and they contain statistical errors. Figures for Finnish forces are correct as listed; they are taken from the Seppälä and Kilkki article and are confirmed in all other reliable sources, e.g., K. J. Mikola, et al., p 267. Independent covering troop battalions mentioned totalled approximately the strength of one additional division. Authorized strength of Finnish infantry divisions was approximately 14,200 men, but that figure is only nominal—most units were understrength in the Winter War. Estimates for Soviet divisions vary between 15,000 and 18,000, but their composition also varied and the lower figure is probably more typical. Soviet infantry divisions normally had an organic complement of about 50 tanks; Finnish divisions had none. An article by "Victor Suomalainen" presents a breakdown of opposing divisions, with the higher figure for the Soviet. (Seppälä and Kilkki give the lower figure for the "average" Soviet division.) "Victor Suomalainen" was pseudonym of Colonel Alpo K. Marttinen, U. S.

Army (Ret.), who—then a captain in the Finnish Army—was 9th Division Chief of Staff at Suomussalmi. Mannerheim read and praised the "Suomalainen" article (author's interview with Colonel Marttinen, 11 June 1968). Covering troop units were independent (or "detached"— Finnish "erillinen") battalions composed of Civic Guards, augmented during hostilities by border guards and local volunteers. (Information on Finnish divisions and covering troops provided by Major Kilkki and other ST personnel.) Data on Murmansk RR (Soviet designation was Kirov RR) from U. S. Military Academy, *The Soviet-Finnish War 1939–1940* (hereinafter cited as USMA), p 2. Finnish underestimation revealed in Mannerheim, p 330. This and subsequent quotations are from the book *The Memoirs of Marshal Mannerheim* by Mannerheim, translated by Count Eric Lewenhaupt, U. S. copyright 1954 by E. P. Dutton & Co., Inc., publishers; British copyright by Laurence Pollinger, Ltd. and published by Cassell and Co., Ltd. Reprinted with permission of all parties.

2. Mannerheim (p 329) admitted the "paralyzing effect" of tanks; Colonel Järvinen (p 215) spoke of "tank terror" which resulted in some places in "panicky" retreat. The general effects on civilian morale revealed in Hannula, p 21. Details of the 30 November raids, ultimatum rumor, and terrified exodus from private correspondence of a competent eyewitness, Colonel (then Major) Frank B. Hayne, U. S. Military Attaché in Helsinki (letters dated 28 December 1939 and 1 April 1940). Number of bombers from U. S. State Dept. *Bulletin,* 2 December 1939, p 610.

3. If opinions on self-evident Soviet invasion strategy are necessary, see Peitsara, pp 46–47, and USMA, p 4.

4. Finnish view on significance of different fronts, Peitsara, p 49. Soviet agreement apparent from subsequent deployments of their reinforcements. Finnish strength (or rather weakness) in Petsamo region also noted in Peitsara, pp 53–54. Unit designation, Mikola et al., p 267. Marshal Meretskov (p 181) claimed that the 14th Army (as well as the 8th and 9th Armies) was designated as a mere Group at the outbreak of hostilities. Even if true, that would not alter the data presented here and below on the designations and strengths of the divisions participating in the initial attacks.

5. Soviet order of battle information (hereinafter referred to as OB), Seppälä and Kilkki. Soviet confirmation of general presentation, Kuz'min, p 262.

6. Improvement of road to border noted on a U. S. War Dept. map in U. S. Library of Congress collection, filed under "Finland, Boundaries —Finnish-Russian Line." Finnish OB, Mikola et al., p 267. Soviet OB, Kuz'min, p 261. Date of Salla capture from Soviet communiqué

(Leningrad Military District), 10 December 1939; confirmed in different terms by Finnish communiqué, 11 December. Finnish concern over this drive, Hannula, p 44. NB: Place names in this area are confusing. Church village (equivalent to an American county seat) in question was called Kuolajärvi until 1937 when it was renamed Salla. Soviet sources continued to refer to it as Kuolajärvi, both during the war and afterwards when they annexed it. The Finns who evacuated the ceded area moved to Märkäjärvi, about 16 miles to the SW, which they renamed Salla. For maps or reports concerning Salla, it is essential to note date of issue.

7. Surprise of new road noted by Mannerheim, p 337. NB: Only the most important "highways" anywhere north of Lake Ladoga had as much as a gravel pavement; most, like the Juntusranta-Suomussalmi road, were merely dirt lanes. Accordingly, the appearance of the road network on the accompanying map (and on other maps of northern areas) is misleading. Many of the depicted "roads" are too poor to appear on maps of much greater scale. They are included to illustrate routes used by the contending forces. The 50-man force in a book written by Finnish commander at Suomussalmi, General H. J. Siilasvuo (*Suom. T.,* p 17). Same source (p 15 ff) confirms Finnish surprise, OB, and Soviet gains. Soviet OB and its disposition from Suomalainen. Zelentsov identified by U. S. Attaché, Helsinki, 2 April 1940 (from Finnish General Staff report), in U. S. Archives, records RG 165, file 2657–D–1054–25.

8. Peitsara, p 51, confirms general scorched earth policy. Colonel Marttinen felt that refugee columns strengthened morale, as the troops had visual evidence of what they were fighting for (11 June 1968 interview); Captain I. Miettinen, who served as a 1st Sgt at Suomussalmi, listed as his most memorable experience during the war "the initial impression . . . was made very depressing when the troops passed the refugees in long lines and when one saw the slaughtered animals they had to leave by the roadside" (questionnaire, July 1967).

9. USMA, p 9; Kuz'min, p 261; Mikola, "The Finnish Wars," p 244; and Mikola et al., p 267.

10. There has been some dispute about Finnish strategic planning for defense of Ladoga-Karelia. Heinrichs, pp 126–127, agreed with a Swedish critic that the region was relatively neglected by Finnish military leaders (Mannerheim excepted) before the war. However, as Mannerheim noted, p 333, maneuvers had often been held there and concrete plans for counterattacks had been formulated. To a neutral party, this appears to be a petty argument over degrees of emphasis. The question it raises to many Finns is simply: what right have the Swedes to criticize? Finnish OB, Mikola et al., p 267 and Mannerheim,

p 325. (Units in this area were 12th and 13th Divisions and 8th, 9th, and 10th Battalions of covering troops.) Soviet OB from Seppälä and Kilkki and confirmed by Kuz'min, p 256, with the exception of the armored brigade which he euphemistically described as a "small quantity of tanks" (actually 190 tanks). Finnish miscalculations and consequent surprise noted by both Heinrichs (pp 127–128) and Mannerheim (pp 330–331). The rail spur from Petrozavodsk towards Suojärvi appears on a map depicting this war in the *History of the Great Fatherland War of the Soviet Union* (see Pospelov, *IVOVSS,* Vol. I, Map No. 13, between pp 264–265) Moscow, 1960, but it did not appear on the pertinent map in the *Bol'shaya Sovetskaya Entsiklopediya* (hereinafter cited as BSE), Second Edition, Vol. 39, between pp 510–511, published in 1956.

11. Suojärvi battle, Heinrichs, p 128. The 30 November losses from ST file 3687. Soviet OB and dispositions in Seppälä and Kilkki. Mannerheim's view in his *Memoirs,* pp 333—334. Peitsara (p 54) felt that the thrusts towards Värtsilä were the most dangerous.

12. Task Force R originally consisted of Independent Btn No. 10, the 9th Battery of Regt 13 (field artillery) and the 8th Co. of JR 37. Reinforced by Independent Btn 112 and Bicycle Btn No. 7. Composition of Task Force R, Tuompo, *Kunnia-Isänmaa* (hereinafter cited as K-I, chapter by Talvela), p 215; supplemental information provided by Major Kilkki of ST. Approximate total strength, Aarnio, p 179. Same source, p 181, mentions that Räsänen was far behind the front; Heinrichs, p 130, confirmed this without mentioning the commander's name. The HQ move recorded in ST file 3687. Aittojoki fighting, Tuompo, *K-I,* p 215.

13. 2 December losses and Mannerheim's "furious" reaction (Heinrichs used the term "fuming") reported in Heinrichs, pp 128—129. The replacement of General Juho Heiskanen (not to be confused with the then Colonel, later Commander-in-Chief, General Kaarlo Heiskanen) confirmed in ST records and Mikola letter to author, 11 April 1969. Activities of Det R on 3 and 4 December in ST file 3687.

14. Järvinen, pp 214—215; Mannerheim, p 334; and Tuompo, *K-I,* p 166.

15. Shooting own men noted in ST file 3687, 5 December 2212 hour entry (blamed on lack of snow capes for some groups). Ägläjärvi defeat, Tuompo, *K-I,* p 215. Fear of night attacks mentioned by Colonel Pajari, ST file 929:5 (Daily Report of Action of Task Force P, 6–23 December). Heinrichs, pp 129–130, confirmed the general morale picture; tank terror documented above.

16. Both Colonel Nihtilä and General Grönvall mentioned presence of spies and saboteurs to the author. Former noted Inkeri tribe, latter

the bodyguards. Few Finns will admit, even today, the fear of treason, but it is implied in certain records, e.g., in Colonel Pajari's writings such as *Hamalainen Sotilaana* (A Man of Häme as a Soldier) ST file 929:5 and another article in same file. Author knows of one case of alleged battlefield treason, but it would be difficult to document.

17. Heinrichs, p 129.

18. Seppälä & Kilkki, p 6.

19. Viipuri's checkered history in any good history of Finland, e.g. Jutikkala, *History* . . ., passim.

20. Term "Mannerheim Line," coined by foreign journalists, was not then used by the Finns. I have employed it for convenience. Finnish OB, Mikola et al., p 267. The four covering troop groups (U, M, L, and R) were named after towns in their sectors, from SW to NE respectively. The data on the Line and frontier zone, Peitsara, p 52 and Öhquist, *Vinterkriget,* p 47. Covering troop strength, Kilkki, "Talvisodan S . . .," p 143. Regarding the resistance offered by these forces, it is pertinent to note that their total fatalities were only about 400, ibid, p 128. Soviet tank strength, Mannerheim, p 328. Seppälä and Kilkki give even higher estimate for tanks employed here. Mannerheim's view in his *Memoirs,* pp 326–327; also Colonel Nihtilä interview.

21. Kuz'min (p 236) revealed that 7th Army employed an average of 11 guns per mile of front when the war began, which would approximate the 600 figure. Seppälä and Kilkki placed total for "guns and mortars" at 900, which is also compatible with artillery strength of about 600 pieces. Numerous Soviet accounts mention the half-hour barrage, e.g., Matrosov, *Boi* . . ., passim. Surprise and capture of border guards from Manninen interview. Retreat to Terijoki 30 November, ST file 3948:5. Other details, Matrosov, *Boi* . . ., Vol. I, pp 73–76; Vol. II, p 305.

22. ST file 3948:5.

23. Heinrichs, p 120.

24. Matrosov, *Boi* . . ., Vol. I, pp 35–38.

25. Use of *heavy* tanks, Finnish General Staff report, 2 December, found in U. S. State Dept. file 760 D.61/582. Other details, Matrosov, *Boi* . . ., Vol. I, p 100.

26. Heinrichs, p 120 and Mannerheim, pp 327–328.

27. The 3 December move verified by Major Kilkki of the ST from the GHQ War Diary.

28. HQ visit from author's interview with Colonel Nihtilä, 20 June 1967, and Österman, pp 207–209; Mannerheim, pp 326–327, explains his views. Considering Österman's bitter memoirs, it seems remarkable that the Finnish Army didn't disintegrate at the top. On at least one prior occasion (in October 1939) he had offered to resign because of

differences with the Marshal (Österman, pp 181–182). By his own admission, Österman (and also Öhquist), questioning the Commander-in-Chief's judgment, deliberately ignored his telephone orders on 2 December to reinforce the U Group with a regiment from the main position (ibid, pp 206–207). Postmortem reports, ST file 3948:5 (cited units were tasked directly by II Army Corps, but Mannerheim's hand is apparent).

29. Prewar differences, reorganization, and friction discussed by Heinrichs, pp 103–111, and Österman, pp 173–194, 265. Mannerheim, pp 326–327, discusses his views on the role of the covering troops.

30. Stiffening resistance, Mannerheim, p 328. Koukunniemi battle, Matrosov, *Boi . . .*, Vol. 1, pp 104–106. Finns considered these lowlands expendable; their main line in this sector was back from the river and uphill (author's interview with General G. Ehrnrooth, 17 July 1967).

31. Soviet Vuoksi claim in Leningrad Military District communiqué for 6 December, quoted in *Pravda* (and other papers), 7 December. Summa penetration, ST file 3948:5, which also mentions panic during withdrawal. Mannerheim's anticipation of this possibility from author's interview with Nihtilä, 29 June 1967. In general, the delaying phase of the fighting ended in the eastern part of the Isthmus by 6 December and in the western sector (where the main defenses were farther from the frontier) by 10 December (Kilkki, "Talvisodan S . . .," p 127).

32. Data on antitank weapons and their effectiveness, Mannerheim, pp 327–328. The most common Soviet tank employed during the Winter War was the light T-26, copied from 15 Vickers tanks purchased from Britain in the early 1930s (Ogorkiewicz, pp 224–225, and Öhquist, "Comments . . .").

33. The role of the reserve officers is a sensitive subject to those involved. There were far too few regular officers in the tiny peacetime army to lead all the troops mobilized during the war, and those few professional officers were mainly employed on various HQ staffs where their specialized knowledge was essential. Consequently, less experienced reserve officers carried the brunt of the actual fighting, suffering proportionally the highest casualties of any group, officer or enlisted. This unfortunate necessity resulted in some bitterness among the reservists, on the one hand, and some criticism of their leadership abilities by the regulars, on the other. Mannerheim properly singled out the reserve officers for his highest tribute in his final Order of the Day on 14 March 1940. Heinrichs, pp 183 and 190, discusses this question. One example of the regulars' criticism in ST file 3948:5, 25 December entry, in which a 5th Division officer states that the battalion commanders of a subordinate unit "cannot carry out

their difficult task because they are leading basic units commanded by reserve officers." The reservists' attitude was brought home to the author in an interview with a Captain (Res.) Oiva M_____, who noted that they were also paid less than regular officers.

34. U. S. State Dept. file 760 D.61/681.

35. Voronov, p 136.

36. Heinrichs, p 182.

37. Radio Moscow in U.S. State Dept. files 760 D.61/551 and 561. Finland's Foreign Minister, Social Democrat Väinö Tanner, described Kuusinen and Rosenberg (both of whom he knew personally) as "fanatics with burning eyes" (U. S. State Dept. file 760 D.61/583). Full composition of Kuusinen's government, *Pravda,* 2 December 1939. Terms of "treaty" in Aleksandrov's *Politicheskiy Slovar'* (pp 604–606), the editorial work on which was completed 2 December. Mazour, pp 238–240, has an English translation.

38. The term for the 1918 fighting is still controversial in Finland. To the communists, it was the "Civil War." To many others, it was the "War of Liberation" (Mannerheim) or the "War for Independence." The Red forces included both tens of thousands of native Leftists and approximately 40,000 Soviet troops from the Russian garrisons stationed in Finland during the First World War. Initially, Soviet troops —and especially munitions—were an important source of support for the Finnish Reds. I have used the term "civil war" because the major forces on both sides were Finns, and it was this class warfare aspect which caused the pernicious aftereffects to linger in Finnish society. (See also Hodgson, Chapter Three.)

39. Among English-language works on modern Finland, two of the better ones are by Mazour and Wuorinen *(A History of Finland);* the figures for starvation are from the latter. The estimate on executions is the result of detailed research by Dr. Jaakko Paavolainen (see bibliography). Percentage of communists in Finnish electorate based on voting statistics before 1930 and after 1944. Of course, the hidden joker in the deck, which Stalin failed to see in 1939, was the fact that very few of those who voted communist were willing to betray their native land in the interests of the U.S.S.R. An interesting discussion of both right and left extremism is found in Rintala's *Three Generations;* that author notes how out-of-touch with Finnish realities Kuusinen became after 1918.

40. Shortage of uniforms, etc., Pospelov, *IVOVSS,* Vol. I, p 276. Same source mentions troops from "S. regions" who were "not prepared for action under winter conditions." This is as close as Soviet sources have come to confirming the freezing to death of scores of non-Slavic soldiers from Soviet Central Asia. Correspondent's report, Soloviev, pp

171–174. One informed opinion of Soviet troops is in Öhquist, "Comments . . .," p 6. For Soviet admissions of use of poorly trained reservists, see Kogan, pp 320 and 337.

41. Oreshin, pp 126–128. The Soviet propaganda apparatus succeeded in creating some anti-Finnish sentiment in the general public; examples of private correspondence illustrating this, Zenzinov, pp 41, 56, and 138.

42. There are numerous contemporary correspondents' accounts of bands playing the Internationale, etc. (e.g., Cox, p 38; Kerr, p 155). Concrete evidence of loudspeaker serenade, including the Marseillaise, ST file 3948:5, 8 December, 2145 hour entry.

43. Author's interviews with General Vaala, 16 June 1967, and Colonel Ekholm, 20 June 1967; Järvinen, p 208.

44. Munitions supply, Mannerheim, p 324. Colonel Nihtilä also emphasized rationing of shells to the author. Soviet confirmation of Finnish 1887 guns on the Isthmus, Matrosov, *Boi . . .*, Vol. I, p 313.

45. Soviet rejection of "Suomi," Voronov, pp 136–137. Appearance in February in *Study of Soviet Tactics,* p 14. Division authorization from ST staff.

46. Finnish tank strength, 11 April 1969 letter Colonel Mikola and Major Kilkki to author, which noted that Renaults were used only for towing and as stationary observation and firing points. Six of the Vickers were lost in action on the Isthmus. That all tanks used on Isthmus confirmed in *Study of Soviet Tactics,* p 63. Finnish air strength, Mikola, "The Finnish Wars," p 243; "open cockpits" were Blackburn Ripon II F aircraft (Luukkanen, pp 64–65). Soviet air power (800 planes), Mannerheim, p 330.

47. Tanner's interrogation noted in Attlee, p 77. Apparently unnoticed (or at least underestimated) in Moscow, a gradual improvement in class relations had begun in the immediate prewar years. In February 1937, Social Democratic and bourgeois Agrarian leaders united to form a coalition cabinet, the first such cooperation since 1917 (Rintala, *Three Generations,* pp 241–242). Mannerheim used the occasion of the 20th anniversary of the end of the civil war, 16 May 1938, to acknowledge this spirit of reconciliation, referring to the unity of all political elements. Responding in a public speech on 17 July, Tanner declared that "the bitterness against the victor in the war, the White General Mannerheim, has disappeared from the working class consciousness" (U. S. State Dept. file 760 D.61/1046). The essence of this unity was eloquently expressed in the plain words of a sergeant who fought at Tolvajärvi. In response to a request for his most unforgettable experience, he wrote, "Although I myself was an active Civic Guards man and known as extremely rightist-minded, while the platoon I led was

put together of leftists, a spirit of complete trust was created between us. It was part of that brotherhood of arms that was born at a moment of common danger, when we felt to be just Finns with a right to live in an independent, free fatherland. It was such a brotherhood of arms I will not forget" (Asunta questionnaire).

48. On 13 November, the same day the last Finnish delegation left Moscow, Tuominen had been offered the post Kuusinen subsequently accepted (Wuorinen, *Finland and World War II,* p 66). Tuominen himself mentions Stalin's astonishment that "tens of thousands of Finnish communists . . . flocked to the [Finnish] colours" (Tuominen, p 220). Heinrichs, pp 111–112, notes that former Red Guards volunteered even during the pre-war mobilization period. Öhquist's tailor incident from author's interview.

49. Mikola letter to author, 2 October 1967, citing Annual Report of the Central Statistical Office.

50. Jutikkala, *History* . . ., pp 273–276, emphasizes anti-Russian sentiment and its origins. Order of the Day excerpts in Hannula, p 18. Mannerheim's sentiments in his *Memoirs,* pp 124–127. Battle order from ST file 3743.

51. Heinrichs, p 107; Mikola, "The Finnish Wars", p 243; Peitsara, p 50; Mannerheim quoted from his *Memoirs,* p 323.

52. U. S. State Dept. file 760 D.61/244 and *The New York Times,* 8–17 October 1939. Many schools had reopened by late October and the stock exchange resumed operations 22 November (*The New York Times,* 28 October and 21 November). At that late hour, the Government was still so parsimonious with defense appropriations that Mannerheim tendered his resignation as Chairman of the Defense Council (Mannerheim, p 319).

53. *Ency. Fennica,* Part 8, 1964; U. S. State Dept file 760 D.61/476 and ST.

54. Luukkonen and Viherjuuri, pp 9–10, and Yrttimaa, passim.

55. Mannerheim, p 368, is one of many sources noting Soviet fear of "the White Death."

56. Oreshin, p 127.

57. Matrosov, *Razgrom,* p 46. A junior Finnish officer recalled as one of his strongest recollections of the war the fact that "the Russian soldiers were quite helpless in the forests; they even were afraid to go there" (Kuusela questionnaire).

58. Mannerheim, p 329.

59. U. S. Army C&GS lesson plan, p 155. Journalists and memorialists sometimes exaggerate the low temperatures of that severe winter; nevertheless, the official weather records show readings on 17 January 1940 at both Vihti and Hyvinkää (some 25 miles NW and N of Helsinki,

respectively) of minus 43.1 degrees Centigrade (-45.6° F)! (*Ilmatieteelliset Havainnot Suomessa* [hereinafter cited *IHS*], *Vuonna* 1940, Helsinki, 1955, pp 52 and 54).

60. Mannerheim, p 332, terms the disposition of reserves "some of the weightiest and most important decisions of the Winter War." Reserve divisions noted ibid and Heinrichs, p 127. Supply battalions, author's interview with Colonel Ekholm, 20 June 1967.

61. Mannerheim, p 332; Heinrichs, pp 137–138; and author's interview with Colonel Marttinen, 11 June 1968.

62. Mannerheim, pp 332–333, and Mikola et al., p 267.

63. Mannerheim's strategy discussed in Hannula, p 45, and Peitsara, p 54.

## CHAPTER II: TOURIST SEASON ENDS

The essence of this chapter was compiled from war diaries and other official records of units and personnel participating in the campaigns of Group Talvela. The cryptic ST reference numbers are explained in the bibliography.

1. Tuompo, *K-I* (Chapter by Talvela), p 212; author's interview with General Talvela, 8 June 1967; Talvela interview with T. Kylmälä in *Suomen Kuvalehti,* No. 7, 18 February 1967; and Mannerheim, p 334.

2. ST file 3687; Tuompo, *K-I*, pp 215, 217, 226.

3. Mannerheim, p 334; Heinrichs, p 130.

4. Mannerheim, pp 333–334; that recapture of Suojärvi contemplated, Talvela, p 214.

5. Mannerheim, p 334; author's interview with General Talvela, 8 June 1967.

6. Talvela in *Suomen Kuvalehti.*

7. Ibid.

8. ST file 929:5 (Daily Report of Action of Task Force P, 6–23 December); Tuompo, *K-I*, p 215.

9. ST file 929:5 (Daily Report of Action of Task Force P, 6–23 December).

10. ST file 3687; Talvela, pp 215–216; Heinrichs, p 131, notes retreat of PPP 7.

11. ST files 3687, 929:5 (Report of . . . commander of 4th Company); 929:7; Pajari file No. 22, Situation Map No. 6; Tuompo, *K-I*, pp 218, 219, 228; Heinrichs, pp 130, 132.

12. Tuompo, *K-I*, pp 218, 220, 221; Mannerheim, p 335; author's interview with Siukosaari et al. (The author is indebted to Major Siukosaari and the following veterans of the Second Battalion, JR 16, who met him in Tampere on 10 July 1967 to discuss the Tolvajärvi campaign:

Paavo Korppoo, Lauri Marttala, Eino Naaralainen, Väinö Rauhalahti, Lauri Rossi, Arvo Saksala, Nestori Uitti, and Oiva Vuorinen.)

13. Tuompo, *K-I*, pp 221–222; ST file 929:5 (Pajari articles "A Man of Häme as a Soldier" and "Some Words on Our Qualifications When Leaving for the Winter War"). These articles reveal Pajari's deep concern about the reliability of the Third Battalion and his emphasis on the incident of 25 May 1933. This author found it incredible that Colonel Pajari would be so worried about the flag affair if—as an interview with a participant had indicated—there was no attendant violence. However, a check of the contemporary account of the episode in Tampere's Social Democratic newspaper—which certainly did not sympathize with the Civic Guards—confirmed the peaceful nature of the event which caused him such lingering anxiety. His fears were unfounded. This Battalion fought as well as the other units.

14. Tuompo, *K-I*, p 222.

15. ST files 3687, T 1117—1122, and 929:5 (Report of . . . commander of 4th Company); Heinrichs, pp 132, 134; deafness from Siukosaari et al. interview.

16. ST file 3687; Heinrichs, p 134.

17. ST files 3687, T 1117–1122, 929:5 (Report of . . . commander of 4th Company); Heinrichs, p 132–134; Tuompo, *K-I*, p 224.

18. ST file 929:5 (Report of . . . commander of 4th Company); Tuompo, *K-I*, p 224.

19. Tuompo, *K-I*, p 225; Mannerheim, p 335; Ylinen.

20. Tuompo, *K-I*, pp 217, 218, 226, 232.

21. Ibid, pp 218, 225.

22. Author's interview with Colonel Ekholm, 20 June 1967.

23. Ibid; Tuompo, *K-I*, pp 219, 229, 232.

24. Tuompo, *K-I*, pp 225, 227; Mannerheim, p 335. Colonel Ekholm told the author about the boots, and the reason for the shortage was explained to him during an interview with Colonel Nihtilä on 29 June 1967. The parsimonious Parliament had provided first for the small peacetime field army; the reservists were expected to bring their own clothing. Rural Finns had warm garments, but Ekholm's replacement battalions were city men who were not well prepared for severe weather.

25. Tuompo, *K-I*, p 228.

26. Mannerheim, p 335; Tuompo, *K-I*, p 229; ST files 1717a and 929:7 (Action of . . . Sgt Reinikka).

27. ST files 929:7 (Action of . . . Sgt Reinikka) and 1085, p 63 ff.

28. Mannerheim, p 335; Tuompo, *K-I*, p 229; ST files 1717a, 929:7 (Action of . . . Sgt. Reinikka) and 1085, p 63 ff; Ylinen.

29. ST file 929:5 (Report of . . . commander of 4th Company).

30. ST file 929:7 (Activities of . . . Captain Kivelä).

31. Tuompo, *K-I,* pp 230–231; ST files 1717a and 1085, pp 70–71.

32. Tuompo, *K-I,* p 231.

33. Ibid, pp 231–232; ST file 1717a.

34. Tuompo, *K-I,* p 230; ST file 1717a; Mannerheim, p 328; photo showing both improvised antitank weapons in Korhonen, p 111.

35. Tuompo, *K-I,* pp 228, 232.

36. ST file 3732; Talvela, pp 231–234; Mannerheim, pp 335–336; Järvinen, pp 219–220.

37. ST file 3732; Siukosaari et al. interview; ST Pajari file 22, Situation Map 6.

38. ST file 3732; Mannerheim, p 336; Kukkonen, Map p 84; ST Pajari file 22, Situation Maps 6 and 7.

39. ST files 4646 and 3732; ST Pajari file 22, Situation Maps 6 and 7.

40. ST file 3732; ST Pajari file 22, Situation Map 7.

41. Tuompo, *K-I,* p 236; ST Pajari file 22, Situation Map 6; ST files 3743 and 929:7 (Activities of . . . Captain Kivelä).

42. Siukosaari et al. interview; ST file 929:5 (Reports of commanders of 4th, 5th, and 6th Companies, JR 16).

43. Ibid. Numerous Finnish officers mentioned the inaccuracy of the voluminous Soviet artillery in the early phase of the war, e.g. General Öhquist during author's interview, 15 June 1967.

44. ST file 929:5 (Reports of commanders of 4th and 5th Companies and 2nd Machine Gun Company).

45. ST file 3737:2; Siukosaari et al. interview.

46. ST file 3737:2, ST file 929:5 (Reports of commanders of 5th and 6th Companies).

47. Tuompo, *K-I,* p 234; ST file 929:5 (Report of commander of 5th Company).

48. Tuompo, *K-I,* pp 234–235; ST Pajari file 22, Situation Map 7; ST file 929:5 (Report of commander of 5th Company).

49. Siukosaari et al. interview; ST files 3737:2 and 929:5 (Report of commander of 5th Company).

50. Same as above paragraph, plus ST Pajari file 22, Situation Map 7.

51. ST Pajari file 22, Situation Map 7; ST files 929:7 (Activities of . . . Captain Kivelä) and 3743.

52. 139th Division commander identified in U. S. Military Attaché report, Helsinki, 2 April 1940, U. S. Archives, records RG 165, file 2657-D-1054–25. Morale effect, ST file 1085. Press release, *The New York Times,* 13 December 1939, p 1. Colonel Nihtilä (20 June 1967 interview) told the author that the reports of Tolvajärvi circulated among the troops were even exaggerated for morale purposes. Colonel Pajari

(ST file 1085) nevertheless felt that the victory merited more publicity than it received.

53. ST files 3737:2 and 929:5 (Report of . . . commander of 6th Company); Siukosaari et al. interview. The shooting at the doorway is described exactly as Major (then Lt.) Siukosaari told it to the author; he said that there was so much firing going on that he could not be certain who killed the regimental commander.

54. Tuompo, *K-I,* pp 236, 238; ST file 3687 (7 December 0945 hour entry); ST file 929:5 (Reports of commanders of 4th and 6th Companies); ST Pajari file 22, Situation Map 7. It is no longer possible to determine why Pajari did not continue the pursuit with the two companies which had remained in reserve, 8/JR 37 and 3/ErP 112. A reasonable guess is that the surprising extent of the victory led to confusion.

55. Tuompo, *K-I,* p 238.

56. ST file 1717a.

57. Ekholm interview, 20 June 1967; temperature from *IHS*—for 1939, pp 78–79 and for 1940, pp 60–61 (readings at Joensuu weather station, about 40 miles W. of Ilomantsi). Snow depth from *Sade ja L* . . ., p 54. These official weather records are more reliable than the memories of participants, many of whom speak of a meter or more of snow. The temperatures that winter were exceptionally severe, but the snow was not unusually deep.

58. Author's interview with Colonel Ekholm, 20 June 1967; Tuompo, *K-I,* pp 226 and 242.

59. ST file 1717a.

60. Ibid; Tuompo, *K-I,* p 240; Siukosaari et al. interview re opinions of Pajari; Mannerheim (p 368) is one of many who praised Russian ability to dig in.

61. Tuompo, *K-I,* pp 241–243; ST file 1717a; Kuz'min, p 256, mentions only the 75th Division as the 8th Army's reserve at the start of the operations.

62. ST files 1717a and 929:7 (Activities of . . . Captain Kivelä, and Activities of Cpl. Mutka).

63. ST files 3687 (15 December 1500 hour entry) and 1717a; Siukosaari et al. interview re condition of replacements.

64. ST file 3687; Siukosaari et al. interview.

65. ST files 1717a and 3687; ST Pajari file 22, Situation Map 17; Kukkonen, Map appendix.

66. ST file 3687.

67. Ibid; ST file 1717a; Aarnio, pp 187–188; Järvinen, pp 223–224.

68. Tuompo, *K-I,* p 231; Mannerheim, pp 336–337; ST files 1717a and 1085.

69. ST files 1717a and 929:7 (Activities of Cpl. Mutka).

70. Tuompo, *K-I,* pp 244–245; Talvela-author interview; ST Pajari file 22, Situation Map 17.

71. ST file 1717a.

72. ST files 929:5 (Report of Battle of Äglajärvi), 4646, and 3737: 2; ST Pajari file 22, Situation Map 17; Siukosaari et al. interview.

73. ST files 929:5 (Report of Battle of Äglajärvi) and 3737:2; Siukosaari et al. interview re battalion commander's behavior. His subordinates considered him too old to command an infantry battalion in the field. The captain's breakdown was apparently only temporary, as his name appears in later records as a major. He was transferred to another unit on 29 December 1939 (ST file 3732:2 [28 December entry]).

74. ST files 929:5 (Report of Battle of Äglajärvi) and 3737:2; ST Pajari file 22, Situation Map 17.

75. ST files 3687, 929:5 (Report of Battle of Äglajärvi), 3737:2, 4646, and 720:5.

76. ST files 3687, 1717a, and 720:5.

77. Mannerheim, p 337 and Kukkonen, p 128, re Finnish losses; Tuompo, *K-I,* p 243; Talvela-author interview; Talvela interview in *Suomen Kuvalahti,* 18 February 1967.

78. Mannerheim, p 336; ST file 1085.

79. ST file 3687; the broader aspects of POWs, psychological warfare, and propaganda are discussed in the next chapter.

80. Pajari quoted, ST file 1085; Heinrichs quoted, p 135. (This and subsequent quotes are made with the permission of Holger Schildts Förlag, AB, publisher of Erik Heinrichs, *Mannerheimgestalten.*)

## CHAPTER III: WHITE CHRISTMAS

1. Meretskov, p 184; Kilkki, "Talvisodan S . . .", p 127; ST file 3948:5.

2. Öhquist, *Vinterkriget,* pp 46–47; Horne, pp 27–28. The Soviet effort to rationalize the Red Army's slow progress against the Mannerheim Line by comparing it to the Rhineland defenses began as early as December 1939. An example is found in the summary of the first three weeks of fighting which appeared in *Pravda, Izvestiya,* and *Krasnaya Zvezda* on 23 December. This official "line" has not changed to this day. Another face-saving gambit is to list all of the bunkers on the Karelian Isthmus (including those in the two lines behind the Mannerheim Line) when discussing the Red Army's belated breakthru. Thus, the authors of *Boi v Finlyandii* (1941) claimed to have overcome 356 reinforced-concrete pillboxes (DOTs) and 2,425 earth-and-timber pillboxes (DZOTs). Marshal Meretskov

gave almost identical figures (350 DOTs and 2,400 DZOTs) in his memoirs published in 1968 (p 190). Even counting some 70 obsolete machine gun emplacements which the Finns had abandoned as useless, it is not possible to reach the figure of 350 DOTs for the entire Isthmus (Kilkki article "Mannerheim-Linjaa . . .," in response to Meretskov's book). These propaganda claims notwithstanding, the Red Army possessed fairly accurate information about the Mannerheim Line. A Soviet battle map (1:20,000 scale, prepared by Colonel Khrenov of the Engineer Service and stamped "SECRET" in Russian) depicts the Muolaanjärvi sector on 23 December 1939 in detail. It clearly shows the true preponderance of earth-and-timber fieldworks in that area. (U. S. Library of Congress, Geography and Map Division, filed under "Finland, War, Viborg, 1940, USSR Military Topographical Service, Leningrad Front").

3. Öhquist, *Vinterkriget,* p 47 and Maps 5–7; Österman, pp 158–159.

4. Soloviev, pp 164–165.

5. U. S. Archives, records RG 165, file No. 2037–2100–31.

6. Österman, p 221; Mannerheim, p 342. The three attacking divisions were the 49th, 90th, and 142nd (Seppälä & Kilkki, p 6).

7. Hannula, p 62; Österman, pp 217–218, 222; ST files 3948:5, T9386, and P506:1.

8. Österman, pp 222–223, 226–227; ST file 3948:5.

9. Österman, pp 222–223; ST file 3948:5.

10. Öhquist, *Vinterkriget,* p 111; Österman, p 223; ST file 3948:5.

11. Österman, p 223; ST file 3948:5.

12. ST file 3948:5.

13. Quoted in Fischer, Louis (ed), *Thirteen Who Fled,* p 216; reprinted with permission of Harper and Row, Publishers, Inc.

14. Österman, pp 223–225; Heinrichs, p 121; Kuz'min, p 237; Mannerheim, p 343; ST file 3948:5.

15. Österman, p 225; Heinrichs, p 123; ST file 3948:5.

16. Heinrichs, p 123; ST file 3948:5.

17. Mannerheim, p 343; Österman, p 225. By 28 December the 5th Division, which bore the brunt of the attacks in the western Isthmus, had destroyed a total of 102 tanks (ST file 3948:5).

18. Österman, pp 229–232; author's interview with Colonel Nihtilä, 29 June 1967. Öhquist ( *Vinterkriget,* p 122) also felt that cancelling the plan on 22 December would have been psychologically deplorable. As usual, no one is anxious to accept the main responsibility for a plan which failed. A detached observer is struck by the fact that General Österman considered it proper to forward the proposal to GHQ in spite of his acknowledgement (p 229) that he "did not personally believe in the ability of the [Finnish] troops to wage large-scale offensive battle,"

and his statement (p 232) that he would have to stop the operation should it fail "as was to be feared." (These and subsequent quotations from his book *Neljännesvuosisata Elämästäni* are made with the kind permission of General Hugo Österman.)

19. Österman, pp 231, 235; Järvinen, p 112; Mannerheim, p 344. The 6th Division had been transferred from the Commander-in-Chief's reserve to the Kannas Army on 20 December (Österman, p 231).

20. Österman, pp 232–234; Järvinen, p 116; Heinrichs, p 124; Mannerheim, p 345; ST file 3948:5.

21. Österman, pp 232–233; Öhquist, *Vinterkriget,* p 124; Palmunen, pp 40–41. The failure to anticipate many of the timing and logistic problems involved in so large an operation is perhaps understandable, because none of the Finnish officers had prior experience in handling comparable forces. The very largest peacetime maneuvers had involved only some 20,000 troops. General Österman (p 234) lists among the deficiencies revealed on 23 December "the inexperience of the leaders and their aides in mobile warfare."

22. Palmunen, pp 42–45 (based on the War Diary of III/2nd Brig/1st Div. and confirmed for the author by the officer who maintained that battalion's diary, Colonel [then 1st Lt.] A. Aakkula).

23. Öhquist, *Vinterkriget,* p 125. The account of the 6th Division in this and following paragraphs is mainly derived from Järvinen, pp 112–115, which, in turn, is based on the battle reports of that division's regimental commanders. Only additional sources are cited below.

24. A small modification in the tail section of the mortar rounds had been made at the depot; apparently no one thought to test fire them after the change (Järvinen, p 113).

25. The 4th Division also complained that its advance was disturbed by the slow advance of the 6th Division (ST file 3948:5).

26. Heinrichs, p 123; ST file 3948:5.

27. Österman, pp 232–234; Palmunen, p 46; Mannerheim, p 345; ST file 3948:5; author's interview with Colonel Nihtilä, 29 June 1967.

28. Österman, p 234; Öhquist, *Vinterkriget,* pp 126, 134. Even the weather was against the Finns; instead of the predicted snowstorm cover and warm temperatures, the day was clear, windy, and cold. The mercury fell from 19° (F) in the morning to zero in the afternoon, and even colder in the evening (Öhquist, pp 122–123). Frostbite was due to the fact that, from the time they left bivouac until they returned, some of the men were exposed to freezing weather for about 24 hours (Palmunen, pp 46–47).

29. Tvardovski, pp 143–145; Matrosov, *Boi . . .,* Vol. II, pp 201–202.

30. Mannerheim, p 345.

31. Österman, pp 221, 236; ST file 86; Mannerheim, p 345.

32. Ehrnrooth, p 58.

33. Ibid; Österman, p 221.

34. ST file 3948:5; Matrosov, *Boi* . . ., Vol. I, p 241.

35. Kuz'min, p 238. On 28 December the Soviet High Command issued a directive to the Military Council of the Front containing instructions for improving tactics, preparing for offensives, etc., ibid, pp 238–239.

36. Tvardovski, pp 121, 130–132. In recent years the liberal editor of the Soviet literary journal, *Novyi Mir,* Tvardovski was then a correspondent for the military paper, *Na Strazhe Rodiny.* He published the personal notebook he had retained from the war period in the 2 February 1969 issue of *Novyi Mir,* pp 116–160. This is probably the most creditable account of events of the Winter War to be found in Soviet sources. (Tvardovski was removed from his position as editor in 1970).

37. USMA, pp 8–9; Mannerheim, p 341; Tuompo, *K-I,* pp 262–263.

38. Tuompo, *K-I,* pp 260–262, 284–288. This is also the source for the following two paragraphs.

39. Gregory Ugryumov in Fischer, pp 216—219.

40. Mannerheim, pp 332–333, 341; Peitsara, p 58.

41. Tuompo, *K-I,* pp 259, 266–267, 275. A Soviet admission that a patrol of some 50 Finns penetrated their border on 1 January is found in Zyryanov, p 128. The Reboly Border Guard Detachment fought a total of nine skirmishes inside Soviet borders during the war (ibid, p 179).

42. The actual linkup occurred at the Koirinoja road junction, about 5 miles SE of Kitelä (Tuompo, *K-I,* p 168).

43. Tuompo, *K-I* (chapter by Hägglund), p 172; Peitsara, p 56; Mannerheim, pp 341–342, 347.

44. Tuompo, *K-I,* p 172; Mannerheim, pp 334, 341, 347; U. S. Archives, records RG 165, file 2037–2100–27, 3 March 1940.

45. Oreshin, pp 129–130, 134–135.

46. Mannerheim, pp 341–342; Seppälä and Kilkki, pp 6, 8. In addition to the 5 Soviet divisions initially engaged in this region, the 75th and 164th Divisions were committed in December.

47. *The New York Times,* 16 January 1940, p 13.

48. Eade, Vol. I, p 137.

49. For examples, see *Le Temps,* 11 January 1940; Jean-Louis Perret, *La Finlande en Guerre,* p 202.

50. *Pravda, Izvestiya,* and *Krasnaya Zvezda,* 23 December 1939.

51. Meretskov, p 185.

52. Although the League Assembly's condemnation of Soviet behavior and the Council's expulsion resolution were technically "unanimous," the abstentions were significant and ominous: Sweden,

Norway, and Denmark were among the seven abstaining states in the Assembly (Citrine, p 11); of the 14 Council members, only the French and British delegates spoke in favor of expulsion. Of the others, 3 were absent, 4 expressly abstained, and 5 made no comment. No formal vote was taken; the President merely declared that "if there are no other observations . . . the . . . resolution has been adopted" (League of Nations Official Journal, 20th Year, Nos. 11–12, Part II, pp 501–508).

53. Tanner, p 164; Gripenberg, p 92; Jakobson, pp 191–192.

54. Schwartz, p 16; Mannerheim, pp 358, 376–377; Tanner, p 133; Gripenberg, p 95; *The New York Times,* 8 December 1939. Despite pro-Finnish and anti-Soviet sentiment in the U.S., the Neutrality Act and isolationist psychology greatly limited the amount of military aid granted. Even the two loans which were extended thru the Export-Import Bank (totalling only $30,000,000) were restricted to the purchase of non-military items (Schwartz, pp 19–25).

55. *Krasnaya Zvezda,* 23 December 1939.

56. Pospelov, *VOVSS-KI,* p 47; Alliluyeva, *Twenty Letters to a Friend,* p 27.

57. Kuz'min, p 238. The Soviet leaders may have given too much credit to the Swedish commanders of 1808. The Finns withdrew because General Klingspor opted for retreat, against the unamimous desire of his subordinates. The subsequent (and transitory) Finnish victories were due to the initiative of the troops and subordinate officers, rather than to any farsighted strategy (Jutikkala, *History,* pp 179–181).

58. Pospelov, *IVOVSS,* Vol. I, pp 266–267; Meretskov, p 181; Kuz'min, p 238; Rotmistrov, p 500.

59. According to Meretskov (p 177), Kuusinen's office was actually in Petrozavodsk, not Terijoki.

60. Karhunen, p 180. The 1st Battalion of "Finland's National Army Corps" was identified at Kivijärvi (east of Vasovaara in the Raate area) in February 1940. A Finnish intelligence source indicated that these men were from Ingermanland and Eastern Karelia (ibid).

61. Author's interview with Manninen, 5 July 1967.

62. Report of Intelligence Department of Finnish Army HQ, July 1940 (cited in Mikola letter to author, 2 October 1967).

63. Jakobson, p 169; author's interviews with Generals K. Valla (16 June 1967) and G. Ehrnrooth (17 July 1967); Sysikumpu questionnaire.

64. Author's interview with General G. Ehrnrooth, 17 July 1967.

65. Oreshin, p 136.

66. Finnish War Museum file No. 329.653; author's interview with Colonel Nihtilä, 29 June 1967.

67. Finnish War Museum file No. 329.668.

68. Author's interview with General G. Ehrnrooth, 17 July 1967.

69. Finnish War Museum file No. 329.661; Soloviev, pp 184–189.

70. Heinrichs, p 150. The Finnish-language edition of Heinrichs' book differs from the Swedish edition on this point (and others).

71. Author's interview with Finnish officer who prefers to remain anonymous.

72. Heinrichs, pp 147–150.

73. As early as 3 December a Soviet officer (killed at Suomussalmi on 18 Decmeber) recorded a cynical entry in his diary about their "liberation" mission (Zenzinov, p 164).

74. *Krasnaya Zvezda,* 14 December 1939.

75. The *politruk's* combat role was also difficult. Often, he was called upon to provide battle leadership when the unit commander fell, and he was seldom prepared for such a task. See Zyryanov, p 175, for a contemporary Soviet acknowledgement that the *politruks* frequently lost their heads under those circumstances, substituting suicidal personal bravery for intelligent command decisions.

76. Heinrichs, p 150; Hannula, p 143; Ehrnrooth, pp 72–73; ST file 3743; author's interview with Siukosaari et al.

77. ST file 3737:2; *Fighting Finns Write Home,* passim; author's interviews with Oiva M____ (29 December 1967) and General Vaala (16 June 1967).

78. ST file 3743; author's interview with Colonel Ekholm, 20 June 1967.

79. U.S. State Dept. files 760 D.61/1347 and /851; Luukkanen, Eino *Fighter Over Finland* (Macdonald & Co., Ltd), pp 34–35. The author relied heavily on this excellent book by Finland's third ranking ace for details of the air war. Thanks are due the publisher for permission to use the data in the appendixes, the reliability of which was confirmed by ST personnel.

80. ST file 1717a; Hannula, p 42.

81. Author's interview with General Grönvall, 12 July 1967.

82. The above ten paragraphs are primarily based on the author's interviews with two officers who were closely associated with the Marshal at Mikkeli, General (then Major) Ragnar Grönvall, and Colonel Valo Nihtilä. Some minor details are taken from reminiscences published in 1967, the centennial of Mannerheim's birth, in the weekly journal *Suomen Kuvalehti* (No. 21, 27 May 1967). The pertinent articles were written by Colonel K. Lehmus and Miss Taru Stenvall, a waitress at the Seurahuone Hotel.

83. The two volumes of *Across Asia from West to East in 1906–1908* were published by the Fenno-Ugrian Society 31 years later, during the

Winter War. Mannerheim somehow found time to write a two-page preface in February 1940.

84. The above 11 paragraphs are primarily derived from Mannerheim's *Memoirs,* his *Across Asia . . .,* and Warner's *Marshal Mannerheim and the Finns.*

85. Hodgson, pp 31 and 51.

86. Mannerheim, pp 109 and 131; Borenius, pp 132–137; author's interview with Colonel P. O. Ekholm, one of the Jägers present at the 1918 meeting with Mannerheim.

87. Smith, p 49.

88. Vivid testimoney to Mannerheim's ambivalent stature in Finland was presented on the centennial of his birth, 4 June 1967. Conservative papers (e.g. *Uusi Suomi*) eulogized him, while the extreme Left pillored him mercilessly. *Kansan Uutiset* featured on its front page a poem by Hannu Salama under a picture of the famous equestrian statue of the Marshal which dominates the street near Helsinki's main post office. After evoking all the old class hatreds, the poem jeeringly referred to the "hobby horse" statue with the hose of the "gelding" hanging under its stomach. In reality, the statue portrays the Marshal's mare *Kate*—a remarkable horse, but not *that* remarkable! (This is an example of "communist truth"; the obscene "hose" exists only in the author's mind.) It may be reasonable to assume that Salama's opinion of Mannerheim is shared by that proportion of his countrymen who vote for the SKDL (communist front) candidates.

89. Mannerheim, pp 134–135, 182–183. Another possible reason for his resignation was the Government's opposition to his plan to continue the war into Russia to help overthrow the Soviet régime (Rintala, *Politics . . .,* p 76).

90. Mannerheim, pp 187–199.

91. Mannerheim, pp 206–209, 220–221, 224; Hodgson, p 152; Rintala, *Politics . . .,* p 77; Jutikkala, *Two Essays,* p 22; Borenius, pp 229–230. Mannerheim was an advocate of the "Greater Finland", at least to the extent that he wished to secure more defensible borders (Hodgson, p 152; Jutikkala, *Two Essays,* p 22). As early as March 1918 he had authorized attacks in the Ukhta (Uhtua) region of Eastern Karelia (Hodgson, p 152; Borenius, p 184). Finnish volunteers (although disavowed by their Government) continued sorties into Eastern Karelia even after the Peace of Tartu—as late as the winter of 1921–1922 (Rintala, *Three Generations . . .,* p 102).

92. Mannerheim, pp 222–225; Rintala, *Politics . . .,* p 81.

93. Mannerheim, p 222.

94. Ibid, pp 229–235.

95. Ibid, pp 243–244; Rintala, *Three Generations* . . ., p 179.

96. Mannerheim, pp 246–250.

97. Ibid, p 236.

98. Ibid, pp 149 and 507; Talvela in *Suomen Kuvalehti,* 18 February 1967; Matti Kurjensaari in *Suomen Kuvalehti,* 27 January 1968.

99. Mannerheim, pp 252–261.

100. Tuominen, p 220; Mannerheim, pp 269–319, passim.

101. Rodzianko, pp 178–179; Borenius, p 248. Mannerheim received a second Marshal's baton on the occasion of his 75th birthday, when he received the unprecedented title "Marshal of Finland" (Mannerheim, p 450).

102. The above five paragraphs from Mannerheim, pp 280–319.

This brief résumé of Mannerheim's career does not begin to cover the complexities of his personality. Neither do his *Memoirs,* which are as noteworthy for their omissions as for their revelations (for example, there is only one line on his marriage and no mention of his separation and divorce). Although much has been written about him, it is probably too early for a definitive biography—he is still too controversial a figure. Yet he looms so large in the history of independent Finland that some tentative evaluation is unavoidable in any discussion of Finnish political, military or diplomatic affairs between 1918 and 1946.

Perhaps the most damning objective commentary about his political predilections is simply the fact that—after serving and observing the utterly incompetent Tsar Nicholas II during that ruler's entire catastrophic reign—Mannerheim still styled himself "a monarchist in principle" (*Memoirs,* p 222).

His haughtiness was prodigious; perhaps only Charles de Gaulle among Twentieth Century leaders of democratic states was his equal in this respect. Even his admirers mention how "aloof" he was; his aide, Major General R. Grönvall, expressed it this way: "he always kept something to himself, even among his family" (personal interview, 12 July 1967). Even as a guest in his house, the Finnish diplomat G. A. Gripenberg found his host "tight-lipped and uncommunicative" (Gripenberg, p 238). During the Winter War an American correspondent was reportedly instructed by his paper to attach himself to the Marshal to write human-interest stories. He cabled back: "Mannerheim impossible. Shall I try Jesus Christ?" (Langdon-Davies, p 84). Even if apocryphal, that anecdote conveys a widely held impression. General Österman remarked that Mannerheim was "extremely sensitive of maintaining his preeminence" (the word he used, *arvovalta,* might also be translated as "prestige"). Although much of Österman's apologia may be discounted, this point of criticism seems valid; as the

General noted, that attitude on the part of the Marshal made it difficult for subordinates to present proposals to him (Österman, pp 263–264). One secret of effective leadership is to avoid "the familiarity which breeds contempt," yet to remain accessible to the ideas of subordinates. Mannerheim achieved the former to perfection, but perhaps this was sometimes at the expense of the latter.

That he may have recognized this problem is indicated by his method of conducting important meetings such as those of the Defense Council: he solicited the views of subordinates before indicating his own (Österman, pp 241–242). Interestingly, Stalin apparently operated in the same manner (Bialer, p 36), which is the only intelligent way to achieve an open discussion when the prestige of one party is so great that all others hesitate to contradict him. In both cases, however, these leaders kept a very tight rein on their subordinate commanders, delegating the minimum of authority (see Bialer, p 36 and Österman, pp 173, 236, and 239).

A perfectionist himself, Marshal Mannerheim was very demanding of senior officers. As noted, General Österman had difficulty in working for him, and General Öhquist admits friction in his relations with the Commander-in-Chief (Öhquist, *Vinterkriget,* p 225). Even General Oesch apparently welcomed the opportunity to transfer from GHQ to the front because he felt he could not please the Marshal (Öhquist, *Vinterkriget,* p 292). Mannerheim was also quite imperious in his dealings with Defense Minister Niukkanen (Heinrichs, pp 151–152).

Yet a reserve officer who had occasion to observe Marshal Mannerheim noted that he was courteous and considerate with the lower ranks (Captain Oiva M_____ interview). Perhaps there was a touch of noblesse oblige in this, as there certainly was in such charitable projects as the Child Welfare Association.

Urbane to the utmost, he could converse entertainingly with kings or waitresses. Although he needed an interpreter to talk to Finnish troops in 1918 (Rintala, "The Politics of G. Mannerheim," p 70), he acquired a reasonable command of that difficult language when in his fifties. Most of his close associates in Finland, as well as his servants, spoke his native Swedish tongue. He was fluent in Russian and French, the latter being the preferred language of the tsarist aristocracy. A subordinate who helped to draft some of his Orders of the Day remarked that—regardless of which language he employed—his style remained French (Kurjensaari in *Suomen Kuvalehti,* 27 January 1968). He also spoke English, German, and Polish.

The Baron's personal library reflects both his linguistic abilities (there are books in all seven languages, but notably few in Finnish) and his interests. These were predominantly military and historical, but there are also a large number of travel books—especially on the Orient. Among the very few works of fiction are ones by Zola, Dumas, and de Maupassant. Perhaps Landtman's *The Origin of the Inequality of the Social Classes* is revealing. (Author's visits to Mannerheim Museum, 1967.)

An inveterate showman, Mannerheim related that, when presenting gifts for the Incarnate Buddha, he pulled a ring off his own finger "to heighten the effect" (*Memoirs,* p 62). Throughout his life he remained keenly conscious of his public "image", yet he was not a mere poseur. In terms of sophistication and refinement, he *was* superior to his Finnish contemporaries. He was also superior to most of them in intelligence and talent.

By the standards of modern democratic and egalitarian societies, his personality was not attractive. He had too little of the natural charm of Dwight Eisenhower and too much of the snobbery of Charles de Gaulle. Yet it is hardly fair to judge him by such standards; he belonged to the older order of the 19th Century aristocracy (or perhaps a century or two earlier). And he was, as one observer has aptly phrased it, both a nobleman and a noble man. His personal integrity is not even questioned by his enemies.

Most importantly, Marshal Mannerheim twice came as near to being "indispensable" as ever happens in the affairs of man. An indisputable instance was in 1944, of which more will be said later. The other time was in those first terrifying days of the Winter War, when public and army alike were on the verge of complete panic in the face of such staggering odds. Had there been the faintest sign of hesitation or faltering at the helm, the ship of state would assuredly have been sunk by the Red Army and the Terijoki "Government". When the chips were down in the game for survival, the Marshal's calculated air of imperturable self-assurance inspired confidence such as no other national figure could approach. Whether they admired him or not, Finns of all classes respected him and rallied behind his determined leadership. That Finland remains a free nation is largely due to that phenomenon, and therein lies the greatness of Carl Gustaf Mannerheim.

## CHAPTER IV: BELAYA SMERT'

1. Soviet intentions derived from 163rd Division orders dated 6 December 0800 hours and 9 December 1000 hours, captured from the 662nd Regiment by Task Force Susitaival. Finnish translations of these orders are attached to Colonel Susitaival's staff study, ST file 207–208/S.N. The author had access to these orders in a private collec-

tion. An abbreviated version of the 9 December order is found in Aarnio, p 128.

2. Tuompo, *Sotilaan T.,* p 184; Aarnio, pp 111–112, 118–121.

3. Tuompo, *Sotilaan T.,* p 184; Aarnio, p 120; Tuompo, *K-I,* p 270.

4. ST file 207–208/S.N. (attached translations of 662nd Regiment reports written 5 December, and messages 11 December 1000 hours and 13 December 1800 hours; see also footnote No. 1 above).

5. Ibid, 662nd Regiment Operations Summaries Nos. 1 (8 December), 9 (15 December), 15 (17 December) and Combat Report, 12 December 1115 hours.

6. Heinrichs, pp 137–138; Mannerheim, p 338; author's interview with Colonel Marttinen, 11 June 1968. Siilasvuo's force was so poorly equipped because, as part of the Commander-in-Chief's reserve, it had transferred many of its weapons and supplies to units which had departed for the Karelian Isthmus during the YH period. It was thought that the reserve would have enough time to reequip, but the surprisingly strong Soviet thrusts in the northern wilds upset this calculation (author's interview with Colonel Lassila, 29 September 1968).

7. Siilasvuo, *Suom. T.,* pp 39, 54; *IHS,* 1939, p 47; Mannerheim, p 338; Hannula, p 58; Heinrichs, p 138; Suomalainen, p 55; author's interview with Colonel Lassila, 29 September 1968.

8. Author's interview with Colonel Marttinen, 11 June 1968.

9. Suomalainen, pp 55–57.

10. Ibid, pp 57–58; Heinrichs, p 138.

11. Suomalainen, p 58; Mannerheim, p 338; Tuompo, *K-I,* p 268.

12. Siilasvuo, *Suom. T.,* pp 73, 86, 101, 114; Suomalainen, p 55; Mannerheim, p 339; Heinrichs, p 139.

13. Tuompo, *K-I,* p 270; Tuompo, *Sotilaan T.,* p 184; Siilasvuo, *Suom. T.,* pp 72, 93; Aarnio, p 132; Usva.

14. Siilasvuo, *Suom. T.,* p 72; Aarnio, pp 130–133; Tuompo, *K-I,* p 270; ST file 207–208/S.N. (662nd Regiment Operations Summary No. 25, 22 December 1200).

15. Tuompo, *Sotilaan T.,* p 196; Tuompo, K-I, p 270; Aarnio, p 137.

16. Tuompo, *Sotilaan T.,* p 197.

17. Siilasvuo, *Suom. T.,* pp 67, 81, 84; Mannerheim, p 339; author's interviews with Colonel Marttinen, 11 June 1968 and 31 March 1970. Details of Finnish cryptanalysis and radio traffic analysis are still not discussed by Finnish officials, but many will privately acknowledge the importance of this source of intelligence, which was directed by Colonel Hallamaa. Mobile intercept detachments directly supported field commanders (*Study of Soviet Tactics . . .* p 83). Captain Marttinen

usually had decoded and translated copies of enemy messages on his desk within 4 to 5 hours of their transmission (author's interview, 11 June 1968). In some cases, such messages were read within 2 hours (author's interview with General Öhquist, 15 June 1967).

18. Suomalainen, p 58.

19. Siilasvuo, *Suom. T.,* pp 81, 84, 101; Järvinen, p 229; War Diary of I/JR 27 (in private collection); author's interview with Colonel Lassila, 27 February 1969.

20. Siilasvuo, *Suom. T.,* p 84; Suomalainen, p 58; author's interview with Colonel Marttinen, 11 June 1968.

21. Järvinen, pp 228, 234.

22. Siilasvuo, *Suom. T.,* p 87.

23. Ibid, pp 88, 94.

24. Ibid, pp 92–95; Mannerheim, p 339.

25. Siilasvuo, *Suom. T.,* pp 93–96.

26. Ibid, pp 93–95; Tuompo, *K–I,* Map p 303.

27. Siilasvuo, *Suom. T.,* p 99.

28. Above 5 paragraphs from Siilasvuo, *Suom. T.,* pp 96–107.

29. Ibid, pp 103–105; author's interviews with Colonel Marttinen, 11 June 1968 and 31 March 1970. Colonel Marttinen felt that his commander was doctrinaire about using his reserves.

30. Siilasvuo, *Suom. T.* pp 106–109.

31. Ibid, p 110.

32. Ibid, pp 110–111; author's interview with Colonel Lassila, 23 April 1970.

33. Siilasvuo, *Suom. T.,* p 112.

34. Ibid, pp 112–113.

35. Ibid, p 113; Tuompo, *K-I,* p 271; author's interview with Colonel Marttinen, 11 June 1968; Luukkanen, pp 193 ff.

36. ST file T1835 a–c.

37. Mannerheim, p 339; author's interview with Colonel Marttinen, 11 June 1968.

38. Heinrichs, p 143.

39. Siilasvuo, *Suom. T.,* p 88; Suomalainen, pp 59–60; author's interview with Colonel Marttinen, 11 June 1968.

40. Suomalainen, p 55; *Study of Soviet Tactics . . .,* p 27. The 44th Division, a regular army unit assigned to the Moscow Military District (Heinrichs, p 140), was originally from the Kiev Military District. According to ST records, two of its regiments were organized at Zhitomir and the third at Berdichev. Most of its troops were Ukrainians who were not familiar with the northern woods. Colonel Siilasvuo had only one obsolete aircraft at his disposal during the Suomussalmi-Raate campaign, but (although it could only be flown at dawn or dusk) it was

effective for reconnaissance because the Russians were plainly visible on the roads (author's interview with Colonel Marttinen, 11 June 1968).

41. Järvinen, pp 229–230; author's interview with Colonel Lassila, 18 May 1970.

42. Siilasvuo, *Suom. T.,* pp 100, 126.

43. Ibid, p 138; Järvinen, p 231.

44. The above six paragraphs are based on the author's extensive interviews with the officer who led this attack, Colonel (then Captain) Eino Lassila, 1968–1971.

45. Siilasvuo, *Suom. T.,* p 129.

46. Ibid, pp 126, 130–131.

47. Ibid, pp 130–131, 144–145; Järvinen, pp 231, 233.

48. Siilasvuo, *Suom. T.,* pp 140–141; Järvinen, p 231.

49. Siilasvuo, *Suom. T.,* pp 138–139; Järvinen, p 232.

50. Siilasvuo, *Suom. T.,* pp 138–139.

51. Ibid, pp 138–140.

52. Ibid., pp 150–151.

53. Ibid, p 152.

54. Ibid, pp 151–152; author's interview with Colonel Lassila, 25 September 1970.

55. Siilasvuo, *Suom. T.,* pp 151–152, author's interview with Colonel Lassila, 25 September 1970.

56. Above five paragraphs from Siilasvuo, *Suom. T.,* pp 140–148.

57. Ibid, pp 142–143, 155; Zyryanov, p 133. The 3rd NKVD (Border Guard) Regiment was probably formed about the turn of the year, the same time the 1st Regiment was organized. Eight NKVD regiments were employed against the Finns in January. Their primary mission was to secure communications behind the field armies, but they sometimes fought side by side with Red Army units, as at Raate. At least two battalions (Nos. I and II) of the 3rd Regiment fought in the area between Kokkojärvi and the border (and in skirmishes east of the frontier) between 2 and 7 January. Sharing the fate of the 44th Division, the 3rd NKVD Regiment sustained heavy losses—including the death of its commander, Major L'vov (see Zyryanov, pp 132 ff).

58. Siilasvuo, *Suom. T.,* pp 143–144.

59. Ibid, pp 153–154. General Siilasvuo's book (mainly ghostwritten by Colonel—then Captain—Marttinen) indicates that Captain Flink led only one reinforced company on 5 January; however, the war diaries of III/JR 65, 8/JR 65 and 3. KKK JR 65 (ST files 1677, 1649–1650, and 1654–1660, respectively) show that he led the 7th and 8th Companies, as well as the 3rd Machine Gun Company.

60. Siilasvuo, *Suom. T.,* pp 154–155.

61. Ibid, p 155; 3rd NKVD Regiment identified from Zyryanov.

62. Above 8 paragraphs from Siilasvuo, *Suom. T.,* pp 156–168.

63. Ibid, p 159; author's interview with Colonel Lassila. According to POW accounts reported in *The Times* (London, 5 February 1940, p 5), Vinogradov's order to retreat was issued at 9:30 P.M. on 6 January.

64. Siilasvuo, *Suom. T.,* pp 169–171.

65. Ibid, p 171; Zyryanov, p 136.

66. Siilasvuo, *Suom. T.,* pp 171–172.

67. Ibid, pp 172–175.

68. Ibid, p 174.

69. Ibid, p 173; Mannerheim, p 340; Järvinen, p 232; *The New York Times,* 9 January 1940.

70. Mannerheim, p 340.

71. *The New York Times,* 12 January 1940, p 2.

72. Author's interview with Colonel Marttinen, 11 June 1968. A recent Soviet source states that L. Z. Mekhlis, sent by Stalin to the 9th Army to investigate the Suomussalmi-Raate fiasco, demanded Vinogradov's execution (Shtemenko, p 22). However, General Shtemenko added that "matters did not go to the length of shooting." This confirms Vinogradov's arrest, but it leaves open the question of who was telling the truth about his execution.

73. ST casualty lists; Russian losses estimated in Major Usva's study.

74. Siilasvuo, *Kuhmo T.,* p 71. The freeing of JR 27 (and other units) for use elsewhere fulfilled the hopes the Marshal had held when he sent that unit from his slim reserves to Suomussalmi. However, it appears that the transfer of JR 27 (and most of Siilasvuo's other forces) to Kuhmo was not his idea. According to Colonel Nihtilä (author's interview, 29 June 1967), Marshal Mannerheim wanted to return those troops to his reserve for possible use on the Karelian Isthmus, but General Tuompo redeployed them to attack near Kuhmo before he learned of it. Rather than interfere with Tuompo's decision at that point, Mannerheim let the Kuhmo operations proceed. As a consequence, the Finnish 9th Division was tied down near Kuhmo for the duration of the war.

75. *The New York Times,* 1, 9, 11, 12 January, 5 February 1940; *The Times,* January 1940, passim, 5 February 1940.

76. *Krasnaya Zvezda, Pravda, Izvestiya,* 28 December 1939—14 January 1940.

77. Tanner, pp 119 and 209.

78. Heinrichs, p 143.

79. Ibid, p 144. One incidental result of this victory, according to General Heinrichs (p 142), was a general sigh of relief in Sweden. Had the 163rd Division succeeded, Sweden would have had the Red Army at its border.

## CHAPTER V: THE LULL BEFORE

1. Luukkanen, pp 52–53; author's interview with General Grönvall, 12 July 1967; Taru Stenvall in *Suomen Kuvalehti,* No. 21, 27 May 1967. Relative to its size, Mikkeli was the most heavily damaged town outside the combat areas; it received 2,885 bombs (Finnish War Museum wall map).

2. U. S. State Dept. file 760 D.61/1347; U. S. Archives records RG 165, files 2682–32–1 (20 March 1940) and 2682–33–3 (21 May 1940).

3. *The New York Times,* 2 January 1940.

4. U. S. Archives records RG 165, file 2682–33–3 (21 May 1940); Hannula, p 100; U. S. State Dept. file 760 D.61/1347; Finnish War Museum wall map.

5. Mannerheim, p 369; U. S. Archives records RG 165, file 2682–33–3 (21 May 1940).

6. Hannula, pp 40, 104; Luukkanen, p 40; Tuompo, *K-I,* p 342; ST file 3948:5.

7. Luukkanen, pp 206–208, 221–223, 245–247; Hannula, p 104; Rotmistrov, p 503.

8. Luukkanen, pp 215–216 and passim; Mannerheim, p 377. Thirty Gloster Gladiator IIs arrived from England in January and February, but those outdated and highly vulnerable fighters proved to be white elephants. After 13 had been lost within a few days, the remaining Gladiators were transferred from fighter to reconnaissance units (Luukkanen, pp 211–212).

9. Luukkanen, p 212.

10. U. S. Archives records RG 165, file 2682–32–1, 20 March 1940.

11. Ibid; Luukkanen, pp 46, 53, 55, 61, 62, 65, 66, 74.

12. Tuompo, *K-I,* p 324; Rotmistrov, p 503; U. S. Archives records RG 165, file 2682–33–2 (2 May 1940).

13. Tuompo, *K-I,* pp 332, 335; Luukkanen, pp 194–196.

14. Tuompo, *K-I,* (chapter by Commodore R. Hakola), p 313.

15. Peitsara, pp 50–51; Mannerheim, p 346.

16. Tuompo, *K-I,* pp 315–317.

17. Ibid, p 318; Mannerheim, p 361; Ignatkovich, p 200 ff; ST records of the Supply Dept., GHQ (re ice road).

18. Tuompo, *K-I* (chapter by Lt. Colonel V. Valtanen), pp 129–132.

19. Ibid, pp 138–140.

20. Ibid, pp 133–135.

21. Ibid, pp 140–141; Luukkanen, pp 35–37, XIV; Hannula, p 65.

22. Tuompo, *K-I,* pp 140–142.

23. Ibid, pp 142–143.

24. *IHS* for 1939 and 1940.

25. *Sade-ja L. . . .,* p 51 ff; Tuompo, *K-I,* p 291.

26. Tuompo, *K-I,* pp 290–291.

27. Ibid, pp 288–290.

28. Ibid, p 266.

29. Ibid, pp 274–276.

30. Ibid, p 276; Sevast'yanov, pp 5–6, 16.

31. Luukkanen, pp 43–60 passim.

32. Author's interview with Colonel Ekholm, 20 June 1967.

33. Siukosaari et al. interview.

34. *The New York Times,* 10 December 1939, p 48 and 12 February 1940, p 4; *The Times* (London), 6 February 1940, p 7; Asunta questionnaire; letter to author, 5 October 1968, from Mr. Paavo Fleming, a veteran of the "Finnish-American Legion". The size of Captain Penttila's force, reported by *The New York Times* correspondent to be 50–300 men, was originally only two squads (about 18 men). By 8 February a total of 330 Finns residing in America had sailed for their native land. A serious limitation on the number of volunteers was the fact that those who were U. S. citizens could not obtain passports (*The New York Times,* 10 December 1939 and 8 February 1940).

35. Tuompo, *K-I* (chapter by General Talvela), p 248; Järvinen, pp 244–251.

36. Järvinen, p 250. This assumption concerning Soviet priorities was substantiated by the fact that the Red Army later transferred six regiments from the Aittojoki area to the Kollaa front.

37. Tuompo, *K-I* (chapter by General Hägglund), pp 168–169, 172.

38. Author's interview with Colonel Nihtilä, 20 June 1967.

39. Tuompo, *K-I,* pp 173–177, Map III; Zyryanov, p 154.

40. Mannerheim, p 348; Hannula, p 90; Tuompo, *K-I,* Map III.

41. Mannerheim, p 348; Tuompo, *K-I,* pp 173–175; Hannula, pp 89–93; Kuz'min, pp 258–260.

42. Tuompo, *K-I,* pp 177–178, Map III; Zyryanov, p 106.

43. Tuompo, *K-I,* pp 174, 176, 180, Map III; Seppälä and Kilkki, pp 8–9; author's interview with Colonel Nihtilä, 20 June 1967.

44. Mannerheim, pp 347–348, 356; Österman, p 237; Öhquist, *Vinterkriget,* p 203.

45. Österman, pp 239, 243; Peitsara, p 53; author's interview with General K. Vaala, 16 June 1967; Kuz'min, p 239; Pospelov, *IVOVSS,* Vol. I, p 267.

46. Mannerheim, pp 351–352; ST file 3948:5.

47. Mannerheim, p 351; Österman, p 237; Öhquist, *Vinterkriget,* p 161; Mikoka et al., p 267.

48. Meretskov, pp 186–187; Bialer, biographical index.

49. Meretskov, p 187; Kuz'min, pp 238, 240.

50. Kuz'min, pp 238–239.

51. *Krasnaya Zvezda,* 12 February 1941; Matrosov, *Boi . . .,* Vol. I, p 383. Meretskov (p 186) stated that his Army somehow obtained maps and plans of the Mannerheim Line. Another Soviet source (Matrosov, *Boi . . .,* Vol. II, pp 5–6) claimed that a captured Finnish sergeant disclosed the defense system of its two strongest fortifications. It should have been easy for Soviet agents to obtain such information, as the Line was accessible to the public in peacetime (Öhquist, *Vinterkriget,* p 50).

52. Mannerheim, pp 350–351; ST file 3948:5, 27 December 2025 hours entry.

53. Matrosov, *Boi . . .,* Vol. II, p 8; Kuz'min, p 246.

54. Matrosov, *Boi . . .,* Vol. I, p 315 and Vol. II, p 6; Meretskov, p 186.

55. Pospelov, *IVOVSS,* Vol. I, p 267; Öhquist, *Vinterkriget,* p 184; Seppälä and Kilkki, p 9 (which estimated the Soviet strength on the Isthmus in February at 600,000 troops).

56. Seppälä and Kilkki, p 9. This Finnish estimate is roughly compatible with the figures for Soviet artillery presented in Kuz'min, chart, p 241. That chart, however, overestimates Finnish strength.

57. Öhquist, *Vinterkriget,* p 164; Peitsara, p 58; Mannerheim, pp 351, 368.

58. Pospelov, *IVOVSS,* Vol. I, p 267; Kuz'min, pp 242–244.

59. Matrosov, *Boi . . .,* Vol. I, p 386 and passim; Tvardovski, p 117.

60. Soloviev, pp 193–196.

61. Kuz'min, p 246; Soviet press, 16 January—22 May 1940, passim.

62. Pospelov, *IVOVSS,* Vol. I, p 268; Meretskov, pp 187–188; Kuz'min, p 250; Rotmistrov, p 500; Öhquist, *Vinterkriget,* pp 173–174; Ogorkiewicz, p 229.

## CHAPTER VI: THE STORM

1. Pospelov, *IVOVSS,* Vol. I, p 267; Hannula, p 78.

2. Matrosov, *Boi . . .,* Vol. II, p 133.

3. Österman, p 245; Järvinen, p 168.

4. Öhquist, *Vinterkriget,* pp 163, 172; Mannerheim, p 353.

5. Österman, p 244; Öhquist, *Vinterkriget,* pp 171–172; Järvinen, pp 165, 168, 170; Hannula, pp 78–80; ST file 3948:5.

6. Öhquist, *Vinterkriget,* p 185 and Map 6; Mannerheim, p 354; Tuompo, *K-I* (section by General K. Heiskanen), p 110.

7. Öhquist, *Vinterkriget,* p 163; ST file 3948:5. The ski shields are pictured in Matrosov, *Boi . . .* Vol. II, p 15.

8. Österman, p 244; Järvinen, p 168.

9. Öhquist, *Vinterkriget,* pp 164–165, 173, 175; Österman, p 244; Järvinen, p 171.

10. Öhquist, *Vinterkriget,* pp 162–169, 183; Ehrnrooth, pp 84, 88.

11. Öhquist, *Vinterkriget,* pp 166, 183–185; Österman, p 246; Matrosov, *Boi . . .,* Vol. I, pp 288–291. Soviet sources usually refer to "Poppius" as DOT 006 or "DOT on hill 65.5," and they call "Million" DOT 45, DOT 0011, or "DOT on *Yazyk.*" The terms can be equated by comparing the geographic descriptions in Pospelov, *IVOVSS,* Vol. I, p 268 and Matrosov, *Boi . . .,* Vol. I, pp 64, 273, 385 and Vol. II, p 20 with those in Öhquist, *Vinterkriget,* p 184 and Map 6.

12. Öhquist, *Vinterkriget,* p 172.

13. Ibid, pp 166–175; Hannula, p 80.

14. Öhquist, *Vinterkriget,* pp 165–167, 172, 176; Tanner, pp 151–153.

15. *BSE,* 2nd edition, Vol. 39, map between pp 510–511; Pospelov, *IVOVSS,* Vol. I, pp 267–268.

16. Matrosov, *Boi . . .,* Vol. I, p 385 and Vol. II, pp 9, 134; Pospelov, *IVOVSS,* Vol. I, p 268.

17. Öhquist, *Vinterkriget,* p 177; Pospelov, *IVOVSS,* Vol. I, p 268; Tvardovski, pp 148, 150; Kuz'min, pp 249–250; Matrosov, *Boi . . .,* Vol. II, pp 8–10, 51, 135, 257. Voronov (p 140) stated that the decision to issue vodka to the front line troops, to counter the cold weather, was made at the end of December.

18. Öhquist, *Vinterkriget,* pp 183–186, Map 6.

19. Ibid, p 185; Pospelov, *IVOVSS,* Vol. I, pp 267–268; Matrosov, *Boi . . .,* Vol. I, p 385 and Vol. II, pp 7, 50–52; Kuz'min, p 250; Tvardovski, p 152.

20. Tvardovski, p 151. Those poor "sons of bitches" who survived the preparatory shelling were far too preoccupied to keep records of that day's action; most of the available details are found in the war diaries of higher echelons which inevitably lag behind the course of events. It is therefore impossible to reconstruct an exact, minute by minute, battle chronology for 11 February. The role of aircraft in the breakthru is also uncertain. According to the scenario, hundreds of bombers were to plaster the Mannerheim Line just ahead of the advancing tanks and infantry, but the weather was poor that morning and Soviet sources contradict each other here. The official Soviet history (Pospelov, *IVOVSS,* Vol. I, p 268) states that planes did not participate in that day's assault, but Colonel Kuz'min (p 249) claims that bombers did precede the infantry. Tvardovski (pp 152–153) noted their appearance on the 123rd Division's sector *after* the initial attack—probably after 12:30. Finnish sources (e.g., ST file 3948:5) confirm afternoon air activity.

21. Tvardovski, pp 152–154; Matrosov, *Boi . . .,* Vol. II, pp 20, 53; Öhquist, *Vinterkriget,* pp 183, 186.

22. Öhquist, *Vinterkriget,* pp 186–188; Matrosov, *Boi . . .,* Vol. I, p 363.

Due to heavy snow cover it received early in the winter, the Munasuo Swamp did not freeze sufficiently to support tanks. Consequently, this was one area where Soviet infantry attacked without tank support on 11 February (Öhquist, *Vinterkriget,* p 184 and Matrosov, *Boi . . .,* Vol. I, p 363).

23. Öhquist, *Vinterkriget,* p 187; Tvardovski, p 153; Kuz'min, pp 250–251; Matrosov, *Boi . . .,* Vol. II, p 12 and appendix.

24. Tvardovski, p 154.

25. ST file 3948:5; Tuompo, *K-I* (section by General K. Heiskanen), pp 107–108; Öhquist, *Vinterkriget,* pp 181–182; Järvinen, p 168.

26. Öhquist, *Vinterkriget,* pp 177–179.

27. Ibid, pp 178–180; Tuompo, *K-I,* p 145; Pospelov, *IVOVSS,* Vol. I, Map 14.

28. Öhquist, *Vinterkriget,* pp 179–182; ST file 3948:5.

29. Öhquist, *Vinterkriget,* pp 179–182; Österman, p 245.

30. Öhquist, *Vinterkriget,* p 180; Hannula, pp 81–82.

31. Öhquist, *Vinterkriget,* pp 179, 185, 189, 191; Österman, pp 247–248; Mannerheim, p 354; ST file 3948:5.

32. Öhquist, *Vinterkriget,* pp 186–187; Matrosov, *Boi . . .,* Vol. II, pp 69–72.

33. Österman, p 248; ST file 3948:5.

34. Tuompo, *K-I,* pp 108–110.

35. Öhquist, *Vinterkriget,* pp 190–191.

36. Ibid, p 190.

37. Ibid, pp 189–192.

38. Ibid, p 190; Ehrnrooth, pp 88, 92.

39. Öhquist, *Vinterkriget,* p 193.

40. Österman, p 248; ST file 3948:5.

41. Österman, pp 248–249; Öhquist, *Vinterkriget,* pp 192–197; ST file 3948:5.

42. Österman, p 249; Öhquist, *Vinterkriget,* pp 192–196.

43. Öhquist, *Vinterkriget,* pp 192–198; Österman, p 249; Mannerheim, p 355; ST files 3948:5 and 3948:7 (Summa-Lähde Battle Report, 11–17 February 1940); author's interview with General Vaala, 16 June 1967.

44. Öhquist, *Vinterkriget,* p 196.

45. Ibid, pp 184, 192, 202; Österman, pp 249–250.

46. Öhquist, *Vinterkriget,* p 200; Österman, p 250.

47. Matrosov, *Boi . . .,* Vol. II, p 59; Pospelov, *IVOVSS.* Vol. I, p 269.

48. Meretskov, p 186.

49. Öhquist, *Vinterkriget,* pp 192–197; Tuompo, *K-I* (chapter by Lt. Colonel Valtanen), p 145.

50. Ehrnrooth, p 88.

51. Öhquist, *Vinterkriget*, pp 193–196; ST file 3948:5.

52. Öhquist, *Vinterkriget*, pp 193–197.

53. Ibid, pp 193–194, 196–197.

54. Ibid, p 195.

55. Ibid, pp 196–200; ST file 3948:5.

56. Öhquist, *Vinterkriget*, p 198.

57. Ibid, pp 199–201; Österman, p 251; Mannerheim, pp 355–356. There were reasonable arguments for both the T and the V lines. Österman (pp 220, 251), Öhquist (p 201), Heinrichs (p 145), and others discuss the opposing views. In light of subsequent events, the Marshal's choice appears fortunate, considering that the main object was to gain time. The overly cautious leadership of the NW Front paused for a full week before assaulting the intermediate line (Pospelov, *IVOVSS*, Vol. I, p 269).

58. Österman, p 262.

59. Ibid, p 252; Öhquist, *Vinterkriget*, pp 199–208; Mannerheim, pp 355–356.

60. Österman, p 252; Öhquist, *Vinterkriget*, pp 200–203.

61. Tuompo, *K-I*, pp 145–146; Öhquist, *Vinterkriget*, pp 202–203.

62. Ehrnrooth, p 92; Öhquist, *Vinterkriget*, pp 202–203. The Soviet force attacking Merkki was probably the 90th Division (see Pospelov, *IVOVSS*, Vol. I, p. 268).

63. Mannerheim, pp 355–356; Tuompo, *K-I* (section by Colonel I. Karhu), p 111; ST file 3948:5. The 5th Division (JR 13, 14, and 15) officially relieved the 3rd Division on 14 February, but a piecemeal transfer of front responsibilities had begun on 12 February (Öhquist, *Vinterkriget*, p 193 and ST file 3948:5). The weary survivors of the 3rd Division were soon transferred to the Viipuri-Tali region to work on the T-Line defenses (Tuompo, *K-I*, p 73).

64. Mannerheim, p 356; ST file 3948:7.

65. Öhquist, *Vinterkriget*, p 47; Tuompo, *K-I*, p 113; Voronov, p 152.

66. Voronov, pp 152–153.

67. Ibid; Pospelov, *IVOVSS*, Vol. I, p 268; *Literaturnaya Gazeta*, 25 February 1964. Timoshenko probably visited one of these divisions at 2 A.M. on 15 February. With him were Meretskov, Voronov, and Commander Vashugin (Matrosov, *Boi . . .*, Vol. I, p 265). No date is given for that visit to the "Khotinen" sector (Soviet maps show Khotinen just south of Summa—e.g., ibid, pp 4–5), but Pospelov (*IVOVSS*, Vol. I, p 268) notes that the "most powerful center of resistance, Khotinensk", was destroyed on 15 February by two divisions of the 19th Corps. Only the fall of Summa seems to match these details.

68. Öhquist, *Vinterkriget*, pp 205–207; Österman, p 255; Pospelov, *IVOVSS*, Vol. I, p 269.

69. Öhquist, *Vinterkriget,* p 206; Österman, pp 254–256.

70. Öhquist, *Vinterkriget,* pp 206–207; Österman, pp 252, 256; Mannerheim, p 356.

71. Öhquist, *Vinterkriget,* p 206.

72. Ibid, pp 206–207; Österman, pp 220, 256–257; Heinrichs, p 145; Palmunen, pp 80–81, 91.

73. Österman, p 220.

74. Ibid, p 256; Mannerheim, pp 356–357; Tuompo, *K-I,* pp 146, 149; Matrosov, *Boi . . .,* Vol. II, pp 308–309.

75. Österman, p 256; Matrosov, *Boi . . .,* Vol. II, pp 10, 61–62; Pospelov, *IVOVSS,* Vol. I, p 269; ST file 3948:5.

76. Österman, pp 256–257; Mannerheim, p 357; Pospelov, *IVOVSS,* Vol. I, pp 269–270. (5th Division losses from ST, daily reports.) The Soviet claim that their offensive was deliberately halted from 21 to 28 February (Pospelov, *IVOVSS,* Vol. I, pp 269–270) is difficult to reconcile with other Soviet accounts of offensive operations involving the 123rd Division and Baranov's tanks during this period (Tvardovski, p 137; Matrosov, *Boi . . .,* Vol. II, pp 405–410). The former claim may be intended to rationalize the limited success of the attacks.

77. Ehrnrooth, p 92; author's interview with General G. Ehrnrooth, 17 July 1967. Any criticism of the Taipale defense should consider that, for sustained stress and sheer horror, that was probably the worst of all fronts. The 7th (10th) Division suffered more than 3,500 casualties *before* the main offensive began on 11 February—and an additional 2,000 by the end of February (Ehrnrooth, pp 84, 109).

78. Heinrichs, p 146.

79. Translation forwarded from U. S. Minister in Finland, U. S. State Dept. file 760 D.61/1349.

80. Author's interview with Colonel Nihtilä, 20 June 1967; Österman, pp 262–263.

81. Österman, p 262; Mannerheim, p 358; ST file 3948:5; author's interview with General Öhquist, 15 June 1967.

82. Österman, p 266; Mannerheim, p 358.

83. Österman, p 252; Tuompo, *K-I* (chapter by General Tapola), p 75; Mannerheim, p 358.

84. Hannula, p 10; Tuompo, *K-I,* p 75.

85. Heinrichs, p 168; Tuompo, *K-I,* pp 292–294; Mannerheim, p 360; Hannula, p 99; U. S. State Dept. file 760 D.61/1429. The Swedish Volunteer Corps was by far the largest foreign contingent serving in Finland. Because they were in action for only a short period, their casualties were light—26 dead, 39 wounded, 10 missing, and 139 suffering frostbite. Among those killed was Lt. Colonel Dyrssen (Tuompo, *K-I,* p 294).

86. Tuompo, *K-I,* p 75.

87. Ibid, pp 74–75; Matrosov, *Boi* . . ., Vol. II, pp 406–410; Tvardovski, p 138; Colonel Mikola letter to author, 11 April 1969 (confirming loss of 5 tanks).

88. Pospelov, *IVOVSS,* Vol. I, pp 269–270; Kuz'min, p 253; Mannerheim, pp 360–361; Tuompo, *K-I,* p 76.

89. Pospelov, *IVOVSS,* Vol. I, p 270.

90. Mannerheim, p 361.

91. Ibid, p 348; Kuz'min, pp 235, 260.

92. Tuompo, *K-I* (chapter by General Hägglund), p 176.

93. Ibid, p 179.

94. Ibid, pp 179, 185–186; Hannula, pp 93–94; Zenzinov, pp 34–35, 40, 168–170.

95. Tuompo, *K-I,* pp 180, 186–187, 190, and Map III; Peitsara, p 57.

96. Tuompo, *K-I,* pp 178–179; Mannerheim, p 348; Peitsara, p 57.

97. Seppälä and Kilkki, pp 8–9; Peitsara, p 57. In order of their arrival, the four divisions at Pitkäranta were the 25th Motorized Cavalry and the 11th, 72nd, and 37th Infantry.

98. Tuompo, *K-I,* pp 177, 187–189, Map III.

99. Voronov, p 155.

100. Tuompo, *K-I,* pp 180, 188–190; Kuz'min, p 260; Järvinen, pp 246–250.

101. Mannerheim, p 349; Sevast'yanov, p 16; Tuompo, *K-I,* pp 279–280; ST file T255–256; author's interview with Colonel Lassila, 23 April 1970.

102. Tuompo, *K-I,* p 283.

103. *Study of Soviet Tactics* . . ., p 86; ST file T255–256; author's interview with Colonel Marttinen, 11 June 1968.

104. *Study of Soviet Tactics* . . ., p 74; Siilasvuo, *Kuhmo T.,* pp 132–157, passim, and Map 5; ST file T255–256; Tuompo, *K-I,* p 280.

105. *Study of Soviet Tactics* . . ., Map 4; Siilasvuo, *Kuhmo T.,* p 137 and Map 5; Tuompo, *K-I,* p 280; ST file T255–256.

106. Tuompo, *K-I,* pp 280–282; Siilasvuo, *Kuhmo T.,* p 206 and Map 6; *Study of Soviet Tactics* . . ., Map 4; author's interview with Colonel Lassila, 18 January 1971.

107. Tuompo, *K-I,* p 282; author's interview with Colonel Lassila, 28 September 1970.

108. Karhunen, p 195 (which gives 2,009 fatalities for the N. Finland Group. Of these, 596 fell at Suomussalmi-Raate, and the remainder at Kuhmo). Author's interview with Colonel Lassila, 18 January 1971.

109. Hannula, p 98; Tuompo, *K-I,* p 290; Kuz'min, p 262.

## CHAPTER VII: THE ELEVENTH HOUR

1. Author's interview with Colonel Nihtilä, 20 June 1967. Soviet recognition of tsarist Russian heritage prior to the German invasion is illustrated by an account of the Winter War published in Moscow early in 1941; it mentions both the 1710 exploit and the crossing of the ice to seize the Åland Islands in 1809 (Matrosov, *Boi* . . ., Vol. II, p 304).

2. Heinrichs, pp 172, 175; Kuz'min, p 253; Meretskov, p 189; Voronov, p 146; Pospelov, *IVOVSS*, Vol. I, Map 14; Mannerheim, p 361. Corps Commander Pavlov's reserve group (mentioned in Pospelov, *IVOVSS*, Vol. I, p 266) was probably the same unit Kuz'min (p 253) identified as the 28th Corps. Pavlov's force consisted of three infantry divisions, a tank brigade, a cavalry corps, and reinforcements. Voronov (p 145) noted that Pavlov's group was concentrated at Kingisepp (east of Narva) to cross the "Gulf of Finland," but it is obvious that this was during a training phase before the attack.

3. Tuompo, *K-I* (chapter by General Tapola), p 76; Mannerheim, pp 361–362, Öhquist, *Vinterkriget,* pp 269, 281–283.

4. U. S. Archives, Records of OKL, frame 19.

5. Öhquist, *Vinterkriget,* p 292; Mannerheim, p 361; Tuompo, *K-I,* pp 77–78; Heinrichs, p 168.

6. Mannerheim, pp 360–361; author's interview with Colonel Nihtilä, 29 June 1967.

7. Tuompo, *K-I,* pp 79, 83; author's interview with General Öhquist, 15 June 1967.

8. Tuompo, *K-I,* pp 79, 83; Kuz'min, pp 253–254; Pospelov, *IVOVSS,* Vol. I, Map 14.

9. Luukkanen, pp 69–73.

10. Mannerheim, pp 362–363.

11. Ibid, p 362; Tuompo, *K-I,* p 80.

12. Heinrichs, p 171.

13. Tuompo, *K-I,* p 80; Mannerheim, p 362; Tanner, p 220; author's interview with General Öhquist, 15 June 1967.

14. Tuompo, *K-I,* pp 80–83; Öhquist, *Vinterkriget,* Map 14; Pospelov, *IVOVSS,* Vol. I, Map 14; Mannerheim, p 364.

15. Tuompo, *K-I,* pp 77–78; Pospelov, *IVOVSS,* Vol. I, pp 269–270. Grendal' was luckier than many of Stalin's unsuccessful commanders (Vinogradov's fate has been noted; D. G. Pavlov was also shot in July 1941 [Bialer, p 635]). Grendal' was promoted to Lt. General in June 1940 (*Krasnaya Zvezda,* 5 June), and when he died in November 1940 at the age of 57, his obituary noted that he was awarded the Order of Lenin for his "selfless actions" during the Winter War (*Pravda,* 17 November 1940).

16. Tuompo, *K-I,* pp 82–84; *BSE,* Vol. 39, Map between pp 510–511.

17. Tuompo, *K-I,* pp 77–78; author's interview with General G. Ehrnrooth, 17 July 1967.

18. Tuompo, *K-I,* pp 80–83; Hannula, pp 106–107; Ehrnrooth, p 161.

19. Mannerheim, p 363; Pospelov, *IVOVSS,* Vol. I, p 270; Tvardovski, p 139; Matrosov, *Boi* . . ., Vol. II, pp 501–510; Tuompo, *K-I,* pp 81–82; author's interview with General Öhquist, 15 June 1967.

20. Mannerheim, p 361; Voronov, p 146; Öhquist, *Vinterkriget,* p 178; Tuompo, *K-I,* pp 80–84; Kuz'min, p 255; *BSE,* Vol. 39, p 512; Matrosov, *Boi* . . ., Vol. II, p 497.

21. Meretskov, p 189; Mannerheim, p 363; *BSE,* Vol. 39, p 512. The claim that Viipuri was captured is one of many falsehoods about this embarrassing war still repeated by Soviet authors (e.g. in Meretskov's memoirs, p 189—published in 1968).

22. Author's interviews with Colonel Nihtilä, 20 and 29 June 1967, and General Grönvall, 12 July 1967.

23. Mikola et al., p 269; Seppälä and Kilkki, p 9; Hannula, p 99; Tuompo, *K-I,* p 84.

24. Peitsara, p 61; U. S. State Dept. file 760 D.61/1207; Tanner, p. 227; Heinrichs, pp 175–176.

25. Heinrichs, p 468.

26. Öhquist, "Comments . . ."; *The Times,* 23 February 1940, p 7.

27. Tanner, p 190.

28. Clark, pp 127–128; Mannerheim, pp 364–377; Tanner, p 115; Schwartz, p 25; Luukkanen, pp 77, 192; U. S. State Dept. file 760 D.61/1433. Quotation from author's interview with General Grönvall, 12 July 1967.

29. Mannerheim, pp 358–359; letter from Mr. Paavo Fleming to author, 5 October 1968. In another case where Soviet historians have retroactively made today's villains yesterday's as well, their official history of the war (published in 1960) states that "about 1,000 American pilots were sent to Helsinki"—an utter fabrication! (Pospelov, *IVOVSS,* Vol. I, p 264).

30. Mannerheim, p 359; Hannula, p 16; Clark, pp 131, 208; *The Times,* 4 March 1940, p 3.

31. The officials who virtually monopolized foreign policy were Prime Minister Ryti, Foreign Minister Tanner, Minister Paasikivi, and—intermittently—President Kallio (Jakobson, p 222 ff).

32. Woodward, p 19.

33. Ibid, p 16.

34. Butler, pp 100, 107, 109–110. Concerning the likelihood of a German invasion of Sweden if Allied forces crossed her border, Churchill

wrote (on 16 December) that England had more to gain than to lose by that eventuality (Churchill, Vol. I, p 546).

35. Tanner, pp 149, 153.

36. Ibid, pp 171, 176–177, 187, 194, 205, 208, 219, 387; Mannerheim, pp 385–386. Tanner's highest figure is 57,000, but Mannerheim's 57,500 is probably correct.

37. Tanner, pp 177, 223, and passim.

38. Ibid, pp 144, 152 ff; Mannerheim, p 382.

39. *Foreign Relations of the United States* (hereinafter cited as *FRUS*), 1939, Vol. I, pp 1008–1010, 1021; Tanner, pp 106–107, 114–115.

40. Jakobson, pp 180–183.

41. *Documents on German Foreign Policy* (hereinafter cited as *DGFP*), Series D, Vol. 8, p 597.

42. Ibid, pp 511–512, 521; Tanner, pp 118, 121; Tuompo, *K-I*, p 316; Jakobson, p 184.

43. *DGFP*, Ser. D, Vol. 8, pp 479–480, 501, 914–915.

44. Ibid, p 631.

45. Tanner, pp 125–128; Jakobson, p 222. The Finnish scholar-diplomat, Max Jakobson, has criticized the arbitrary assumption of power by the triumvirate of Ryti, Tanner, and Paasikivi. Tanner subsequently admitted that he did not inform the other Cabinet members of the peace feelers because he knew most would have opposed his policy. He did not even let President Kallio or Mannerheim in on the secret immediately. (Jakobson, pp 221–223; Tanner, p 151; Mannerheim, p 379.)

46. Jakobson, pp 208–211; Tanner, pp 123–131; *Sovetskaya Istoricheskaya Entsiklopediya* (hereinafter cited as *SIE*), Vol. 7, p 502.

47. Tanner, pp 124–151 passim; Jakobson, p 210.

48. Jakobson, pp 161, 230–231; Tanner, pp 131, 142–145, 150; Mannerheim, p 376.

49. Tanner, pp 128–130, 142–148.

50. Ibid, pp 150, 157; Mannerheim, p 381.

51. *DGFP*, Ser. D, Vol. 8, pp 293–297, 863; Tanner, pp 157–160.

52. Tanner, pp 160–163; Jakobson, pp 231–233.

53. Tanner, p 170; Mannerheim, p 382.

54. Tanner, pp 172, 179–182; Mannerheim, p 382.

55. Tanner, pp 180–182.

56. Ibid, pp 181–184.

57. Ibid, p 185.

58. Ibid, pp 188–190; Mannerheim, pp 383–384.

59. Tanner, pp 191–195; Jakobson, pp 238–239.

60. Tanner, pp 192, 195–196.

61. Ibid, p 197.

62. Ibid, pp 196–200; Woodward, pp 26–27; Churchill, Vol. I, p 573.

63. Tanner, pp 201–202; Jakobson, p 246; Woodward, p 27. On 8 July 1940, about four months after her categorical rejection of the Allied request, Sweden granted transit rights to Nazi troops enroute between occupied Norway and Germany (*DGFP,* Ser. D, Vol. 8, p 158). The author once discussed Sweden's policies in World War II with a sophisticated Swedish colonel. To the question of neutral Sweden's probable fate had Hitler won the war in Europe, the colonel's astonishingly frank reply was that the Swedes would not have been greatly affected, because Hitler approved of the Nordic race!

64. Tanner, pp 197–204, 207; Jakobson, p 242.

65. The above 5 paragraphs are based on Tanner, pp 204–223.

66. *FRUS,* 1940, Vol. I, pp 301, 305. Subsequently, the Finnish Prime Minister declared that "this démarche of the U.S. was the only influence which had served to moderate the Russian terms" (ibid, p 306, note 89). As there was little "moderation" in those terms, this remark was probably only a goodwill gesture by Ryti. In fact, there was considerable resentment of American policies in Finland, due to the legalistic interpretation of the Neutrality Acts which prohibited the sale of arms to belligerents (Jakobson, p 195). Profuse expressions of sympathy procured precious little military hardware. A former Foreign Minister, Antti Hackzell, told a member of the U. S. Legation that the attitude of the U. S. in the Winter War was "only less disappointing to the Finnish people than that of Germany" (*FRUS,* 1940, Vol. I, p 290).

67. Tanner, pp 221–225.

68. *FRUS,* 1940, Vol. I, p 307; Tanner, pp 198, 228, 234; Jakobson, p 251.

69. Tanner, pp 226–230; Mannerheim, p 387; Wuorinen, *Finland and World War II,* p 78.

70. Tanner, pp 226, 240; Mannerheim, p 365.

71. Tanner, pp 210, 231–249 passim; Heinrichs, p 180; author's interview with General Talvela, 8 June 1967.

72. Tanner, pp 234, 237.

73. Ibid, pp 235–238. After the war, two newsmen were sentenced to prison for this "scoop," which originated when one of them overheard two members of the Committee discussing the decision in a café (Heinrichs, p 179 and Tanner, p 238). Marshal Mannerheim was furious when he learned of the leak; it confirmed his conviction that neither the Parliament nor its Foreign Relations Committee could be trusted with important state secrets (Heinrichs, p 179).

74. Tanner, p 237; Pakaslahti in *Suomen Kuvalehti,* 30 October 1970, p 33.

75. Tanner, p 241.

76. Clark, p 183; Tanner, pp 239–244; Wuorinen, *Finland and World War II,* p 79; Butler, p 113; Mazour, p 126; Kallio quoted in Tanner, p 244.

77. Tanner, pp 245, 248. Information subsequently published by Sweden and Germany indicates that the Norwegians contemplated only formal resistance if the Allies attempted to force a passage across Norway. Sweden's likely response is more problematical. (Jakobson, p 244.)

78. Tanner, pp 250, 265.

## CHAPTER VIII: ENTR' ACTE

1. Heinrichs, p 181.

2. Hannula, p 116.

3. ST file T255–256 and author's interview with Colonel Lassila, 25 September 1970.

4. Sevast'yanov, pp 58–59.

5. ST files 1204, 3737:2, and 3732, respectively.

6. Author's interview with General Grönvall, 12 July 1967.

7. Tanner, p 250. Quotation from *The Times* (London), 14 March 1940, p 8.

8. Jakobson, p 253; Tanner, pp 172, 244, 251; Hannula, p 142; Mazour, p 130; ST file 1204; International Boundary Study No. 74, pp 5, 8.

9. Mikola, "The Finnish Wars," p 245; Jakobson, p 254; Hannula, p 142; Tanner, p 251; Mazour, pp 130–131.

10. Tanner, p 266; Heinrichs, p 182.

11. Tanner, pp 255–260, 265.

12. Heinrichs, p 182; author's interview with Mr. Vilho Manninen (a former POW), 5 July 1967; U. S. Archives, Records of OKW, frames 5647901-02.

13. The precise number of Russian POWs, according to an authorized statement in the Finnish press, was 5,468 (U. S. State Dept. file 760 D.61/1455). Soloviev, p 199; Alliluyeva, *Only One Year,* pp 370, 375; letter from Professor Artemiev to author 18 July 1967. (Mr. Artemiev became a Professor of Military Science at the U. S. Army Institute of Advanced Russian and East European Studies)

14. *Pravda,* 30 March 1940.

15. *SIE,* Vol. 7, pp 30–37 and Vol. 8, p 339. The Karelian Isthmus, including Viipuri, was annexed by the R.S.F.S.R.

16. Pospelov, *IVOVSS,* Vol. I, p 266.

17. Maisky (Maiski), pp 48–49; Pospelov, *IVOVSS,* Vol. I, p 272; Meretskov, p 189. Tanner, p 191, probably erred in giving 26 February as the date Maiski asked the British to transmit the peace terms to

Finland. Tanner noted that these were the same terms *later* presented thru Sweden, and he said (p 172) they were transmitted via Stockholm on 23 February. Soviet sources consistently give 24 February as the date of the British refusal to mediate.

18. *Pravda,* 30 March 1940; Khrushchev [?], p 155; Colonel Mikola letter to author, 15 June 1959; Pospelov, *IVOVSS,* Vol. I, p 277.

19. *The Fighting Forces,* Vol. 16, No. 6, p 493 and Vol. 17, No. 1, pp 42–53.

20. Halder, Vol. 5, p 85.

21. *DGFP,* Ser. D, Vol. 8, p 877.

22. Mannerheim, p 392.

23. Ibid, p 430; Pospelov, *VOVSS-KI,* p 602. A Soviet Admiral, I. S. Isakov, acknowledged that Hanko had not been "suitably fitted for defense" by the time of the German attack, nor had artillery collaboration from the southern shore been arranged yet (Isakov, p 21).

24. *Pravda,* 23 February 1941; Pospelov, *IVOVSS,* Vol. I, pp 276–277.

25. *Spravochnik;* Kuz'min, p 273.

26. Kuz'min, pp 268–271.

27. Ibid, pp 271–272; Bialer, p 137 (quoting Marshal Biriuzov); Liddell Hart, pp 86, 462.

28. *Study of Soviet Tactics . . .,* p 48; Timoshenko quoted in Mannerheim, p 371.

29. Kuz'min, p 263; Bialer, biographical index, passim; Burroughs, passim; Shtemenko, p 396; Voronov, p 195; Matrosov, *Boi . . .,* Vol. II, p 23; Erickson, p 859.

30. Data provided by Major Kilkki from ST records. Slight variations in Finnish sources are due to differing criteria, e.g., killed in action vs killed in action plus died later of wounds; permanently disabled vs wounded.

31. Mannerheim, p 373. The Marshal (p 391) made a strong case for the proposition that Finland also saved Sweden. Had the Red Army achieved its goal of reaching the Swedish border near the vital iron ore fields, Sweden would probably have become a battleground during the Nazi-Soviet war.

## CHAPTER IX: EPILOGUE

1. Sherwood, pp 303–304; *FRUS,* 1941, Vol. I, pp 788–789, 812, 814–815.

2. Degras, Vol III, p. 424; Upton, *Finland in Crisis,* pp 50–53.

3. Upton, *Finland in Crisis,* p 87.

4. Degras, Vol. III, pp 453–456; *Nazi-Soviet Relations,* pp 156, 169–171; *FRUS,* 1940, Vol. I, p 368.

5. Degras, Vol. III, p 466; Upton, *Finland in Crisis,* pp 105–109; *FRUS,* 1940, Vol. I, p 372; Mannerheim, pp 396–397. For a detailed discussion of the complex negotiations relating to the nickel concession, see H. Peter Krosby, *Finland, Germany, and the Soviet Union, 1940–1941, The Petsamo Dispute* (University of Wisconsin Press, 1968).

6. Upton, *Finland in Crisis,* p. 113; *DGFP,* Ser. D, Vol. X, p 158 and Vol. XI, p 149.

7. Upton, *Finland in Crisis,* pp 100, 106, 115–116, 119–122; Degras, Vol. III, p 466; Krosby, p 56; *Nazi-Soviet Relations,* p 170; House Report No. 2684, Part 13, p 12; *Outline History of the U.S.S.R.,* p 426.

8. Upton, *Finland in Crisis,* pp 118, 124; Wuorinen, *Finland and World War II,* p 85. The special Soviet hatred reserved for Tanner was probably due to his successful leadership of the Social Democratic Party, always an object of Stalin's deepest enmity. Communist antipathy for Social Democracy exists on two levels, theoretical and practical. From a Marxist viewpoint, even capitalists are preferable, as they are *necessary* evils at a certain stage of history, whereas democratic socialists of any hue are *unnecessary* perversions of the proletariat. Pragmatically, the improvements of the workers' lot effected by Social Democracy decrease the incentive for (and delay) the class revolution. If there were no other reasons, Stalin would have opposed Social Democratic Parties merely because they were not under his control.

9. Upton, *Finland in Crisis,* pp 117, 124–125; Krosby, pp 56, 64; *FRUS,* 1940, Vol. I, p 338; *DGFP,* Ser. D, Vol. X, p 460.

10. Mannerheim, p 398; Upton, *Finland in Crisis,* pp 78–85.

11. U. S. Army, *The German Campaign in Russia . . .,* pp 1–6.

12. *DGFP,* Ser. D, Vol X, p 512.

13. Upton, *Finland in Crisis,* pp 134–138; Krosby, pp 65–66; Mannerheim, pp 399–400. Ryti denied that Mannerheim consulted with him on the evening of 18 August, but the Marshal's version is more credible (see Upton, p 137).

14. Upton, *Finland in Crisis,* pp 140, 145–146; Mannerheim, p 400; *DGFP,* Ser. D, Vol. XI, pp 148–149.

15. Subsequently, on 25 June 1941, Sweden—in contrast to her policy towards the Allies during the Winter War—granted permission for a full German division to cross her territory enroute to Finland. German aircraft were permitted to overfly Sweden, while Russian planes would encounter opposition (Halder Diary entry for 24 June 1941, in *DGFP,* Ser. D, Vol XIII, p 21).

16. Upton, *Finland in Crisis,* pp 85, 139; *DGFP,* Ser. D, Vol X, p 512.

17. Upton, *Finland in Crisis,* p 235 ff.

18. Ibid, pp 150–189 passim, 202; Mannerheim, p 403.

19. Upton, *Finland in Crisis,* pp 192–193; *DGFP,* Ser. D, Vol XI, p 841.

20. Upton, *Finland in Crisis,* pp 205–206; *DGFP,* Ser. D, Vol XI, p 1139; Mannerheim, p 404.

21. Upton, *Finland in Crisis,* p 173; *Nazi-Soviet Relations,* pp 217–254, passim.

22. *Nazi-Soviet Relations,* p 258.

23. U. S. Army, *The German Campaign in Russia . . .,* pp 18–22.

24. *DGFP,* Ser. D, Vol. XI, pp 722–723, 813.

25. Upton, *Finland in Crisis,* pp 139–140, 189, 207.

26. Ibid, pp 207–209; Mannerheim, p 405; *DGFP,* Ser. D, Vol XI, p 1231.

27. *DGFP,* Ser. D, Vol XII, pp 122–123.

28. Ibid, pp 122–126; Upton, *Finland in Crisis,* p 215 ff; Mannerheim, p 405.

29. *DGFP,* Ser. D, Vol XII, pp 879–885; Mannerheim, pp 407–408; Halder, Vol. 6, p 133.

30. Halder, Vol. 6, p 145. See Upton, *Finland in Crisis,* p 262 ff, for details on Kinzel's visit, during which the Germans gained the definite impression that the Finns agreed to participate in the attack on the Soviet Union.

31. Upton, *Finland in Crisis,* pp 254–256, 260–264.

32. Halder, Vol. 7, p 399; Mikola, "The Finnish Wars," pp 247–248; Mannerheim, pp 410–411; Upton, *Finland in Crisis,* pp 273–274; *DGFP,* Serv. D, Vol. XII, p 1038.

33. Mannerheim, p 412; Beloff, Vol. II, p 384; *DGFP,* Serv. D, Vol. XII, p 1079; Upton, *Finland in Crisis,* p 282. (Author's italics)

34. Upton, *Finland in Crisis,* p 282.

35. Ibid, pp 282–288; Mannerheim, pp 412–413; Mikola, "The Finnish Wars," pp 247–248. A Soviet source (Viktorov et al., pp 19–20) acknowledges raids on 19 Finnish airfields on 25 June, claiming heavy damage.

36. *DGFP,* Ser. D, Vol. XIII, p 20.

37. Upton, *Finland in Crisis,* pp 283, 289–290.

38. *FRUS,* 1941, Vol. I, p 44.

39. *DGFP,* Ser. D, Vol. XII, p 963.

40. Lundin, p 212.

41. *FRUS,* 1941, Vol. I, pp 54, 108, 114–115; Jutikkala, *History,* p 282.

42. Wuorinen, *Finland and World War II,* pp 140, 172–175; *FRUS,* 1944, Vol. III, pp 606–607.

43. Mannerheim, pp 426–428; *FRUS,* 1941, Vol. I, pp 61–64, 74–76; *DGFP,* Ser. D, Vol XIII, p 399; Pospelov, *VOVSS-KI,* p 83; Halder, Vol. 7, p 80.

44. Wuorinen, *Finland and World War II,* p 123; Jutikkala, *History,* p 282; *The New York Times,* 15 July 1942, p 3; *DGFP,* Ser. D, Vol XIII, p 477.

45. *DGFP,* Ser. D, Vol. XIII, p 418.

46. *FRUS,* 1941, Vol. I, pp 48–50; Lundin, pp 124–125, 130 ff.

47. *The USSR and Finland,* pp 61–62. There is a slightly different translation in Degras, Vol. III, pp 407–412.

48. Halder, Vol. 6, p 204 and Vol. 7, pp 18, 42, 92.

49. U.S. Army, *Warfare in the Far North,* pp 2–3.

50. Mikola, "The Finnish Wars," pp 249–250; Pospelov, *VOVSS-KI,* p 83.

51. Mikola, "The Finnish Wars," pp 250–252; Mannerheim, p 432; Pospelov, *VOVSS-KI,* p 83.

52. Mikola, "The Finnish Wars," pp 250–252.

53. Ibid, p 251.

54. Mannerheim, pp 440–441; *DGFP,* Ser. D, Vol. XIII, pp 396, 418, 720; Wuorinen, *Finland and World War II,* p 127.

55. Mannerheim, pp 463–474; Wuorinen, *Finland and World War II,* pp 145–154, 171.

56. Wuorinen, *Finland and World War II,* pp 163–169; *FRUS,* 1944, Vol. III, pp 588–589.

57. Mannerheim, pp 474–475; Lundin, pp 206–208; Wuroinen, *Finland and World War II,* p 171.

58. Upton, "End of the Arctic War," p 2226; Mannerheim, p 489; Wuorinen, *Finland and World War II,* pp 171–172; Pospelov, *IVOVSS,* Vol. IV, pp 137–138.

59. Mikola, "The Finnish Wars," p 253; Pospelov, *IVOVSS,* Vol. IV, p 140; Mannerheim, pp 475–476.

60. Mannerheim, pp 475–477, 483–484; Mikola, "The Finnish Wars," p 254; Upton, "End of the Arctic War," pp 2227–2230.

61. Wuorinen, *Finland and World War II,* p 172; Pospelov, *IVOVSS,* Vol. IV, p 142; Mannerheim, p 480; Upton, "End of the Arctic War," pp 2227–2228; Lundin, p 212.

62. Wuorinen, *Finland and World War II,* p 173; *FRUS,* 1944, Vol. III, p 603; Mikola, "The Finnish Wars," pp 254–255; Upton, "End of the Arctic War," pp 2231–2232; Pospelov, *IVOVSS,* Vol. IV, p 145; Mannerheim, pp 181–182; Lundin, p 213.

63. Wuorinen, *Finland and World War II,* pp 173–174; Lundin, p 216; Mannerheim, pp 482–483.

64. Lundin, p 217; Wuorinen, *Finland and World War II,* p 174; *FRUS,* 1944, Vol. III, pp 596, 604–607.

65. Mannerheim, pp 485, 489; Upton, "End of the Arctic War," pp 2230–2231; Mikola, "The Finnish Wars," p 254; Pospelov, *IVOVSS,* Vol. IV, p 143.

66. Mannerheim, pp 486–487; Upton, "End of the Arctic War," p 2232; Mikola, "The Finnish Wars," p 255; Pospelov, *IVOVSS,* Vol. IV, p 147.

67. Mannerheim, pp 485–487; Upton, "End of the Arctic War," p 2232; Mikola, "The Finnish Wars," p 255.

68. Mannerheim, pp 486, 491–492; Wuorinen, *Finland and World War II,* pp 175–176; Lundin, p 222; *FRUS,* 1944, Vol. III, pp 611–612.

69. Wuorinen, *Finland and World War II,* p 178; Mannerheim, pp 493–495; Lundin, pp 225–227.

70. Mannerheim, pp 497–498; Wuorinen, *Finland and World War II,* pp 178, 189; Mazour, p 249; *FRUS,* 1944, Vol III, p 617.

71. Lundin, pp 228–230; Mannerheim, p 501; Wuorinen, *Finland and World War II,* p 180.

72. Mannerheim, pp 499–500, 503–505; Wuorinen, *Finland and World War II,* pp 189–190; Lundin, pp 239–249; Mikola, "The Finnish Wars," pp 256–257.

73. Mannerheim, p 505; Meretskov, pp 392–393; Pospelov, *IVOVSS,* Vol. IV, pp 368–371; Upton, "End of the Arctic War," p 2232.

74. *FRUS,* 1944, Vol. III, pp 574, 579, 583, 614; Mannerheim, p 502.

75. Mannerheim, p 512.

76. Gripenberg, pp 366–367.

77. Wuorinen, *History,* pp 436–437, 452–453, and *Finland and World War II,* pp 202–207; Mazour, pp 171–173, 179–187; Mannerheim, pp 507–510.

78. Wuorinen, *Finland and World War II,* p 205; Mazour, p 263.

79. Wuorinen, *Finland and World War II,* pp 181, 193, 201.

80. Ibid, pp 193, 203.

81. Hodgson, p 225; Schöpflin, p 317; Wuorinen, *History,* p 430.

82. Hodgson, pp 205, 225; Wuorinen, *History,* p 442. For a discussion of the 1948 coup affair, see Hans Peter Krosby, "The Communist Power Bid in Finland in 1948," *Political Science Quarterly,* June 1960, pp 229–243 (Vol. LXXVI, No. 2).

83. *Current History,* May 1948, pp 304, 305; Jackson, p 511; *Milestones of Soviet Foreign Policy,* pp 122–123.

84. *Milestones of Soviet Foreign Policy,* pp 122–123.

85. Wuorinen, *History,* pp 456–457; Forster, p 349.

86. *Milestones of Soviet Foreign Policy,* p 123; Wuorinen, *History,* p 453.

87. Forster, p 345.

88. Ibid, p 346; Wuorinen, *History,* pp 431, 445–447; *Finnish Foreign Policy,* pp 206–207.

89. For a breif and circumspect discussion of this topic, see J. Nousiainen, "The Parties and Foreign Policy," in *Finnish Foreign Policy,* especially pp 187–188.

90. Hodgson, pp 225, 230.

91. Mikola, "The Finnish Wars," p 257.

# BIBLIOGRAPHY

Aarnio, Matti A., *Talvisodan Ihme* [The Miracle of the Winter War], Jyväskylä, K. J. Gummerus, 1966.

Aleksandrov, G., et al. (eds), *Politicheskiy Slovar'* [Political Dictionary], Moscow, Gos. Izdat. Pol. Lit., 1940.

Alliluyeva, Svetlana, *Twenty Letters To A Friend,* N. Y., Harper & Row, 1967.

———, *Only One Year,* N. Y., Harper & Row, 1969.

Attlee, C. R. et al., *Labour's Aims in War and Peace,* London, Lincolns-Prager, n.d.

Beloff, Max, *The Foreign Policy of Soviet Russia,* Vol. II, 1936–1941, London, Oxford University Press, 1949.

Bialer, Seweryn (ed.), *Stalin and His Generals: Soviet Military Memoirs of World War II,* N. Y., Pegasus, 1969.

*Bol'shaya Sovetskaya Entsiklopediya* [Large Soviet Encyclopedia] 2d. ed., Vol. 39, Moscow, Izdat. "B.S.E.," 1956.

Borenius, Tancred, *Field-Marshal Mannerheim,* London, Hutchinson, 1940.

Burroughs, E. G., *Who's Who in the Red Army,* Watford, Farleigh Press, 1944.

Butler, J. R. M., *Grand Strategy,* Vol. II, September 1939—June 1941, London, HMSO, 1957.

Churchill, Winston S., *The Second World War,* Vol. I, *The Gathering Storm,* Boston, Houghton Mifflin, 1948.

Citrine, Sir Walter, *My Finnish Diary,* N. Y., Penguin Books, 1940.

Clark, Douglas, *Three Days to Catastrophe,* London, Hammond, Hammond, 1966.

Cox, Geoffrey, *The Red Army Moves,* London, Victor Gollancz, 1941.

*Current History,* "Stalin's Letter to Finnish President," May 1948, pp 304–305.

Deborin, G., *The Second World War: A Politico-Military Survey,* Moscow, Progress Publ., n.d.

Degras, Jane (ed.), *Soviet Documents on Foreign Policy,* Vol III, 1933–1941, London, Oxford University Press, 1953.

*Documents on German Foreign Policy 1918–1945,* Series D (1937–1945):

    Vol. VIII *The War Years, September 4, 1939–March 18, 1940* (State Dept. Publication No. 5436, Government Printing Office, 1954).

    Vol. X *The War Years, June 23—August 31, 1940* (State Dept. Publication No. 6491, Government Printing Office, 1957).

    Vol. XI *The War Years, September 1, 1940—January 31, 1941* (State Dept. Publication No. 7083, Government Printing Office, 1960).

    Vol. XII *The War Years, February 1—June 22, 1941* (State Dept. Publication No. 7384, Government Printing Office, 1962).

Vol. XIII *The War Years, June 23—December 11, 1941* (State Dept. Publication No. 7682, Government Printing Office, 1964).

Eade, Charles (compiler), *The War Speeches of the Rt Hon. Winston S. Churchill,* Boston, Houghton Mifflin, 1953.

Ehrnrooth, Colonel Gustaf, *Talvisota: III AK:n Taistelut* [The Winter War: Battles of the III Army Corps] , Helsinki (unpublished staff study written for the ST).

Erickson, John, *The Soviet High Command: A Military-Political History, 1918–1941,* London, St. Martin's Press, 1962.

*Fighting Finns Write Home,* Helsinki, Finlandia News Service, 1940.

*The Fighting Forces,* February 1940, pp 492–500, "The Russo-Finnish War".

——, April 1940, pp 42–53, "The Russo-Finnish War".

*The Finnish Blue Book: The Development of Finnish-Soviet Relations During the Autumn of 1939, Including the Official Documents and the Peace Treaty of March 12, 1940,* Philadelphia, J. B. Lippincott (published for the Finnish Ministry of Foreign Affairs), 1940.

*Finnish Foreign Policy: Studies in Foreign Politics,* Helsinki, Finnish Political Science Association, 1963.

Fischer, Louis (ed.), *Thirteen Who Fled,* N. Y., Harper & Row, 1949.

*Foreign Relations of the United States,* 1939, Vol. I, *General,* Dept. of State Publication No. 6242, Government Printing Office, 1956.

——, 1940, Vol. I, *General,* Dept. of State Publication No. 6818, Government Printing Office, 1959.

——, 1941, Vol. I, *General,* Dept. of State Publication No. 6642, Government Printing Office, 1958.

——, 1944, Vol. III, *The British Commonwealth and Europe,* Dept. of State Publication No. 7889, Government Printing Office, 1965.

Forster, Kent, "The Silent Vote in Finnish Politics," *International Journal,* Summer 1963, pp 341–352.

Gripenberg, G. A., *Finland and the Great Powers: Memoirs of a Diplomat,* Lincoln, University of Nebraska Press, 1965.

Halder, General Franz, *The Halder Diaries,* Washington, D. C., The Infantry Journal, 1950.

Hannula, J. O. and Fagerström, Briger, *Finland Fights: for Home, Faith and Country, 1939–1940,* Helsinki, Suomen Kirja [1940].

Heinrichs, General Erik, *Mannerheimgestalten: 2. Marskalken av Finland* [Mannerheim's Image: Vol. 2, Marshal of Finland], Helsinki, Holger Schildts, 1958.

Hodgson, John H., *Communism in Finland: A History and Interpretation,* Princeton, Princeton University Press, 1967.

Horne, Alistair, *To Lose A Battle: France 1940,* Boston, Little Brown, 1969.

House Report No. 2684, Part 13, 83rd Congress, 2nd Session, Union Calendar No. 929, "Communist Takeover and Occupation of Lithuania," 31 December 1954 (Government Printing Office, 1955).

Ignatkovich, G. R. (ed.) *Flot v Boyakh s Belofinnami: 1939–1940* [The Fleet in Combat with the White Finns: 1939–1940], Moscow, Voenno-Morskoe Izdat. NKVMF SSSR, 1942.

*Ilmatieteelliset Havainnot Suomessa* [Meteorological Observations in Finland], *Vuonna 1939* [in 1939], Vol. 38, Part 1, Helsinki, Ilmatieteellinen Keskuslaitos, 1953.

——, *Vuonna 1940* [in 1940], Vol. 40, Part 1, Helsinki, I. K., 1955.

International Boundary Study No. 74, *Finland—USSR Boundary,* issued by The Geographer, U. S. Dept. of State, 1 February 1967.

Isakov, Admiral I. S., *The Red Fleet in the Second World War,* London, Hutchinson, 1947.

*Izvestiya,* Moscow, 1939 et seq.

Jackson, J. Hampden, "Finland Since the Armistice," *International Affairs,* London, October 1948, pp 505–514.

Jakobson, Max, *The Diplomacy of the Winter War,* Cambridge, Harvard University Press, 1961.

Järvinen, Colonel Y. A., *Suomalainen ja Venäläinen Taktiikka Talvisodassa* [Finnish and Russian Tactics in the Winter War], Helsinki, Werner Söderström, 1948.

Jutikkala, Eino, *A History of Finland,* N. Y., Frederick A. Praeger, 1962.

——, *Two Essays on Finnish History* (reprinted from *Introduction to Finland, 1960*), Helsinki, Werner Söderström, 1960.

*Kansan Uutiset,* 4 June 1967.

Karhunen, Veikko, *Raatteen Tie* [The Raate Road], Helsinki, Werner Söderström, 1970.

Kerr, Walter, *The Russian Army—Its Men, Its Leaders, and Its Battles,* N. Y., Alfred A. Knopf, 1944.

Khrushchev, Nikita S [?], *Khrushchev Remembers,* Boston, Little Brown, 1970.

Kilkki, Pertti, "Talvisodan Suojajoukkotaistelut Karjalan Kannaksella" [Covering Troop Operations on the Karelian Isthmus during the Winter War], *Tiede ja Ase,* No. 27, 1969, pp 100–157.

——, "Mannerheim-Linjaa Lännestä ja Idästä [Mannerheim Line From West and East (article in response to Meretskov's memoirs)], *Uusi Suomi,* 12 January 1969, p 3.

Kogan, Ya. and Tolchenova, N. (eds.) *Boi na Karel'skom Peresheike* [Combat on The Karelian Isthmus], Moscow, OGIZ Gospolitizdat, 1941.

*Komsomol'skaya Pravda,* 8 March 1940.

Korhonen, Arvi, *Viisi Sodan Vuotta* [Five Years of War], Porvoo, Werner Söderström, 1963.

*Krasnaya Zvezda* [Red Star], 1939 et seq.

Krosby, Hans Peter, *Finland, Germany, and the Soviet Union, 1940–1941: the Petsamo Dispute*, Madison, University of Wisconsin Press, 1968.

———, "The Communist Power Bid in Finland in 1948," *Political Science Quarterly*, June 1960, pp 229–243.

Kukkonen [General], E. W., *Tolvajärven ja Ilomantsin Taistelut vv 1939–1940* [The Battles of Tolvajärvi and Ilomantsi], Helsinki, Otava, 1955.

Kuz'min [Colonel], N. F., *Na Strazhe Mirnogo Truda (1921–1940 gg)* [In Defense of Peaceful Labor], Moscow, Voennoe Izdat. M.O. SSSR, 1959.

Langdon-Davies, John, *Invasion in the Snow*, Boston, Houghton Mifflin, 1941.

Liddell Hart, B. H. (ed.), *The Red Army*, N.Y., Harcourt, Brace, 1956.

*Literaturnaya Gazeta*, 25 February 1964.

Lundin, C. Leonard, *Finland in the Second World War*, Bloomington, Indiana University Press, 1957.

Luukkanen, Eino, *Fighter Over Finland*, London, Macdonald, 1963.

Luukkonen, Fanni and Viherjuuri, H. J., *Lotta-Svärd*, Helsinki, Otava, 1937.

Maisky, Ivan, *Memoirs of a Soviet Ambassador: the War 1939–43* (transl. by Andrew Rothstein ) London, Hutchinson, 1967.

Mannerheim [Marshal], Carl G., *The Memoirs of Marshal Mannerheim* (transl. by Count Eric Lewenhaupt), N. Y., E. P. Dutton, 1954.

———, *Across Asia from West to East in 1906–1908*, 2 Vol., Helsinki, Suomalaisen Kirjallisuuden Seuran Kirjapaino, 1940.

Matrosov, F. F. (ed.), *Boi v Finlyandii* [Combat in Finland], 2 Vol, 2nd ed., Moscow, Voennoe Izdat. N.K. Oborony, 1941.

———, *Razgrom Linii Mannergeyma* [Destruction of the Mannerheim Line], 2nd ed., Moscow, Voennoe Izdat. N. K. O. SSSR, 1941.

Mazour, Anatole G., *Finland Between East and West*, Princeton, D. Van Nostrand, 1956.

Meretskov [Marshal], K. A., *Na Sluzhbe Narodu* [In the Service of the Nation], Moscow, Izdat. Pol. Liter., 1968.

Mikola, Keijo J. et al. (eds.), *Suomen Puolustusvoimat Ennen ja Nyt* [The Finnish Defense Forces Yesterday and Today], Helsinki, Werner Söderström, 1959.

———, "The Finnish Wars, 1939–1945", *La Revue Internationale d'Histoire Militaire*, No. 23, 1961, pp 241–257.

*Milestones of Soviet Foreign Policy 1917–1967*, Moscow, Progress Publ., 1967.

*Nazi-Soviet Relations 1939–1941; Documents from the Archives of the German Foreign Office,* ed. by Raymond J. Sontag and James S. Beddie, U. S. Dept. of State, Government Printing Office, 1948.

*The New York Times,* 1939 et seq.

Ogorkiewicz, Richard M., *Armour: A History of Mechanized Forces,* London, Stevens & Sons, 1960.

Öhquist [General], Harold, *Vinterkriget 1939–1940: Ur Min Synvinkel* [The Winter War, 1939–1940: From My Viewpoint], Stockholm, Fahlcrantz and Gumaelius, 1949.

———, "Comments on the War in Finland, 1939–1940" (unpublished translation from *Militar-Wochenblatt,* 4 April 1941, by Translation Section, Army War College, Washington, D. C.).

Oreshin, *Politruk Oreshin Päiväkirja—Dnevnik Politruka Oreshina —The Diary of Politruk Oreshin,* Helsinki, Tilgmannin Kirjapaino (private printing in 152 copies for Lord Carlow), 1941.

Österman [General], Hugo, *Neljännesvuosisata Elämästäni* [A Quarter Century of My Life], Helsinki, Werner Söderström, 1966.

*Outline History of the USSR,* Moscow, FLPH, 1960.

Paavolainen, Jaakko, *Poliittiset Väkivaltaisuudet Suomessa 1918* [Political Terror in Finland in 1918], Vol. I, Helsinki, Tammi, 1967.

Palmunen, Einar, *Tampereen Rykmentin Suojapataljoona Talvisodassa* [The Covering Troop Battalion of the Tampere Regiment in the Winter War], Hämeenlinna, Arvi A. Karisto, 1963.

Peitsara, Major T., "A Short General Survey of the War Between Finland and Russia in the Winter of 1939–1940," *The Army Quarterly,* London, October 1941.

Perret, Jean-Louis, *La Finlande en Guerre,* Paris, Payot, 1940.

Pospelov, P. N. et al. (eds.), *Istoriya Velikoi Otechestvennoi Voiny Sovetskogo Soyuza 1941–1945* [History of the Great Fatherland War of the Soviet Union 1941–1945], Moscow, Voennoe Izdat. M.O. SSSR, Vol. I—1960 and Vol. IV—1962.

———, *Velikaya Otechestvennaya Voina Sovetskogo Soyuza 1941– 1945: Kratkaya Istoriya* [The Great Fatherland War of the Soviet Union 1941–1945: Short History], Moscow, Voennoe Izdat. M.O. SSSR, 1965.

*Pravda,* Moscow, 1939 et seq.

Rintala, Marvin, *Three Generations: The Extreme Right Wing in Finnish Politics,* Bloomington, Indiana University Press, 1962.

———, "The Politics of Gustaf Mannerheim," *Journal of Central European Affairs,* April 1961, pp 67–83.

Rodzianko, Paul, *Mannerheim: An Intimate Picture of a Great Soldier and Statesman,* London, Jarrolds, 1940.

Romanov, P., *Finlyandiya i Eye Armiya,* Moscow, Voennoe Izdat. N. K. Oborony, 1937.

Rotmistrov [Marshal], P. A. (ed.), *Istoriya Voennogo Iskusstva* [History of Military Art], Moscow, Voennoe Izdat. M. O. SSSR, 1963.

*Sade-ja Lumihavaintoja Suomesta Vuonna 1940* [Precipitation and Snowfall Observations in Finland in 1940], Vol. 40, Part 2, Helsinki, Ilmatieteellinen Keskuslaitos, 1951.

Schöpflin, George, "The New Finnish Government," *The World Today,* August 1970, pp 317–321.

Schwartz, Andrew J., *America and The Russo-Finnish War,* Washington, D. C., Public Affairs Press, 1960.

Seppälä, H., and Kilkki, P., "Neuvostoliiton Maavoimat Talvisodassa 1939–40" [The Soviet Land Forces in the Winter War 1939–1940], *Sotilas Aikakaus Lehti,* January 1967, pp 5–10.

Sevast'yanov, Brigade Commissar, G. (ed.), *Istoriya 54-i Strelkovoi Divizii* [History of the 54th Rifle Division], Leningrad, Na Strazhe Rodiny, 1941.

Sherwood, Robert E., *Roosevelt and Hopkins: An Intimate History,* rev. ed., N. Y., Harper & Bros., 1950.

Shtemenko, General S. M., *The Soviet General Staff at War,* Moscow, Progress Publ., 1970.

Siilasvuo, H. J., *Suomussalmen Taistelut* [The Battles of Suomussalmi], Helsinki, Otava, 1940.

――――, *Kuhmo Talvisodassa* [Kuhmo in the Winter War], Helsinki, Otava, 1944.

Smith, C. Jay, *Finland and the Russian Revolution 1917–1922,* Athens, University of Georgia Press, 1958.

Soloviev, Mikhail, *My Nine Lives in the Red Army,* N. Y., David McKay, 1955.

*Sovetskaya Istoricheskaya Entsiklopediya* [Soviet Historical Encyclopedia], Moscow, Izdat. "Sov. Ents.", Vol. 7 and 8, 1965.

*The Soviet Union—Facts and Figures 1960,* London, Soviet News, 1960.

*Spravochnik Po Vooruzhennym Silam Belo-Finlyandii* [Handbook on the Armed Forces of White Finland], [Moscow], RKKA (marked "For Official Use"), n.d. [1940].

SSSR v Tsifrakh v 1967 Godu [USSR in Figures in 1967], Moscow, Izdat. "Statistika", 1968.

ST (Sotahistoriallinen Tutkimuslaitos) [Institute of Military History], Helsinki, archival files:

86 War Diary of Third Army Corps, 21.12.39–8.1.40.

207–208/S.N. Staff Study of Task Force Susi's Operations by Colonel Paavo Susitaival.

720:5 War Diary of Bicycle Battalion PPP 7, 18.10.39–24.4.40.

Colonel A. O. Pajari files:

929:5 (Pajari file No. 5) Battle Descriptions and Documents from the Front of Tolvajärvi

4/JR 16 Report of statement of commander of 4th Company, Reserve Captain U. Isotalo.

5/JR 16 Report of [5th] company commander, Reserve Captain A. Heinivaho. Addenda to above report by Reserve Lt. Pohjavirta of Second Machine Gun Company.

6/JR 16 Report of [6th] company commander, Reserve 2nd Lt. M. Siukosaari.

The action of the Third Battalion in the so-called Sausage Rebellion 10–11 December.

Daily report of action of Task Force P., 6–23 December.

Report of the battle of Äglajärvi, 21.–22.12.39.

A man of Häme as a soldier.

Some words on our [JR 16] qualifications when leaving for the Winter War.

929:7 Battle activities of those who distinguished themselves in the battles of Tolvajärvi-Aittojoki as described in the recommendations for decoration.

Description of activities of the commander of the 9th Company of JR 16, Reserve Captain Eero Kivelä.

Description of action of Sergeant 1st Class Vilho H. Reinikka.

Description of activities of Reserve Corporal Toimi S. Mutka.

1085 Survey of the most important battle phases of Task Force P. on the Tolvajärvi-Aittojoki Front in the war of 1939–40. (Written in 1941 by Colonel A. O. Pajari.)

1204 War Diary of Task Force Pajari, 19.2–26.3.1940 (see also ST file 3687 below).

1649–1650 War Diary of 8th Company, JR 65.

1654–1660 War Diary of Third Machine Gun Company, JR 65.

1677 War Diary of Third Battalion, JR 65.

1717a War Diary of Detachment Hannell, 9.10.39–7.12.39 and Group Talvela, 8.12.39–13.3.40.

3687 War Diary of Task Force Pajari, 7.12.39–18.2.40 (see also ST file 1204 above).

3688 War Diary of Third Battalion, JR 16, 28.12.39–30.3.40 (see also ST file 3743 below).

3732 War Diary of First Battalion, JR 16, 29.10.39–30.3.40.

3737:2 War Diary of Second Battalion, JR 16, 13.10.39–30.3.40.

3743 War Diary of Third Battalion, JR 16, 5.12.39–27.12.39 (see also ST file 3688 above).

3948:5 War Diary of Fifth Division, 14.10.39–25.2.40.

3948:7 Battle Reports and Copies of War Diaries of JR 13, 11.2–13.3.40.

4646 War Diary of Independent Battalion ErP 9, 7.10.39–24.1.40.

P 506:1 War Diary of First Division, 9.12.39–6.1.40.

Pajari File 22 (Battle maps of Tolvajärvi campaign).

T248–249 War Diary of Tenth Division, 25.11.39–7.4.40.

T255–256 War Diary of Ninth Division.

T1117–1122 War Diary of 9th Company, JR 16.

T1835a-c General Tuompo's operational order to 9th Division and Task Force Susi, 30 December 1939.

T9386 War Diary of First Brigade, 6.12.39–29.12.39.

*Study of Soviet Tactics and Techniques* [Staff study by Eino Lassila and Erkki Lahdenpera], The Infantry School, Fort Benning, Ga. 1949 [1950].

Suomalainen, Victor [pseud. of Colonel Alpo Marttinen], "The Battle of Suomussalmi," *Military Review,* Fort Leavenworth, December 1949, pp 54–62.

*Suomen Kuvalehti,* 18 February 1967, 27 May 1967, 27 January 1968, 30 October 1970.

Tanner, Väinö, *The Winter War: Finland Against Russia 1939–1940,* Stanford, Standford University Press, 1957.

*The Times* [London], 1939 et seq.

Tuominen, Arvo, "The Northern Countries and Communism," *The Norseman,* July-August 1954, pp 217–229.

Tuompo, General W. E. and Karikoski, Colonel V.A.M. (eds.) *Kunnia-Isänmaa: Suomen ja Neuvostoliiton Sota 1939–40* [Honor and Fatherland: Finno-Russian War 1939–40], Helsinki, Kivi, 1942.

Tuompo, General W. E., *Sotilaan Tilinpäätös* [A Soldier's Summation], Helsinki, Werner Söderström, 1967.

Tvardovski, Aleksandr, "S Karel'skogo Peresheika: Zapici 1939–1940 gg" [From the Karelian Isthmus: Notes 1939–1940], *Novyi Mir,* No. 2, 1969, pp 116–160.

Upton, Anthony, *Finland in Crisis 1940–1941: A study in small-power politics,* London, Faber & Faber, 1964.

———, "End of the Arctic War," *History of the Second World War,* (London, Purnell & Sons, in cooperation with the Imperial War Museum), Vol. 5, No. 16, pp 2225–2232.

United States [National] Archives:

OKL—Records of HQS, German Air Force High Command, Microfilm No. T-321, Roll 126, Document OKL 2614, Frame 19 [German intelligence report on General (Kurt) Martti Wallenius].

OKW—Records of HQS, German Armed Forces High Command, Microfilm No. T-77, Roll 896, Frames 5647901–02 [On Finns held as Russian POWs during Winter War].

RG 165, War Dept. General Staff M.I.D.:

File No. 2037–2100–27, 3 March 1940. Military Attaché Huth-steiner, Helsinki, to G2, relaying Finnish GHQ report on Soviet land forces as of 25 February 1940.

File No. 2037–2100–31, 9 May 1940. Military Attaché, Helsinki, to G2, transmitting translation of orders issued by Soviet corps commander on 9 December 1939, etc.

File No. 2657–D–1054–25, 2 April 1940. Huthsteiner to G2, relay-ing Finnish General Staff report on Soviet land forces as of mid-February 1940.

File No. 2682–32–1, 20 March 1940. Huthsteiner to G2, report on visit of Captain R. M. Losey to Finnish air units and discus-sions at same.

File No. 2682–33–2, 2 May 1940. Military Attaché M. F. Scanlon, London, to G2, relaying data on Finnish aircraft losses ob-tained from Finnish Minister in London.

File No. 2682–33–3, 21 May 1940. Huthsteiner to G2, relaying data from Finnish General Staff on Soviet bombing raids, damages, casualties.

U. S. Army Command and General Staff School, Lesson Plan R6480/6, School Year 1965–1966, "Division Operations—Mountain and Northern Regions," Annex B, "Historical Example: The Battle of Suomussalmi-Kuhmo 1939–40."

U. S. Army, *The German Campaign in Russia: Planning and Opera-tions (1940–1942)*, Department of the Army Pamphlet No. 20–261a, March 1955.

———, *Warfare in the Far North*, Department of the Army Pamphlet No. 20–292, October 1951 (prepared by Dr. [General] Waldemar Erfurth).

U. S. Military Academy, *The Soviet-Finnish War 1939–1940*, West Point, 1943. (Because this pamphlet was classified when first pub-lished, its distribution was limited to appropriate U. S. Govern-ment offices.)

*The USSR and Finland*, N.Y., Soviet Russia Today, 1939.

*USSR in Figures for 1959*, Moscow, FLPH, 1960.

U. S. State Department, *Bulletin*, Vol. I, No. 20, 11 November 1939.

———, Vol. I, No. 23, 2 December 1939.

———, Vol. I, No. 25, 16 December 1939.

U. S. State Department files:

760 D.61/

244 Min. Schoenfeld (Helsinki) to State, 12 October 1939, re evacuation of cities, etc.

476 Schoenfeld to State, 24 November 1939, relaying Military At-taché (Hayne) report on mobilization.

510 Schoenfeld to State, 30 November 1939, re Soviet air raids on Helsinki that date.

512 Attaché Hayne to State, 30 November 1939, relaying Finnish Army reports of Soviet air, artillery, and patrol action.

551 Thurston (Moscow) to State, 1 December 1939, re Soviet radio announcement on outbreak of hostilities.

561 Ambassador Steinhardt (Moscow) to State, 1 December 1939, re Soviet radio statement on "People's Government of Finland."

582 Schoenfeld to State, 3 December 1939, relaying Finnish General Staff reports on military operations as of 2 December 1500 hours.

583 Schoenfeld to State, 3 December 1939, re Tanner's opinion of members of "Terrijoki Government."

681 Steinhardt to State, 8 December 1939, re Potemkin's remark to member French Embassy on duration of war.

1046 Schoenfeld to State, 4 January 1940, relaying McClintock memo of 1 January on background of war.

1207 Min. Florence Harriman (Oslo) to State, 10 February 1940, re conversation with publisher William L. White on his visit to Finnish front.

1297 Higgs (Secretary of U. S. Legation in Finland) to State, 6 February 1940, transmitting Finnish Information Central pictures of air raid damage.

1347 McClintock to State, 29 February 1940, memo on war, 10 December 1939—1 Mar. [sic] 1940.

1349 Schoenfeld to State, 20 February 1940, transmitting translation of Mannerheim's 17 February proclamation to troops and comments thereon.

1429 Attaché (Helsinki) report, 9 April 1940, on Swedish volunteer corps.

1433 Schoenfeld to State, 26 April 1940, relaying McClintock memo, 25 April, on conclusion of war and boundary settlement complications.

1455 Schoenfeld to State, 28 May 1940, transmitting press report on completion of POW exchange, with numbers involved.

701.6160 P/22 Wiley (Riga) to State, 11 May 1940, re Derevyanski.

*Uusi Suomi,* 4 June 1967.

Usva [Major], K., "Battles of the Winter War in Northern Finland" (unpublished study financed by Suomen Sotatieteellinen Seura for the ST, 1971).

Viktorov, I. G., et al., *SSSR v Velikoi Otechestvennoi Voine 1941–1945* [The USSR in the Great Fatherland War, 1941–1945], Moscow, Voennoe Izdat. M.O. SSSR, 1970.

*Voennaya Mysl'* [Military Thought], 1940 et seq.

Voronov [Marshal], N. N., *Na Sluzhbe Voennoi* [On Active Duty], Moscow, Voennoe Izdat. M. O. SSSR, 1963.

Warner, Oliver, *Marshal Mannerheim and the Finns,* London, Weidenfeld & Nicolson, 1967.

Woodward, Sir Llewellyn, *British Foreign Policy in the Second World War,* London, H.M.S.O., 1962.

Wuorinen, John H., *A History of Finland,* N.Y., Columbia University Press, 1965.

_____ (ed.) *Finland and World War II,* N.Y., The Roland Press, 1948.

Ylinen, Pekka, "Tolvajärven Taistelun Kokemuksia" [Experiences of the Battle of Tolvajärvi], *Kansa Taisteli,* 15 February 1969, pp 36–38.

Yrttimaa [Rev.], J., "The Part Played by Women in the Present Struggle in Finland" (substance of a lecture given 28 January 1940, distributed by Rev. J. Yrttimaa, Montreal).

Zenzinov, V. M., *Vstrecha s Rossiei: Kak i Chem Zhivut v Sovetskom Soyuze, Pis'ma v Krasnuyu Armiyu* [Encounter with Russia: How they live in the Soviet Union, Letters to the Red Army], N. Y. (privately published), 1945.

Zyryanov, P. I et al. (eds.), *Pogranichnye Voiska SSSR 1939-iyun' 1941* [Border Guard Forces of the USSR 1939–June 1941], Moscow, Izdat. "Nauka," 1970.